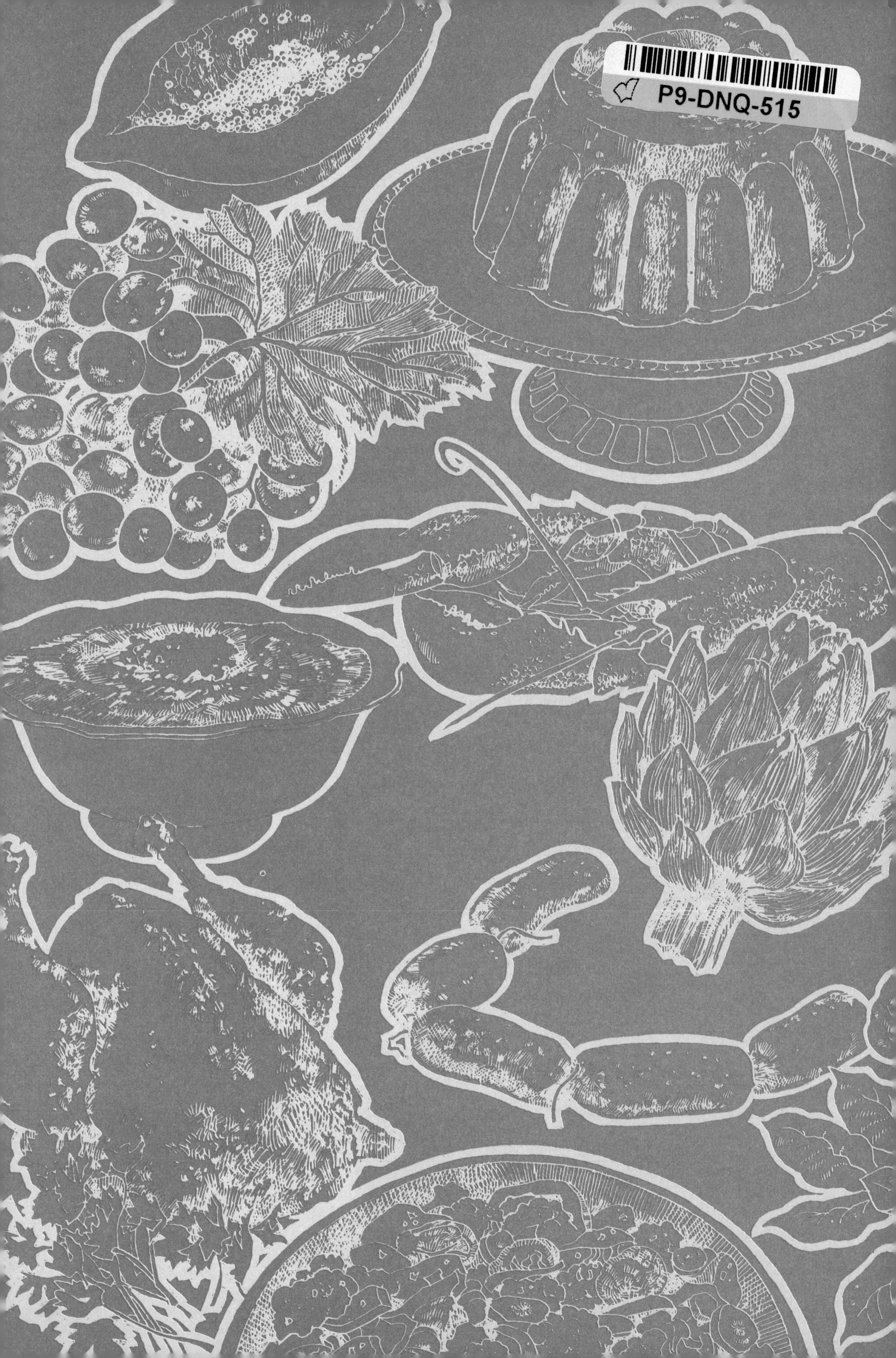

The Helen Corbitt Collection

BOOKS BY HELEN CORBITT

Helen Corbitt's Cookbook (1957)

Helen Corbitt's Potluck Cookbook (1962)

Helen Corbitt Cooks for Looks (1967)

Helen Corbitt Cooks for Company (1974)

Helen Corbitt's Greenhouse Cookbook (1979)

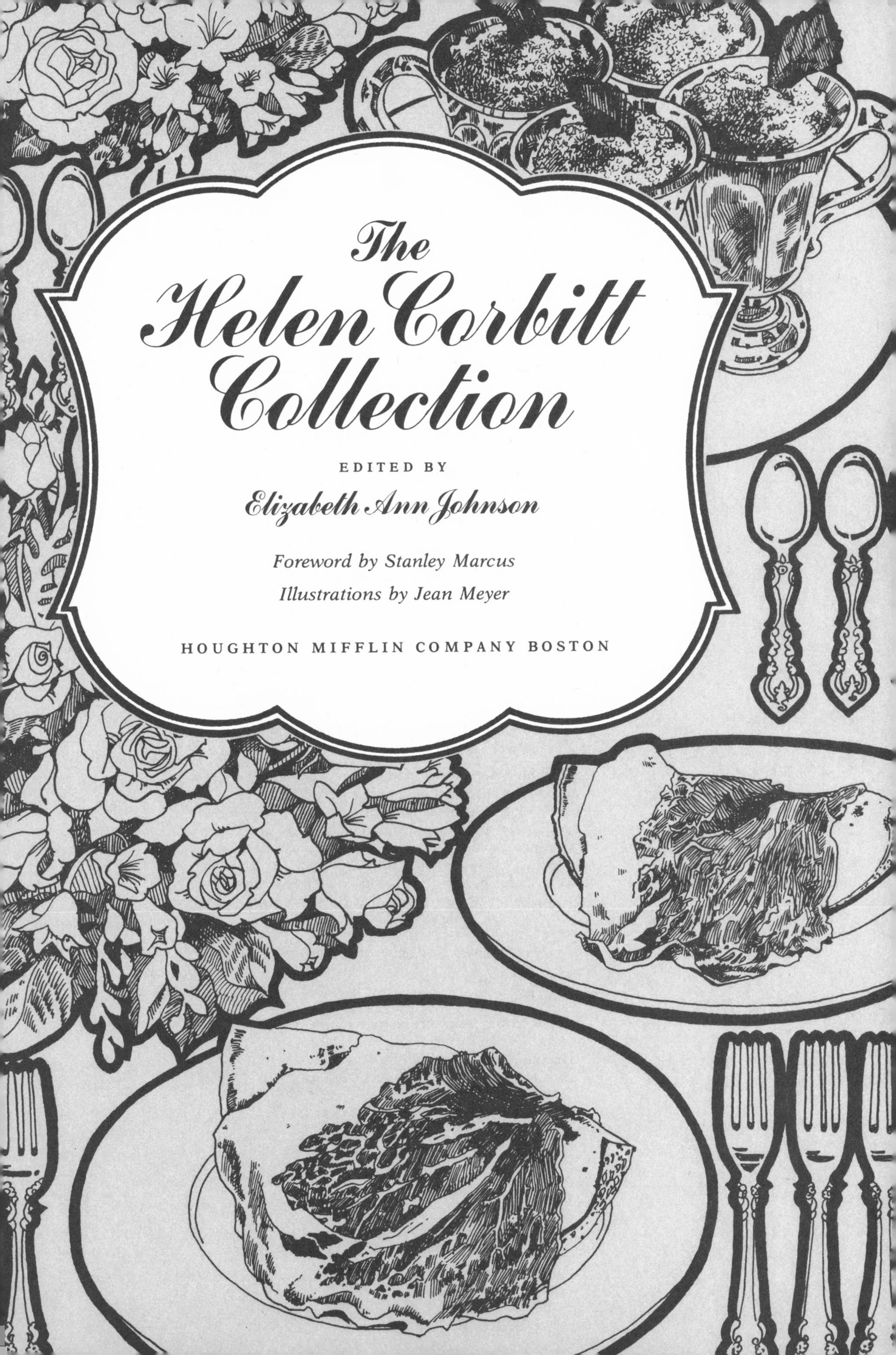

The Helen Corbitt Collection

EDITED BY

Elizabeth Ann Johnson

Foreword by Stanley Marcus

Illustrations by Jean Meyer

HOUGHTON MIFFLIN COMPANY BOSTON

Library of Congress Cataloging in Publication Data

Corbitt, Helen.
The Helen Corbitt collection.

A selection from the author's previously published works.
Includes index.
1. Cookery. I. Johnson, Elizabeth Ann. II. Title.
TX715.C7994 641.5 81-4259
ISBN 0-395-31295-7 AACR2

Printed in the United States of America

M 10 9 8 7 6 5 4 3 2

To Helen Corbitt's friends and followers all over the world

Contents

Foreword

Many people remember Helen Corbitt as the culinary genius who made the Zodiac Room at Neiman-Marcus the best table in town; many recall her as the author of half a dozen cookbooks that contributed to their own gastronomic skill; others have vivid memories of her didactic cookery-school lectures and demonstrations.

I like to think of her as a professional who knew her business, and all aspects of it, so well that she could trade recipes with the best of chefs, who could step into any vacancy in the kitchen — from the range to the bakery to the dishwashing — and do a better job than the person for whom she was substituting. She was difficult, for she knew the difference between better and best, and she was never willing to settle for second best. That sense of perfection made her difficult to work for or with, but she offered no apologies to a waiter, a cook, a hostess, or her boss if she knew they were wrong.

She combined her many abilities with the talent to create new taste sensations by unexpected mixtures of components. She recognized the importance of the appearance of a food, as well as its nutritional content, and to that end she maintained a discipline of color harmony in the plates that came out of her kitchen. That is why I dubbed her the Balenciaga of Food. I think she relished this title more than any of the many significant awards she won.

Helen Corbitt died in 1978, and her memory not only lingers on but increases with the lapse of time. *That* is immortality.

Stanley Marcus

Introduction

By the 1970s, when American cuisine was finally being recognized as worthy of world attention, Helen Corbitt had been an eminent figure in the American food world for more than a quarter century. Famous as a gracious hostess, she was, in the eyes of one sharp-eyed observer, "probably the most civilizing influence on the Southwest in the past fifty years." The observer was Stanley Walker, the legendary city editor of the *New York Herald Tribune,* who spent his last years seeking out the good things of his native Texas.

Dick Hitt's *Dallas Times Herald* column described her as "a curious combination of elegance and gusto, impatience and painstaking perfectionism, femininity and jaunty zest. She was subtle and imperious, ebullient and unerringly correct. Lots of things you wouldn't think would go together in a person went together in Helen Corbitt. She was a bouillabaisse of a person, part administrator, part hostess, part duchess, part Mother Superior." She was a woman whose manner could be endearing or awesome. She was a genius as a cook. On the lecture platform or before a class she could be very funny or very stern. But she loved people without stint and entertained them with a generous and skillful hand.

Helen was not a Texan. She was born in Benson Mines, New York. Her father was a gregarious attorney who loved good food and sharing it with friends. Her talented and versatile mother was expert at preparing fine meals for her husband, her daughter, Helen, and son, Michael, and the many friends who came to the Corbitt home.

Helen began to cook before she started school. By the time she was in high school she had seized responsibility for refreshments for school parties, and the 1928 yearbook of Skidmore College, in Saratoga Springs, New York, called her "the campus culinary expert."

Armed with a Bachelor of Science degree, Helen entered the field of food and its preparation. "There were," she said, "my hospital days, over ten years of them, at Presbyterian Hospital in New Jersey and Cornell Medical Center in New York. During the depression in New York City I used to get up at three o'clock on Saturday mornings to bake chocolate cakes for special orders for extra money. Then there was Texas. My first Texas job was teaching Foods, Catering, and Restaurant Management at the University of Texas in Austin. The University Tea Room was our workshop. About two years later I went to the Houston Country Club as manager and stayed five strenuous happy years. I didn't even mind wartime rationing; I was having such a good time producing great food for appreciative Texans. As director of food services at Joske's of Houston, I met the public at large in the Garden Room, a restaurant where all day long hundreds came in for coffee and homemade coffee cake and hundreds more for lunch. I had three, almost four, years at the Driskill Hotel in Austin, the state capital. And in 1955 my last stop was as director of restaurants for Neiman-Marcus, where I found the discriminating tastes of urbane Dallasites a year-round challenge and Foreign Fortnights an unprecedented culinary experience."

Every commercial establishment with which she was associated immediately became famous for the best food, certainly in the state of Texas, maybe in the whole Southwest. The Zodiac Room at Neiman-Marcus was described by restaurant critics as "one of the best restaurants this side of Paris."

Helen was teaching others to cook at the same time that she directed the operations of large restaurants. Coupled with her consummate skill in creating fine food was her ability to explain and demonstrate procedures to others so that they could execute the most intricate steps in any kitchen maneuver. Her talent for conducting a class may have begun at the University of Texas, but it was most likely a natural ability because she thought about food in an orderly manner. Her explanations and demonstrations enabled every person in her audience to know exactly how to make each dish Helen described. In the 1940s she began giving lectures on cooking and entertaining. For the next thirty-five years she was one of the most popular lecturers in the country, often appearing in Canada and with a schedule in the United States that rivaled a hit Broadway show on the road.

She achieved early and marked success in each of her three compatible roles — cooking, teaching, and lecturing. Later, a fourth role, that of writer, fit naturally into her career. Helen's philosophy of food was that it must be of the finest quality, properly prepared, and beautifully and imaginatively served. She was unswervingly dedicated to those principles during her almost fifty years in the food business. She inspired her own staff to produce miracles in the many commercial kitchens she managed. And through her lectures, cooking schools, and books, she led the women of America "back to the kitchen" and urged them "to forget short cuts, mixes, instant foods, and packaged meals."

In *Helen Corbitt Cooks for Company* she wrote: "The dining room is one of the last outposts of civilization. Let's keep it that way. As the hostess you can set the tone of your party. I feel that the food can be a part of the decoration, so in planning a menu you should see the food in your mind's eye. The color, texture, and flavor of your menus are what a discriminating guest will notice. And your family deserves as much consideration as your guests. So make the habit of planning meals carefully."

For those who were not fortunate enough to eat her food or hear her lecture or until now read her books, I shall try to explain this charming and puzzling lady and a few of her opinions about food and life.

If Helen liked you there was no limit to the unexpected nice things she might do for you. And it was the same with her employees in all the kitchens she managed. In spite of her well-deserved reputation as a perfectionist and for being something of a tyrant in the kitchen, the loyalty of her employees matched her devotion to them. Some worked for her for fifteen to twenty years and leaned on her for much guidance and inspiration.

"I spent 85 percent of my working day in the kitchen. It was the fun part — with the employees," Helen recalled. "I was always more interested in the back of the house."

Helen took responsibilities very seriously. Her early ambition had been the medical profession — a hope canceled out by the depression of the 1930s. But if she had become a doctor, she could not have taken the responsibilities of that profession any more earnestly than she regarded the obligation of the resolute dietitian she became. Lecturing in 1971 to the Louisiana Heart Association in Shreveport, Helen chided the doctors for putting their patients on diets but "not telling them how to make the food palatable. Even sick people get hungry and like the taste of food."

The challenge of making low-calorie food delicious and irresistible was one Helen accepted with twofold enjoyment. She had been told by her doctors to lose weight and she reveled in making the chore of dieting easier, if not downright pleasurable.

Helen was always ready to try new procedures and new ways of doing old tasks. She liked the food processor and used hers a great deal. The ice-cream maker that works in the freezer was a great boon to low-calorie dessert making and she recommended it highly.

With an almost perverse pleasure Helen turned traditionally unpopular foods into dishes alluring to look at and so delicious that everyone wanted the recipes. If she found out a friend could not stand parsnips or turnips or snails or yogurt, she served those very foods in such a way that the friend asked for more, never suspecting what he was eating. According to Ann Criswell, food editor of the *Houston Chronicle,*

"Helen Corbitt could make a cowpuncher eat rhubarb and love it."

Helen also took special delight in finding odd foods, such as new vegetables that were not commonly in the markets, and presenting them in handsome combinations. Cardoons, fennel, and flageolet were all new to most people and proved popular. Her imagination in serving food knew no limits. A much-reported example of a Corbitt touch was the dusting of candied violets she put on old-fashioned rice or tapioca pudding. She also suggested using pistachio dust as a topping for various desserts. "Call it ground pistachios," Helen warned, "and nobody will care, but 'pistachio dust' they love it."

As James Beard wrote in his *American Cookery,* "Helen Corbitt, who has furthered the cause of good food in Texas over a great period of years, understands American food as few people do, and she is a genius at preparing things that will enchant the eye and the palate at the same time."

Interest in color contrast prompted Helen to serve white cole slaw in a hollowed-out red cabbage years before it became a common sight on buffet tables, and to add inch-square pieces of handsome fresh red pepper to my flavorful but pale pickled green chiles. "This," she said, "gives the chiles just the color and the crunch they need." She liked the recipe well enough to include it in *Helen Corbitt's Greenhouse Cookbook,* of course giving credit to Mary Wallbanks, whose recipe it originally was. Helen loved raspberries, strawberries, and blueberries and enjoyed thinking up fresh ways to use them, ways new to the food world and new to her.

"She had a great flair for combining foods and an artistic way of serving and arranging her color combinations," said Adele Simpson, the designer whose clothes were favorites of Helen's. "She had a wonderful knack of making everything harmonize. As a dress designer, I appreciated that."

Certain Texas favorites she came to know only as an adult. Most non-Texans confronting black-eyed peas for the first time would shrug and say, "Not for me." But Helen knew how popular they were in the South, so she invented Texas Caviar by pickling the peas. Before long, Texas Caviar put up in cans with clever Neiman-Marcus wrappers appeared under Christmas trees all over the country.

One of Helen's most cherished friendships was with President and Mrs. Lyndon Baines Johnson. Remembering that, I wrote to Mrs. Johnson about the present collection and want to share with you excerpts from her gracious answer:

> It made me smile to think back across the long stretch of years we knew Helen and to remember Lyndon teasing her about coming to cook for him. She was a legend in our family, as she was in the lives of the many who admired and enjoyed her special talents.

Helen's genius in the kitchen was a combination of so many things — flair, imagination, and artistry were as much among the "staples" as her knowledge of good nutrition and sound health habits. Her creative hand at the table and her sensible advice made one *want* to eat right. And, her energy and "can-do" spirit were infectious both in person and through the pages of her books.

It was — and is — a delight to have Helen's skills and recipes deliciously grace our mealtimes, and very much a joy to have had her as a friend.

Beginning in 1955, Helen's special province was the Zodiac Room of Neiman-Marcus, Dallas, where superb food was served with elegance to the thousands who visited the store, including an endless stream of celebrities. Her lectures and cooking schools took her to all parts of the country and her itinerary for a week might include White Sulphur Springs, Atlanta, Mobile, and New Orleans, and the sponsorship might be a medical association, the Junior League, a symphony group, or even a bank. On vacation, often abroad, she invariably made a study of the local cuisine and reported on it in her various newspaper columns.

She traveled many miles every year to attend meetings of food and restaurant associations. And she lectured to restaurateurs and club managers; she was bluntly truthful with them, good-naturedly scolding those who served canned or frozen vegetables when the same vegetables could be had fresh in their areas. Forthright as she was, she was asked back again and again and rewarded with their highest honors.

For years Helen Corbitt's customers and friends had been urging her to write a cookbook. Finally, at the prodding of Stanley Marcus, Helen got down to work on it. I was on vacation with my family on Cape Cod in the summer of 1956 when a letter came from her asking me to be her literary agent. The longhand letter reads in part:

> I am sure you think Helen Corbitt is a myth, her cookbook too, but it is on its way, good or bad. The book is an accumulation of recipes and ideas used in the various places I have worked. Everywhere I have managed to give the impression that I do everything differently and all by myself. Goodness knows why — the Luck of the Irish I guess.
>
> I don't care who publishes it — really. I would like to sell it and as long as it is done well and promoted, it doesn't matter. It is in your hands. I think we will have fun.

Cookbooks had interested me for a long time. For eighteen years in my bookshop — McMurray's, the Personal Bookshop, in Dallas (I had sold it just months before Helen came to Dallas) — I had tried to discover the best cookbooks for my customers. So I began to read Helen's manuscript with great interest. I finished convinced that there never had been a cookbook like it. It was happy, natural, informal, and full of inspired recipes with directions anyone could follow. And it had humor.

We met in New York at the Algonquin Hotel and talked half the night about the cookbook and our plans for it. I knew from that first meeting that working with Helen would never be dull or seem like work. Whether she visited us in New England or California or I went to Dallas, we always had lots to thrash out, laugh about, and decide.

After our New York meeting I submitted the manuscript of the cookbook to Houghton Mifflin, the distinguished Boston publishing firm. They liked it and made a formal offer. Just one month after I had mailed out the manuscript Helen had her first book contract and her first advance. The rest is cookbook history. Houghton Mifflin published all five of her books, the last one, *Helen Corbitt's Greenhouse Cookbook,* posthumously.

Helen was a cosmopolitan being. Prior to her move to Texas she had been a New Yorker for eleven years (though she always stressed her "upstate" origins), and she had a thorough knowledge of the best restaurants and clubs in the city as well as the special food suppliers. She enjoyed lifelong friendships with professionals such as those she met at the 21 Club: Mac Kriendler (with whom she served on the board of governors of the Culinary Institute of America), Bob and Pete Kriendler, Jerry Berns, and Sheldon Tannen.

Recognition of Helen's eminence came from many quarters — from culinary classicists, from restaurateurs, from food writers, and from the thousands who came to her first as customers and returned again and again as disciples. She received the Golden Plate Award, the highest honor of the food industry, the Escoffier Gold Plaque of the Confrérie de la Chaîne des Rotisseurs, board membership of the Chevaliers du Tastevin, and the University of Dallas Athena Award. In 1977, the year before her death, her alma mater, Skidmore College, gave her an honorary Doctor of Letters for her career as an "American-born genius in the kitchen who shared her accumulated wisdom through her cookbooks."

Helen, busy though she was, energetically supported civic, educational, and cultural activities in Dallas and elsewhere. She conducted special cooking schools for the benefit of the Dallas Symphony that raised more than $150,000. She actively supported the University of Dallas and many charities, Catholic and nondenominational. Over the years she anonymously contributed to the education of needy college students in various schools. Her estate was divided equally between Skidmore College and the University of Dallas, which established a fund supporting the annual Helen Corbitt Lecture on Excellence. Another memorial fund has been created to furnish the Helen Corbitt

Room in Castletown House, Celbridge, County Kildare, Ireland, which is under the direction of the Irish Georgian Society.

To sum up the extraordinary career of Helen Corbitt is impossible, but the wording on the Gold Plaque of the Confrérie de la Chaîne des Rotisseurs, awarded to her in 1968, spells it out very well: "To Helen Corbitt in recognition of her unfailing dedication to the highest principles of pure gastronomic product in fact, word, and deed."

Editor's Note

The idea of a collection of "the best of Helen Corbitt" originated with the editors of Houghton Mifflin, Helen's publishers. Because of my long association as Helen's literary agent, they asked if I would compile such a volume. Very naturally, I was eager to tackle the job.

The editors and I agreed that we wanted the book to be all Corbitt, with the recipes and her introductory notes to be as she had written them originally or had described in a lecture or newspaper column, or in an interview given during the twenty-two years covered by my Corbitt file. We wanted Helen's bedrock knowledge of foods and her astringent humor to dominate this collection, just as they had dominated her books and her professional life.

After many careful rereadings of all the cookbooks and cooking columns, I have selected representative recipes from all categories. Three of Helen's books furnished most of the recipes, since they were the books designed for general use: *Helen Corbitt's Cookbook, Helen Corbitt's Potluck Cookbook* and *Helen Corbitt Cooks for Company.* A number of special recipes were chosen from *Helen Corbitt's Greenhouse Cookbook,* which, in addition to low-calorie recipes, contains two chapters, "Greenhouse Indulgences" and "A Potpourri," that feature dishes Helen served successfully during the last years of her life.

I felt the presence of cooks of all descriptions and degrees of expertise as I worked at selecting the more than 900 recipes for this volume. Professional chefs, experienced hostesses, housewives with big families and small budgets, teachers in cooking schools, and the men and women of Helen's two famous Dallas cooking classes all seemed to be looking over my shoulder ready to lobby for their pet Corbitt recipes. Remembering that Corbitt fans are fiercely proprietary about "their" Corbitt recipes persuaded me to proceed with caution.

Choice of what to leave out was based on many considerations, one of which was the availability of recipes for the same dish in standard cookbooks. But here too there were difficulties. I planned to omit Helen's recipe for Scalloped Potatoes because it is found in almost all general cookbooks. Then I remembered a long-time friend who gave many gift copies of Helen's first book, always calling the recipient's attention to the simple trick in Helen's Scalloped Potatoes that set her recipe apart from others. So the Corbitt recipe is back where it belongs in this volume, with the vegetables. Ultimately I had to face the fact that every recipe I left out could be someone's favorite and that it was going to be impossible to please everyone.

In *Helen Corbitt Cooks for Company* the author wrote: "This is a very personal book and I say many times that no one has to agree with me. My friends demanded the I approach and I am glad they did because it is as casual and conversational as if we were sitting down to have a cup of tea and to talk recipes and cooking."

That is the way we want the reader to feel about *The Helen Corbitt Collection.* With minor clarifications, the recipes are as Helen wrote them. At times I have felt that a comment or explanation was needed, in which case I have tried to be brief and my words are in italics. And readers of other Corbitt cookbooks will be familiar with our practice of capitalizing names of dishes for which a recipe has been provided; you can easily locate any recipe by consulting the index. We have not attempted to update the recipes. Throughout her life Helen used the most modern wonders in her kitchen, and in her later years she certainly depended on the food processor for chopping, blending, puréeing, and more.

Because the editors and I have always been charmed by the spontaneity of the Corbitt cookbooks, we have included a large section of "This and That," among which are some tips that are true Corbitt but just haven't yet been in circulation.

Part 1

Hors d'Oeuvres
Soups · Sauces

Hors d'Oeuvres

When I give a cocktail party, I like to prepare for the individual tastes of my guests — those who drink and those who don't; those who watch their weight and others who do not care. For non-drinkers I provide a cold or hot soup. There is nothing worse than spending an evening with a dumb glass of tomato juice or a soft drink in one's hand. I find too that the soup table is usually more popular than the bar. For those who drink, you can no longer provide just whiskey. Wine, beer, and champagne are becoming the usual rather than the exception. Too, I think something sweet is a good idea. Some people shudder at the thought of liquor and sweets. Go ahead and shudder. There is never a crumb left. Don't forget coffee, and, of course, plates and forks. No dribbles on the rug.

The cocktail buffet table should look heavily laden whether it is or not; I find a round or oval table helps to create this illusion. Guests today expect food to hold them over until they go somewhere else for dinner or home for breakfast.

EGGPLANT CAVIAR

---

1 eggplant, medium size
½ cup finely chopped onion
1 clove garlic, crushed
1 tomato, peeled, seeded, and chopped fine
3 tablespoons olive oil
2 tablespoons vinegar
1 teaspoon sugar
Salt and cracked pepper
4 tablespoons chopped parsley

Bake the eggplant whole at 400° for 30 minutes. Cool and peel. Chop fine and mix with onion, garlic, tomato, oil, vinegar, and sugar. Season with salt and cracked pepper. Cover with chopped parsley and chill several hours. Serve with slices of dark rye bread or Lahvash (an Armenian cracker bread) — or on a thick slice of tomato as a salad.

MARINATED FRESH ARTICHOKES

I like to serve these as a cocktail tidbit. They are low in calories and light enough not to interfere with the main course.

8 fresh artichokes
½ lemon, sliced
Few slices onion
2 tablespoons olive oil

Wash artichokes in cold salted water, drain, and snip off the sharp tips of the leaves with scissors. Stand in a kettle and cover with fresh cold salted water, lemon, onion slices, and olive oil. Cover and boil until leaves pull away easily. Remove, turn upside down, and drain. Cool. Turn right side up and pour marinade over. Refrigerate for several hours or overnight.

Marinade:
½ cup salad oil
½ cup olive oil
Juice of 2 lemons
2 tablespoons chopped chives or green onions
¼ cup chopped parsley
¾ teaspoon dry mustard
1½ teaspoons each salt and cracked pepper

Mix thoroughly all ingredients and pour over artichokes. To serve, lift the artichokes onto plates and pour over a little of the marinade.

ASPARAGUS TIPS

A rare hot hors d'oeuvre is 1 or 2 pounds of asparagus tips cut in 1-inch lengths and covered with:

½ teaspoon anchovy paste
¼ pound butter

blended together and softened to spreading consistency. Keep very hot and generously sprinkle with chives. Toothpicks to spear them with.

Fingers are O.K. It is also wonderful to leave the asparagus in whole stalks, especially when it is fresh, and suck on it as you get down toward the end.

It is well to leave a pretty bowl of warm water and cocktail napkins near. To wash the fingers, of course. Personally I think a finger bowl should always be present somewhere near an hors d'oeuvre table. Inconspicuous, but there, nonetheless.

CAVIAR WITH HOT FLAGEOLETS

A tin of fresh caviar costs a great deal of money and comes in a very plain package. I like to dress up caviar by putting it in a cabbage to keep cool. Put a medium-sized cabbage in warm water and let it stand in the water all night. Then peel back the outside leaves to form a crown. Cut away the center of the head. Refrigerate in a plastic bag or put in ice water. When ready to use, drain and set the tin of caviar in the center. This will keep the caviar cold and pretty up the tin. Spoon caviar onto this mixture:

⅓ cup sliced green onion
4 tablespoons butter
4 cups canned flageolets
Salt and fresh ground pepper
Chopped parsley

Sauté the onion in the butter 1 minute. Add beans which have been drained. Correct seasonings. Cover and bake at 350° for 20 minutes. Sprinkle with chopped parsley and serve warm.

AVOCADO BUTTER

FOR ONE POUND

I keep Avocado Butter in my deep freeze to bring out for a quick cocktail treat and find it always fascinates guests. Do some in a crock and give it for a Christmas gift.

1 large ripe avocado
2 tablespoons fresh lime juice
1 pound sweet butter, softened
¼ teaspoon ground ginger
Natural almonds or filberts

Peel and remove seed from the avocado. Chop it in a blender with the lime juice. Add the butter and ginger and blend until smooth. Form into a ball; roll in chopped nuts. Chill. This is also good to use as a butter for any kind of sandwich, or on steak. I also like it with radishes.

CRAB IMPERIAL

¼ cup butter
1 tablespoon finely chopped shallots or onion
1 cup sliced mushrooms
¼ cup flour
1½ cups milk
½ cup dry sherry
1 teaspoon salt
2 teaspoons Dijon mustard
1 pound crabmeat, fresh, frozen, or canned
2 tablespoons mayonnaise

Melt butter, add shallots or onion, sauté 1 minute. Add mushrooms and sauté until limp. Add flour and cook until foamy. Pour in milk, stirring constantly until mixture is thick. Mix in the sherry and seasonings. Cook until thickened again. Add crabmeat, cool, and stir in mayonnaise. Correct seasonings. Spoon into lightly buttered coquilles or a 1½-quart shallow casserole. Place in oven at 300° to heat for 15 to 20 minutes. Run under broiler to brown. May be prepared ahead of time.

CRABMEAT GRUYÈRE

1 cup canned crabmeat
¼ cup shredded Gruyère cheese
1 tablespoon Sauterne
½ teaspoon salt
Mayonnaise to moisten

Mix and pile high on sautéed rounds of white bread and run into a 450° oven until hot.

SNAILS IN PASTA SHELLS

Snails I like but not in their shells. (Somehow I feel the snails might resent them.) I like to serve snails in the pasta shells you find in the grocery stores — the large seashell macaroni is best. Drain and wash the snails, and for 2 dozen, which is the small can size, sauté in 2 tablespoons butter and 2 cloves of finely chopped garlic for about 5 minutes. Cool and stuff each snail into a cooked macaroni shell. Cover with the following butter mixture: ½ cup softened butter, 1 teaspoon chopped shallots, 2 tablespoons chopped parsley, 1 clove finely minced garlic, juice of half a lemon, and a few drops of Worcestershire sauce. Let stand several hours, then bake in 350° oven until sizzling. You eat the snail with the pasta and all the butter. I find they disappear like magic. You can prepare these several days ahead and freeze.

CHAFING-DISH OYSTERS

This one is good too. In your chafing dish sauté ½ cup of finely chopped scallions — young onions to many of us — in:

2 tablespoons of butter

Then add:

1 cup catsup
2 tablespoons Worcestershire sauce
1 pint oysters, drained

Drop oysters in sauce and heat until the edges curl. Serve with tiny pastry shells to hold the sauce that clings to them. I make these shells by shaping piecrust over a teaspoon and placing them on a cookie sheet so the edges touch to bake.

FRESH CRABMEAT WRAPPED IN BACON

FOR SIX OR EIGHT

1 tablespoon chopped onion
4 tablespoons butter
2 tablespoons chopped parsley
3 cups fresh crabmeat
1 cup thick Cream Sauce
2 tablespoons bread crumbs
Salt
Bacon

Sauté onion in the butter; add parsley and crabmeat and sauté 1 minute. Add cream sauce and crumbs, season with salt, cool; form into balls about the size of a walnut, and wrap each in a ½-by-4 inch slice of bacon. Fasten with toothpicks. When about ready to serve, place in oven at 350° and bake until the bacon is brown. Remove toothpicks, drain, and serve with marinated cucumbers. A really good cocktail savory also. This recipe makes 36 rolls. You can make these up and freeze them for a few days. Really nice for entertaining.

CHICKEN SATÉS

FOR EIGHT TO TEN SATÉS

1 broiler-sized chicken
6-inch bamboo skewers (from Oriental or gourmet shops)
1 cup soy sauce
2 slices fresh ginger
2 cloves garlic, mashed
Fresh ground pepper, a twist or two
½ cup dry white wine or sake

Remove skin from chicken and cut off all the meat from the carcass. Cut into ½- to 1-inch pieces and thread 5 or 6 onto each skewer. Place in a shallow pan and cover with the marinade consisting of remaining ingredients. Refrigerate for several hours. Remove from marinade. Place on a shallow pan or rack and broil, about 5 minutes, on each side. Baste with marinade. Serve hot or warm. Beef, lamb, shrimp, scallops, pork — try any of them.

Sometimes I have Peanut Sauce handy to dip the satés into before eating. Be sure you leave enough space at the end of the skewer to hold on to.

PEANUT SAUCE

⅔ cup peanut butter
2 tablespoons butter
6 tablespoons soy sauce
2 tablespoons lemon juice
2 teaspoons fresh garlic juice
⅔ cup whipping cream

Cook all except cream over hot water until hot. Add cream. Keep warm. Use for egg rolls and tempura, too.

TERRINE PÂTÉ

1 pound chicken livers
¼ teaspoon salt
⅛ teaspoon poultry seasoning
1 tablespoon Cognac
½ pound fresh pork
½ pound veal
¼ cup dry sherry
Dash of salt and pepper
¼ pound salt pork, sliced paper-thin
1 egg, well beaten
1 bay leaf

Dice half of the livers. Add the salt, poultry seasoning, and Cognac. Refrigerate for a few hours. Put the rest of the livers, the pork, and veal through your meat grinder. Add the sherry, salt, egg, and pepper and mix well. Line the bottom and sides of the terrine or casserole with salt pork. Put in a layer of the ground mixture, then a few pieces of diced liver. Repeat until terrine is filled, ending with mixture layer. Top with more salt pork. Place a bay leaf on top. Cover the terrine and seal the edges with foil. Place in a pan of hot water and bake at 375° for 2½ hours. Remove cover and bay leaf, and refrigerate 24 hours. You may add truffles if you feel extravagant. Slice and serve on soft lettuce or watercress with or without Melba toast. A garnish of sliced olives adds.

CHICKEN LIVER PÂTÉ

This pâté substitutes very well for the imported pâté de foie gras. Bring 1 pound chicken livers to a boil in chicken broth barely to cover and simmer them for 15 to 20 minutes in a covered saucepan. Drain and put the hot livers through the finest blade of the food chopper. Mix this with 2 teaspoons salt, a pinch cayenne, ½ cup softened butter, ½ teaspoon dry mustard, and 2 tablespoons finely minced onion. Blend well, add 1 tablespoon dry sherry; pack the mixture in a crock and chill in the refrigerator. You may freeze.

SCALLOPS RAMAKI

Boiling water
12 slices bacon
24 sea scallops
24 whole water chestnuts
2 tablespoons soy sauce
½ cup dry white wine

Pour boiling water over bacon and let stand 5 minutes; drain and dry. Stretch the bacon as long as you can and then cut each slice in half. Wrap around a scallop and a water chestnut and secure with a toothpick. Cover with the soy sauce and wine in a shallow pan. Marinate for several hours. Drain and bake in a 350° oven until bacon has cooked. Remove toothpicks and replace with fresh or plastic ones. Serve hot. These are better than the old standby of bacon and chestnuts with chicken livers.

HOOMIS

Borrowed from the Middle East, this is an inexpensive cocktail spread. Serve with Lahvash (an Armenian cracker bread) or cold relishes.

3 cups cooked chickpeas, puréed
1 cup lemon juice
1 cup sesame oil
6 cloves garlic, minced
2 teaspoons salt
Chopped parsley

Mix the puréed chickpeas; slowly add the lemon juice and sesame oil, alternately. It will become a thick and smooth paste. Add the garlic mixed with the salt. Correct seasonings. Place in a bowl or mold and cover with the chopped parsley.

SHRIMP CANAPÉS

FORTY TO FIFTY

1 pound large shrimp, 20 to 25 count
1 garlic clove
½ lemon
½ cup mayonnaise
½ teaspoon curry powder
¼ cup Major Grey's chutney
12 slices white bread
Caviar
Pimento
Chopped parsley

Cook the shrimp until shells turn pink, 5 to 8 minutes, in enough water to cover, with a clove of garlic and half a lemon, sliced. Peel, clean, and chill. Mix the mayonnaise with the curry power and chutney, chopping the pieces of mango, if necessary, to make a smooth dip. Cut the bread into half-moons. Use a round cutter, if you haven't a half-moon one, and then cut in half. Spread with the mayonnaise mixture. Cut the shrimp in half lengthwise and place on the half-moon pieces, fitting them to the shape of the shrimp. Place a dot of caviar for an eye and circle it with a fine strip of pimento. Sprinkle the chopped parsley on the inner curve of the shrimp and bread. These are pretty to look at and intriguing to eat. They take time, but are worth it. A nice "tea" sandwich, also.

A thin slice of cold ham cut to fit squares of whole-wheat bread, spread with the same mayonnaise mixture, and a good-sized sliver of the mango from the chutney placed on top, makes a conversation piece, too.

SHRIMP À LA HELEN

Peel one pound of raw shrimp (20 to 25 count to the pound). Wash well and put in a pan and cover with:

2 tablespoons finely minced parsley
2 cloves of garlic, minced
1 cup salad oil (olive oil is better but it is expensive)

Leave in refrigerator all day — and night, too, if you have the time. When ready to serve, place shrimp on a shallow pan with the oil that clings to them and broil 3 minutes on each side. Salt lightly. Be sure you do not overcook them or they will be tough and stringy. Sprinkle with freshly ground black pepper. Good, too, to charcoal-broil out-of-doors. Spear with toothpicks.

PICKLED SHRIMP

TWENTY TO THIRTY SHRIMP

No one will deny that pickled shrimp are delicious:

1 pound cooked and cleaned shrimp
2 tablespoons olive oil
1 cup vinegar
2 tablespoons water
¼ cup paper-thin slices of onion
8 whole cloves
1 bay leaf
2 teaspoons salt
1 teaspoon sugar
A dash of cayenne pepper

Dribble the oil over the shrimp. Bring to a boil the rest of the ingredients and pour over shrimp while hot. Cool and then refrigerate for at least 24 hours.

SHRIMP IN THE SHELL

FORTY TO FIFTY SHRIMP

There are many arguments against serving shrimp in their shells to guests, but for football parties, with informal clothes and informal attitudes, they are wonderful. And a pat on the back for the hostess; she doesn't have to peel them herself — some kind guest will peel one for her.

2 pounds large shrimp
1 teaspoon salt
2 teaspoons pickling spice
3 bay leaves
½ teaspoon cracked pepper
½ cup salad or olive oil
¼ cup water
¼ cup vinegar

Mix together, put in a saucepan with a tight-fitting lid, bring to a boil, then simmer for 10 minutes. Dump into a serving bowl that will keep them warm, and let your guests do the rest. For a good dunk:

½ cup salad oil
2 tablespoons tarragon vinegar
1 teaspoon dry mustard
1 teaspoon Creole mustard or any prepared type
¼ cup finely chopped celery
⅛ cup finely minced green onion or chives
A dash of garlic salt
A dash of Tabasco sauce

Mix together and let stand overnight. Use for dunking — and it's good on a green salad too.

ANGELS ON HORSEBACK

Angels on Horseback (oysters broiled, wrapped in bacon) are the usual. Be unusual with this Irish version.

4 dozen medium-sized oysters
1 cup chili sauce
2 tablespoons chopped green pepper
2 tablespoons Worcestershire sauce
12 slices uncooked bacon
¾ cup grated Parmesan cheese

Place oysters, well drained, in a skillet or saucepan; cover with chili sauce mixed with green pepper and Worcestershire sauce. Place in oven at 350° until oysters begin to puff. Remove and sprinkle with the bacon cut in fine dice and the cheese. Return to oven and bake 10 minutes. Keep hot while serving; and give your guests a square of dark rye bread to rest them on.

STUFFED SHRIMP

FOR FOUR

1 pound large shrimp (15 to 20 count)
1 3-ounce package cream cheese
¼ cup Roquefort cheese
3 tablespoons Madeira
⅛ teaspoon garlic salt (you may omit)
Chopped parsley (lots of it)

Cook shrimp; peel and clean. Split each shrimp halfway through (from the vein side) and chill.

Mash the cream cheese and Roquefort with the Madeira, and add garlic salt; stuff the shrimp. Roll stuffed side in chopped parsley and serve on a chilled serving dish.

SEAFOOD SPREAD

FORTY TO FIFTY CANAPÉS

1 cup finely chopped lobster
1 cup chopped shrimp
1 cup chopped crabmeat
¾ cup Russian dressing
¼ cup chopped pistachio nuts

Mix seafoods and Russian dressing; refrigerate for at least an hour. Serve on thin crackers or Melba toast, and sprinkle, as served, with chopped salted pistachio nuts.

FISH BALLS

FOR ONE HUNDRED

Pass them while they are hot!

2 cups cooked finely flaked fish
½ teaspoon salt
½ teaspoon dry mustard
1 tablespoon lemon juice
1 cup thick Cream Sauce
1 tablespoon chopped parsley
½ teaspoon onion juice

Combine all ingredients and chill. Shape into balls. Fry until golden in deep fat at 375°. Drain on paper. A dip is nice to dunk them in, but not necessary. Serve with cocktail sauce, or a sour cream and French-fried-onion mixture.

HOT CREAM-CHEESE CANAPÉS

One of my favorites!

1 3-ounce package cream cheese
1 egg
1 teaspoon onion juice
1 tablespoon lemon juice
1 teaspoon salt
Chutney

Mix first five ingredients in an electric blender or by hand until smooth and airy. Pile high on well-buttered toast rounds, spread top with chutney, place on buttered cookie sheet and bake at 450° until bubbly, about 5 to 8 minutes. Pass right away!

CHEESE SPREAD SANDWICHES

THREE DOZEN

1 pound Cheddar cheese, grated
1 cup finely chopped onion
1 clove garlic, minced
1 4-ounce can Ortega green chiles, seeded and chopped
1 4-ounce jar stuffed olives, chopped
2 tablespoons vinegar
1 8-ounce can tomato sauce
1 teaspoon Worcestershire sauce
2 tablespoons salad oil (I prefer peanut oil)
French bread or baguettes

Mix together; spread on thin slices of French bread. I buy baguettes that are about the size of a silver dollar in circumference. Broil, as far away from the heating element as possible, until bubbly and edges of bread are brown. A good cocktail snack also. The spread keeps well and is nice to have on hand.

CHEESE BALL

1 pound Cheddar cheese, soft type
1 pound cream cheese
¼ pound blue cheese
¼ pound smoked cheese
1 tablespoon prepared mustard
1 tablespoon onion salt
¼ teaspoon garlic salt
Port
2 tablespoons Horseradish Sauce
½ cup finely chopped pickled beets

Mix all the cheeses, except 1 cup of the cream cheese, with the mustard, onion and garlic salts, and enough port to soften. Form into a log or a ball and cover with a coating of the 1 cup of cream cheese mixed with the Horseradish Sauce and chopped beets. Refrigerate for several hours and dust with finely chopped parsley. Arrange on a tray with an assortment of crackers, Melba toast, and rye or pumpernickel bread. If you think the pinkness of the beets will annoy you, leave them out, but I like the added flavor.

CHEESE STRAWS

FIVE DOZEN

1 cup butter or margarine
1 cup grated sharp cheese
2 cups flour
1 teaspoon salt
⅛ teaspoon cayenne pepper
Parmesan cheese

Have butter and cheese at room temperature. Mix all ingredients and either put through a cookie press or roll out very thin and cut into narrow strips. Sprinkle lightly with Parmesan cheese. Bake at 350° for 15 minutes.

Sometimes I use grated Gruyère in place of the sharp cheese and add 1 teaspoon *fine herbes*. Whatever kind of cheese you use, be sure you grate it finely.

LIPTAUER CHEESE

3 8-ounce packages cream cheese
1 cup sour cream
Watercress or parsley
¼ cup chopped chives or green onion
2 tablespoons paprika
4 tablespoons chopped capers
2 tablespoons cracked pepper
2 tablespoons salt
¼ cup chopped parsley

Mix cheese and sour cream; form into a ball. Place in center of serving tray. Surround with watercress or parsley. Around the edge, about 1 inch from the ball, make separate piles of each remaining ingredient. Serve with a small flat-bladed knife, and let the guests mix whatever seasoning they wish with their cream cheese. Serve with dark bread. This also keeps your guests busy.

CHEESE AND RED CAVIAR

1 cup cream cheese
2 tablespoons cream
1 teaspoon onion juice
1 teaspoon lemon juice
2 tablespoons red caviar

Soften the cream cheese with cream and onion juice (obtained by grating onion and straining — you will weep bitterly, but it is good for you). Add lemon juice and mix the caviar in carefully to avoid breaking the eggs.

Dark-rye-bread squares are mighty good with it.

ALMOND–PARMESAN CHEESE SPREAD

3 tablespoons chopped almonds
3 tablespoons butter
6 tablespoons grated Parmesan cheese
3 tablespoons minced parsley
3 tablespoons heavy cream
Salt and pepper to taste
12 toast strips (buttered)

Sauté almonds in butter until golden. Add cheese, parsley, cream, salt, and pepper. Spread on buttered toast strips. Heat thoroughly in a 400° oven before serving.

PRAIRIE FIRE

1 quart red beans, cooked and put through a sieve
½ pound butter
½ pound grated Provolone cheese
4 jalapeños (pickled hot peppers), chopped very fine
1 teaspoon jalapeño juice
2 tablespoons minced onion
1 clove garlic, chopped very fine

Mix all ingredients and heat over hot water until cheese is melted. Serve hot from chafing dish with fried tortillas or potato chips.

ANCHOVY STICKS

Anchovies have an affinity for cheese. Sometime try these anchovy sticks. First, you fry pieces of bread in butter until crisp, then cut them in fingers wide enough to lay an anchovy fillet on each. Mix Parmesan cheese and a little chopped parsley and moisten with dry sherry to make a paste. Spread the paste rather thickly over the anchovy fingers; sprinkle with melted butter and grill under the broiler. Serve very hot!

SAUSAGE BISCUITS

1 10-ounce bar extra sharp cheese
1 pound hot sausage (Owens, if available)
3 cups biscuit mix
1 teaspoon salt

Grate cheese and let stand at room temperature. Mix all the ingredients with your hands. Shape into small balls or patties. Bake at 375° for 12 to 15 minutes. Serve hot. You may bake and freeze, then put frozen in a 300° oven for 10 minutes.

PICKLED FRANKFURTERS

Pickled tiny frankfurters are a good try for both gastronomical and conversational delight, and if you ask long and loud enough of your butcher, he can sell them to you by the pound, rather than having to get small jars of them, which makes both cost and effort greater. Remember that the law of supply is governed by the law of demand, or the wheel that squeaks the loudest get the grease, and frankfurters should be on the *must* list.

Cover 1 pound of tiny frankfurters with boiling water to which has been added:

¼ cup thinly sliced onions
½ teaspoon peppercorns
6 cloves
1½ tablespoons salt

Cook slowly until tender. Drain and pack in sterilized jars and cover with:

1 cup white vinegar
1 tablespoon sugar
1 clove of garlic

Keep refrigerated until ready to serve, and serve cold.

These tiny frankfurters are especially good, too, broiled in mustard butter or barbecued — I have served them for many years at parties, and young men about town have dubbed them my "sophisticated frankfurters." Mustard butter is made by mixing ½ cup of butter with 2 tablespoons of prepared mustard — the Louisiana type, I think, is best.

TEXAS CAVIAR

In the South the black-eyed pea is the traditional good-luck food for New Year's Day and a good Texan eats them sometime during the day to ensure prosperity for the coming year — whether he likes them or not. I came to Texas wide-eyed and innocent about such shenanigans — I didn't like the peas either. So-o-o, I pickled them. Since then I serve few parties at *any* time of the year without them.

2 No. 2 cans black-eyed peas
1 cup salad oil
¼ cup wine vinegar
1 clove garlic — or garlic seasoning
¼ cup thinly sliced onion
½ teaspoon salt
Cracked or freshly ground black pepper

Drain liquid from the peas. Place peas in pan or bowl, add remaining ingredients, and mix thoroughly. Store in jar in refrigerator and remove garlic after one day. Store at least two days and up to two weeks before eating. You'll need a plate and fork for these. Red kidney beans and garbanzos do the same.

CRABMEAT-STUFFED MUSHROOMS

You may stuff mushrooms with all sorts of things — fish, fowl, or meat, but I do think that the crabmeat-stuffed ones are the best. Sauté the mushrooms in butter and fill the cavities (made when stem is pulled out) with this crabmeat mixture (for 24 small or 8 large mushroom caps):

2 tablespoons fine white bread crumbs
¼ cup mayonnaise
¼ cup medium Cream Sauce
1 pound fresh or canned crabmeat, flaked and cut in small pieces
¼ teaspoon Worcestershire sauce
Parmesan cheese

Mix ingredients and stuff the mushrooms; sprinkle liberally with grated Parmesan cheese. Bake at 350° for 15 minutes, then run under the broiler to brown. Serve hot! For cocktails spear with plastic toothpicks. For an entrée, serve on, for instance, fried eggplant rings.

HAM-STUFFED MUSHROOMS

½ pound ground cooked ham
1 clove finely minced garlic
1 cup finely minced parsley
1 cup finely minced mushroom stems
½ cup fine white bread crumbs
½ cup grated Parmesan cheese
Salt and pepper
24 medium-sized mushrooms
Pine nuts
½ cup butter, melted

Mix ham, garlic, parsley, mushroom stems, crumbs, and cheese. Add salt and pepper as needed. Stuff the mushrooms (you have removed the stems for mincing). Decorate with the pine nuts. Place in a buttered casserole, pour butter over, and bake at 375° for 25 minutes.

Mushroom lovers may freeze these and other mushroom canapés. Fill the sautéed caps with any stuffing you desire — crabmeat or lobster salad, minced ham with mayonnaise, a good savory dressing — most anything at all; just freeze and take out and pop into a hot oven until the filling is brown.

OYSTERS AND MUSHROOMS

For a smart cocktail item, pass hot oysters and mushrooms. Sauté fresh mushrooms (or canned broiled-in-butter ones) in butter in which a bud of crushed garlic has been swished around. Place an oyster on each mushroom, top with a dash of butter, and bake at 350° until the edges of the oyster curl. Pass quickly while hot — with toothpicks! And cocktail napkins to catch the drip.

MEATBALLS

TWENTY BALLS

1 pound ground beef
1 small can Smithfield ham spread
Salt
Freshly ground pepper
Roquefort cheese
Dry red wine
Butter

Mix ground beef and ham spread together. Sprinkle lightly with salt and pepper, cut pieces of Roquefort or blue cheese into small squares, and mold the meat around them. Place in a bowl, china or crockery, and cover with dry red wine. Let stand in refrigerator for at least 3 hours. Then put a small amount of butter in a skillet (or frying pan — depending on how you say it), add a little of the wine the meat has soaked in, and pan-fry the meat patties to medium doneness. Remove to a hot platter or chafing dish for serving.

HAM BALLS

THIRTY BALLS

1 pound finely ground fresh lean pork (the butcher will do it)
1 small can Smithfield ham spread
1 cup fresh bread crumbs that have soaked in enough milk to soften
1 egg, uncooked
¾ cup red wine

Mix together all ingredients but the wine — your hands will do it best — and roll into small balls. Brown in butter in the skillet part of your chafing dish, pour wine over, put chafing dish cover on, and simmer slowly until thoroughly cooked. Keep hot as you serve them.

SAUSAGE BALLS IN CHILE CON QUESO

I find you can take short cuts in many ways, so for Chile con Queso I make or buy a cheese sauce and add canned Rotel (tomatoes and green chiles). If I wish it hotter, I add some chopped jalapeño peppers. Form sausage balls, bake in the oven, drain on paper towels, and cover with the Chile con Queso. You may prepare this the day before; the sauce freezes well. If I have sausage and sauce left, I combine them with slices of eggplant, floured and sautéed in salad oil. It makes a delicious vegetable and can also be used for a supper entrée. I call it "Mamacita's Supper Dish." I also make it when I do not have leftovers. It is not a one-helping dish. 'Tis good!

CHIPPED BEEF AND HORSERADISH

Cream cheese answers the needs of many hostesses when they want a cocktail standby that takes little time and money. Made into a ball, or log, this one is amazing.

2 3-ounce packages cream cheese
2 teaspoons horseradish
1 teaspoon prepared mustard
2 2½-ounce jars dried chipped beef
2 tablespoons butter

Soften cream cheese with horseradish and mustard. Chop the dried beef until fine and sauté in the butter until well frizzled. Form cheese mixture into a ball, or log, and roll in the dried-beef mixture. Wrap in wax paper and chill. I like to serve these with any buttery crackers, toasted, of course.

Or, you may divide cream cheese into as many parts as you wish flavors; for instance, crushed garlic or garlic powder in one part; Beau Monde seasoning salt in another; chopped anchovies in another; chopped black and green olives in another; curry powder in another. Put together into a ball or a loaf, keeping each flavored cheese as separate as possible. Then roll the whole thing in chopped parsley or nuts and chill. When the guests knife into it they cannot tell what they are getting and it causes a furor. I like to have a bit of garlic somewhere in it; and sometimes I roll the whole works in chutney. Any kind of crackers or thin breads keep your guests coming back for more.

HAM AND CHUTNEY

2 cups ground cooked ham
¾ cup chopped Major Grey's chutney
½ cup mayonnaise
⅛ teaspoon curry powder

Mix and serve with hot buttered Melba toast made with thin slices of icebox rye bread. This mixture makes a good sandwich, too!

ROLLWITCHES

For this hors d'oeuvre I use canned biscuits. I split each in half, press my thumb in the middle to make an indentation, and fill with crabmeat, lobster, tuna fish, shrimp, chicken, or ham salad with a little curry powder added to the mayonnaise (especially if I am using seafood). I then cover generously with grated Gruyère cheese and bake according to directions on package. These are good! I know that when I have them on a cocktail buffet, as I do when I'm in a hurry, I need lots — and someone to keep them coming out of the oven.

DIPS

When Helen Corbitt wrote her first book, Helen Corbitt's Cookbook, *cocktail dips were very popular, but even then dips bored Helen. In 1974 in* Helen Corbitt Cooks for Company *she wrote: "Dips are passé. Aren't you glad? I always resented dipping. I either had too much or too little on that piece of whatever was provided to dip with."*

But the Corbitt dips were sensational and are still prized and used by many hostesses. For quick production of something good, here are five great Corbitt dips. If you put an individual butter knife on the plate with the dip and an assortment of good crackers and small pieces of whole-wheat and rye bread your guests will spread instead of dip.

CHEESE-CRAB DIP

½ cup Roquefort or blue cheese
⅓ cup cream cheese
2 tablespoons mayonnaise
½ teaspoon Worcestershire sauce
1 small clove of garlic, finely chopped (you may leave it out)
1 teaspoon lemon juice
½ cup crabmeat, fresh or canned, but fresh is better, as always

Mix the two cheeses together until soft and add the rest of the ingredients in order given. Place in a bowl on a large tray or plate and surround with potato chips that have been sprinkled with garlic salt and heated.

One of the simplest and best hot appetizers I ever had was up in the mountains of New Jersey when a football crowd dropped in on my hostess. She quickly cut baker's bread in 1-inch squares, spread mayonnaise on topsides and covered with grated Parmesan cheese, and put them in the oven at 450° to brown. Were they good! I finally pitched in and helped because they plain disappeared too fast.

□

A hot Roquefort Cheese Puff smells to high heaven, but is so good you can hardly wait for a second. Merely mix Roquefort cheese with a little Worcestershire sauce and butter. Pile high on toast rounds, or better yet, pastry bases you make yourself from piecrust. Place in oven at 450° until hot. (You will be amazed at their acceptance.) Mix with toasted chopped almonds for a more delightful experience.

□

If there are going to be more men than women at a large gathering for pick-up food, sea trout or red snapper (or even catfish) — cut in 1-inch squares, rolled in cornmeal and fried in bacon fat or butter and drained thoroughly on paper — would meet with approval. Put it in a "dunking" dish, with a real tartar sauce beside it, and that is all there is to it — except to keep the supply coming!

□

In these days of waist watching, honeydew or cantaloupe balls, encircled with a thin slice of ham and held together with a toothpick or plastic spear, makes an interesting taste experience. The better the ham, the better the morsel.

□

Mash together equal quantities of sweet butter and Roquefort or Danish blue cheese. Sandwich a little of the mixture between two walnut or pecan halves. Chill before serving.

□

There is nothing better (nor higher in calories) with sautéed chicken livers than Béarnaise Sauce — a good cocktail delicacy.

Soups

Helen Corbitt liked to make and serve soup and often served it before dinner in a demitasse cup. She enjoyed inventing soups no one has ever dreamed of and then watched with amusement and interest as they became more popular than the old standbys like cream of tomato soup. She once wrote: "A good soup does fine things for the soul at times . . ."

CONSOMMÉ BELLEVUE WITH AVOCADO

FOR EIGHT

2 10½-ounce cans chicken consommé
2 cups clam juice
2 cups diced avocado
⅓ cup sherry
½ cup whipping cream

Heat consommé and clam juice to a rolling boil. Add avocado and sherry. Pour into cups or an oven-proof tureen. Whip the cream and spoon on top. Run under the broiler to brown.

VELVET ASPARAGUS SOUP

FOR SIX OR EIGHT

1 10-ounce can white asparagus
1 6-ounce breast of chicken, boned and uncooked
1 quart cold chicken broth
1 egg white
2 tablespoons cornstarch
Cold water
Salt to taste
¼ cup slivered ham

Using a sharp knife, slice asparagus open and scrape out the delicate portions of the stem and tip. Mash to a pulp and mix with ½ cup of the juice the asparagus was canned in. Set aside. Mince the chicken and pound to a pulp with the blunt end of a cleaver or edge of a heavy plate. Mix with ½ cup of the cold chicken broth and beat until light, removing any sinews. Beat the egg white until frothy and add to chicken mixture. Dissolve the cornstarch in a little cold water. Bring broth to a boil; add asparagus pulp and slowly stir in the cornstarch. Simmer for 15 minutes. Add salt to taste and beat in the chicken and egg white. Remove from heat and allow chicken to cook in the heat of the soup. Sprinkle with the ham as served.

ARTICHOKE SOUP

FOR TEN TO TWELVE

---

1 14-ounce can artichoke bottoms
3 10½-ounce cans chicken consommé
1 clove garlic (you may omit)
Approximately 1 cup dry white wine
Salt and pepper

Mash the artichoke bottoms. Add the consommé and garlic. Bring to a boil. Pour in the wine, reheat, season with salt and pepper, and add a dash of Tabasco if you wish it spicier. Remove garlic before serving.

BLACK BEAN SOUP

FOR TWELVE

---

4 cups dried black beans
4 quarts cold water
1 cup sliced onion
2 cloves garlic, chopped
4 stalks celery, chopped
8 peppercorns
1 bay leaf
2 carrots
Few sprigs parsley
A ham bone or ½ pound salt pork or leftover ham scraps
Salt and pepper

Cover beans with the water, bring to the boiling point, and simmer for 10 minutes. Cool. Add remaining ingredients and cook about 4 hours below the boiling point until beans are soft. Add more water if necessary. Remove ham bone or salt pork, and put beans and vegetables through a Foley mill or purée in your blender. Correct seasonings. If you like, add sherry or Burgundy to taste. Sometimes I add rice, bits of avocado, sour cream, lemon, or eggs poached in the soup. You may add the ham scraps too if you wish.

No time? Use canned Black Bean Soup as label directs; dry sherry or Burgundy will help it.

CHICKEN CONSOMMÉ ORIENTAL

FOR EIGHT

5 cups canned chicken consommé, or make your own
½ cup diced water chestnuts
½ cup sliced canned or fresh mushrooms
1 cup fresh spinach leaves, slivered
1 egg white
Salt and white pepper

Bring consommé to a boil. Add the water chestnuts and mushrooms. Cook 1 minute. Add spinach, again cooking 1 minute only. Pour egg white in slowly, stirring with a fork. Correct seasonings and serve at once. For a few more calories, add a handful of bean threads (rain noodles) and cook until transparent before adding the spinach.

CANADIAN CHEESE SOUP

FOR EIGHT

By far the most asked-for soup everywhere I have been is Canadian Cheese Soup. Where it comes from I do not know; it has been a part of my life so long it could have come with the stork.

¼ cup butter
½ cup finely diced onion
½ cup finely diced carrots
½ cup finely diced celery
¼ cup flour
1½ tablespoons cornstarch
1 quart chicken stock
1 quart milk
⅛ teaspoon soda
1 cup processed Cheddar-type cheese
Salt and pepper
2 tablespoons parsley, chopped fine

Melt butter in the pot you are going to make the soup in; add onions, carrots, and celery and sauté over low heat until soft. Add flour and cornstarch and cook until bubbly. Add stock and milk and make a smooth sauce. Add soda and the cheese, grated. Season with salt and pepper. Add parsley a few minutes before you serve.

CHICKEN AND CORN SOUP

FOR SIX

½ cup fine noodles
1 quart chicken stock
½ cup cooked chicken, finely diced
¼ cup corn kernels, ground
Salt and pepper to taste
1 teaspoon chopped parsley
1 hard-cooked egg, put through a sieve

Wash noodles in cold water and add to the chicken stock. Cook until soft; then add the chicken and corn. Season with salt and pepper; add the parsley and egg. Serve hot with an inch square of French bread on each cup. Chicken and Corn Soup is of German descent. It is especially popular with my Yankee friends.

LEMON RICE SOUP

FOR EIGHT

1 egg yolk
1 tablespoon lemon juice
4 tablespoons Parmesan cheese
4 cups (about 2 cans) chicken consommé
¾ cup cooked rice

Mix egg yolk, lemon juice, and cheese. Fork-stir into boiling chicken consommé. Add rice and serve. Nice with a variety of thin bread sandwiches.

FRENCH ONION SOUP

FOR SIX

This takes time.

1 pound onions, sliced paper-thin
4 tablespoons butter
6 cups stock, preferably chicken

Brown onions carefully in the butter, turning constantly to prevent burning. Add the stock and cook slowly until onions are soft. Remove from heat and let stand several hours. Reheat and serve with 2-inch squares of French bread sprinkled with grated Parmesan cheese and oven browned. Add a teaspoon of grated Parmesan cheese on top of each cup.

GIN SOUP

FOR SIX TO EIGHT

Here's a different twist in the soup department — especially good on a cold day.

2 tablespoons butter
2 tablespoons finely diced onion
2 tablespoons finely diced celery
2 cups canned clam juice
2 cups canned chicken broth
2 cups whipping cream
2 tablespoons cornstarch
⅔ cup gin
1 teaspoon dill weed
2 tablespoons chopped chives
2 tablespoons chopped parsley
Salt and pepper

Melt butter in large saucepan. Add onion and celery, and sauté for 1 minute. Add clam juice, broth, and cream. Bring to a boil. Mix cornstarch with the gin and add. Bring to a boil again. Reduce heat; simmer for 10 minutes. Add dill, chives, and parsley, and season with salt and pepper to taste.

MINESTRONE

FOR SIX

Italian Minestrone is a good stick-to-your-ribs soup, and especially adaptable for that one-dish meal we all dream about. This needs real crusty French bread put in the oven with butter and a suspicion of garlic. Then serve really hot!

½ cup minced raw onion
1 small clove garlic, minced
2 tablespoons minced parsley
½ cup salt pork, diced fine
1 cup minced ham

Put these in the pot you are going to make the soup in and sauté until the onions are yellow and soft. Add:

2 quarts boiling stock

and cook slowly for 20 minutes. Add:

½ cup diced fresh tomatoes, or canned
½ cup carrots, diced
½ cup celery, diced
½ cup diced raw potatoes
½ cup cooked navy beans or chick peas

Cover and cook over low heat until vegetables are tender. Add:

1 cup fresh spinach, cut in shreds
¼ cup elbow macaroni

Cook until tender. Just before serving, add:

2 tablespoons grated Parmesan cheese
Salt and pepper to suit you

Serve very hot as soon as it is done — with plenty of extra cheese. Freezes well.

OLD-FASHIONED POTATO SOUP

FOR EIGHT

Good old-fashioned potato soup is asked for time and again. If any is left, I reheat it the next day, add lots of chopped watercress, and serve it with toasted almonds.

2 quarts raw potatoes, pared
3 leeks or ¼ cup chopped onion
2 quarts boiling water
2 teaspoons salt
½ cup butter
2 tablespoons flour
2 quarts milk
2 tablespoons parsley

Put potatoes and leeks or onion through food chopper, or chop fine. Cook in the boiling water with the salt until potatoes and water are thick. Melt butter, add flour, stir until smooth, and add the milk. Cook until thickened and smooth. Add potato mixture and chopped parsley.

RUSSIAN BORSCHT

FOR SIX

2 cups chopped canned beets
2 tablespoons butter
½ cup chopped onion
1 cup chopped celery
Beet juice and water to make 4 cups
2 cups canned consommé
2 teaspoons salt
¼ teaspoon pepper
3 tablespoons lemon juice
Sour cream

Chop the beets very fine. Melt butter, add onion and celery, and cook until soft but not brown. Add beets, juice and water, and consommé, and simmer uncovered for 30 minutes. Season with salt and pepper and lemon juice. Pour into hot cups and drop a tablespoon of sour cream on top. Serve at once. Or serve cold, in chilled cups, adding a dash of caviar to the sour cream.

MULLIGATAWNY

FOR SIX

If you want to be exotic, make that India-born creation, full of subtle flavors, which became a favorite American dish a century ago. Mulligatawny, a fascinating name, a fascinating dish; and definitely a soup any guest in your house will rave about.

2 tablespoons butter
½ cup onion, chopped fine
1 small clove garlic, crushed
2 tablespoons flour
1 tablespoon curry powder
1 pint half-and-half
1 quart chicken stock
1 raw apple, peeled and chopped
1 tablespoon salt
A dash of pepper

Melt the butter in the pot you are going to make the soup in. Add onion and crushed garlic and cook over low heat until the onion is soft. Remove the garlic, add the flour and curry powder, and cook 2 minutes. Add half-and-half and chicken stock; cook over hot water until smooth. Add apple 10 minutes before serving. Season with salt and freshly ground pepper — just a dash. It is the apple that throws them; no one can figure it out, unless they are Mulligatawny addicts.

COCK-A-LEEKIE

FOR TWELVE TO FOURTEEN

1 4- to 5-pound chicken or wings and backs
3 quarts water or chicken broth
4 cups washed and stored leeks, white part only
10 to 12 cooked prunes, sliced
Salt and white pepper
Finely minced parsley

Cook the chicken (and giblets) in the water or broth. When tender remove and add the leeks. Cook until leeks are soft. Add the prunes, some of the chicken, and giblets cut in julienne pieces. If you wish to use this as a main dish, cut the chicken in serving pieces. Correct seasonings and add the parsley.

Cock-a-Leekie appears in cookbooks pertaining to the British Isles. No doubt its origin is Scotch, or Irish, or whatever. Who cares? You find it everywhere the sun sets on British soil. Texans like it!

CREAM OF CAULIFLOWER SOUP

FOR SIX

One of my long-time favorites for cold weather.

1 small head of cauliflower
4 cups boiling water
2 cups hot milk
4 tablespoons butter
2 tablespoons sliced onion
2 tablespoons flour
2 teaspoons salt
Pepper to taste
1 egg yolk
2 tablespoons grated Cheddar cheese
¼ cup cooked crumbled sausage

Cook the cauliflower in boiling water, uncovered, until tender. Remove and mash the cauliflower through a food mill or purée in electric blender. Add to the hot milk. Melt the butter, add the onion, and sauté until yellow but not browned. Add the flour and seasonings. Add the milk and cauliflower mixture and cook until thick. Add the egg yolk and cheese, whipping briskly. As you serve, sprinkle the cooked sausage over the soup.

CREAM OF PEANUT SOUP

FOR SIX

1 tablespoon butter
2 tablespoons finely chopped onion
1 tablespoon flour
1 quart milk
½ cup peanut butter
¼ teaspoon celery seed
½ cup finely chopped dry roasted peanuts (you may omit)
Salt and pepper

Melt butter, add onion, and sauté until soft but not brown. Add flour and cook until foamy. Add milk, peanut butter, and celery seed. Cook over hot water until creamy. Strain through a fine sieve. Add peanuts, and salt and pepper to taste.

CHICKEN VELVET SOUP

FOR EIGHT

Chicken Velvet Soup was, I think, named by my good friend Veronica Morrissey. It tastes the way it sounds.

⅓ cup butter
¾ cup flour
6 cups chicken stock
1 cup warm milk
1 cup warm cream
1½ cups finely diced chicken
½ teaspoon salt, and pepper to your taste

Melt butter, add flour, and cook over low heat until well blended. Add 2 cups hot chicken stock and the warm milk and cream. Cook slowly, stirring frequently, until thick. Add remaining 4 cups of the chicken stock and chicken, and heat to boiling. Season with salt and pepper.

CREAM OF CORN SOUP

FOR SIX

This is my favorite soup.

2 strips of bacon, finely diced
2 tablespoons finely chopped onion
2 cups frozen or fresh corn
2 tablespoons butter
2 tablespoons flour
2 cups milk
1 teaspoon salt
½ teaspoon pepper
2 cups light cream

Fry bacon until crisp; add onion and sauté until soft. Put corn through a food chopper, add to onion and bacon, and cook until it begins to brown. Add butter, and then the flour. Cook slowly for 3 minutes. Add milk, salt, and pepper and cook until thickened; then add cream and heat until smooth. Serve with hot crackers.

ZUPPA PAVESE

FOR FOUR

I can think of nothing better to soothe one's nerves.

4 slices French or Italian bread
2 tablespoons butter
4 eggs
2 cans hot chicken consommé
½ cup grated Parmesan cheese

Trim the crusts from the bread and cut into round shape with a cookie cutter. Sauté in the butter until brown on both sides. Soft-poach the eggs in salted water. Place the eggs on the toast, pour the consommé over them, and ladle the cheese over all.

What a nice dish to come home to after a cocktail party or the theater or opera.

CLEAR TOMATO SOUP

FOR SIX

Here is a hot, spicy soup that will stimulate your appetite.

¼ cup diced celery
¼ cup diced carrots
¼ cup diced onion
2 tablespoons butter
2 sprigs parsley
4 cups canned tomato juice
½ teaspoon white pepper
6 whole cloves
1 bay leaf
1 teaspoon salt
⅛ teaspoon thyme
2 cups hot consommé

Sauté celery, carrots, and onion in the butter for 5 minutes. Add rest of the ingredients except consommé and bring to a boil. Cover and simmer over low heat for 1 hour. Strain, add the consommé, reheat, and serve.

MUSHROOM AND CHIVE BISQUE

FOR EIGHT

½ cup butter
2 cups finely chopped mushrooms (I use stems, too.)
4 tablespoons flour
¼ teaspoon dry mustard
1 teaspoon salt
2 cups chicken broth
2 cups half-and-half
¼ cup dry sherry
¼ cup finely chopped chives
¼ cup whipping cream

Melt butter, add mushrooms, and sauté until soft. Add flour, mustard, and salt; cook 1 minute. Pour in chicken broth and cook until thickened. Add half-and-half, sherry, and chives. Heat thoroughly and let stand over hot water until ready to serve. Whip the cream and float on top of soup. If serving cold, I put everything but the whipped cream in the blender, and chill.

CREAM OF SPINACH SOUP WITH CHEESE

FOR SIX

When men ask for spinach, even in soup, I mark the soup as popular.

¼ cup boiling water
2 cups frozen spinach
¼ cup finely chopped onion
4 tablespoons butter
4 tablespoons flour
4 cups milk
1 teaspoon salt
A dash of Ac'cent
Provolone cheese

Add water to the spinach and allow to stand until spinach is heated through. Put through a food mill or purée in an electric blender. Brown onion in the butter and stir in the flour. Cook until bubbly; add the milk, stirring rapidly until thickened. Add spinach, salt, and Ac'cent. Let stand at least 15 minutes. When serving, put a teaspoonful of coarsely grated Provolone cheese on top, or Swiss, or American, but the Provolone is the catch.

PURÉE OF SPLIT PEA SOUP

FOR SIX

Another all-time favorite that only takes time.

2 cups split peas
8 cups cold water
Ham bone, or ends of baked ham
3 tablespoons chopped onion
1 teaspoon salt
⅛ teaspoon pepper

Soak peas overnight, wash, and drain. Add to the water with the ham bone and onion, and cook until thick. Put the soup through a food mill. Season well. Serve with croutons. If this should get too thick, thin with hot cream. Dried beans may be substituted for the peas. If you have a smoked turkey carcass, use it with the ham bone.

QUICK MUSHROOM CONSOMMÉ

FOR EIGHT TO TWELVE

10 cups canned beef consommé
1 cup thinly sliced fresh mushrooms
1 cup water
½ cup sherry or Burgundy
Few slices raw mushrooms

Put first three ingredients in a saucepan and simmer for 10 minutes. Add dry sherry or red Burgundy; bring to a rapid boil. Remove and serve with floating slices of raw mushrooms.

CHICKEN GUMBO

FOR EIGHT OR TEN

Gumbo is as southern as fried chicken, and you may go any route you like — chicken, seafood, ham, vegetable, or leftovers. Use it as a soup or a main dish.

½ cup chopped onion
½ cup green pepper, slivered
1 cup chopped celery
Butter or salad oil
3 cups chicken broth
2 cups canned or peeled fresh tomatoes
1 bay leaf
¼ teaspoon thyme
1 cup sliced okra, fresh, frozen, or canned
2 tablespoons chopped parsley
¼ teaspoon Tabasco
½ teaspoon gumbo filé (you may omit)
Salt to taste
3 cups chicken pieces (or less)

Sauté the onion, green pepper, and celery until soft in very little butter or salad oil. Add the rest of the ingredients except chicken and simmer for 30 minutes; add chicken and heat thoroughly. Add additional salt to taste.

If you freeze the gumbo for future use, and like the flavor of filé, add when you reheat. Vary this recipe adding whole cooked shrimp or pieces of ham or both. Serve as a main course on hot rice. Always serve with a slice of lemon whether used as a soup or an entrée. One needs only a salad and perhaps a bowl of fruit for a satisfying meal.

P.S. Dip green pepper in boiling water for one minute before cutting. It cuts more easily and the unpleasant oily taste that many object to is lessened.

LOUISIANA SEAFOOD GUMBO

FOR SIX

Once you meet the Deep South in your travels you find all kinds of interpretations of gumbo. This recipe is a compromise; add more shrimp and crabmeat or oysters and pour it over a mound of hot cooked rice and you have an entrée; serve it as written for a soup.

¼ pound bacon
¼ cup chopped onion
¼ cup diced green pepper
1 cup diced celery
3 sprigs parsley
2 cups fresh or canned tomatoes
4 cups stock
1 cup raw cleaned shrimp
1 cup fresh or frozen crabmeat
2 cups okra
1 cup cooked rice

Dice and sauté the bacon in the pot you plan to make the soup in. Add onion, green pepper, and celery and sauté until onion is yellow. Add parsley, chopped fine, and the tomatoes and stock. Cook until all the vegetables are soft. Add the raw shrimp and crabmeat, the okra, and the rice. Cook for 10 minutes and serve hot. This is not a soup to serve if the meal that follows is bountiful.

OYSTER BISQUE

FOR SIX

Oyster Bisque is a delightful soup for entertaining and this recipe I like best.

1 quart small oysters
½ clove garlic
¼ cup finely chopped onion
½ cup butter
2 cups milk
2 cups cream
½ cup soft white bread crumbs
Salt
Chopped parsley

Chop the oysters with the garlic and mix with the chopped onion. Sauté at low heat in butter until oysters curl. Combine with milk and cream, previously heated. Add bread crumbs and season with salt to your taste. Let stand over hot water for at least 15 minutes before serving. Sprinkle with chopped parsley when serving.

OYSTER AND SPINACH SOUP

FOR FOUR TO SIX

4 tablespoons butter
¼ cup finely chopped onion
1 clove garlic, minced
1 pint oysters, chopped
4 tablespoons flour
3 cups half-and-half or milk
1 cup chicken broth
¾ cup spinach purée (made in blender from fresh or frozen uncooked spinach)
Salt and pepper

Melt the butter; add the onion and garlic. Sauté at low heat until soft. Add oysters and cook until they curl. Push oysters aside; add flour and cook until foamy. Add half-and-half; cook until thickened. Mix in chicken broth and spinach. Bring to a boil. Remove from heat. Correct seasonings and serve.

OYSTER STEW

FOR SIX

1 pint small oysters
¼ pound butter
6 cups half-and-half, scalded
½ teaspoon salt
⅛ teaspoon freshly ground pepper
A dash of paprika

Sauté oysters over low heat in the butter until edges curl. Add hot half-and-half and seasonings. Let stand a few minutes over hot water before serving. Sometimes I substitute raw shrimp for the oysters, and I like it equally well. (Sauté the shrimp until they turn pink.)

SHE-CRAB BISQUE

FOR SIX TO EIGHT

After serving She-Crab Bisque at a dinner party, I received many requests for the recipe. You do have to order the she-crab with eggs ahead of time from your fish man.

2 tablespoons butter
1 tablespoon onion, chopped fine
¼ teaspoon dry mustard
1 tablespoon flour
1½ cups milk
1½ cups half-and-half
1½ cups she-crabmeat with eggs
1 teaspoon salt
A pinch of white pepper
1 teaspoon chopped parsley (you may omit)
Dry sherry

Melt butter; add onion and sauté until soft. Add mustard and flour; cook until well blended. Pour in milk and half-and-half; bring to a boil. Remove from stove to add crabmeat and seasonings. Return pot to stove and keep over hot water until ready to serve. Add parsley before serving. I like to put a teaspoon of hot sherry into the hot cups before ladling the soup. You may add hot sherry to a soup tureen when serving from it. If you cannot obtain she-crab with eggs, use lump crab and add ¼ cup hard-cooked egg yolk, riced.

LOBSTER BISQUE

FOR SIX TO EIGHT

3 tablespoons butter
3 tablespoons finely minced onion
2 cups chopped lobster meat, fresh or frozen
3 tablespoons flour
5 cups half-and-half or milk
1 teaspoon salt
⅓ cup dry sherry

Melt the butter; add the onion and sauté until soft but not brown. Add the lobster and cook at low heat until thoroughly heated. Remove the lobster; add the flour and cook until bubbly. Add half-and-half and cook until thickened. Return the lobster, add salt, and let stand over hot water until ready to serve. Heat the sherry and float on top. It will mix as the bisque is ladled out into cups.

CREAM OF BROWN SCALLOP SOUP

FOR EIGHT

2 tablespoons chopped onion
1 quart diced fresh scallops
½ cup butter
4 tablespoons flour
4 cups milk
Salt and coarsely ground pepper
1 cup cream
Blanched almonds

Brown onion and scallops in the butter, stirring so that the scallops are evenly browned. Add flour and cook until well blended. Add milk and cook over low heat until thickened. Season with salt and freshly ground pepper; add the cream just before serving and reheat until very hot. Serve with slivered blanched almonds for a different flavor.

NEW ENGLAND FISH CHOWDER

FOR SIX

Being a Yankee, Friday to me always means Fish Chowder Day, and I find others are becoming addicted, too — the Yankee infiltration into many ports, no doubt. As they say up there, when the frost is on the pumpkin, there isn't anything better than a bowl of chowder, especially with hot Johnnycake (cornbread to you) dripping with butter. Chowder made with red snapper is wonderful, but any fish will do. During cold weather, I like to use smoked haddock or finnan haddie. And when I am really homesick, I use clams, fresh, frozen, or canned.

1 cup chopped onion
½ cup diced salt pork or bacon
1 cup butter
1 cup raw potatoes, diced fine
½ cup water
2 tablespoons flour
2 cups milk
1 cup cream
2 cups flaked cooked fish

Sauté onion and salt pork in the butter and cook until soft but not brown. Add potatoes and water and cook until the potatoes are soft. Add flour, cook 2 minutes, and add the milk. Cook 5 minutes, stirring constantly; add the cream and fish, then cook until hot.

BISQUE OF CORN AND CRABMEAT

FOR TEN OR TWELVE

I always like the combination of flavors and textures in soup. This is one of my favorites for Sunday night entertaining.

¼ cup chopped onion
¼ cup butter
2 tablespoons flour
½ teaspoon curry powder
4 cups fresh or frozen corn (uncooked)
4 cups milk
1 cup cream
Salt and pepper
1 pound crabmeat (I prefer lump)

Sauté the onion in the butter until soft. Add the flour and curry and cook 1 minute. Add corn, chopped by hand or in an electric blender. Cook for 5 minutes. Add milk and cream, salt, and pepper, and bring to a boil. Stir in the crabmeat and serve at once from the pot.

PORTUGUESE SOUP

FOR TEN OR TWELVE

1 cup dry red kidney beans
1 cup navy beans
3 pounds boneless chuck
Salt and pepper
1 cup coarsely chopped onion
4 smoked sausages or chorizo (Spanish sausage)
1 quart shredded cabbage
1 pound fresh spinach, shredded

Cover beans with cold water and let stand overnight. Season meat with salt and pepper and refrigerate overnight. Heat oil; add meat and brown on all sides. Add onions and 2 quarts of water. Simmer slowly for about 2 hours. Add drained beans; cover and cook until beans are tender. Remove meat, dice, and return to pot. Add sausage and cook 5 minutes. Remove the soup from the burner and cool. Then refrigerate or freeze. When ready to serve, reheat. Add cabbage and spinach. Cover and cook 5 minutes. Correct seasonings. Serve with dark rye bread and a cheese with bite to it.

AVOCADO SOUP

FOR EIGHT OR TEN

Cold Avocado Soup is beautiful to look at and to taste. I serve it in a ceramic tulip cup. I also serve canned jellied madrilène with avocado mashed with lime on top, and canned jellied chicken consommé with halves of white grapes and sometimes strips of ham on top.

4 tablespoons butter
4 tablespoons flour
2 cups milk
2 cups cream
3 avocados
¼ teaspoon powdered ginger (you may omit)
Grated rind of 1 orange
Salt to taste

Melt butter; add flour. Cook until bubbly. Add milk and cream. Cook until thickened and smooth. Cool. Peel and mash avocados. Add to the cream sauce with the ginger and orange rind. Purée in electric blender until smooth as velvet. Chill. Serve very cold with diced avocado on top, and whipped cream if you like, and grated orange peel.

JELLIED CONSOMMÉ HELENNAISE

FOR EIGHT

4 cups canned jellied beef consommé
1 cup seeded cucumber, finely diced
2 cups seeded tomatoes, peeled and finely diced
½ cup thinly sliced green onion
1 cup finely diced celery
½ cup diced avocado
1 tablespoon olive oil
2 tablespoons red wine vinegar

Lightly mix together all ingredients and refrigerate. Serve from a punch bowl or in individual soup cups. You may serve with or without sour cream. Caviar is a nice addition, but expensive. I sometimes add diced cooked shrimp, chicken, or roast beef.

CREAM OF FRESH PEA SOUP

FOR SIX

One of the most popular cream soups that I have served is Cream of Fresh Pea. In the summer I add finely chopped fresh mint just before serving, or chopped fresh chives. Every time I serve it I always have requests for the recipe or for a jar to take home. You know, cream soups of any kind are much better if just before serving you add a bit of the freshly chopped vegetable you are using; for example, freshly chopped celery to cream of celery, chopped tomatoes to cream of tomato, etc. It just does something to them. Try it sometime.

3 cups fresh or frozen peas
1 pint water
A dash of sugar — what you can get on the tip of a teaspoon
½ cup chopped onion

Cook peas in water, adding sugar, in saucepan until peas are soft but still green. Force onions, peas, and liquid through a food mill or sieve, or purée in an electric blender. Make a cream sauce of:

3 tablespoons butter
3 tablespoons flour
½ teaspoon salt
⅛ teaspoon pepper
3 cups milk

Melt butter in top of a double boiler, add flour, salt, and pepper; then cook over direct heat until bubbly. Add milk; cook and stir over hot water until smooth. Combine the pea mixture with cream sauce and heat in double boiler. Chopped mint or chives are added 10 minutes before serving. A dash of nutmeg added last makes people sit up and take notice. It is good served icy cold in the hot days of summer —and the color is lovely.

GAZPACHO

FOR FOUR OR SIX

A taste treat from Spain has many interpretations.

4 large ripe tomatoes, peeled
½ cucumber, peeled
¼ cup chopped green pepper
A dash of Tabasco
4 tablespoons olive oil
4 teaspoons wine vinegar
1 cup tomato juice
½ teaspoon salt
1 teaspoon grated onion
Fresh-ground pepper

Chop the tomatoes and cucumber fine, and add rest of ingredients. Strain through a sieve and chill, or purée in an electric blender. Serve with an ice cube floating in the center of the chilled cup. Pass a tray containing separate bowls of chopped cucumbers, chopped tomatoes, tiny croutons, and one of chopped chives or parsley for each to add their own; and a bowl of sour cream would not be amiss.

Served in ceramic tomatoes it is a beautiful first course — and did you ever stop to think that both children and adults might like any soup, even canned, served in containers such as these? Serve in a punch bowl for a buffet or for an added touch at a cocktail party.

GAZPACHO BLANCO

FOR TWELVE

3 small cucumbers, peeled and diced
1 clove garlic, crushed
3 cups chicken broth
2 cups sour cream
1 cup plain yogurt
3 tablespoons white vinegar
Salt and pepper to taste
4 medium tomatoes, peeled and diced
½ cup diced green onions (white part only)
½ cup chopped parsley
4 ounces slivered toasted almonds

Purée cucumbers, garlic, and 1 cup of the chicken broth in blender. Remove from blender and add remaining broth, sour cream, yogurt, vinegar, salt, and pepper. Mix thoroughly and chill. Present it in a chilled bowl, with the tomatoes, onions, parsley, and almonds served separately in small bowls.

ICED SPINACH SOUP

FOR FOUR TO SIX

3 cups sour cream or yogurt
2 cups chopped raw spinach
3 tablespoons finely chopped onion
½ cup finely diced cucumber
¼ cup peeled, seeded, and chopped tomatoes
8 ice cubes
Salt and pepper
Dash of Tabasco

Mix and chill. Good for dip too; just leave out the ice cubes. Keeps well for several days in a covered container.

SPINACH VICHYSSOISE

FOR SIX TO EIGHT

¼ cup butter
4 leeks, white part only
¼ cup chopped onion
2 large Idaho potatoes, peeled and sliced
1 carrot, sliced
4 cups chicken broth
1 teaspoon salt
1 pound blanched spinach
2 cups half-and-half or milk

Melt butter; sauté leeks and onions at medium heat until yellow, not brown. Add potatoes, carrot, chicken broth, and salt. Cover and simmer until potatoes and carrot are soft. Cool. Purée potato mixture in blender with blanched spinach. Add half-and-half, correct seasonings, and chill. Serve soup in very cold cups. If potato mixture becomes too dry during cooking, add more chicken broth.

VEGETABLE CONSOMMÉ

FOR SIX

4 cups chicken consommé, beef consommé, or half of each
½ cup thinly sliced cucumber, chopped
½ cup peeled, seeded, and chopped tomatoes
½ cup diced avocado
2 tablespoons minced green onion
1 tablespoon wine vinegar
1 teaspoon olive oil
Salt and pepper

Mix, season, and chill. Serve very cold. Sometimes I add diced fresh mushrooms, any kind of seafood, or cooked chicken.

COLD ROQUEFORT SOUP

FOR EIGHT

2 cups crumbled Roquefort (you may use blue cheese)
16 ice cubes
4 tablespoons chopped parsley
4 tablespoons chopped green onions
4 cups sour cream
Salt and pepper

Put cheese, ice cubes, parsley, and onions in blender. Whip until smooth. Add sour cream and salt and pepper. Carry to a picnic in a vacuum jug. You will need all of it. For a cup at home, use half the recipe and add red or Romanoff caviar or finely diced shrimp or lobster. Leftovers? Add 1 tablespoon melted unflavored gelatin to 1 pint of soup. Pour into individual molds and refrigerate. A superb salad with beef.

COLD YOGURT SOUP

FOR SIX

½ cup raisins
1 cup cold water
3 cups yogurt
½ cup light cream
1 hard-cooked egg, chopped
6 ice cubes
½ cup finely chopped cucumber
¼ cup finely chopped green onion
1 teaspoon salt
½ teaspoon pepper
1 tablespoon chopped parsley
1 tablespoon chopped fresh dill (or 1 teaspoon dried)

Soak raisins in 1 cup cold water. Put yogurt in mixing bowl with the cream, egg, ice cubes, cucumber, onion, salt, and pepper. Stir well. Add the raisins and cold water. Refrigerate for several hours. Serve with chopped parsley and dill.

ICED CUCUMBER VICHYSSOISE

FOR SIX

This soup provides a change in flavor when you feel you must.

1 medium onion, finely chopped
4 leeks, white part only
¼ pound butter
4 medium cucumbers, peeled and chopped
2 quarts chicken stock, or canned chicken broth
6 sprigs of parsley
2 large potatoes, chopped
Light cream
Salt and white pepper
Chopped chives or parsley

Sauté chopped onion and thinly sliced leeks in the butter until soft but not brown. Chop cucumbers and parboil 10 minutes in 1 cup of slightly salted chicken stock; drain and combine with onion and leeks, from which all butter has been drained. Reserve. Add parsley and potatoes to remaining chicken stock and cook until potatoes are soft. Put through a sieve and store in refrigerator until needed. Then combine the reserved cucumber mixture with an equal amount of light cream. Add to chilled potato mixture and stir until blended. Season with salt and pepper and serve in chilled cups with chopped chives or parsley on top. The color is pale green and it looks and is a cool, delightful soup. Thin cucumber sandwiches are a nice accompaniment. I served this from a punch bowl to a group one night, and who was impressed? The husbands!

CHLODNIK

FOR TEN TO TWELVE

At large cocktail parties I like to serve Chlodnik in the living room in a crystal bowl and let my guests help themselves. The color is divine.

1 pint chopped cooked beets
1 cup chopped shrimp
1 hard-cooked egg, chopped fine
½ medium cucumber, chopped fine
2 tablespoons chopped chives or green onions
½ teaspoon dill
2 cups sour cream
1 cup beer
Salt and pepper
1 sliced lemon
A few whole shrimp
Ice cubes
Chopped parsley

Mix together first eight ingredients and chill. Season with salt and pepper. Serve in individual soup cups or in a crystal bowl with sliced lemon and shrimp and an ice cube. I usually dip the lemon edges in chopped parsley. Leftovers? Add melted gelatin, 1 tablespoon to 1 pint Chlodnik, and make a salad ring to fill with seafood salad.

SUMMER SOUP

FOR EIGHT TO TWELVE

4 cups sour cream
2 cups ice water
2 cups finely chopped fresh spinach (raw)
3 tablespoons finely chopped green onion
½ teaspoon dried dill
Salt and pepper

Mix together and chill. Correct seasonings. When ready to serve add:

½ cup peeled, seeded, and chopped tomato
½ cup seeded cucumber, chopped
A dash of cayenne pepper

CHILLED CREAM VICHYSSOISE

FOR EIGHT

Mention Vichyssoise and immediately the housewife goes into a dither. In reality it is the easiest soup there is to make. No fuss about getting it on the table hot, no worrying the guests or family to hurry. Everyone loves the refrigerator in the hot or more-hot months. Cold soup does not stimulate the appetite, so in using it make it a part of the meal instead of the "come-on" to bigger and better things. Amazing, too, is the fact that almost all cream soups are good cold — but they have to be really cold.

4 leeks, white part, finely sliced
¼ cup finely chopped onion
¼ cup butter
5 medium-sized potatoes (Idaho variety)
1 carrot
1 quart chicken stock
1 teaspoon salt
2 cups milk
3 cups cream
Chopped chives

Sauté leeks and onion in butter until yellow. Add potatoes, carrot, chicken stock, and salt. Bring to a rapid boil, cover, reduce heat, and simmer until potatoes and carrot are soft. Mash and rub through a fine strainer. Return to heat and add the milk. Season to taste, and cool. Add cream and chill thoroughly. Serve in very cold cups with a sprinkling of finely chopped chives.

SENEGALESE SOUP

FOR SIX

This will be a talked-about addition to your menu.

2 tablespoons finely diced onion
2 tablespoons butter
2 teaspoons curry powder
1 tablespoon flour
3½ cups chicken stock
4 egg yolks
2 cups heavy cream
¼ cup finely diced white meat of chicken (or cooked shrimp)

Sauté onion in the butter until soft, but do not brown. Add curry powder and flour and cook slowly for 5 minutes. Add stock and bring to a boil, stirring until smooth. Whip in the egg yolks and cook for 1 minute. Put through a fine sieve and chill. Add the chilled cream and chicken. Serve very cold in bowls surrounded by crushed ice, with a nasturtium blossom and leaf peeping from under, if you go for such. I do.

COLD CURRIED CRABMEAT SOUP INDIENNE

TEN OR TWELVE SMALL CUPS

---

1 tablespoon chopped chives or green onion tops
2 tablespoons butter
2 teaspoons curry powder
2 tablespoons flour
3 cups milk
2 cups crabmeat (fresh, frozen, or canned) cut in small pieces
¼ cup dry sherry
2 cups light cream

Sauté the chives in the butter for 1 minute. Add the curry powder and flour and cook until well blended. Add the milk and cook until thick. Heat the crabmeat in the sherry, add the cream, and bring to a boil. Add to the curry mixture and cool. Serve very cold surrounded by ice, for informal entertaining.

The flavor is best if it is made the day before.

COLD SQUASH SOUP

FOR EIGHT

¼ cup butter
1½ cups finely chopped onion
4 cups sliced small summer squash
2 cups chicken broth
¼ teaspoon sugar
2 cups whipping cream
Salt and white pepper
Pinch of nutmeg
Chopped parsley or chives

Melt the butter, add the onion, and cook at low heat until soft but not brown. Add the squash and chicken broth. Cook until squash is tender. Add the sugar. Put mixture through a sieve or purée in the blender. Cool, add the cream, and season with salt, pepper, and nutmeg. Chill. Serve very cold sprinkled with chopped parsley or chives — good!

COLD FRUIT SOUP

FOR SIX

Cold Fruit Soup gives a different twist to your taste buds. Swedish in origin, it is especially good for a luncheon party.

6 whole cloves
3 cups orange juice
2 cups pineapple juice
⅓ cup sugar
3 tablespoons cornstarch
¾ cup lemon juice

Heat cloves, orange juice, and pineapple juice to boiling. Mix sugar and cornstarch, add to the juice, and cook until thick and clear. Cool and add the lemon juice. Chill and serve in very cold cups with French rolls, sliced very thin the round way, spread with butter, sugar, and cinnamon and dried out in a 200° oven until crisp and brown.

CURRIED APPLE SOUP

FOR EIGHT

1 cup white onions, chopped
¼ cup butter or margarine
2 tablespoons curry powder
2 tablespoons cornstarch
¼ cup cold water
4 cups chicken broth
4 egg yolks, slightly beaten
1 cup whipping cream
2 apples — peeled, cored, and diced
Juice of 1 lemon
Salt and freshly ground pepper
Thin slices of unpeeled ripe red apple

Cook onions in butter until soft but not brown. Stir in curry powder. Cook 1 minute. Blend cornstarch with cold water; add to onions and curry with broth. Stir over low heat until slightly thickened and clear. Add a little of the hot mixture to egg yolks; return to remaining mixture; cook and stir about 1 minute. Add cream. Remove from heat. Add diced apples. Purée in an electric blender or food processor. Add lemon juice. Season to taste with salt and pepper. Serve chilled, garnished with thin slices of unpeeled red apple.

QUICK COLD SOUPS FOR A HOT SUMMER

Soaring temperatures bring demands on you to make you forget how cool you would like to be. Your families are irritable, your friends have lagging appetites, and you are bleak. Cheer up, plan your meals around cold soups.

The easy way is to resort to canned or frozen soups, and each year they improve. Any *jellied consommé* has a gourmet appeal when topped with sour cream and chives or capers, and for the extravagant touch, caviar spooned over rather generously. A dot of it won't do. Serve with any type of sandwich made with rye bread, which likes to be seen with sour cream: sliced smoked salmon or sturgeon for the more cultivated palate, salmon or egg salad for the budget minded.

□

Specifically, *jellied madrilène* with avocado mashed with lime juice is cool looking and tasting; or chopped black olives with sliced scallions, sour cream, and a light dusting of curry; or chopped fresh vegetables like beans, peas, carrots, and summer squash, stirred in at the last minute and dusted with minced parsley. *Jellied chicken consommé* with fresh minced mint, or rosemary; with cooked fresh vegetables spooned in just before serving; with slivers of chicken and ham and halves of white grapes; with chopped truffles and very fine, oh very fine, slivers of salami.

□

Jellied green turtle soup mixed half and half with madrilène, topped with lump crab or small shrimp, and sour cream. Why go on? Use your imagination.

□

Condensed cream of chicken soup becomes a specialty when finely shredded cucumber is added with the cream or milk to dilute it. Heat only enough to blend the flavors, then chill, or do the whole thing in a blender and sprinkle with chopped chives or watercress. This I think could make a quick delightful supper dish with whole cold shrimp and halves of hard-cooked eggs, with mayonnaise whipped with lime juice to dunk them in, and salty rye crisp wafers.

□

Canned condensed cream of celery soup diluted with cream, as in the previous one, and generously combined with finely cooked chopped broccoli, or raw spinach served icy cold with chopped fresh tomato floating in the center and a faint dusting of curry powder, goes well with a make-your-own-sandwich tray of assorted breads and cheese.

□

Cream of green pea soup combined with fresh mint, served cold with well-chilled fresh fruit and lime dressing would make a summer luncheon party a joy for both hostess and guests, with crisp cheese wafers — store-bought, of course, and one of my favorites, *black bean soup* diluted with beef consommé, put in a blender with sour cream for 30 seconds, no more, served icy cold.

Sauces

The sauce to meat is ceremony, according to Lady Macbeth. But what would the ceremony be without the sauce? I'm sure the hostess who serves a really superb sauce feels at times she is playing god to the mortals who partake of it. And why not? It takes patience to make a sauce that will enhance, not disguise.

Any sauce, whether simple or complex, takes time — to blend the proper proportions of fat, flour or egg yolks, and whatever liquid that goes into it. A good rule in blending is to follow the sauce recipe, and carefully; but let your imagination inspire your seasoning.

Trite as it may seem, every cook should know how to make a smooth cream sauce — thick, thin, or medium. It is the foundation of many a sauce, soup, scallop, and casserole; and saves many a hostess an embarrassing moment when a meal planned for two must be stretched for more.

Several times in the collection the sauce recipe is given following the dish for which Helen thought it was the perfect accompaniment. The index will locate any sauce you cannot find in this section.

BASIC CREAM SAUCE

ONE CUP

1 tablespoon butter
1 tablespoon flour
¼ teaspoon salt
1 cup milk (or half milk and half cream)

Melt butter in top part of double boiler, add flour and salt, and cook until bubbly. Slowly add milk and stir briskly. Cook over hot water until thick and smooth, stirring occasionally. (A French whip or wire whisk is, or ought to be, a must in the kitchen drawer, especially for stirring sauces of all kinds.) With the new heavy-based saucepans, it is not necessary to use a double boiler if low heat is maintained. But all cream sauces should be cooked until there is no starchy taste remaining.

For a medium Cream Sauce, increase the butter and flour to 2 tablespoons of each, and for a thick Cream Sauce (to use in croquettes or soufflés) use 4 tablespoons.

Variations of Cream Sauce, using medium Cream Sauce:

Seafood Sauce for Fish: Add ½ cup sautéed oysters and shrimp with 1 teaspoon lemon juice.

Add ½ teaspoon grated onion and 1 teaspoon anchovy paste for a sauce for fish or asparagus.

Egg Sauce: Add 2 chopped hard-cooked eggs, 1 tablespoon chopped parsley, 1 teaspoon chopped chives or grated onion. Serve with fish.

Supreme Sauce: Add 1 slightly beaten egg yolk with ¼ cup heavy cream and a pinch of nutmeg. Serve with fish or chicken croquettes or soufflés.

Vegetable Sauce: Add ½ cup cooked vegetables heated with 1 tablespoon butter. Serve with soufflés and pastry meat rolls and turnovers.

Surprise Sauce: Add ½ cup diced sharp cheese just as served. Do not blend.

HOLLANDAISE SAUCE

ONE-HALF CUP

½ cup butter
2 egg yolks, slightly beaten
1 tablespoon lemon juice
A dash of cayenne

Divide butter in half and put half in a small saucepan with the egg yolks and lemon juice. Hold the saucepan over hot water (do not allow water to boil) and stir constantly until butter is melted. Add remaining half of butter and stir until thick. Remove and add cayenne pepper. Serve at once with any vegetable or fish. (If the sauce curdles, beat in 1 tablespoon of cream.) If left over, you may reheat. Set in a pan of warm water and stir until ready to serve. If it breaks again, add the cream again. This can go on indefinitely.

Variations using Hollandaise Sauce:

Béarnaise Sauce: Substitute 2 teaspoons tarragon vinegar for lemon juice; add a dash of mushroom catsup (if you have it, or skip it), 1 tablespoon chopped parsley, ¼ teaspoon freshly ground pepper, 1 teaspoon chopped chives. Serve with tenderloin steak.

Mousseline Sauce: After sauce is thickened, fold in ¼ cup whipped cream. Serve on fish and asparagus or Brussels sprouts.

Lobster or Shrimp Hollandaise: Add ¼ cup finely chopped cooked lobster or shrimp to finished sauce. Serve over poached fish of any kind.

Véronique: Combine ½ cup medium Cream Sauce with 1 cup Hollandaise. Add ½ cup grapes (white is usual) cut in half. Serve over poached fish, or white meat of turkey, or chicken and ham. Run under broiler to brown.

Maltaise: Whip 2 tablespoons of orange juice plus ½ teaspoon grated orange rind into ½ cup Hollandaise. I like it with salmon.

BÉCHAMEL SAUCE

TWO CUPS

---

2 tablespoons finely diced onion
½ carrot, finely diced
½ cup butter
2 cups chicken stock
1 bay leaf
2 sprigs parsley
4 peppercorns
¼ cup flour
1½ cups scalded milk
Salt and pepper

Sauté onion and carrot in half the butter until onions are yellow. Add chicken stock, bay leaf, parsley, and peppercorns. Bring to a boil and then simmer for 30 minutes. Melt remaining half of the butter in top of a double boiler; add flour and cook over direct heat until bubbly. Add milk and cook until thick and smooth. Strain the first mixture and combine with the cream sauce. Season to taste.

I like this sauce to serve over croquettes, soufflés, and such, and to use in the place of Cream Sauce for creaming chicken, for instance.

HORSERADISH SAUCE

ONE CUP

---

1 tablespoon chopped onion
3 tablespoons butter
2 tablespoons flour
1 cup milk or light cream
¼ cup prepared horseradish

Brown onion slightly in butter; add flour, then milk or cream, to make a sauce. When thick add horseradish. Always associated with boiled meats, Horseradish Sauce is especially good on boiled brisket of fresh beef — and corned beef, without saying.

Variation:

Mustard Sauce: In place of the horseradish, substitute 3 tablespoons prepared mustard and ½ teaspoon Worcestershire sauce. Serve over fresh pork, spareribs, pork butts, and regular hams.

CUMBERLAND SAUCE

ONE-HALF CUP

A delicious and easy sauce to serve with ham or cold turkey (you can keep it on hand in the refrigerator and take it out a few minutes beforehand to serve at room temperature).

3 tablespoons red currant jelly
2 tablespoons port
2 tablespoons orange juice
1 tablespoon lemon juice
1 teaspoon dry mustard
½ teaspoon ground ginger
1 teaspoon paprika
3 tablespoons orange rind, finely shredded (white part removed), covered with cold water and brought to a boil and drained

Melt jelly over low heat until liquid. Cool and add rest of ingredients.

IMPERIAL SAUCE

TWO AND ONE-HALF CUPS

A sauce to make a fish dish a delectable entrée any day, and especially for company.

2 tablespoons finely chopped onion
¼ cup finely diced mushrooms
1 tablespoon butter
1 cup thick Cream Sauce
1 cup mayonnaise
1 teaspoon lemon juice
2 tablespoons finely chopped sweet mustard pickles
1 tablespoon finely chopped pimento
¼ teaspoon Worcestershire sauce

Sauté onion and mushrooms in butter; add cream sauce, mayonnaise, lemon juice, pickles, pimento, and Worcestershire. Completely cover any boned fish — red snapper, sea trout, filet of sole, or similar fish —

and bake at 300° for 40 minutes. Part of the sauce cooks into the fish and part stays on top. I use it also combined with shrimp, lobster, and crabmeat, and baked in individual casseroles for a luncheon dish, and find it popular as a hot hors d'oeuvre served with pastry scoops: pie-crust molded on a tablespoon, placed close enough to touch on a baking sheet and baked at 400° until light brown and crisp.

FRESH MINT SAUCE

ONE CUP

Lamb, of all kinds, calls for a variety of sauces. There is nothing the matter with mint jelly — it's just overworked. Try this instead.

1 cup lamb drippings
1 tablespoon vinegar
¼ cup currant jelly
2 tablespoons fresh mint, chopped

Cook drippings, vinegar, and jelly together until jelly is melted. Add the fresh mint, finely chopped, just before serving.

LAMB SAUCE ANITA

ONE CUP

A rather hot sauce, delicious with lamb.

½ cup brown sugar
½ cup currant jelly
1 tablespoon dry mustard
3 egg yolks
½ cup vinegar

Mix brown sugar, jelly, dry mustard, and egg yolks and cook in double boiler until thick. Add vinegar slowly, beating after each addition.

MORNAY SAUCE

ONE AND ONE-HALF QUARTS

Mornay Sauce has as many definitions as there are people who make it. If you must be technical, it is a "cheesed" sauce. Start or finish how you wish, but cheese it you must. This one is easy, keeps well, and can be used for many things.

¼ pound butter
1 cup flour
4 cups milk
2 pounds Cheddar cheese
12 ounces beer

Melt butter; add flour and cook until bubbly. Add milk and cook until smooth. Boil 1 minute. Cut cheese in small pieces and beat into hot cream sauce. I recommend an electric beater and beat at medium speed for a minimum of 15 minutes; longer beating improves the sauce. Add beer a little at a time to obtain consistency desired. Pour over whatever vegetable, fowl, fish, or meat you wish; put a level teaspoon of Hollandaise on top, and run it under the broiler until brown. Or sprinkle with grated Swiss or Parmesan cheese before browning. If you make the sauce and keep it several days, beat it again before using to restore its light consistency.

Using the cheesed sauce as a base you can add all sorts of things to make it interesting:

Welsh Rabbit: Add 1 egg yolk and ½ teaspoon dry mustard.

Almond Sauce: For fish. Add 2 tablespoons blanched almonds, slivered and browned.

Fresh Tomato Cheese Sauce: Add ¼ cup finely diced fresh tomatoes and serve over toasted seafood sandwiches or croquettes.

Sherry Sauce: Add 2 tablespoons sherry.

CURRY SAUCE

FOR EIGHT

Curried meats are becoming more and more popular for entertaining. This recipe is good for chicken, ham, or seafood, and is not complicated:

2 tablespoons chopped onion
2 tablespoons chopped celery (may be omitted)
½ cup butter
½ teaspoon salt
1 tablespoon curry powder
½ cup flour
3 cups milk (or half milk, half chicken stock)
1 cup cream
2 tablespoons dry sherry (may be omitted, but I like)
3 cups cooked chicken (or what you have) cut into large dice

Sauté onions and celery in the butter until onions are yellow; add salt and curry powder and mix thoroughly; add flour and cook until bubbly. Add milk and cream, stirring briskly until smooth and thick, and cook until all the starchy flavor has disappeared. Add sherry and chicken and serve with rice cooked with a bit of curry powder in the water.

Curry of Smoked Turkey I think wonderful for using up the dark meat.

With curry, the accompaniments are important. In India each accompaniment is served by a servant boy, so we call curry "Five-boy," "Seven-Boy," or however many accompaniments we use. These are usual, and served in individual bowls:

Chutney, of the Major Grey variety
Diced crisp bacon
Finely diced hard-cooked egg whites and yolks, diced separately
Finely chopped salted peanuts or pecans or almonds
Finely chopped French-fried onions
Shredded coconut, fresh if possible
Shredded Bombay Duck (an Indian fish delicacy available in fine food shops)
A tart jelly
Finely chopped sweet pickles
Pappadums (a special wafer from India)
French-fried shrimp
Olives, ripe and stuffed, slivered
Seedless raisins

MEAT SAUCE

FOR SIX TO EIGHT

A good meat sauce is one thing you can keep in your icebox or deep freeze, and this one I like because it is gentle with my taste buds.

¼ pound salt pork, diced
½ cup minced onion
1 cup minced celery
½ cup minced carrots
1 tablespoon butter
2 pounds ground beef
¼ cup white wine
1½ cups fresh tomatoes, peeled and chopped
2 cups light cream

Sauté the salt pork until brown. Add the onion, celery, and carrots. Cook until they are transparent. Add the butter, meat, wine, and tomatoes. Simmer for 1½ hours. Add cream and continue cooking until thick.

This is wonderful with lasagna, using a mixture of Parmesan and Gruyère cheese with it. You cook the noodles. Make a thin cream sauce made with light cream instead of milk, with a pinch of nutmeg added.

Place a layer of cream sauce in bottom of casserole, then noodles, then meat sauce, then cheese; repeat for two layers of each and end up with cream sauce and cheese on top. Bake at 350° until bubbling hot.

Combine this sauce with any pasta and sprinkle with Parmesan cheese. Why be in a rut, though, for pastas? At least change the shape. Try mostaccioli for a change. It is interestingly and amusingly shaped like a mustache and comes in at least three sizes in many Italian grocery stores.

RAISIN SAUCE

FOUR CUPS

1 cup sugar
½ cup water
1 cup seedless raisins (white, if you can find them)
1 cup oranges cut fine, with rind left on
2 tablespoons butter
2 tablespoons vinegar
⅛ teaspoon Worcestershire sauce
½ teaspoon salt
¼ teaspoon ground cloves
⅛ teaspoon mace
1 cup currant jelly
¼ cup ham drippings (if you have them)
2 teaspoons cornstarch

Mix together all the ingredients except ham drippings and cornstarch, and bring to a boil. Cook until raisins are plump. Add drippings and cornstarch dissolved in a little cold water. Cook until clear.

Sauce for ham should be light-bodied and thin. This is a good one to keep in your refrigerator. Besides ham, use it on corned beef, Canadian bacon, or smoked tongue. It is especially nice to dress up leftover ham made into timbales or loaves.

SAUCE PROVENÇAL

ONE CUP

With a roast of veal, I like a faint suspicion of garlic.

2 tablespoons chopped onion
1 garlic bud, crushed
1 tablespoon olive oil
½ teaspoon flour
1 cup veal drippings from roast (add water to make 1 cup)
1 fresh tomato cut in eighths or 8 small cherry tomatoes
1 tablespoon chopped parsley
Salt, if needed

Sauté onions and garlic in olive oil until onions are soft. Remove garlic and add flour. Cook for 1 minute; add drippings and cook until thickened, which will be very slightly. Add tomatoes, parsley, and salt; heat, but do not cook. Extravagant? Add sautéed mushrooms.

À LA KING SAUCE

THREE CUPS

À la King Sauce can be used as a basis for many things, and for the most part everyone I know likes à la king foods for a light, though ample, luncheon dish. Chicken, of course, leads the parade, but seafood of any kind, especially shrimp or lobster, ham, whole mushrooms, asparagus, eggs, just about anything can be "à la kinged" to perfection. Too, you can make it ahead of time, and keep it in the refrigerator for a few days — or in your deep freeze for a few weeks. However, as with most sauces, it is better the day you make it.

½ cup butter
½ cup flour
Paprika
2 cups chicken stock or canned chicken broth
¼ cup milk
½ cup cream
2 egg yolks, beaten (may be omitted)
½ cup pimentos cut in strips
1 cup fresh mushrooms, sautéed (canned ones will do)
¼ cup green peppers cut in strips and cooked in water until tender (may be omitted)
1 teaspoon salt
White pepper (to suit you)
2 tablespoons dry sherry

Melt butter; add flour and few grains of paprika. Cook for 5 minutes. Add chicken stock, milk, and cream. Bring to a boil, put over hot — not boiling — water and cook 15 minutes. Remove from heat and add beaten egg yolks, pimentos, mushrooms, and cooked green peppers. Season with salt and pepper and sherry.

To this amount of sauce you would add 2 cups of cooked chicken or turkey cut in large cubes, or the same amount of shrimp, ham, or whatever you choose to "à la king."

À la king foods may be served on all sorts of bases: hot buttery toast (crisp), pastry shells, squares of pastry or toast that have been spread with deviled ham or cheese, hot biscuits or cornbread, or a bed of rice or noodles — Chinese noodles give it a crispness that most people enjoy. À la king foods call for a sweet accompaniment like spiced peaches or apricots, spiced watermelon pickles, preserved oranges, or your favorite preserve.

The sauce may be used over toasted sandwiches, croquettes, and soufflés.

MUSHROOM SAUCE

ONE CUP

½ cup sliced mushrooms
2 tablespoons butter
2 tablespoons flour
¾ cup chicken stock
½ cup cream
Salt
1 tablespoon dry sherry (may be omitted)

Sauté the mushrooms in butter until soft. Add flour, stock, and cream to make a cream sauce. Season with salt, and sherry if you like.

Variation:
Add ½ cup slivered toasted almonds and ½ cup grated sharp cheese, and serve over asparagus or broccoli as an entrée.

LEMON SAUCE

ONE CUP

A sauce less expensive than Hollandaise or Maltaise, which are both elegant but expensive.

2 egg yolks
1 tablespoon flour
1 cup liquid from fish poaching, or chicken broth
1 tablespoon fresh lemon juice
2 tablespoons chopped parsley
Salt and white pepper

Mix egg yolks with the flour; add liquid and stir with your French whip until thick. Add lemon juice and parsley and correct seasonings. Add more lemon juice if you desire.

MICHAEL SAUCE

ONE CUP

A Corbitt favorite for asparagus and zucchini.

¾ cup sour cream
2 teaspoons tarragon vinegar
2 egg yolks
½ teaspoon paprika

Cook over hot water, not boiling, until thick and smooth. You must stir constantly. For hot vegetables. Good over poached fish, too!

LEMON BUTTER SAUCE

ONE-FOURTH CUP

¼ cup butter
1 tablespoon chopped parsley
1 tablespoon lemon juice

Cream butter; add parsley and lemon juice. Mix and serve over steak, fish, or vegetables.

Variations:

Parsley Butter: Add 2 tablespoons chopped parsley.

Anchovy Butter: Substitute 1½ teaspoons anchovy paste for parsley.

Mustard Butter: Add 1 teaspoon prepared mustard. Serve over broiled fish.

CREOLE SAUCE

THREE CUPS

½ cup chopped onion
1 clove garlic, crushed
½ cup diced celery (may be omitted)
¼ cup diced green pepper
2 tablespoons olive oil
2½ cups canned tomatoes
1 bay leaf
2 teaspoons salt
2 teaspoons sugar
2 teaspoons chopped parsley
4 cloves
1 teaspoon flour

Sauté the onion, garlic, celery, and green pepper in olive oil until soft, but not brown. Add remaining ingredients, except flour, and cook over low heat until thick. Remove garlic and cloves and add flour, dissolved in a little water. Use over meat loaf, cutlets, and with cooked shrimp over rice. Leftover sauce may be poured over canned green beans, okra, eggplant, and similar vegetables.

STEAK SAUCE

ONE AND ONE-HALF CUPS

A good sauce to spoon over steaks as you cook them (preferably on the grill in the back yard).

1 cup mayonnaise
½ cup chili sauce
1 teaspoon Kitchen Bouquet
½ teaspoon Worcestershire sauce
1 teaspoon prepared mustard
½ teaspoon hickory-smoked salt

Cover the bottom surface of the steak with the sauce before putting it on the grill, and keep swishing it on as the steak cooks. A good dash of red wine helps, too.

SHERRY SUPREME SAUCE

ONE CUP

A more delicate sauce to use with white meat of turkey or chicken.

2 tablespoons flour
2 tablespoons butter
½ cup cream
½ cup chicken broth
¼ cup grated Swiss or Gruyère cheese
2 tablespoons dry sherry
Salt

Make a cream sauce with the flour, butter, cream, and chicken broth. Add cheese and stir until thoroughly blended. Add sherry and season to your taste.

I use this sauce over thin slices of white meat of turkey or chicken, over rice seasoned with a very little curry. I put a bacon curl on top, and a crisp link sausage on each side. With a grilled tomato it is an excellent blend of flavors.

ONION BUTTER
for steaks

4 tablespoons grated Bermuda onion
4 tablespoons minced parsley
4 tablespoons butter
1 teaspoon Worcestershire sauce
½ teaspoon salt
¼ teaspoon dry mustard
½ teaspoon cracked or freshly ground pepper

Mix together and spread over steak as you remove it from the broiler. The heat of the steak will melt the butter.

BARBECUE SAUCE

ONE AND ONE-HALF CUPS

Barbecue Sauce should be among a housewife's prized possessions, especially if she is south of the Mason-Dixon line. This one I like to keep on hand and use, especially for barbecuing chicken and pork ribs.

1 cup bouillon or chicken stock
¼ cup vinegar
½ teaspoon prepared mustard
½ teaspoon Worcestershire sauce
2 tablespoons chili sauce
1 tablespoon lemon juice
Grated rind of ½ lemon
½ clove garlic, finely minced
¼ cup finely minced onion
¼ cup butter
¼ teaspoon Tabasco sauce
1 bay leaf
¼ teaspoon whole cloves
2 tablespoons sugar
2 tablespoons flour

Combine all ingredients except flour and cook until onion is soft and the sauce smells heavenly. Add flour moistened with water and cook until thick. For barbecuing chicken I oven-roast them until nearly done, coat with the barbecue sauce, cover, and cook at least 45 minutes at 325°; uncover and bake another 15 minutes at 400° or run them under the broiler until crisp on top.

Pour the sauce over a turkey or ham and use it to baste for the last hours of its cooking.

Mix it with prepared barbecue sauce (I like Sexton's brand) half and half and use for beef short ribs or chuck roast, increasing the time for cooking after the sauce is added to 2 hours. It will keep indefinitely if refrigerated.

FRENCH MUSTARD

Every so often someone gets ambitious enough to want to make French mustard. If you are one, here is a recipe that will make both your eyes and your mouth water.

Into 1 cup of vinegar slice one medium-sized onion and let stand overnight. Pour off vinegar into a saucepan and discard the onion. Mix together:

1 teaspoon ground black pepper
1 teaspoon salt
1 tablespoon sugar
½ cup dry mustard

Rub mustard mixture with enough of the vinegar to make a smooth paste. Heat remaining vinegar and add to mustard mixture, stirring to a smooth paste. Place in a saucepan, bring to a boil, and boil for 5 minutes. Remove and let stand overnight. It will keep in a covered jar indefinitely.

MUSTARD SAUCE

A good sauce for ham and corned beef.

1 pint light cream, heated
4 tablespoons dry mustard
1 cup sugar
1 cup vinegar
Salt to taste
2 egg yolks, well beaten
2 tablespoons flour

Mix thoroughly and cook in double boiler for at least an hour. When cold, drained horseradish may be added, or whipped cream.

BROWN SAUCE

ONE CUP

What do you mean by a brown sauce? Everyone agrees on one thing — you make it from meat stock. So, brown gravy, brown sauce, and Espagnole are all basically the same.

2 tablespoons butter or meat drippings
1 tablespoon minced onion
1 tablespoon minced carrot
½ bay leaf
2 tablespoons flour
1 cup meat stock
Salt and pepper

Melt the butter or drippings; add onion, carrot, and bay leaf and cook over low heat until butter is brown. Stir in flour and cook until bubbly. Add stock and cook until thick and smooth. Strain and season.

Variations:

Add 1 cup sliced mushrooms, sautéed, and 1 tablespoon sherry. Serve with roasts, meat loaf, or cutlets.

Substitute ½ cup orange juice for ½ cup stock from roasting ducks. After sauce is strained, add 2 tablespoons slivered orange rind. Serve with duck.

NEWBURG SAUCE

TWO AND ONE-HALF CUPS

Newburg Sauce should be as important to a good hostess as Hollandaise. Keep various cans of seafood on the emergency shelf. A Newburg whipped up in a hurry can save face many a time.

2 tablespoons butter
2 tablespoons flour
¾ teaspoon salt
A dash of cayenne
2 cups thin cream (or half-and-half)
4 egg yolks, well beaten
¼ cup dry sherry (or half brandy)

Melt butter; stir in flour, salt, and cayenne. When well blended, add the cream and cook over low heat until smooth and the mixture boils. Stir a little of the sauce into the egg yolks and add to the rest of the sauce. If using the sauce over fish, add the sherry and heat. If using for lobster or shrimp or other seafood, sauté the seafood, or what you have, in a little butter and the sherry. This amount will serve six or eight people.

SEAFOOD SAUCE

FOUR AND ONE-HALF CUPS

3 tablespoons butter
3 tablespoons flour
1 cup half-and-half
1 cup chicken broth
½ cup dry white wine
2 cups cooked seafood or chicken
Salt and pepper

Melt the butter; add the flour and cook until bubbly. Add half-and-half, chicken broth, and wine. Cook until thickened, stirring constantly with a French whip. Mix in seafood and season to taste. Simmer about 5 minutes at low heat. Keep hot over hot water.

TARTAR SAUCE

ONE CUP

1 cup mayonnaise
2 tablespoons chopped gherkins
2 tablespoons chopped green olives
2 tablespoons chopped onion
2 tablespoons chopped parsley
1 tablespoon chopped capers

Mix and serve.

SAUCE LOUIS

THREE AND ONE-HALF CUPS

2 cups mayonnaise
½ cup chili sauce
2 tablespoons lemon juice (1 lemon normally yields 3 tablespoons of juice)
6 drops Angostura bitters (you may omit)
½ cup whipping cream

Mix mayonnaise, chili sauce, lemon juice, and bitters. Whip cream and fold into the mixture. Chill. Good with any kind of seafood.

SAUCE VERTE

ONE CUP

1 cup yogurt
1 hard-cooked egg, finely chopped
2 teaspoons lemon juice
2 tablespoons finely chopped green onion or chives
2 tablespoons chopped parsley
Few drops of Tabasco
Salt and pepper to taste

Mix and refrigerate. Good on green salads and seafood.

COCKTAIL SAUCE

FOUR AND ONE-HALF CUPS

2 cups catsup
2 cups chili sauce
¼ cup cider vinegar
6 drops Tabasco
½ cup prepared horseradish
¼ cup finely minced celery
¼ cup finely minced onion
2 teaspoons Worcestershire sauce

Mix together and refrigerate. Use for all seafood cocktails.

RÉMOULADE SAUCE

ONE AND ONE-HALF CUPS

1 cup mayonnaise
2 teaspoons chopped anchovy
½ teaspoon dry mustard
1 tablespoon wine vinegar
1 tablespoon tarragon vinegar
2 tablespoons dry sherry
½ cup chopped parsley
¼ teaspoon garlic powder
4 tablespoons capers
1 tablespoon onion juice

Mix together and keep in refrigerator at least one day before using. This sauce is traditionally used on cold shrimp, but is also good as a dressing for hard-cooked eggs or any green salad.

PIQUANT SAUCE FOR SEAFOOD

⅓ cup salad oil or olive oil (or half of each)
2 tablespoons red wine vinegar
½ cup finely chopped parsley
2 tablespoons lemon juice
2 tablespoons finely chopped green pepper
1 clove garlic, minced
A few chives, chopped
Salt and cracked pepper

Mix and pour over seafood. A nice flavor change from the usual.

SPAGHETTI SAUCE

FOUR CUPS

½ cup finely chopped onion
1 teaspoon finely chopped garlic
1 teaspoon finely chopped celery
1 teaspoon finely chopped parsley
½ cup olive oil
2 cups canned tomatoes
2 cups tomato purée
⅛ teaspoon paprika
Salt and pepper
¼ cup dry sherry

Sauté finely chopped onion, garlic, celery, and parsley in olive oil until celery and onions are soft. Add tomatoes, purée, and paprika. Cook until well blended and thick and season with salt and pepper. Add sherry and serve at once. Combined with fresh crab flakes or chicken it is a good buffet supper dish. Serve with a dish of grated Parmesan cheese nearby.

PIQUANT SAUCE FOR VEGETABLES

1 cup mayonnaise
1 tablespoon lemon juice
½ teaspoon salt
1 cup peeled, seeded, and diced tomatoes

Mix mayonnaise, lemon juice, and salt. Keep hot over water. Add tomatoes when ready to serve. Especially good with asparagus or broccoli.

Part 2

Salads
Salad Dressings
Vegetables

Salads

There are probably more opinions given on the subject of salad making than on any other gastronomical feat. Some say the male half of the universe are the only ones who are "in the know" as to how much or how little oil and vinegar goes where; others give the fair sex equal honors. Being a woman, I do not care, but salad should be a thing of beauty, fresh, chilled, and delectable to eat!

Everyone has his own idea of a green salad — I like to say a salad of "everything green." Combinations of any greens, and the more the tastier, but definitely, if at all possible, the cool crisp tanginess of watercress somewhere; lettuce (head or leaf), escarole, chicory, Belgian endive, if the budget allows; tender leaves of spinach, romaine, a few chives, chopped fine. A fan am I of Bibb or Limestone lettuce! Green peppers, if sliced almost too thin to see; if you like, and if you grow them, young nasturtium leaves; fresh tarragon and sweet basil leaves give intrigue, but take them easily. All greens should be thoroughly washed and dried, and chilled. From there you are on your own.

Dressings should be sprinkled rather than poured, and the greens tossed gently until thoroughly coated. When I can, I like to use only the best olive oil, equal parts with red wine vinegar, a faint whiff of garlic, and freshly ground pepper for a green salad.

AVOCADOS WITH SHRIMP MAYONNAISE

Avocados cut in large dice, dipped in Fruit Fresh (you buy it in the markets) or in lemon juice to keep their color, arranged around a bowl of shrimp mayonnaise, add both color and interest to your table. I find I can count on about 18 pieces to a large avocado. Be sure it is ripe, but not soft. Sometimes I mix it with chunks of cantaloupe. The dressing, good for both, is made merely by adding cooked shrimp, chopped fine (buy the broken pieces), to homemade mayonnaise (1 cup shrimp to ½ cup mayonnaise), a little onion juice, lemon juice, Tabasco, and a bit of anchovy paste.

APPLE AND WATERCRESS SALAD

FOR EIGHT TO TEN

---

2 bunches watercress, washed and crisped
2 heads Belgian endive, thinly sliced
2 unpeeled cored red Delicious apples, thinly sliced
¼ cup salad oil
¼ cup olive oil
4 tablespoons white vinegar
½ teaspoon salt
½ teaspoon sugar
¼ teaspoon dry mustard
Cracked pepper
1 clove garlic
½ cup dry bread crumbs or ¼ cup wheat germ, browned in butter

Wash and dry the watercress and endive. Toss with the apples, oils, vinegar, and seasonings in a salad bowl rubbed with garlic. Sprinkle with the browned bread crumbs or wheat germ.

ASPARAGUS SALAD

FOR EIGHT

---

1 head ruby lettuce or watercress
1 ripe avocado
1 tablespoon lemon juice
8 stalks asparagus, cooked and chilled
1 tablespoon capers
4 slices bacon, cooked crisp and crumbled
2 tablespoons additional lemon juice
⅓ cup salad oil
Salt and pepper

Make a bed of the lettuce leaves or watercress in a bowl or on a tray. Peel avocado, halve it lengthwise, remove seed, and slice thinly lengthwise. Sprinkle with fresh lemon juice. Arrange avocado and asparagus on the lettuce and sprinkle with capers and bacon. Mix lemon juice and salad oil, season to your taste, and sprinkle over lightly. Will keep in refrigerator for a few hours.

GUACAMOLE I

FOR FOUR TO SIX

2 cups mashed avocado
2 tablespoons lemon juice
½ tablespoon grated onion
2 tablespoons chili sauce
4 drops Tabasco sauce
Salt to taste

Mix together thoroughly and chill. Place in bowl that has been rubbed with garlic and serve with tortilla chips or Fritos that have been warmed in the oven. I like to dunk raw cauliflower florets in it. It is good, too, on top of green salad or on thinly sliced tomatoes. If you make it ahead of time, leave the avocado pit in the mixture until ready to use — it keeps the mixture from turning dark.

GUACAMOLE II

FOR FOUR

Guacamole fans are as apt to kibitz as not. Try them out on this one. I like it best of all.

2 avocados
1 tablespoon salad oil
1 tablespoon lime juice (or vinegar)
¼ pound Parmesan cheese, grated
1 tablespoon chili sauce
1 tablespoon finely minced onion
1 tablespoon finely minced green pepper (you may omit)
Salt and pepper

Peel and mash the avocados, and mash and mash. Add the oil, lime juice, cheese, chili sauce, and onion. Then the green pepper, if you wish. Taste for salt and pepper.

CAESAR SALAD

FOR FOUR

20 or 30 croutons (see below)
Garlic
2 heads lettuce
Sprig of watercress
¼ teaspoon dry mustard
¼ teaspoon black pepper
½ teaspoon salt
4 ounces Parmesan cheese, grated, or Roquefort, crumbled
6 tablespoons French olive oil
4 tablespoons tarragon vinegar
2 eggs
1 2-ounce tin anchovies
1 teaspoon capers

For croutons: Place about 20 or 30 cubes of French or whole-wheat bread in a pan and set in oven at 200°. When the croutons are browned, toss them in olive oil that has been lightly flavored with garlic; then set aside to drain, to be added to the salad at the last minute.

Into a garlic-rubbed wooden salad bowl cut or tear into small pieces two heads of chilled greens (either romaine or head lettuce) and a sprig of watercress. Sprinkle with dry mustard, black pepper, and salt. Add Parmesan or Roquefort; then add olive oil and tarragon vinegar. Break the eggs, which have been coddled for 2 minutes (or use raw eggs at room temperature), on the greens. (To coddle eggs, place in boiling water after pot has been removed from the heat.) Then add anchovies and capers. Toss enough to mix thoroughly — but not vigorously; leaves should be marinated but not "waterlogged." Do not have excess liquid in the bowl. Just before serving, add the croutons, tossing the salad again just enough to mix in the croutons without making them soggy.

COBB SALAD

FOR EIGHT

1 head romaine, finely chopped
8 slices crisp bacon, crumbled
4 ounces Roquefort cheese, crumbled
3 tomatoes, peeled, seeded, and finely diced
2 avocados, peeled, seeded, and finely diced
2 hard-boiled eggs, finely chopped
4 strips pimento

Put romaine in bowl. Arrange remaining ingredients in decorative sections on the lettuce, like wedges of a pie. Refrigerate. Serve with Basic French Dressing or whatever sounds good to you.

CHICKEN SALAD

There is no doubt about it, Chicken Salad is a popular dish if it isn't abused. Almost everyone has chicken meat on the pantry shelf, or in the deep freeze. It is extended with everything under the sun, depending on how many one has to serve or how important the people are who are going to eat it. The simple method is, as usual, the best. A simple rule for any kind of meat salad is to divide the ingredients into fourths. For one quart:

2 cups diced chicken (or other meat)
1 cup diced celery
1 cup mayonnaise or dressing

The meat should be in medium or large dice so one knows what one is eating, the celery diced but not minced, and the dressing of whipped-cream consistency. The seasoning is up to you. In using roasted chicken or turkey for salads, if the skin is crisp, a couple of tablespoonfuls ground up and added to the mayonnaise gives it a wonderful flavor, but do not use it if it is fat and greasy. (And if you use turkey it is a bit better, I think, if marinated first in a tart French Dressing, or if a dash of wine vinegar is added to the mayonnaise.)

Chicken Salad should be served on cold, crisp salad greens — lettuce, to be exact. You can let your imagination run wild on the accompaniments. If you stuff a tomato with the salad, it should be peeled, chilled, and stuffed just before serving. A few things like capers, slivered and browned almonds, chopped chives, chopped hard-cooked egg if you are from the Carolinas, are good to add to the mixture; count it as the celery, or serve on top, but do it just before combining and serving. My favorite garnish and extender is fresh pineapple, or white grapes — and fresh strawberries when they are at the height of the season.

CHICKEN SALAD SUPREME

FOR EIGHT

2½ cups diced cold chicken
1 cup celery, chopped fine
1 cup sliced white grapes
½ cup shredded browned almonds
2 tablespoons minced parsley
1 teaspoon salt
1 cup mayonnaise
½ cup whipping cream, whipped

Combine and serve in lettuce cups with thin slices of chicken on top, garnished with stuffed olives, sliced thin, or chopped ripe olives.

This same mixture can be made into a delicious mold. Use the same eight ingredients, plus:

1½ tablespoons gelatin
4 tablespoons water
½ cup chicken stock

Mix the chicken, celery, grapes, almonds, parsley, and salt. Soak gelatin in the cold water for 5 minutes and dissolve in hot chicken stock. When cold, add mayonnaise and whipped cream. Stir until thick and fold in the chicken mixture. Pack in individual molds or a large ring. Serve garnished with your favorites — artichoke hearts, for instance.

CHICKEN AND FRUIT SALAD

FOR EIGHT

A most popular dish for a luncheon.

2 cups white meat of chicken, cubed
1 orange, sectioned
¼ cup grapes, cut in half and seeded
¼ cup salted almonds, halved
1 banana
¾ cup mayonnaise

Cut the white meat from a boiled fowl into medium-sized pieces. Place in a chilled bowl and add the rest of the ingredients. Stir as little as possible and serve at once. I like to pile it on slices of fresh pineapple and use lots of watercress with it; and serve yesterday's rolls buttered and heavily sprinkled with cinnamon and sugar and oven-toasted.

CUCUMBER COLE SLAW

FOR FOUR TO SIX

Start with a head of cabbage, shredded fine. Wash, drain, put in a covered container, and chill in refrigerator early in the day. Mix and cook until thick:

2 eggs
½ cup vinegar
1 tablespoon salt
1 tablespoon sugar
2 teaspoons dry mustard
¼ teaspoon white pepper

Cool and add 2 cups sour cream. Add 2 cups shredded cucumbers and ¼ cup sliced green onion to the cold crisp cabbage — and as much dressing as you wish. The dressing is wonderful for potato salad, too.

GERMAN COLE SLAW

FOR FOUR TO SIX

Cover one head of cabbage, shredded fine, with boiling water for five minutes. Drain and add:

2 tablespoons finely chopped onion (or leave it out)
¼ cup vinegar
3 tablespoons olive oil
½ teaspoon salt
¼ teaspoon pepper
3 tablespoons chopped parsley

Toss together, and add a cup of sour cream.

COLE SLAW WITH BEER DRESSING

FOR FOUR TO SIX

1 head cabbage, medium-size
1 green pepper
½ cup beer
1 cup mayonnaise
1 teaspoon salt
1 teaspoon celery seed
¼ teaspoon Tabasco

Shred cabbage finely. Slice thinly the green pepper after you have seeded it and removed the white ribs. Mix rest of ingredients and toss with the cabbage and green pepper mixture.

This slaw has more character than you would think from the spices and ingredients prepared for the dressing. Use the ingredients given and taste before you decide that more seasonings are needed.

Dressing will not hold more than one day.

CRUDITÉS SALAD

FOR EIGHT TO TWELVE

A green salad is wonderful if made with fresh crisp salad greens — no cabbage, radishes, and such — but that doesn't mean you have to serve it every time you entertain. I like to make a salad from crudités — refreshing and good for you.

6 stalks fresh asparagus
½ cup raw cauliflower florets
½ cup slivered celery
1 small zucchini, sliced thin
½ cup fresh Brussels sprouts, cut in half
½ cup sliced raw mushrooms
2 Belgian endive, sliced
1 small cucumber, sliced thin
¼ cup sliced green onions
A few sliced radishes or cherry tomatoes
Sherry French Dressing
8 onion brushes (whole trimmed green onions made into brushes by slitting the whole portion 4 or 5 times about 3 inches into the onion)
Chopped parsley

Cut asparagus on the diagonal; put in a large strainer. Add the cauliflower, celery, zucchini, and Brussels sprouts. Pour boiling water over. Drain and cool. Toss with the mushrooms, endive, cucumber, green onions, and radishes. Pour dressing over and refrigerate for at least 1 hour. Drain off the dressing. Serve on very cold salad plates and decorate with the onion brushes and sprinkle with chopped parsley. No lettuce. The salad leftovers are good the following day. You may substitute slivered snow peas, yellow squash, very thinly sliced carrots. What I have listed is merely a guide. This is a great buffet salad, especially for a walk-around supper.

A clear crystal bowl or transparent soufflé dish for a salad of layered vegetables always adds interest to a table. Toss the vegetables while guests watch.

FENNEL SALAD

FOR FOUR

This is my favorite salad.

2 medium-sized fennel bulbs
4 tablespoons salad oil
2 tablespoons wine vinegar
Whites of 2 hard-cooked eggs, chopped fine
2 tablespoons capers
2 tablespoons chopped parsley

Place fennel in ice water for an hour. Remove, dry, and slice very thin. Mix oil, vinegar, egg whites, capers, and parsley. Pour over fennel and toss.

BELGIAN ENDIVE AND MUSHROOM SALAD

FOR EIGHT TO TWELVE

4 Belgian endive
8 large fresh mushrooms
Juice of 2 lemons
2 cups slivered celery, blanched 1 minute, drained, and cooled
1 teaspoon salt
1 tablespoon chopped chives
¼ teaspoon dried fines herbes
¼ cup olive oil
¼ cup salad oil
Cracked pepper
1 bunch watercress

Cut the endive lengthwise in as thin slices as possible. Place in ice water and refrigerate for several hours. Wash and dry mushrooms. Slice very thin. Pour lemon juice over. Toss drained endive with the celery. Add the mushrooms with the lemon juice. Add rest of ingredients except watercress. Toss lightly. Correct seasonings. Sprinkle with cracked pepper and pile on salad plates. Garnish with watercress (or parsley).

FLAGEOLET SALAD

FOR EIGHT

6 cups canned flageolets, drained, or cooked dried flageolets
¾ cup finely chopped parsley
½ cup thinly sliced green onion
1 clove garlic, finely minced
6 tablespoons olive oil
4 tablespoons vinegar
Salt and cracked pepper

Mix and marinate overnight. Serve with or without salad greens.

BLUE LAKE GREEN BEAN SALAD

FOR SIX OR EIGHT

2 No. 2 cans Blue Lake green beans
1 onion, thinly sliced
1 tablespoon salad oil
1 tablespoon vinegar
Salt and freshly ground pepper

Drain green beans; add onion, oil, and vinegar; sprinkle with salt and pepper. Let stand at least an hour; drain and add enough Horseradish Sour Cream Dressing to coat the beans generously. Serve from a salad bowl with or without greens.

BOUILLABAISSE SALAD

FOR EIGHT TO TWELVE

2 heads Boston lettuce, washed and crisped
3 heads curly endive, washed and leaves separated
1 pound fresh crabmeat
1 lobster tail, cooked
1 pound cooked shrimp
½ cup slivered celery, blanched 1 minute in boiling water
2 ripe tomatoes, peeled
2 hard-cooked eggs, finely chopped
1 tablespoon chopped chives
Salt and pepper
¼ cup thinly sliced green onion or small white onion
1 bunch watercress

Line a large shallow salad bowl with lettuce leaves. Add the endive leaves. Arrange seafood, celery, and tomatoes on top. Sprinkle with the chopped eggs, chives, and salt and pepper. Heap the onion on top; put half a bunch of watercress on either end of bowl. When guests come to the table, toss salad with:

Caviar Dressing:

1 cup sour cream
1 cup mayonnaise
2 tablespoons horseradish sauce
¼ cup caviar, black or red

But do let your guests see the salad before tossing.

BUFFET SALAD BOWL

FOR SIXTEEN OR MORE

---

1 head ruby lettuce
2 heads Boston lettuce
1 head romaine
6 stalks celery, sliced thin in diagonal pieces and blanched
1 small head cauliflower, broken into florets and blanched
½ cup sliced green onions
2 hard-cooked eggs, chopped
⅓ cup red wine vinegar
2 tablespoons lemon juice
⅓ cup olive oil
⅓ cup salad oil
1 tablespoon Dijon mustard
2 tablespoons chopped parsley
½ teaspoon salt
¼ teaspoon fines herbes
Cracked pepper

Wash and break salad greens. Mix with the celery and cauliflower. Cover and refrigerate. Mix rest of ingredients except cracked pepper and toss with the greens when ready to serve. Correct seasonings. Sprinkle with cracked pepper. Add other vegetables such as green beans, mushrooms, cherry tomatoes, artichoke hearts, slices of avocado. This is a good clean-out-the-icebox salad.

GARBANZO (CHICKPEA) SALAD

FOR EIGHT

---

5 cups canned chickpeas
½ cup olive oil
¼ cup salad oil
¼ cup red wine vinegar
1 teaspoon diced onion or shallot
1 teaspoon sugar
½ teaspoon salt
½ teaspoon cracked pepper
1 garlic clove, finely chopped
⅓ cup chopped parsley
2 tablespoons chopped pimento

Wash the chickpeas. Drain. Mix rest of ingredients and pour over. Let marinate for 24 hours.

MARINATED LEEK SALAD

FOR EIGHT TO TWELVE

8 leeks
¼ cup chopped parsley
1 clove garlic, finely minced
¼ cup salad oil
¼ cup olive oil
3 tablespoons vinegar
Salt and white pepper
¼ cup thinly sliced green onion
2 tablespoons green peppercorns
2 tablespoons chopped pimento or sweet red pepper

Cut away green tops of leeks. Wash well. Slice thin and steam until tender, about 4 minutes. Cool. Mix rest of ingredients and toss with leeks. Serve on watercress or fresh spinach.

PAPAYA ORIENTAL

FOR EIGHT

3 cups cooked tiny shrimp or diced shrimp
2 cups fresh grated coconut or Angel Flake
2 teaspoons grated fresh ginger
4 papayas, peeled and cut in half
½ cup fresh lime juice
Preserved ginger

Mix the shrimp, coconut, and fresh ginger. Pile into papaya cavities. Pour lime juice over. Decorate with thin slices of preserved ginger. Chill. This makes a nice luncheon salad.

GRAPEFRUIT AND SPINACH SALAD

FOR EIGHT OR MORE

1½ pounds fresh spinach
4 pink grapefruit
2 tablespoons Roquefort cheese
½ cup Sherry French Dressing
Salt and cracked pepper

Remove stems from spinach. Wash thoroughly and put in a closed plastic bag to crisp. (Do the day before, if you wish.) Peel and section the grapefruit. Mix the Roquefort with the Sherry French Dressing and toss with the spinach and fruit. Sprinkle with salt and cracked pepper. Substitute oranges for the grapefruit sometimes.

SPINACH AND JERUSALEM ARTICHOKE SALAD WITH CREAMY ITALIAN DRESSING

FOR EIGHT

With hot French bread, good cheese, and red wine, this makes a great supper.

1 cup olive oil
⅓ cup red wine vinegar
¼ cup sour cream
½ teaspoon dry mustard
2 tablespoons sugar
¼ cup chopped parsley
2 cloves garlic, minced
1½ teaspoons salt
1¼ pounds fresh spinach
4 ounces Jerusalem artichokes, sliced
8 slices crisp bacon, diced

Mix the oil, vinegar, sour cream, mustard, sugar, parsley, garlic, and salt. Wash and trim spinach and place in large salad bowl. Add the artichokes and bacon and toss with enough dressing to coat. You may also add sliced or diced pickled beets, avocado, sliced hard-cooked egg, or halved cherry tomatoes.

The dressing will not keep, so be sure to use it up.

SNOW PEA SALAD WITH SESAME SEED DRESSING

FOR SIX TO EIGHT

1 large head iceberg lettuce, shredded fine
1 pound snow peas, steamed 30 seconds
½ cup chopped parsley

Toss with:

¼ cup sesame seeds, lightly browned in oven
⅔ cup salad oil
2 tablespoons lemon juice
2 tablespoons vinegar
2 tablespoons sugar
1 clove garlic, crushed
1½ teaspoons salt

Put all ingredients in a blender except sesame seeds and mix well. Add seeds. This dressing will store well. I like to pile this salad on red or ruby lettuce leaves, if only for color.

RUSSIAN SALAD

FOR SIX

1 cup cooked green beans, cut in small pieces
1 cup cooked diced carrots
1 cup cooked peas
1 cup cooked diced potatoes
½ cup cooked diced celery
¾ cup mayonnaise
Salt and pepper
2 hard-cooked eggs, chopped fine
½ cup cooked diced beets

Combine the first six ingredients. Season with salt and pepper. Cover with chopped eggs and beets.

WILTED SPINACH AND MUSHROOM SALAD

FOR EIGHT OR MORE

½ pound bacon, diced
½ cup sliced scallions
4 tablespoons lemon juice
2 tablespoons salad oil, not olive
1 pound washed and trimmed spinach
1 pound thinly sliced fresh mushrooms
Salt and pepper

Cook bacon until crisp. Remove bacon and all but 4 tablespoons of fat; add scallions and sauté until soft. Add lemon juice and salad oil. Pour over spinach and mushrooms. Toss in bacon and add salt and pepper to taste. I sometimes add 1 cup diced avocado for this amount and a few cherry tomatoes or sliced pickled beets and sliced hard-cooked eggs. This is a good basic salad using spinach as the greens.

TOM HUNT'S SPINACH SALAD WITH GREEK OLIVES

FOR TEN OR MORE

1 pound fresh spinach
¼ cup thinly sliced green onion
1 clove garlic, finely minced
1 cup sliced Greek olives (in brine)
2 cups slivered blanched celery
2 cups finely grated raw carrot
1 cup diced feta cheese
2 cups yogurt
2 tablespoons Dijon mustard
1 teaspoon salt
Cracked pepper

Wash spinach, pulling out any heavy stems. Put in a plastic bag and refrigerate until crisp. Put into a salad bowl with the onion, garlic, olives, celery, grated carrots, and cheese. Mix the yogurt with the mustard and salt and toss with the salad ingredients. Correct seasonings and sprinkle with cracked pepper. Refrigerate for an hour before serving. Use this dressing for other salad greens, cold seafood, and on hot vegetables.

ORIENTAL VEGETABLE SALAD

FOR EIGHT

---

4 cucumbers
3 green peppers
1 sweet red pepper
1 bunch radishes, sliced
2½ cups canned bean sprouts, washed and drained, or fresh
6 tablespoons salad oil
1 tablespoon sugar
4 tablespoons vinegar
1 teaspoon soy sauce
½ teaspoon salt
2 heads Boston lettuce (you may omit)

Slice cucumbers very thin. Remove seeds from peppers and slice thin. Toss with the radish slices and bean sprouts. Chill. When ready to serve, toss with the dressing (made by mixing salad oil, sugar, vinegar, soy sauce, and salt) and put into a salad bowl with lettuce.

FRUIT BOWL

FOR EIGHT

A fruit bowl is nice to serve on a buffet, especially when you know your guests do not like salad greens. Make it the night before, too!

1 cup orange sections
1 cup fresh pineapple, diced
1 cup fresh strawberries, halved
1 grapefruit, sectioned
1 banana, sliced

Cover with half maple syrup, half simple syrup, reserving the banana to add just before serving. Place in refrigerator for at least 12 hours. These are suggested fruits, but you may use any that are in season. This makes a good first course also, served in stemmed crystal dishes that have been chilled or frosted.

MOLDED SALADS

There is nothing quite as cool as a shimmering molded salad. Every kitchen, regardless of size, should support a few molds of various shapes, inexpensive or otherwise, but decorative. You may turn out some works of art as your imagination runs riot. Just give everything enough time: allow at least three hours for gelatin to "set" — six hours is better — and when making a large mold for a summertime meal, make it the day before you use it. Let's talk about such molds; it will simplify your menu planning. A few things to remember:

When you make a large mold (over 1 quart) use 1¾ cups of liquid instead of 2, and keep this proportion throughout.

□

Grease your salad molds with mayonnaise before pouring your molded salads; they come out more easily and the mayonnaise gives them an extra nice flavor.

Before unmolding, moisten both the plate and the molded salad with *wet* fingers. The moist surfaces make it easy to slide the mold into the center of the plate after unmolding. To unmold a salad quickly, dip the mold in hot water, then loosen sides with a silver knife. Tap it with your hand and the salad will come out easily.

□

Remember that everything shows in a molded salad, so when adding fruit, bear in mind that *these fruits sink:* canned apricots; Royal Anne cherries; canned peaches and pears; whole strawberries; prunes and plums; fresh orange sections; grapes. *These foods float:* fresh apple cubes; banana slices; grapefruit sections; fresh peach or pear slices; raspberries; strawberry halves; marshmallows; broken nut meats.

□

Jell-O and gelatin are not the same, so watch your recipes and use whichever is called for.

□

Add whatever you are adding to the gelatin mix *only* when the mixture is thoroughly chilled or even partly congealed. If you are making a pattern, allow for a thin layer of gelatin to "set" before you begin.

□

Never boil gelatin and never add fresh pineapple to it.

□

Too much gelatin or a scarcity of seasoning makes a poor molded salad. Do not add more gelatin to bring it along, as you get the rubbery glue taste that goes with an overdose of it.

□

If they are good, they are delicious; if they are bad, they are very, very bad.

JELLIED ASPARAGUS SALAD

FOR EIGHT

4 cups canned green asparagus spears
1 tablespoon unflavored gelatin
¼ cup cold water
Liquid from asparagus cans, plus water, to make two cups
1 teaspoon sugar
6 tablespoons lemon juice
1 teaspoon salt
½ cup chopped celery
½ cup sliced stuffed olives
½ cup slivered blanched almonds
¼ cup chopped parsley

Drain asparagus, reserving the juice. Soften gelatin in the cold water. Heat the asparagus liquid and water. Add the softened gelatin to it. Remove from heat; add sugar, lemon juice, and salt. When partially set add celery, olives, almonds, and parsley. Arrange asparagus standing around sides of a ring mold or bundt pan. (I'll admit I use bundt pans a lot.) Cut up remaining asparagus and add to mixture. Pour into mold and refrigerate for several hours. Unmold on a bed of watercress. Serve with Green Herb Dressing.

GREEN HERB DRESSING

ONE AND ONE-HALF CUPS

½ cup parsley leaves
½ cup watercress leaves
8 peeled shallots or scallions
2 teaspoons dry mustard
1 teaspoon horseradish
1 teaspoon Worcestershire sauce
2 egg yolks
1 cup salad oil
⅓ cup tarragon vinegar
1 teaspoon mixed dried herbs

Put in a blender and whip until thickened.

AVOCADO MOLD

FOR SIX OR EIGHT

2 tablespoons unflavored gelatin
½ cup cold water
2 cups avocado
1 cup sour cream
1 cup mayonnaise
2 tablespoons chopped onion
1 teaspoon salt
⅛ teaspoon white pepper
¼ cup lemon juice

Dissolve gelatin in cold water. Melt over hot water. Put all the ingredients including melted gelatin in a blender or food processor until smooth. Pour into a lightly greased 1½-quart ring mold and cover with plastic wrap or foil. Refrigerate until set. Unmold onto a bed of watercress or soft lettuce, such as Boston. Fill center with any seafood tossed with sour cream and mayonnaise, or chicken salad made with white grapes and a few capers in place of the celery, or fresh fruit, especially fresh pineapple, which has an affinity for avocado.

ROQUEFORT MOUSSE

FOR EIGHT TO TWELVE

Make this mousse the day before, and freeze it if there are any leftovers. I use it for many occasions — with a salad course at dinner, as a dessert with fruit, as an edible centerpiece for a cocktail table — oh, many ways.

6 egg yolks
½ cup cream
1½ tablespoons unflavored gelatin
½ cup cold water
¾ pound Roquefort cheese
1½ cups cream, whipped
3 egg whites, stiffly beaten

Beat egg yolks with cream; heat over hot water until creamy and thick. Add gelatin dissolved in the cold water. Remove from heat, add the cheese (put through a sieve) and cool. Fold into the whipped cream. Fold in egg whites. Pour into a lightly buttered 1½-quart mold. Refrigerate overnight. Danish or American blue cheese may be substituted, but the Roquefort is more delicate. Turn out onto a plate and decorate as you wish. I use only watercress — in a bunch, not spread out here and there.

HAM MOUSSE

FOR TWELVE

For buffet suppers, Ham Mousse has great possibilities for hungry appetites.

1 tablespoon unflavored gelatin
¼ cup cold water
2 cups ground cooked smoked ham
½ cup finely minced celery
1 tablespoon minced parsley
2 tablespoons prepared horseradish
1 cup heavy cream, whipped

Stir gelatin and cold water together and let stand 5 minutes. Set over boiling water and stir until gelatin is dissolved; remove from heat; stir in ham, celery, parsley, and horseradish. Whip cream and fold into mixture. Pack into a ring mold and place in the refrigerator to set. Unmold on a round, flat platter and heap Waldorf salad in the center of the ham ring. Surround the ring with small lettuce leaves and place on them overlapping half slices of oranges and artichoke halves, and black olives here and there.

CHICKEN MOUSSE

FOR EIGHT

1 tablespoon unflavored gelatin
2 tablespoons cold water
3 egg yolks
1½ cups chicken broth
1 teaspoon salt
2 cups cooked chicken, chopped
½ cup chopped blanched almonds
2 tablespoons minced pimento
½ cup cream, whipped

Soak gelatin in cold water for 15 minutes. Beat egg yolks and add chicken broth. Cook in top of double boiler until mixture coats the spoon. Add gelatin and salt. When partially congealed, add chicken, almonds, pimento, and whipped cream. Pour into well-oiled mold and chill. Unmold on bed of lettuce and garnish with chilled quarters of peeled ripe tomatoes and peeled canned apricots dusted with chopped pistachio nuts.

MOLDED GAZPACHO SALAD

FOR EIGHT OR TEN

6 large ripe tomatoes, peeled and seeded
1 cucumber, peeled
⅓ cup green pepper, chopped and blanched
1 tablespoon plus 1 teaspoon unflavored gelatin, dissolved in ¼ cup cold water
1 teaspoon salt
¼ teaspoon white pepper
⅛ teaspoon Tabasco
1½ cups tomato juice, heated
4 tablespoons olive oil
1½ tablespoons wine vinegar
1 tablespoon chopped green onion

Chop the tomatoes and cucumber fine. Add the green pepper, salt, white pepper, and Tabasco. To the dissolved gelatin add the hot tomato juice. When gelatin is partially congealed, add vegetables and oil and vinegar, as well as the chopped green onion. Pour into individual molds lightly rubbed with mayonnaise. Chill until firm. Turn out on salad greens and serve with: ½ cup mayonnaise mixed with ½ cup sour cream and 1 cup finely diced celery.

This salad is such a nice change from tomato aspic. I really think it is worth the effort to chop the fresh vegetables by hand, but if you don't, use your blender.

TOMATO MEDLEY SALAD

FOR TWELVE

3 tablespoons unflavored gelatin
3 cups peeled, seeded, and diced tomatoes, drained and added to enough tomato juice to make 5 cupfuls
3 tablespoons red wine vinegar
2 tablespoons Horseradish Sauce
Few drops Tabasco
1 tomato, sliced
2½ cups canned artichoke hearts, cut in half
1 cup thinly sliced green pepper, blanched
1 cup thinly sliced celery, cut on diagonal, blanched
½ cup green onion, sliced thin
1 cup thinly sliced cucumber, well scrubbed and skin left on
Salad greens

Dissolve gelatin in ½ cup of the tomato juice. Heat the remaining 4½ cups of tomatoes and juice and add the gelatin mixture. Add vinegar, Horseradish Sauce, and Tabasco. Alternate a slice of tomato with an artichoke half in bottom of a 2-quart ring mold that has been rubbed lightly with mayonnaise. Cover with a thin layer of the gelatin mixture. Refrigerate until set. Layer the rest of vegetables to fill the mold. Pour remaining gelatin mixture in as it begins to congeal. (I like to blanch celery and green pepper in boiling water for 1 minute. The color is better.) Refrigerate for several hours. Turn out onto salad greens and fill center with Russian Salad. Sliced canned tomatoes may be used successfully.

PÂTÉ MOLD

FOR TWELVE

A favorite party salad to serve for a buffet supper (and I like it for a cocktail tidbit—so does everyone else!).

1 tablespoon unflavored gelatin
1 pint canned beef consommé (or green turtle, if you are extravagant)
2 3-ounce packages cream cheese
2 tablespoons cream
⅛ teaspoon garlic powder
½ teaspoon Beau Monde seasoning
½ cup of mashed, sautéed chicken livers, pâté de foie gras, or liverwurst, depending on your pocketbook

Dissolve gelatin in ¼ cup of consommé. Heat the rest to boiling and add dissolved gelatin. Soften cream cheese with the cream; add garlic powder and Beau Monde. Pour half the consommé in a ring mold and chill until it starts to congeal; then drop the pâté, livers, or liverwurst, softened to a creamy consistency, by teaspoonsful into the consommé. When set, spread softened cream cheese over all, pour the rest of the consommé into the mold, and return to the refrigerator. When thoroughly chilled and set, unmold on crisp salad greens and serve with a chive mayonnaise and salty slices of rye Melba toast. For a cocktail tidbit skip the lettuce.

CRANBERRY MOLD

FOR TEN

This holiday mold is especially pretty for Christmas entertaining.

1 package cherry Jell-O
1 cup hot water
¾ cup sugar
1 tablespoon lemon juice
1 tablespoon plain gelatin dissolved in 1 cup pineapple juice, then melted over hot water
1 cup ground raw cranberries
1 orange and rind, ground fine
1 cup crushed pineapple, drained
1 cup chopped celery
½ cup chopped pecans
Lettuce

Dissolve Jell-O in hot water; add sugar, lemon juice, and pineapple juice–gelatin mixture and stir until blended. Chill until partially set; add remaining ingredients; pour into ring mold. To serve, unmold on lettuce leaves, garnish with turkey or chicken salad, using grape halves in place of celery.

PRUNE ASPIC

FOR TWELVE

A most-often-requested molded salad.

2 tablespoons unflavored gelatin
½ cup cold water
3½ cups canned prune juice, hot
4 cups canned prunes, pitted and coarsely chopped
2 tablespoons lemon juice

Dissolve gelatin in the cold water. Add to hot prune juice and when partially congealed add prunes and lemon juice. Pour into a ring mold and chill. Turn out on a silver tray and garnish with whatever you please. Fill the center with cream cheese beaten with light cream until the consistency of whipped cream. Sprinkle top with grated lemon or orange peel. Prune Aspic is particularly good with turkey and ham.

CHICKEN AND LOBSTER RING

FOR EIGHT

Combining chicken and lobster meat in an aspic for a summer luncheon or supper is truly different; but good!

1½ tablespoons gelatin
2 cups cold chicken broth
1 cup cooked lobster meat
1 cup diced cooked chicken
½ cup diced cucumber (you may omit)
½ cup diced celery
1 tablespoon lemon juice
½ teaspoon onion juice
½ teaspoon dry mustard
Salt and pepper to taste

Soften gelatin in ¼ cup of the cold chicken broth. Heat remainder of broth to boiling point and add to the softened gelatin. When cold, add rest of the ingredients. Chill until firm and turn out on a bed of curly bleached endive. Fill the center with cottage cheese and sliced black olives; and serve with mayonnaise whipped up with avocado.

CUCUMBER MOUSSE

FOR EIGHT TO TEN

This is a good salad to accompany any fish entrée. I like to make it in a ring mold for a buffet and fill the center with seafood salad.

¾ cup boiling water
1 package lime-flavored gelatin
1 cup cottage cheese
1 cup mayonnaise
2 tablespoons grated onion
¼ cup cucumber grated with peel left on
1 cup slivered almonds (you may omit)

Pour boiling water on gelatin, cool; add cottage cheese, mayonnaise, grated onion, cucumber, and nuts. Pour into a wet mold and refrigerate.

SPECIAL SALAD LUNCHEON

I have a special salad luncheon that everyone likes. It can be prepared ahead of time, refrigerated, and assembled in five minutes. Since I have been in the restaurant business for many years, I am tired of seeing lettuce used for luncheon salads go to waste. So I have designed a salad lunch without lettuce and called it a potpourri of salads.

You may use three small coquilles (per guest) or small dessert dishes. The coquilles may be china, foil, or the shells you buy from any kitchenware counter. In one coquille I put an assortment of fresh fruit; in another, chicken salad made with capers in the mayonnaise; and in the third, a seafood or a rice salad. Sometimes I make a hot Crab Imperial for one coquille while I'm assembling the other dishes. I place the round edge of the coquilles to the outside of the plate so there is room in the center of the plate for a wine glass or parfait glass filled with a citrus ice or sherbet. I like to use pink grapefruit ice. You may tuck sprigs of watercress or parsley in between the coquilles. I usually serve a thin Melba toast or toasted crackers and coffee. Do not forget to pass Poppy Seed Dressing for the fruit. This is such a pretty luncheon with no jumping up for dessert; it is all there. The menu would be a good suggestion if you were entertaining in a club or restaurant too, as it is pretty to look at and uncomplicated for the cook. Sometimes I use large artichoke bottoms to hold the seafood and the chicken salads, and fill a scooped out orange or papaya with the fruit. You may also use a hollowed-out orange to hold the sherbet.

MORE SALAD IDEAS

In making fresh fruit salads, there are only a few "musts" that should be observed. Fruit should be ripe, but not too ripe; it should be cut in large enough pieces to be able to tell what it is, at least; and should be served cold — really cold. If combined with cheese, or meats of any kind, they should be cold, also, and easily identified — and sherbets are good with them. Mushiness has no place in a salad. The greens that are served with it should be crisp and fresh — and watercress puts the finishing touch to any salad plate.

It is easy to section grapefruit; so they should be sectioned. It is difficult to obtain perfect sections from an orange; so why not slice them? Melon cut in ball-shaped pieces or slices is more attractive than cubed; whole berries of any kind look and taste better than cut up. Last, but not least: a salad plate should look as if it had been made with a light and airy touch — do not flatten it out or follow a too definite pattern. Exaggerating a little, stand a bit away and pitch the fruit onto the plate rather than guide your hand with your nose.

The following combinations are thought out as far as availability is concerned. For main-course salads:

Orange slices, grapefruit sections, and melon balls, with creamy cottage cheese in a bed of romaine in the center of the plate; dates stuffed with ripe olives. Watercress and cinnamon bread finger sandwiches to serve with it.

□

Cantaloupe slices, fresh peach halves, whole strawberries, orange slices, and fresh green grapes left in clusters; balls of cream cheese rolled in freshly chopped mint on well-bleached curly endive or chicory, depending on how you say it.

□

Canned hearts of artichokes cut in half, with grapefruit sections (pink ones and white ones) arranged in a sunburst fashion with thin slices of oranges. Dust all lightly here and there with chopped chives and serve with it a sandwich made of whole-wheat bread with cooked carrots and peas mixed into mayonnaise for a filling.

□

Orange slices and avocado quarters, piled hit or miss in a bed of center pieces of lettuce, and sprinkled with watermelon balls and any fresh berry in season, especially raspberries.

□

Grapefruit sections alternating with ripe tomato quarters, topped with a generous portion of guacamole and served with rolled thin pancakes, filled and covered with grated Cheddar cheese and run under the broiler at the last minute.

Slices of white meat of chicken, pink grapefruit sections, hearts of palm sliced thick, and thin slices of orange piled high on fresh romaine is a meal in itself. Serve with it? — salty rye Melba toast.

□

Sliced oranges, thin slices of fresh pineapple (prepared the day before and mixed with fresh mint and powdered sugar and left in the refrigerator overnight), long slices of honeydew melon, and fresh apricot halves arranged helter-skelter in a bed of watercress, and topped with a ball of lime sherbet rolled in granulated sugar. You can fix your lime sherbet the night before, roll in waxed paper, and put in the deep freeze.

□

Just about any fruit you find in the greengrocer's — but make it *big* enough and *good* enough and *pretty* enough.

□

Dressings should be passed for such fruit dishes — any dressing will do.

□

Texas Pink or Ruby Red grapefruit, with generous crumbles of Roquefort and a simple vinegar and oil dressing, is both beautiful and tasty.

□

Try grapefruit sections and thin slices of sweet onion with Poppy Seed Dressing.

□

The salad to complement shrimp is made of grapefruit sections left whole, combined with slices of avocado. A good French Dressing, combined half and half with chili sauce, gives the spiciness desired with the piquant flavored shrimp.

□

A molded salad with a different twist to serve with shrimp or any seafood dish is made with lemon Jell-O, using half hot water and half hot chili sauce and served with mayonnaise, to which has been added a dash of hot mustard.

Salad Dressings

BASIC FRENCH DRESSING

ONE AND ONE-FOURTH CUPS

2 teaspoons salt
1 teaspoon cracked pepper
1 teaspoon paprika
½ teaspoon powdered sugar
½ teaspoon dry mustard
Few grains of cayenne
¼ cup vinegar
1 cup olive or salad oil

Mix dry ingredients with the vinegar, then add the oil. Shake or beat before using. If you like the flavor of garlic in your dressing, drop a button of garlic into the bottle you keep it in. And if you want a French Dressing with more body to it, add the beaten yolk of an egg before you add the oil.

FRENCH THOUSAND ISLAND DRESSING

ONE CUP

A tart and fresh variation.

2 tablespoons capers
2 tablespoons chopped green pepper
3 tablespoons chopped red pepper or pimento
2 tablespoons chopped stuffed olives
1 cup Basic French Dressing
½ teaspoon Worcestershire sauce

Mix and put in the refrigerator. Shake well before adding to the green salad.

ONION MINT DRESSING

ONE-HALF CUP

A very oniony dressing for salad greens.

1 large bunch of fresh mint
2 tablespoons minced onion
½ green pepper, sliced paper-thin
½ cup Basic French Dressing

Chop mint leaves and the onion really fine — tears will flow. Add green pepper, then the French Dressing. Chill. I like this dressing when I'm serving a buffet with cold meats such as lamb, ham, and turkey.

OTHER VARIATIONS ON BASIC FRENCH DRESSING

With a good Basic French Dressing you may add your choice of ingredients to give variety to your salads. To 1 cup of French Dressing you might add any of the following: 3 tablespoons chopped anchovy and 2 tablespoons capers; 4 tablespoons Major Grey's chutney; 2 finely chopped hard-cooked eggs, 2 tablespoons chopped pimento, 2 tablespoons chopped green pepper, and ¼ cup cooked beets. For Lorenzo Dressing add 4 tablespoons chili sauce and 4 tablespoons watercress; this is delicious served over chilled canned pears with salad greens. For Vinaigrette — which I love on cold cooked asparagus, canned or fresh — add 2 tablespoons finely minced green pepper, 1 tablespoon finely minced parsley, 2 tablespoons finely minced sweet pickle, and 1 tablespoon finely minced chives (or 1 teaspoon scraped onion and 1 tablespoon finely minced capers). For Roquefort Dressing, add ½ cup coarsely crumbled Roquefort cheese and whip with a beater, or use an electric blender to mix thoroughly.

HERB FRENCH DRESSING

ONE AND ONE-HALF CUPS

½ cup wine vinegar
1 cup olive oil
1 teaspoon salt
½ teaspoon dry mustard
¼ teaspoon basil
¼ teaspoon tarragon
2 twists of the pepper mill
½ teaspoon Worcestershire sauce

Put in a jar and shake until you are tired.

SHERRY FRENCH DRESSING

FIVE CUPS

This is a light, mildly flavored dressing that goes well with any greens, fruit, or vegetable. It does not fight with whatever wine you may be drinking. I like it especially on sweet red and green peppers.

1 egg
1 teaspoon sugar
2 teaspoons salt
½ cup vinegar
4 cups salad oil (half olive oil makes it even better)
½ cup dry sherry
2 cloves garlic

Mix egg, sugar, and salt together; add oil and vinegar alternately until all the oil is added; then drip the sherry in slowly. Add garlic cloves, barely crushed, and store in a Mason jar until ready to use. Toss among any collection of salad greens you may find and your salad will be a success. This dressing has a special affinity for Roquefort cheese, too.

LIME HONEY DRESSING

ONE AND TWO-THIRDS CUPS

⅓ cup lime juice
⅓ cup honey
1 cup salad oil
½ teaspoon paprika
½ teaspoon prepared mustard
½ teaspoon salt
Grated peel of 1 lime

Blend all ingredients thoroughly and keep in a cool place.

MIMOSA DRESSING

THREE-FOURTHS CUP

A dressing that likes Jerusalem artichokes, or sun chokes as they are sometimes called.

1 tablespoon Dijon mustard
2 tablespoons lemon juice
2 tablespoons vinegar
6 tablespoons olive oil
6 tablespoons salad oil
1 hard-cooked egg, chopped fine
2 tablespoons chopped parsley
Salt and pepper

Put first five ingredients in a bowl and beat for 1 minute with a French whip. Add egg and parsley. Season with salt and pepper to taste.

STRAWBERRY SOUR CREAM DRESSING

TWO AND ONE-HALF CUPS

2 cups thick sour cream
1 teaspoon salt
½ cup frozen strawberries

Fold the fruit into the salted cream. It is especially good on fruit of any kind, and I like it on chilled canned pears for a dessert.

SOUR CREAM DRESSING

TWO CUPS

Sour cream dressings are good anyhow. Here are some more. This one is especially good with cabbage.

1 cup sour cream
1 tablespoon grated onion
¼ cup tarragon vinegar
2 tablespoons sugar
½ teaspoon celery seed
⅛ teaspoon white pepper
1½ teaspoons salt
½ cup whipping cream

Mix all but the whipping cream in order given. After mixing with shredded cabbage, fold in the whipped cream. I like this, too, for Waldorf salad; also on a mixed fresh fruit salad.

HORSERADISH SOUR CREAM DRESSING

ONE AND ONE-HALF CUPS

Especially for use on Blue Lake Green Bean Salad.

1 cup sour cream
½ cup mayonnaise
1 teaspoon lemon juice
¼ teaspoon dry mustard
1 tablespoon prepared horseradish
¼ teaspoon onion juice
2 teaspoons chopped chives (optional)

Mix all ingredients and store in a jar in the refrigerator. Make the day before use if possible.

Blue Lake Green Bean Salad was demonstrated at a Smith College Alumni Cooking School in Houston with this dressing, and made such an impression that sour cream became popular overnight, confounding the dairymen. A teaspoon of anchovy paste added to the dressing gives an intriguing flavor.

Confidentially, I like this dressing on green salad, cold thick slices of tomato, cucumbers, potato salad — oh well, almost anything but vanilla ice cream.

Or, add a tablespoon of melted gelatin, mold, and serve with cold meats or roast beef.

WARM LEMON DRESSING

ONE CUP

I like to use this very simple dressing on spinach and green salads if I am not using Sherry French Dressing.

⅔ cup salad oil
2 tablespoons sliced scallions
1 clove garlic, crushed
⅓ cup lemon juice
Salt and cracked pepper

Heat the oil and sauté the scallions and garlic for 1 minute. Add lemon juice, remove garlic, and pour over salad. Season with salt and pepper.

BACON DRESSING

ONE-HALF CUP

For young greens like turnip greens, beet greens, spinach, dandelion greens, and especially the curly lettuce you grow in your own yard, a bacon dressing is best. Good for potato salad, too.

6 slices bacon
½ cup vinegar
½ teaspoon sugar
Salt and pepper

Dice bacon, fry, and let the fat render out. Remove from heat and slowly add vinegar, sugar, and salt and pepper to taste. Mix thoroughly and pour over the salad while warm.

MAYONNAISE

ONE AND ONE-FOURTH CUPS

1 teaspoon salt
½ teaspoon dry mustard
½ teaspoon sugar
2 egg yolks
2 tablespoons vinegar or lemon juice
1 cup salad oil
A whiff of cayenne (less than a pinch)

Mix salt (you may prefer using ½ teaspoon), mustard, and sugar. Add egg yolks and 1 tablespoon of the vinegar and make a paste. Add the oil slowly, beating constantly (high speed on a mixer). As it thickens, add the remaining 1 tablespoon of vinegar and the cayenne. Continue beating until stiff. Keep refrigerated — or the raw egg will cause it to spoil. Thin with cream (sweet or sour) or lemon juice, and add any flavor you wish before using.

These variations of mayonnaise I have found most popular over the years:

Russian Dressing:
1 cup mayonnaise
2 tablespoons finely diced celery
2 tablespoons finely diced green pepper
1 tablespoon chopped pimento
2 tablespoons finely diced sweet pickles (I like Pic-l-joys)
2 tablespoons chili sauce
1 tablespoon tomato catsup

For Molded Vegetable Salads:
1 cup mayonnaise
½ cup finely diced celery or shredded cucumber
1 teaspoon chopped chives or green onion tops

1 cup mayonnaise
½ cup any mixed cooked vegetables
¼ cup finely diced American cheese

1 cup mayonnaise
½ cup finely diced fresh tomatoes
1 tablespoon chopped fresh tarragon or basil

1 cup mayonnaise
¼ cup finely diced cooked shrimp or crabmeat
1 tablespoon lemon juice

For Fresh Fruit Salads or Molded Fruit:
1 cup mayonnaise
¼ cup cubed cream cheese
¼ cup orange sections
Grated rind of 1 orange
¼ cup chopped pecans (omit or add for variation)

And sometimes:
2 tablespoons chopped candied ginger

Green Mayonnaise for Seafood:

1 cup mayonnaise
1 tablespoon finely chopped chives
1 tablespoon finely chopped parsley
1 tablespoon finely chopped tarragon
1 tablespoon finely chopped spinach
1 tablespoon finely chopped capers

Green Goddess Dressing for Assorted Salad Greens:

1 cup mayonnaise
¼ cup finely chopped parsley
½ cup heavy cream
1 teaspoon chopped chives
½ clove garlic crushed with:
⅛ teaspoon salt, and
½ teaspoon dry mustard
4 tablespoons anchovies, chopped fine
or
2 tablespoons anchovy paste

Quick Creamy Roquefort Dressing:

1 cup mayonnaise
1 tablespoon lemon juice
1 cup light cream
½ pound Roquefort or blue cheese

POPPY SEED DRESSING

THREE AND ONE-HALF CUPS

I would like to tell a story of a dressing designed for fruits. Where it originated I have no idea; I remember having it served to me in New York so many years ago I hate to recall. Rumors extend hither and yon that I created it; I hasten to deny this; but I did popularize it when I realized that on the best grapefruit in the whole wide world (Texas grapefruit) it was the most delectable dressing imaginable. Today there is hardly a restaurant or home in Texas that does not have some kind of poppy-seed dressing. The recipe I use has been in demand to the point of being ludicrous and, strange as it may seem, the men like it — a few even put it on their potatoes. So here it is!

1½ cups sugar
2 teaspoons dry mustard
2 teaspoons salt
⅔ cup vinegar
3 tablespoons onion juice
2 cups salad oil, not olive oil
3 tablespoons poppy seeds

Mix sugar, mustard, salt, and vinegar. Add onion juice and stir in thoroughly. Slowly add oil, beating constantly, and continue to beat until thick. When you think the mixture is thick enough, beat 5 minutes longer. Add poppy seeds and beat for a few minutes. Store in a cool place or in the refrigerator, but not near the freezing coil.

This dressing is easier and better to make with an electric mixer or blender, using medium speed, but if your endurance is good you may make it by hand with a rotary beater. The onion juice is obtained by grating a large white onion on the fine side of a grater, or dropping a medium onion in an electric blender, then straining. (Prepare to weep in either case.) If the dressing separates, pour off the clear part and beat again, adding the poppy seed mixture slowly, but it will not separate unless it becomes too cold or too hot.

SESAME SEED DRESSING

THREE CUPS

Sesame seeds are in to stay! The use of toasted sesame seeds was taught to us by the Chinese cooks. The seeds add a delightful flavor and texture to salad dressings, breads, cakes, cookies, candies. This dressing will perk up a green or avocado salad.

1 cup sugar
1 teaspoon paprika
½ teaspoon dry mustard
1 teaspoon salt
1 teaspoon Worcestershire sauce
1 tablespoon onion juice
2 cups salad oil
1 cup cider vinegar
½ cup toasted sesame seeds

Put sugar, seasonings, and onion juice in a bowl and beat until thoroughly combined. Add the oil gradually, then the vinegar, a little at a time. Add toasted seeds last. Keep in a covered jar in the refrigerator.

To toast sesame seeds, place on a shallow pan or baking sheet in 200° to 250° oven; watch closely and stir frequently. They should be just golden brown to bring out the flavor, but will become bitter if toasted until they are dark.

CELERY SEED DRESSING

ONE QUART

A salad dressing that adds a touch of the unusual.

2¼ cups powdered sugar
1 tablespoon dry mustard
1 tablespoon salt
½ cup plus 1 tablespoon vinegar
3 cups salad oil
1 tablespoon paprika (to color)
1 tablespoon celery seed

Combine and mix all but the last three ingredients. Let stand 3 hours, stirring frequently (about every 30 minutes) until a honey consistency.

Heat half the oil and add paprika. Strain and cool. Add paprika oil to remainder of oil, and when cool add to first mixture slowly, as for French Dressing. Last, add the celery seed and let stand 24 hours before using. Really good on fruit salads of all kinds, and on frozen salads especially.

BASIC COOKED DRESSING

TWO CUPS

When salad dressings get to be routine, it is time to go back a few years. My mother's kitchen always boasted cooked dressings that I remember today with joy. For potato salads and slaws they are a delightful change, and worth the time it takes to make them.

2 teaspoons dry mustard
3 tablespoons sugar
1 teaspoon salt
½ cup flour
1⅓ cups milk
2 eggs, well beaten
½ cup vinegar
2 tablespoons butter

Mix dry ingredients; add milk, stirring until smooth. Cook over hot water until thick (about 30 minutes); then add eggs, beating constantly, and continue to cook for 3 minutes. Remove from heat and add vinegar and butter. Stir until smooth and thick. Use as is or combine with mayonnaise or sour cream — and whipped cream for old-fashioned mixed fruit salads.

ROQUEFORT DRESSING

TWO CUPS

Roquefort Dressing recipes are numerous. This one is asked for time and again.

1 3-ounce package cream cheese
⅓ cup Roquefort (blue cheese may be substituted)
¼ teaspoon salt
⅛ teaspoon garlic powder
¼ teaspoon prepared mustard
½ teaspoon Beau Monde seasoning (may be omitted)
½ cup light cream
½ cup mayonnaise

Blend cheeses with the seasonings; add the mayonnaise alternately with the cream. Whip until smooth. Sometimes add sour cream!

AVOCADO DRESSING

THREE CUPS

3 avocados, puréed
1 cup sour cream
1½ teaspoons salt
2 tablespoons lime juice

Combine all ingredients and chill 30 minutes.

AVOCADO CREAM DRESSING

TWO CUPS

¾ cup mashed avocado
1 cup heavy cream, whipped
¼ cup powdered sugar
½ teaspoon salt
Grated orange peel

Fold avocado into whipped cream, sugar, and salt. Pile lightly on the salad you choose and sprinkle with grated orange peel.

This dressing is also good served on fresh fruit desserts and baked custards.

Vegetables

To begin with, either grow or buy *fresh* vegetables, and use what is available. If the green beans are tired looking, let them rest. If you are planning on spinach and there isn't any, don't have a nervous breakdown . . . Be flexible, there is always — not sometimes, but always — a fresh vegetable around.*

Second, learn to *undercook* to preserve those precious minerals and vitamins, and taste. The "dressing up" that follows finishes them.

HOW TO COOK ASPARAGUS

In preparing asparagus, remove the "scales" with a paring knife and wash many times in cold water. Sand sticks like mad to these scales and in the tiny ridges of the stalk. The white part of the stalk should be broken off, too. Tie the stalks in a small bunch and stand in a deep pot, or lay flat in a shallow pan, cover, and boil until tender, about 3 to 6 minutes.

ASPARAGUS POLONAISE

In Europe fresh asparagus is used a great deal as a first course. Why not try it for your next dinner party? Either simply dressed with sweet

*Helen did find some canned vegetables handy to have on hand. Beets, hearts of palm, mushrooms, celery hearts, and baby carrots were on her emergency shelf. Frozen green beans, asparagus, and broccoli were in her freezer for unexpected needs.

butter and a squeeze of lemon, or with riced hard-cooked egg sprinkled over before the butter, and a whiff of nutmeg. Perfect with Hollandaise. A new twist is with freshly chopped ripe tomato added to hot mayonnaise and a few bits of chopped basil.

ASPARAGUS SOUR CREAM

FOR FOUR

1½ pounds asparagus
1 cup sour cream
¼ cup mayonnaise
2 tablespoons lemon juice
Buttered bread crumbs

Combine sour cream, mayonnaise, and lemon juice. Heat and pour over asparagus that have been boiled and drained. Brown 2 tablespoons of dry white bread crumbs in butter and sprinkle over the cream mixture. Run under the broiler until bubbly.

ASPARAGUS WITH MUSHROOMS

FOR SIX

A tempting dish to serve with ham.

1 tablespoon chopped green onions or chives
3 cups cut-up freshly cooked asparagus
¼ cup butter
1 cup sliced sautéed or canned mushrooms
½ cup heavy cream

Sauté onion and asparagus in butter for 5 minutes. Add mushrooms and cream. Heat until *hot* and serve.

HAM AND ASPARAGUS GRUYÈRE

FOR FOUR

1 pound fresh asparagus, cooked
8 thin slices cooked ham
1 cup whipping cream or a thin Cream Sauce, (1 cup milk, 1 tablespoon butter, 1 tablespoon flour)
½ cup grated Gruyère cheese
1 tablespoon Parmesan cheese

Place the asparagus in a shallow oven-proof casserole and cover with the ham. Pour the cream over; cover with the cheeses. Bake at 450° about 10 minutes until a golden brown. This is a lovely blending of flavors.

ANCHOVY GREEN BEANS

FOR SIX

Try anchovy sauce on any green vegetable, but especially on fresh green beans.

½ cup butter
1 teaspoon lemon juice
1 teaspoon chopped parsley
1 tablespoon anchovy paste
1½ pounds green beans, freshly cooked

Cream butter and lemon juice; add parsley and anchovy paste. Put on top of the beans and let it melt through them. (If you cook the beans ahead of time, keep the fresh taste by covering with ice, and then reheating with little or no liquid except what clings to them.)

GREEN BEAN CASSEROLE

FOR EIGHT

3 cups fresh green beans or frozen, "kitchen-cut"
1 cup slivered celery, cut slantwise
½ cup thinly sliced onion
1 cup sliced water chestnuts
½ cup sour cream
¼ cup mayonnaise
⅛ teaspoon curry powder
Salt and pepper

Cook the beans, celery, and onion in water to cover, until *al dente*. Drain and add water chestnuts. Mix with the sour cream, mayonnaise, and curry powder. Season to your taste. Pour into a shallow casserole and bake in a 300° oven until hot, about 20 minutes. Run under broiler to brown.

GREEN BEANS WITH FLAGEOLETS

FOR EIGHT

2 tablespoons butter
2 tablespoons finely chopped onion
1 pound snipped green beans, cooked
2½ cups canned flageolets, drained
¼ cup finely chopped parsley
Half-and-half
Salt and pepper

Melt the butter; add onion and sauté until yellow. Add green beans, flageolets, parsley, and enough cream to just hold all ingredients together. Season to taste and serve. Or if you like, place in a buttered shallow casserole, sprinkle with buttered bread crumbs, and run under broiler to brown.

MORE GREEN-BEAN IDEAS

I have to be a green-bean fan. It is one vegetable that people are not afraid to taste. So I dress them up with lots of butter and things thrown in, like:

Almonds or Brazil nuts, sliced and browned in the butter.

□

Dry bread crumbs tossed and sautéed in the butter and poured over the beans, with or without garlic.

□

Fresh chopped mushroom stems sautéed with a dash of Beau Monde seasoning. Swish the cooked beans around in them.

□

Finely diced bacon and onion sautéed together until the bacon is crisp and the onion soft. This gives the southern touch to green beans.

□

One teaspoon *prepared mustard* or *horseradish added to* ¼ cup butter.

□

Little pickled pearl onions, sliced water chestnuts, bamboo shoots, here and there in butter.

□

And, when I first started eating out in New York, I used to see on menus in Italian restaurants Asparagus Buca Lapi. The name always fascinated me, so one day I tried it. I have never dared use the name, but I have Buca Lapied every vegetable known to man ever since. You merely pour hot melted butter over hot cooked vegetables, especially

Wash and scrape the carrots. Cook in boiling salted water until tender. Drain and leave whole or slice. Melt the butter; add flour, salt, and pepper, and cook until bubbly. Add milk and mustard and cook until smooth. Toss in the carrots and heat until hot. Sprinkle with chopped chives or green onion tops.

DILLED CARROTS

FOR FOUR

1 cup thinly sliced carrots
1 teaspoon whipped margarine
A pinch of sugar
½ teaspoon vegetable salt
1 tablespoon fresh or 1 teaspoon dried dill weed
¼ teaspoon cracked pepper

Steam carrots for 4 minutes. Melt margarine in a skillet. Add carrots and remaining ingredients. Cook until thoroughly heated.

CARROTS IN COGNAC

FOR FOUR

Two carrot recipes, sixteen years apart, perfectly illustrate Helen Corbitt's genius with adaptations. Both versions are given here, with the suggestion that the butter in the first recipe can be sharply reduced without injuring the flavors and that the second recipe might be enhanced by a teaspoon to a tablespoon of butter or margarine.

2 cups slivered raw carrots
1 teaspoon sugar
1 cup butter
⅓ cup Cognac

Place in covered baking dish and bake at 350° until tender, about 30 minutes. (Marsala in the same quantity may be substituted for the Cognac.)

CAULIFLOWER

FOR SIX

Cauliflower is a rugged individualist and there is nothing prettier than fresh cauliflower cooked whole and served in various ways. Here is the simplest and most flavorful.

1 whole fresh cauliflower
2 quarts boiling water
¼ teaspoon salt
½ cup milk
Cracker crumbs
Butter
Paprika

Wash cauliflower and cook in an open kettle in boiling salted water and milk (the milk is added to ensure keeping the cauliflower white) until tender, about 20 minutes. Drain, place on an ovenproof tray, cover with cracker crumbs (made from the buttery kind), sprinkle with butter and paprika, and place in the oven at 350° to brown. Remove and serve at once.

You cannot reheat cauliflower very successfully; it takes on a strong, unpleasant taste and usually turns dark.

Cook the cauliflower leaves as you would broccoli, and do them au gratin.

CELERY AMANDINE

FOR FOUR

4 canned celery hearts
2 tablespoons butter
1 cup canned consommé
1 teaspoon arrowroot or cornstarch
2 tablespoons cold water
Salt and freshly ground pepper
½ cup slivered natural almonds (I like these browned in butter)
2 tablespoons chopped parsley

Brown the celery in the butter. Add the consommé and simmer for 5 minutes. Add the arrowroot or cornstarch to the cold water and add to the celery and consommé. Cook until thickened, about 8 to 10 minutes, stirring constantly. Season to taste. Sprinkle nuts on the top and run under broiler for 1 minute. Sprinkle with parsley. Divine! And especially good with beef.

BRAISED CELERY

FOR EIGHT

4 bunches celery
2 tablespoons butter
½ cup finely chopped onion
2 cups canned beef consommé
Chopped parsley

Cut off tops of celery and tough outer stalks. Split the bunches lengthwise, cover with boiling water, and cook for 5 minutes. Remove and cool with cold running water. Melt the butter and sauté the onion until soft and yellow. Fold the celery over to make a serving about 4 inches long. Place in a buttered shallow casserole. Sprinkle with the sautéed onion and pour over the consommé. Cover and bake at 375° for 1 hour or until celery is tender. Remove celery to serving platter or tray (keep warm) and continue cooking the liquid until reduced to about ¾ cup. Pour over celery and sprinkle with chopped parsley. If you use canned celery hearts for a quicker preparation, reduce baking time to 30 minutes and proceed.

ABOUT CORN

Corn is corn, especially when it comes wrapped in its green husk. I think corn on the cob should be eaten almost as a ritual, with nothing else but corn. It is good such a short time — and the shortest time between picking and consuming is the best time for eating. Be sure fresh corn is fresh, canned corn is of a good label, and frozen corn is properly frozen.

CORN-ON-THE-COB RINGS WITH HORSERADISH BUTTER

Corn on the cob cut in 1-inch rings steamed (or boiled with little water) 5 minutes, dressed with melted butter and lots of horseradish makes a surprisingly popular cocktail bit. I usually attach them with picks onto a head of cauliflower or a grapefruit. Plan on each guest eating several.

FRESH CORN SAUTÉ

Two medium-sized ears for each one-half cup corn

Husk and clean corn, removing the silk carefully. Cut or scrape the kernels from the cob (be sure to get the milk) and place in a skillet with sweet butter. Cover and cook slowly until the corn is no longer starchy tasting, turning frequently with a spatula. Season with salt and pepper; and if there is any left after you finish tasting as you go along, serve it hot. I sometimes add 2 tablespoons of cream for each cup of corn as I sauté it. Allow at least ½ cup of corn per person — it's better to allow a whole cup.

CORN PUDDING

FOR EIGHT

¼ cup butter
¼ cup flour
2 teaspoons salt
1½ tablespoons sugar
1¾ cups milk
3 cups fresh or frozen corn, chopped (use an electric blender)
3 eggs

Melt butter in saucepan; stir in flour, salt, and sugar. Cook until bubbly, add milk, and cook until thick. Stir in the corn, either chopped or whole, but chopped makes a smoother pudding. Stir in the eggs, which have been beaten until frothy. Pour into a well-buttered casserole and bake in a hot-water bath at 350° about 45 minutes. For a soufflé, fold in egg whites separately.

CORN AND TOMATOES

FOR EIGHT

2 cups canned tomatoes
¼ cup chopped onion
1 cup corn kernels
2 tablespoons butter
2 strips bacon

Cook tomatoes and onions until onions are soft. Add corn and butter and cook slowly for 30 minutes. Dice and fry bacon until crisp and add the last minute before serving — or leave it out!

FRESH CORN AND YELLOW SQUASH

FOR EIGHT

A good summertime vegetable.

4 tablespoons butter
½ cup thinly sliced onion
4 ears of corn, kernels cut off, or 1 package frozen corn kernels
3 cups diced fresh tomatoes
1 pound sliced yellow squash
1 teaspoon salt
White pepper
¼ cup chopped parsley

Melt butter and add onion; cook until limp but not brown. Add rest of ingredients except parsley. Cover and cook 10 minutes. Correct seasonings if necessary. Sprinkle with parsley and serve.

ESCALLOPED CUCUMBERS

FOR EIGHT

6 medium-sized cucumbers
Salt and white pepper
1½ cups buttered white bread crumbs
Chopped parsley

Peel and slice cucumbers ¼ inch thick. Sprinkle with salt and pepper. Place in alternate layers with the buttered crumbs in a buttered shallow casserole, ending with crumbs on top. Bake at 350° until tender but not mushy, approximately 20 minutes. Sprinkle with chopped parsley.

EGGPLANT PROVENÇAL

FOR EIGHT

Eggplants in the market are a thing of beauty. I love to look at their satiny Victorian purples and reds; and after discovering they have an affinity for olive oil, I find them most succulent. And popular with all ages.

1 large peeled eggplant, cut into 8 one-inch circles
1 teaspoon salt
½ teaspoon white pepper
3 tablespoons olive oil
3 tablespoons butter
1 cup chopped onion
2 cloves minced garlic
2 cups peeled, seeded, and chopped tomatoes
Pinch of thyme
Salt and white pepper
¼ cup chopped parsley
½ cup white bread crumbs
1 cup grated Swiss or Gruyère cheese

As the eggplant slices change in circumference, trim so that they are all the same size. Place in a shallow oiled pan. Sprinkle with the salt and pepper. Broil 5 minutes. Heat the oil and butter; add onion and garlic. Cook until yellow. Add tomatoes and trimmings of eggplant; cook until thick. Stir in thyme, salt, pepper, parsley, and bread crumbs. Correct seasonings. Pile on the broiled eggplant. Cover with the cheese. Bake at 350° until cheese is melted. Good cold, too, as an hors d'oeuvre or salad.

FRIED EGGPLANT

FOR FOUR

Cut a medium-sized eggplant into ¼-inch slices; soak in salted water (2 cups water, 2 tablespoons salt) for one hour. Drain and dry. Sprinkle with salt and pepper and roll in flour. Sauté slowly in butter or olive oil until brown on both sides, turning only once. Drain on paper. I like to use this as a base for stuffed mushrooms.

EGGPLANT AND MUSHROOM CASSEROLE

FOR EIGHT

3 medium eggplants, peeled
1 cup finely chopped onion
8 tablespoons butter
4 eggs, beaten
1 cup mayonnaise
1 pound finely chopped fresh mushrooms
Salt and pepper to taste
9 tablespoons cream cheese, softened
¼ cup finely chopped parsley
A pinch of thyme
3 tablespoons grated Gruyère cheese
¼ cup fine white bread crumbs

Cover eggplants with water and 1 tablespoon salt, and let stand for 30 minutes. Drain and cook in fresh water until tender. Drain well. Cut in cubes and place in large bowl. Sauté the onion in 2 tablespoons butter, until yellow. Add to eggplant. Stir in eggs and mayonnaise. Sauté mushrooms in 4 tablespoons butter. Add to the eggplant mixture. Mix thoroughly. Season to taste. Place in a buttered 2-quart casserole. Mix cream cheese with parsley, thyme, Gruyère, and bread crumbs. Spread over top of casserole mixture. Sprinkle with 2 tablespoons melted butter. Bake at 350° until set and browned, about 40 minutes. You can make this ahead of time and refrigerate it until you're ready to bake and serve it.

EGGPLANT PARMESAN

FOR SIX

1 eggplant
4 cups dry bread crumbs
1 egg
Olive oil or shortening for frying
1 onion, chopped
½ green pepper, chopped
2½ cups canned or fresh tomatoes
1 teaspoon salt
⅛ teaspoon pepper
1 teaspoon sugar
1 cup Parmesan cheese

Slice the eggplant in ¼-inch slices, peel, dip in bread crumbs, then egg (slightly beaten and mixed with ½ cup water), and again in the crumbs. Fry in oil or shortening until brown. Sauté the onion and green pepper until soft; add tomatoes, salt, pepper, and sugar and cook until well blended. Place the eggplant in a casserole in alternate layers with cheese and the sauce, having the top layer end with cheese. Bake covered at 350° for 15 minutes. Remove cover and continue baking until crusty and brown.

EGGPLANT AND OYSTERS

FOR EIGHT

Eggplant combined with oysters I find the most popular dish I can serve with turkey, especially on Christmas Day.

1 eggplant, medium size
4 tablespoons finely chopped onion
¼ cup butter
½ cup dry bread crumbs
½ teaspoon salt
1 pint oysters
½ cup light cream

Peel and cut the eggplant in 1-inch cubes. Cook in boiling salted water until soft; drain. Sauté the onion in the butter until yellow and add bread crumbs and salt. Heat oysters slowly in their own liquid just until the edges curl. Put a layer of eggplant in a buttered casserole, sprinkle with crumbs, then oysters, then crumbs, repeating until the casserole is filled, with crumbs on top, and cover with light cream. Bake at 350° until brown on top. Good cold the next day, too!

FENNEL AU GRATIN

FOR EIGHT

There is no vegetable more exciting to the taste buds than fennel, either in a salad or cooked.

4 bulbs fennel
⅓ cup butter
⅔ cups whipping cream or thin Cream Sauce
Salt and white pepper
¼ cup grated Parmesan cheese
¼ cup grated Gruyère cheese

Wash fennel well; trim and discard the tops. Slice the bulbs and cook in boiling salted water until tender, not soft. Drain. Melt the butter and sauté the fennel until a light brown. Transfer to a serving casserole, cover with the cream, and sprinkle with salt and pepper. Cover with the combined cheeses. Run under broiler to brown. You can prepare this ahead of time and refrigerate. To warm, bake at 350°.

MUSHROOMS AND ARTICHOKES IN MUSTARD CREAM

FOR FOUR

8 large mushrooms
¼ cup butter
1 tablespoon flour
½ cup milk
½ cup light cream
1½ teaspoons prepared mustard
1½ cups artichoke hearts (canned or frozen)
Pastry shells
1 tablespoon chopped chives

Sauté the mushrooms in the butter until tender. Remove. Add the flour, cook until bubbly, and add the milk, cream, and mustard. Cook until thick. Add the mushrooms and the artichokes heated in their juices. Serve on thin pastry shells with the chives sprinkled on top. Especially nice for a Friday luncheon — and you could use canned mushrooms if you wish, and serve from the skillet you prepare it in.

MUSHROOMS WITH GREEN SAUCE

FOR FOUR

16 large mushrooms, washed and dried
¼ cup chopped onion
Water
Salt and pepper

Remove stems and chop fine with the onion. Add to caps and just cover with water. Cover and simmer 15 minutes. Remove and chill. Serve on lettuce leaves with the Green Sauce poured over:

1 cup watercress leaves
½ cup parsley, leaves only
1 clove garlic
3 tablespoons light olive or salad oil
1 tablespoon lemon juice

Put watercress, parsley, and garlic in blender. Purée, slowly adding oil and lemon juice.

MUSHROOMS PAPRIKA

FOR TWO OR FOUR

1 pound fresh mushrooms
¼ cup butter
2 tablespoons finely chopped onion
¼ teaspoon salt
1 teaspoon paprika
1 tablespoon flour
¼ cup white wine
1 cup sour cream

Wash mushrooms, and peel if you wish, but it is not necessary. Sauté in the butter with the onion, salt, and paprika until done. Add the flour and cook 1 minute. Add wine, continue cooking, and add sour cream. Bring almost to a boil, but do not let it boil.

Serve on Melba toast, thinly buttered.

STUFFED MUSHROOMS

FOR FOUR

12 large mushrooms
½ cup thick Cream Sauce
½ cup mayonnaise
1 cup finely diced chicken
1 cup finely diced ham
2 tablespoons minced parsley
Salt and pepper
¾ cup light cream

Prepare and sauté mushrooms. Mix cream sauce and mayonnaise with the chicken, ham, and parsley; season and stuff into the mushroom cavities, piling as high as possible. Then take a silver knife and spread a thin film of mayonnaise over the top. Put in an oven-proof dish and pour the cream around the mushrooms. Bake at 350° until the mixture is hot and the top is a lacy brown. Serve on sautéed rounds of bread or fried eggplant.

MUSHROOMS AU CRESSON IN CRÊPES

SIXTEEN CREPES

---

2 pounds mushrooms, fresh or canned, browned in butter
½ cup butter
½ cup finely chopped onion
½ teaspoon salt
2 tablespoons flour
½ cup dry white wine
2 cups sour cream
3 cups watercress leaves, not minced but leaves removed from stems (about 2 bunches)
½ teaspoon Worcestershire sauce
16 thin crêpes

Wash and slice the mushrooms. Sauté in the butter with the onion and salt. Add the flour; cook until bubbly. Pour in the wine and cook until thickened. Add the sour cream, watercress, and Worcestershire sauce and heat only. Correct seasonings. Put 2 tablespoons in each crêpe, roll, and place in a shallow 8-by-12-inch casserole or in a crêpe suzette pan. Bake at 350° until hot. Run under broiler to brown. Without the crêpes this is a good hot cocktail dip for steak bits or meatballs. Sometimes I add a tablespoon of Dijon mustard to the mixture. This is also a good first course for a seated dinner.

ABOUT ONIONS

A good cook will, no doubt, approach the pearly gates with an onion in one hand and a pound of butter in the other. So, you had better learn your p's and q's about onions. The American variety of onion should be bought and used before it has begun to sprout, and in picking out your onions buy them with tight necks and crisp skin, regardless of color.

A few things to remember about cooking onions:

Red Spanish onions are best for baking and frying.

White mild sweet onions are for salads, or the purple ones if you can find them.

Yellow ones are for stuffing and French-frying.

Small white ones are for boiling and creaming. Add a dash of vinegar or lemon juice to keep them white.

FRENCH-FRIED ONIONS

French-fried onions are popular with steak, or just as a vegetable. And for a cocktail party. Peel Spanish onions, cut in ¼-inch slices, and separate into rings. Dip in milk, drain, and dip in flour. Fry in deep fat at 370°. Drain on paper and sprinkle with salt. If you dip them in sour cream instead of milk they are so much better.

BROILED ONIONS ON TOAST

A taste teaser to be served with beef of any kind, or I like them with an all-vegetable dinner, or baked beans.

Slice large Bermuda onions paper-thin. Place on a long shallow pan or oven-proof casserole. Pour a little olive or salad oil over and broil to a delicate brown on both sides, turning carefully with a spatula. Place on heavily buttered toast rounds. Sprinkle with Parmesan cheese and run them under the broiler again for a few seconds before serving.

ONION PIE

FOR EIGHT

Prebake upside down a pastry shell in 400° oven for 10 to 12 minutes, using your favorite piecrust recipe. Place an empty pie tin on top of the piecrust to help keep the shell smooth. Sauté 2 medium-sized onions, that have been chopped coarsely, in butter until yellow and soft. In the meantime break 5 whole eggs into a bowl, add 2½ cups milk, and mix well together. Add 4 tablespoons flour moistened with a little of the milk, and season with salt and pepper. Cook quickly in a saucepan, stirring constantly, and add ¾ cup of grated Swiss cheese and 2 tablespoons Parmesan cheese. Stir until smooth. Season with salt, pepper, and a dash of nutmeg. Strain. Add onions, pour into pie shell, and bake at 350° about 30 minutes. Brush with melted butter when finished, and serve hot. I like to serve this with beef dishes of all kinds.

ONIONS AND LEEKS IN CREAM

FOR EIGHT

8 medium-sized leeks, white part only
4 medium onions
1½ cups whipping cream
Salt and pepper
¾ pound bacon, finely diced
Chives (you may omit)

Wash and thinly slice the leeks. Peel the onions and slice paper-thin. Steam both vegetables or cook in very little water until tender. Mix with the cream and season to taste. Pour into a shallow 1½-quart casserole. Bake at 350° until hot. Fry bacon until crisp; drain and sprinkle over the onions with the chives. Especially good with beef or turkey.

SCALLOPED ONIONS AND ALMONDS

FOR SIX

12 small boiling onions
1 cup diced cooked celery
4 tablespoons butter
3 tablespoons flour
1 teaspoon salt
⅛ teaspoon pepper
1 cup milk
½ cup light cream
½ cup blanched almonds
Paprika

Wash and peel onions and cook in boiling salted water until tender. Drain. Prepare the celery the same way. Make a cream sauce: Melt butter in saucepan, add flour, salt, and pepper; cook over low heat until bubbly; add milk and cream and cook until thick. Place the onions, celery, and almonds in layers in buttered casserole. Cover with the cream sauce, sprinkle with paprika, and bake at 350° until bubbly and brown. Add grated Parmesan cheese, too, if you like.

PEAS IN SOUR CREAM

FOR EIGHT

A great company dish.

20 ounces frozen or fresh peas
1 cup sour cream
1 teaspoon horseradish
1 teaspoon chopped fresh mint
1 teaspoon Pernod (optional)
2 tablespoons thinly sliced scallions
1 apple, unpeeled, finely diced
Salt to taste

Thaw peas if frozen; cook until just tender, if fresh. In a large bowl, mix sour cream, horseradish, mint, Pernod, and scallions. Add peas and apple. Season with salt. Chill. Serve as a salad or a cold vegetable.

GREEN PEAS WITH LEEKS

FOR EIGHT

6 leeks
4 cups green peas (about 3 pounds fresh or 3 packages frozen)
¼ cup plus 2 tablespoons butter
⅓ cup boiling water
Salt and pepper

Trim the roots of leeks and cut off the tops, leaving 1 inch of the green part. Wash thoroughly under cold running water many times. Slice thin and steam 5 minutes or cook covered in very little water about 8 to 10 minutes. Put the peas in a shallow skillet with the ¼ cup butter until butter is melted and peas are covered. Add the boiling water. Cover the peas and cook 10 minutes, shaking frequently to keep them moving. Or cook them in your steamer for about 8 minutes, and add the butter at the end. Season with salt and pepper to taste. Put peas in serving container and pile the leeks in the center, or around the peas, but do not mix. Do the same with green beans in place of peas.

PEAS IN ASPIC

FOR EIGHT TO TEN

1 tablespoon plus 1 teaspoon unflavored gelatin
⅓ cup dry white wine or water
2 cups chicken broth
Salt and pepper
2 cups cooked frozen petits pois
2 tablespoons fresh mint
2 cups cooked julienne carrots

Soften gelatin in the wine or water. Heat the chicken broth to boiling point, remove from heat, and add gelatin. Season to taste. Coat the bottom of a 1½-quart mold with gelatin mix. Refrigerate. Add the peas and pour in enough gelatin mixture to hold them in place. Refrigerate to set. Chop the mint very fine (no stems), add to the carrots, and arrange over the peas. Add rest of gelatin mixture as it begins to congeal. Refrigerate overnight. Unmold and surround with fresh mint leaves on Boston lettuce. Serve with Mint Dressing. If you can find only frozen peas in butter sauce, defrost and wash thoroughly.

MINT DRESSING

TWO CUPS

½ cup vegetable salad oil
¼ cup red wine vinegar
½ cup fresh mint leaves, finely chopped
1 garlic bud, crushed
½ teaspoon cracked pepper
1 teaspoon salt

Put in a container and shake.

PEASE

FOR EIGHT OR TWELVE

I find I fall back on frozen peas and green beans when few good fresh vegetables are available, but I purée them in my blender or put them through a food mill. Peas are peas, but when you purée them and top them with Hollandaise they become Pease.

3 packages frozen peas
2 tablespoons butter, melted
⅓ cup whipping cream
Salt and white pepper

Defrost peas and put in blender just long enough to smash. Pour into a skillet with the melted butter and cream. Cook 2 minutes, after the mixture begins to boil. Season to your taste. Place in serving dish and cover with Hollandaise.

BAKED POTATOES

There is nothing that smells better than potatoes baking. Idaho potatoes are the popularized ones, but California and Maine produce a fine type for baking or any other style of cooking. For me, the Idaho takes the lead for baking because of its shape — long, flat, quicker cooking than the round kind. Just scrubbed and placed in a 350° oven and baked until done, about 1 hour, but timed to come out when you are ready to sit down; or rubbed in salad oil and salt; or wrapped in brown paper or aluminum foil to keep them from cooling off. Just bake them, and the whole family will succumb — even the curvaceous ones. Serve with sweet butter or sour cream, chopped chives, grated cheese, crisped salt pork — or all of them.

AU GRATIN POTATOES

FOR EIGHT

2 quarts diced cold baked potatoes
2 cups Mornay Sauce
1 cup medium Cream Sauce
A dash of Angostura bitters
Grated Parmesan cheese
Paprika

Mix the diced potatoes with Mornay and Cream sauces; add Angostura bitters. Pour into a buttered 3-quart casserole and cover with grated Parmesan cheese. Sprinkle with paprika. Bake at 350° for 40 minutes.

RÖSTI

FOR EIGHT

3 pounds potatoes
1 tablespoon shortening, not butter
4 tablespoons butter, melted
½ teaspoon salt
2 tablespoons hot water
¼ cup cooked bacon or ham, diced

Boil potatoes in their skins. Cool and peel. Shred on large side of shredder. Heat the shortening in a heavy skillet or griddle. Sprinkle potatoes over evenly. Cook 1 minute; add butter. Add salt and hot water and cover. Cook about 10 minutes, or until potatoes are crusty on bottom, at medium heat. Shake frequently to prevent sticking. Add bacon and turn out on a serving platter, brown side up.

LEMON-CHIVE POTATOES

FOR FOUR

1 quart cooked peeled new potatoes
⅓ cup butter or margarine
4 teaspoons minced chives or parsley
1 tablespoon lemon juice
1 teaspoon grated lemon peel (grated through colored part only; white is bitter)
½ teaspoon salt
⅛ teaspoon white pepper

Place potatoes in saucepan and set over medium heat to heat thoroughly. Meanwhile, melt the butter or margarine in a small saucepan;

stir in the minced chives or parsley, lemon juice, lemon peel, salt, and pepper. Keep the mixture warm. Pour butter mixture over potatoes and, using a spoon, turn potatoes to coat thoroughly. Serve hot!

GARLIC POTATOES

FOR FOUR

16 small new potatoes
¼ cup melted butter
1 garlic clove, crushed, or ½ teaspoon garlic salt
½ cup chopped parsley
1 teaspoon salt

Boil potatoes covered for 5 minutes. Drain and sauté in the butter until tender and golden. Shake frequently. Add the garlic, parsley, and salt and serve at once.

GNOCCHI

FOR FOUR

2 cups mashed potatoes (left over)
1½ tablespoons flour
1 egg
½ cup grated Parmesan cheese

Mix and knead to a smooth paste. Make into small balls, flatten, and roll lightly in flour. Drop in boiling water or stock and cook for 3 to 5 minutes. Serve with melted butter and Parmesan cheese sprinkled over.

POTATOES IN JACKETS

New potatoes have a flavor all their own, and especially if part of their skin is left on. Potatoes in their jackets make a pretty dish too.

Wash new potatoes (not more than 1½ or 2 inches in diameter). Allow 3 potatoes per serving. Take half an inch of peeling off around center of potatoes. Place in cold water to prevent discoloration. When ready to cook, pour off cold water and cover with hot water and a pinch of salt. Cover and boil gently until potatoes are soft, about 30 minutes. Pour off water and shake potatoes in pan over heat to dry.

Season with salt and pepper and sauté 5 minutes in butter and chopped parsley.

I often sprinkle them with Parmesan cheese as served.

Peeled new potatoes or potato balls cut with a melon-ball scoop are prepared the same way. Sometime try sautéing them with finely chopped almonds in place of the parsley, and add crumbled bacon and garlic.

ABOUT SWEET POTATOES

Sweet potatoes are truly American. They were already here when Columbus arrived; the first settlers in the South made them one of their favorite foods, and southerners still think a real dinner incomplete without sweet potatoes in one form or another. They have lots of vitamin A, and enough of vitamin C. Sweet potatoes are dry and mealy and a light yellow in color; yams are darker and sugary.

SWEET POTATO SOUFFLÉ

FOR SIX

6 medium-sized sweet potatoes
3 tablespoons butter
1 egg, beaten
2 tablespoons dry sherry
Salt and pepper
⅛ teaspoon nutmeg
1 tablespoon butter

Bake scrubbed potatoes at 450° until done. Remove skin, and mash with 3 tablespoons butter. Add egg to potatoes with the sherry and beat until light and fluffy. Season with salt and pepper, pour into buttered casserole, sprinkle with nutmeg, and dot with 1 tablespoon butter. Bake at 350° for about 30 minutes.

SWEET POTATOES FLAMBÉE

FOR SIX

6 small sweet potatoes, boiled
Salt
4 tablespoons butter
½ cup sugar
½ cup rum

Peel and cut potatoes in half, season with salt, and sauté in the butter in a frying pan until a light brown. Remove to a chafing dish or casserole, sprinkle with sugar, and pour remaining butter from skillet over. Heat. Just before serving pour rum on top and ignite.

PECAN SWEET POTATOES

FOR SIX

6 yams
Salted water
½ cup brown sugar
⅓ cup chopped pecans
1 cup orange juice
1 tablespoon grated orange rind
⅓ cup dry sherry
2 tablespoons butter

Cook yams in boiling salted water until tender. Peel and cut in half lengthwise. Place in a casserole one layer thick, sprinkle with sugar and pecans, and pour over orange juice, rind, and sherry; dot with butter, cover, and bake at 350° for about 45 minutes or until all the juice has cooked into the potatoes.

SWEET POTATO CHIPS

These will surprise your guests when served with a salad or as a cocktail snack. Peel and slice crosswise into very thin slices as many sweet potatoes as desired. Soak in cold water overnight, or in ice water a few hours. Drain and dry. Fry in hot deep fat (375°) until crisp. Drain and sprinkle with salt or a very little powdered sugar.

SWEET POTATOES MARSALA

FOR FOUR TO SIX

4 medium sweet potatoes
½ cup butter
1 cup Marsala

Peel and cut the potatoes into fingers. Place in skillet with butter and wine; cover and simmer at low heat until done, and wine and butter is cooked into them.

SPINACH AND WHITE BEANS

FOR EIGHT TO TEN

2 pounds fresh spinach
4 tablespoons butter
½ cup finely diced cooked ham
2 cups cooked white navy beans
2 tablespoons whipping cream
Salt and pepper
Nutmeg

Wash spinach and cut away heavy stems. Cook for 1 minute (with only the water that adheres after washing) in a covered container. Drain and put in electric blender until finely chopped. Melt the butter in a large skillet. Add the spinach, ham, and beans. Stir in cream and cook until the consistency of mashed potatoes. Season with salt and pepper and add just a whiff of nutmeg. This is a good way to get your children to eat spinach.

STIR-FRIED SPINACH

FOR SIX OR EIGHT

2 pounds fresh spinach
⅓ cup butter or margarine
Salt and pepper

Wash spinach and remove any heavy stems. Melt the butter in a large skillet. Add the spinach and cook over high heat, stirring constantly with a long fork. You may add very thinly sliced onion or mushrooms. Cook only 1 minute; then add seasonings. No water is used in cooking, only the water that remains on the spinach from washing. Add brown butter if you wish, toasted sesame seeds, a little grated raw beet or carrot for color; I like to toss in a few capers.

SPINACH RING

FOR SIX

2½ cups chopped cooked spinach
1 cup milk
3 tablespoons butter
3 tablespoons flour
⅓ teaspoon nutmeg
1 teaspoon grated onion
1 tablespoon lemon juice
2 eggs, well beaten
1 teaspoon salt

Combine all ingredients and pour into a well-buttered 1-quart ring mold. Place in a hot-water bath, and bake at 375° until firm, about 30 minutes. Unmold on a hot round tray or plate, and fill the center with a creamed vegetable or creamed seafood or chicken. Or make into individual molds and fill with creamed chicken (cut in 1-inch cubes) or shrimp or lobster, and serve as a luncheon entrée.

SAVORY SPINACH

FOR SIX

¼ cup light cream
¼ cup chopped onion sautéed in butter
¼ cup chopped bacon, sautéed until crisp
3 cups hot chopped spinach
Salt and pepper

Add the cream, cooked onion, and crisp bacon to the spinach and heat thoroughly. Season with salt and pepper to your taste.

SPINACH CRÊPES VÉRONIQUE

FOR EIGHT

Vegetables can be used to greater advantage than we think and with little preparation. I like to put some, like spinach, in crêpes.

First, prepare the

Blender Hollandaise:
6 egg yolks
2 tablespoons lemon juice
⅛ teaspoon salt
1 cup melted butter

Warm the blender container with hot water. Put egg yolks in the container with the lemon juice and salt. Cover and set blender on high for 3 seconds. Remove cover and add the melted butter in a steady stream while blender is on high speed; turn off as soon as all the butter has been added.

2 pounds fresh spinach
¼ cup plus 1 cup whipping cream
2 tablespoons butter
Salt and pepper
Pinch of nutmeg
16 crêpes (2 per person)
1 cup Blender Hollandaise
2 cups peeled and seeded grapes or canned white grapes

GRILLED TOMATOES

Grilled Tomatoes, misnamed, are really baked tomatoes and are done as follows. Wash and cut in half crosswise medium-sized ripe tomatoes. Place on a buttered pan and pile ½ inch high with bread crumbs sautéed in butter until crisp. I like to use stale rolls for the crumbs because you have more crust. Season with salt and pepper and bake at 350° until the tomatoes are soft but not mushy. And rye bread crumbs give them a dash!

TOMATO SUPREME

Here is another special tomato treat to serve with chicken.

Wash and cut in half crosswise 6 medium-sized ripe tomatoes and cover with a mixture of ½ cup sour cream, ½ cup mayonnaise, and ½ teaspoon curry powder. Place on a buttered pan and bake at 350° until soft, 20 to 30 minutes.

Tomatoes are good, too, sliced and covered with heavy cream, salt, and pepper and broiled until the cream bubbles. And sometime broil them plain with a thin slice of onion on top, and Cheddar cheese. Heavens, put anything on them and broil — make them glamorous in your own inimitable fashion!

FLORENTINE TOMATOES

FOR FOUR OR EIGHT

4 tomatoes
1 package frozen spinach or 1½ pounds fresh
1 tablespoon chopped onion
1 tablespoon butter
Salt and pepper
Pinch of nutmeg
Parmesan cheese

Cut tomatoes in half and place in a 325° oven in a buttered casserole for 10 minutes. Heat frozen spinach with onion only until ice is melted, or until leaves are wilted if using fresh. Drain. Chop fine in electric blender, or by hand. Mix with the butter, salt, pepper, and nutmeg. Cook until hot. Pile on top of the tomato halves. Sprinkle generously with the cheese and put back in the oven for 10 minutes.

CHILE TOMATOES

FOR SIX

3 large ripe tomatoes
1 cup sour cream
1 teaspoon sugar
1 tablespoon flour
2 tablespoons minced onion
2 tablespoons minced canned green chiles (Ortega brand the best)
Salt and pepper
1 cup grated Cheddar cheese
½ cup grated Monterey Jack or Gruyère cheese

Cut tomatoes in half and hollow out. Drain upside down on a towel. Mix sour cream, sugar, flour, onion, and chiles. Season with salt and pepper. Spoon into the tomato cavities. Place under the broiler until the mixture is bubbly. Sprinkle cheese over and return until cheese is melted and lightly browned. (When using chiles, buy whole and wash and dice or cut in strips.

SIMPLE ZUCCHINI

Zucchini, of the squash family, is another vegetable that should be courted. It is delicate in flavor and I find it generally popular. The easiest way to serve is to slice it thin with the skin left on. Cook in boiling salted water until tender, drain well, "dress" with melted butter, and sprinkle with grated Parmesan cheese. Or peel, cut in half lengthwise (leave the seeds in), cook until tender in boiling salted water, and serve with Hollandaise Sauce — a dish fit for a king.

ZUCCHINI MAISON

FOR SIX

6 medium-sized zucchini
¼ cup thinly sliced onion
4 tablespoons olive oil
2 tablespoons chopped parsley
2 ripe tomatoes, peeled and thinly sliced
Salt and pepper
Parmesan cheese

Wash, slice the zucchini about ½ inch thick, and cook in boiling salted water to cover until tender. Sauté onion in olive oil until yellow. Add parsley and remove from heat. Drain zucchini, put in a casserole in layers with the sliced tomatoes and olive oil and onion mixture. Sprinkle with salt and pepper and grated Parmesan cheese. Bake at 375° for 30 minutes. It is almost as good without the cheese.

STUFFED ZUCCHINI

FOR EIGHT

8 medium zucchini
2 eggs, beaten
1 cup cooked rice
2 cups small-curd cottage cheese
½ cup chopped onion
2 tablespoons chopped parsley
½ teaspoon salt
Dash Tabasco
Cheese Sauce or slices of American or Gruyère cheese

Wash, trim ends, and halve zucchini lengthwise. Parboil until tender-crisp, drain. When cool, scoop out center pulp and arrange shells in buttered casserole. Chop pulp; mix with beaten eggs, rice, cottage cheese, onion, parsley, salt, and Tabasco. Stuff shells and bake at 375° for 20 minutes. Spoon hot Cheese Sauce over or arrange cheese slices and run under broiler to brown.

ZUCCHINI COLLAGE

FOR SIX

1 pound zucchini
¼ cup butter
¼ cup finely diced onion
½ clove garlic, finely diced
½ cup cherry tomatoes, halved (or one small tomato sliced thin)
Salt and pepper to taste
2 tablespoons toasted sesame seeds
¼ cup finely chopped parsley

Wash zucchini and slice diagonally approximately ¼ inch thick. Blanch 1 minute. Drain. Melt butter, add onion and garlic, and sauté until soft and golden. Add zucchini; cover, and cook 2 minutes. Add tomatoes; cover, and cook 1 minute. Season with salt and pepper. Toss with sesame seeds and parsley.

FAVORITE VEGETABLE COMBINATION

FOR SIX

For my vegetable combination, I use 1 pound fresh green beans, 1 cup bean sprouts, 1 cup sliced water chestnuts (canned, as a rule), 3 tablespoons melted butter, and about ½ teaspoon Kikkoman soy sauce. The fresh beans I cook in a steamette — and if you do not own one, buy one. You'll enjoy all your vegetables cooked in it; they will look better, taste better, and have a better texture. I do green beans about 3 minutes, snow peas 30 seconds, fresh asparagus 3 minutes. There is no timetable. You find your own time to suit your taste (double the time for frozen vegetables), but it takes so little time, you cannot complain.

FAVORITE LAYER VEGETABLES

FOR EIGHT

This is my favorite combination:

Little white onions (fresh boiled, canned, or frozen) seasoned with salt and pepper. Sprinkle with sugar and butter, and heat only until sugar begins to caramelize.

Canned celery hearts, heated in consommé.

"Kitchen-cut" frozen beans, taken out of their pouch and cooked in a covered skillet for 5 minutes. (If fresh, cut slantwise in very small pieces, cooked *al dente,* seasoned, and buttered.)

Then assemble. Put the onions on the bottom, the celery in the middle, the green beans on top. Sprinkle finely chopped parsley over all. Help yourself to all three layers, as I do.

RATATOUILLE

FOR EIGHT TO TWELVE

This is the most versatile of all vegetable dishes. You may use it hot or cold, as an hors d'oeuvre, salad, or main dish; keep it covered in your refrigerator for several days. I like to put ratatouille in crêpes and use for a luncheon or brunch.

3 medium-sized zucchini
1 medium-sized eggplant, peeled
4 tomatoes, peeled
2 green peppers
1 cup thin-sliced onion
¼ cup salad oil or half olive oil
1 clove garlic, finely minced
Salt and pepper

Slice zucchini and eggplant into ¼-inch slices. Cut tomatoes in medium dice. Seed the peppers, slice thin, and blanch. Sauté the onion in the oil until soft; do not brown. Add tomatoes, cook 1 minute. Mix in rest of ingredients, cover, and bring to boiling point. Cook 5 minutes. Remove cover and simmer until all liquid has evaporated. Season with salt and pepper to taste; sprinkle with chopped parsley (for added color).

RATATOUILLE IN CRÊPES

Put ¼ cup of ratatouille in each crêpe, roll loosely, and place in a buttered shallow casserole. Sprinkle with grated Parmesan or with half Swiss cheese. Place in a 350° oven until hot and run under broiler to brown. Allow two crêpes per person. I serve these as a vegetable with roast beef or lamb, but then I would serve ratatouille with anything, because my guests think me smarter than I am. No doubt because I can pronounce ratatouille.

BAKED BEAN BASH

FOR TWENTY-FIVE

This is a good inexpensive dish to use any time, especially as a money-making entrée for large groups such as the PTA.

3 pounds ground beef
2 teaspoons salt
½ teaspoon pepper
5 cups sliced or chopped tomatoes, and their juice
2 cups thinly sliced onions
¼ cup butter
10 cups canned baked beans
½ cup dry red wine or beef consommé
½ cup bread crumbs
½ cup grated sharp cheese

Brown beef in skillet; season with salt and pepper. Add juice from the tomatoes and cook until liquid has evaporated. Sauté onions in butter until yellow but not brown. Place a layer of beans, a layer of cooked meat, and one of onions and tomatoes in a buttered 2-quart shallow casserole. Repeat. Add the red wine; sprinkle the crumbs and cheese over the top. Place foil over top and bake at 350° until bubbling. Remove foil and bake for 10 minutes longer, or until browned on top. Make the day before and bake when you serve.

KIDNEY BEANS ITALIANESQUE

FOR EIGHT

Kidney Beans Italianesque is a dish I can always serve when I'm not sure of the likes and dislikes of my guests, for I have found that everyone laps it up. Wonderful for a buffet supper and a good Lenten meal.

2 tablespoons onion, chopped
1 tablespoon butter
1 pound Provolone or Bel Paese cheese, grated
6 cups red kidney beans, drained
1 canned pimento, chopped
1 No. 2 can tomatoes
½ cup dry Sauterne

Sauté onion in butter. Add grated cheese. When melted add beans, pimento, and tomatoes. Mix. Add wine and cook until cheese, wine, and tomatoes are thick. Put in casserole and bake 1 hour at 300°. Dark rye bread or pumpernickel is good to have around with this dish.

BARLEY CASSEROLE

FOR EIGHT

6 tablespoons butter
2 cups barley, not quick-cooking
2 cups diced onion
1 cup diced mushrooms, fresh or canned
4 cups chicken broth
¼ cup toasted chopped almonds or pine nuts

Melt butter; add barley and brown, stirring constantly. Spoon into a 2½- to 3-quart casserole. Sauté the onion in the butter until soft, and add. In the same skillet, sauté the mushrooms and add to the barley. Pour in 2 cups of chicken broth and bake covered at 350° for 45 to 60 minutes. Stir, add rest of broth, and continue cooking until liquid is absorbed and barley is soft, about 10 minutes. Stir again and if not soft, and it is dry, add more broth and continue cooking. Just before serving add almonds or pine nuts.

KASHA

FOR EIGHT

When you ask your guests to have groats, they usually say an embarrassed "no thank you," but kasha, yes.

1 cup butter
1 cup pine nuts
1 cup thinly sliced onion
2 cups thinly sliced mushrooms
2 cups groats
6 cups chicken or beef broth

Melt half the butter in the casserole you will cook in and sauté the pine nuts until a golden brown. Remove the nuts; add the onions and mushrooms. Sauté until onions are soft, about 1 minute. Stir in the groats and broth; cover and bake for 1 hour. Add rest of butter and nuts; toss lightly. Kasha is delicious with beef, lamb, and chicken. You may prepare rice the same way as this kasha recipe.

Part 3

Egg and Cheese Dishes
Rice · Pasta
Bread and Muffins

Egg and Cheese Dishes

OMELET SHORTCAKE

8 eggs, separated
1 teaspoon salt
⅛ teaspoon white pepper
4 tablespoons flour
2 tablespoons butter
1 shallot, minced
Chopped parsley or truffles, or sautéed diced mushrooms

Beat the egg yolks until lemon-colored and smooth. Beat in salt, pepper, and flour. Melt the butter; add the shallot and sauté 1 minute. Pour the butter mixture into two 9-inch cake pans and rub over bottoms and sides until completely covered. Beat the egg whites until stiff and fold the egg mixture into them. Spread over pans evenly. Bake at 350° until a cake tester comes out clean — about 15 minutes. Invert one pan on a serving tray, cover with Seafood Sauce (see following recipe) or chicken in a wine-flavored cream. Cover with second layer and more sauce. Sprinkle with chopped parsley, truffles, or sautéed diced mushrooms.

SEAFOOD SAUCE

FOUR CUPS

3 tablespoons butter
3 tablespoons flour
1 cup half-and-half
1 cup chicken broth
½ cup dry white wine
2 cups cooked seafood or chicken, chopped
Salt and pepper

Melt butter; add the flour and cook until bubbly. Add half-and-half, chicken broth, and wine. Cook until thickened, stirring constantly with a French whip. Mix in seafood, and season to taste. Simmer about 5 minutes at low heat. Keep hot over hot water.

PIPÉRADE

FOR EIGHT

Pipérade is a wonderful egg dish, but as someone once said, never before 10:00 A.M. unless you are addicted to garlic. It does disappear like magic on a brunch buffet.

2 tablespoons butter
1 tablespoon olive oil (you may omit)
2 cloves garlic, crushed
½ cup thinly sliced onion
2 green peppers, slivered and blanched
4 ripe tomatoes, peeled and chopped
1 tablespoon plus 1 teaspoon salt
⅛ teaspoon white pepper
¼ cup chopped parsley
12 eggs
Cracked pepper
Chopped chives (or parsley)

Melt the butter, add the olive oil, and sauté the garlic, onion, and green peppers 1 minute. Add tomatoes and slowly cook until all the liquid from the tomatoes has evaporated. Add 1 tablespoon salt and the white pepper and parsley. Beat the eggs lightly with 1 teaspoon salt and stir gently into the tomato mixture. Let them cook over low heat until set. They should never be hard-cooked. Slide onto a heated platter or serve in the skillet. Sprinkle with cracked pepper and chives. For a large group, I soft-scramble the eggs and pile on top of the tomato mixture. Eat as soon as possible in either case. Anchovies are a nice addition for supper, but not for breakfast. I use smoked sausage frequently.

TEASED EGGS

FOR EIGHT

8 hard-cooked eggs
3 tablespoons butter or margarine
3 tablespoons flour
2 cups milk
1 cup sour cream
1 tablespoon grated onion
1½ tablespoons horseradish
A few drops hot pepper sauce
Salt and pepper to taste
1 pound cooked shrimp, chopped fine, or shredded crabmeat
½ cup Parmesan or grated Swiss cheese

Halve the eggs and mash the yolks. Melt the butter; add flour and cook 1 minute. Add milk and cook over medium-high heat, stirring, until thickened. Add sour cream and seasonings. Combine half a cup of this sauce with the seafood and the mashed yolks, and stuff it into the whites. Arrange them in a buttered shallow casserole, stuffed side up. Pour the remaining sauce over them and sprinkle them with cheese. Bake at 300° until hot and bubbly, about 30 minutes. Serve with link sausage, hot biscuits, and hot broiled fruit. You can substitute cooked chicken or ham for the seafood. I find it a most satisfactory brunch dish.

SCRAMBLED EGGS

FOR TWO

Being a career woman, I am many times caught with my emergency shelf bare. Scrambled eggs I always do, and everyone has asked me to include my recipe.

2 tablespoons butter
4 eggs
¾ cup dry cottage cheese
½ teaspoon salt
Fresh-ground or cracked pepper

Melt the butter in a skillet and remove from fire. Break the eggs into the skillet and beat with a fork. Add the cottage cheese and salt. Return to the heat and cook over low heat, stirring constantly. Sprinkle with fresh-ground or cracked pepper as served.

MOLDED EGGS AND SHRIMP

FOR SIX TO EIGHT

4½ teaspoons unflavored gelatin (1½ envelopes)
⅓ cup dry white wine or cold water
2½ cups seasoned chicken broth
6 hard-cooked eggs, peeled and sliced thin
2 pounds cooked shrimp, sliced if large
1 truffle or several large black olives

Soften the gelatin in the white wine (or cold water if you do not want the wine flavor). Set aside. Heat the chicken broth to boiling, remove from heat, and add the softened gelatin. Cool until syrupy in texture. Pour a thin layer of the gelatin mixture in a 1½-quart mold and one layer of the sliced eggs and slivers of the truffle, black olives, or any other decoration you might prefer. Refrigerate. When firm, fill mold with alternate layers of the shrimp and eggs, and the remaining truffles. Pour the rest of the syrupy mixture over, cover with wax paper or foil, and refrigerate for several hours. Use this as a quick method for molding seafoods, chicken, and vegetables. For meats I prefer beef consommé but still use the white wine for flavor.

EGGS WITH ASPARAGUS

FOR SIX

1 bunch fresh asparagus
¼ cup butter
1 clove garlic, minced
6 eggs, well beaten
Salt and pepper
6 English muffins, toasted
Anchovy paste

Cook the asparagus and drain. Cut in 1-inch pieces, and heat in the butter with the clove of garlic; add the eggs and seasonings. Cook over hot water until of creamy consistency. Serve on toasted English muffins spread with the anchovy paste.

GLORIFIED EGGS

FOR SIX

6 eggs, slightly beaten
¾ cup milk or thin cream
¾ teaspoon salt
⅛ teaspoon pepper
2 tablespoons butter

Cook in double boiler, stirring frequently until smooth and creamy. Serve in place of scrambled eggs.

CHEESE TORTE

FOR SIX OR EIGHT

A good cheese torte can be the answer to many demands. It is extra special for a cocktail table, where each guest may cut his own piece. It is the answer for Friday entertaining or just family. Most of all, I like it to "carry" creamed foods like chicken, seafood, leftover ham, chipped beef, or almost anything. Gets away from the toast bit, and the cheese flavor compliments any food. Save your scraps of cheese and make a real potluck taste. Even if it does not turn out perfectly (and it should), it is still good.

4 egg yolks
1½ cups light cream or milk
1½ cups grated Swiss cheese (or other)
⅛ teaspoon salt
⅛ teaspoon nutmeg
4 egg whites
Unbaked pie shell

Beat egg yolks with the cream; add cheese, salt, and nutmeg. Fold in stiffly beaten egg whites. Pour into an unbaked pie shell or pastry-lined torte pan and bake at 350° for 30 minutes or until custard is set.

This is a good entrée as is, but may be dressed up with stuffed mushrooms, broiled mushrooms, or any seafood or chicken in a light cream sauce. Leftovers reheat successfully — but do not freeze.

SWISS FONDUE

FOR SIX

4 tablespoons flour
4 tablespoons melted butter
1 cup light cream
2 cups milk
½ cup dry Sauterne or kirsch
½ pound Swiss cheese, shredded
Thick slices of hot French bread, plain or garlic-buttered

Mix the flour and butter and cook for 1 minute in a chafing dish. Add the cream and milk. Cook until smooth and thick. Add the wine and cheese and heat thoroughly, beating constantly. Serve over the French bread, or let everyone dunk.

LOBSTER QUICHE

TWENTY-FOUR SMALL TARTS

2 eggs
1 cup half-and-half
2 cups grated Swiss cheese
1 cup cooked chopped lobster meat
¼ teaspoon salt
¼ teaspoon dry mustard
Tart tins lined with unbaked piecrust

Beat the eggs; add the cream, cheese, lobster, salt, and mustard. Mix and pour into the pastry-lined tins. Bake at 400° for 15 minutes. Remove tarts immediately from tins by running the tip of a knife under one side and slipping out. Do not let them cool in the tins. For variation, add a bit of chutney before baking.

This recipe will make an 8-inch quiche, but the piecrust will need to have been partially baked (at 450° for 10 minutes) before filling is added. Then bake at 350° for 30 minutes or until custard is set.

QUICHE LORRAINE

FOR SIX

This is the recipe I use.

8-inch pie tin lined with pastry and baked at 450° for 10 minutes
4 slices crisp bacon, chopped
4 thin slices onion, sautéed until soft
8 paper-thin slices ham, shredded
8 paper-thin slices imported Swiss cheese
3 eggs
¼ teaspoon dry mustard
1 cup light cream, heated
Nutmeg

Sprinkle the bacon and onion over bottom of piecrust. Add half the shredded ham. Distribute 4 slices of the cheese over the ham. Add rest of ham and the cheese on top. Beat the eggs and mustard, add the hot cream, and continue beating. Pour over the ham and cheese; let stand 10 minutes. Sprinkle a tiny bit of nutmeg on top and bake at 350° until custard is set, about 30 minutes.

BROCCOLI QUICHE

FOR SIX

2 12-ounce packages frozen broccoli
4 eggs
1 cup whipping cream
Salt and freshly ground white pepper
1½ cups grated Gruyère
9-inch pie shell

Cook broccoli according to directions on package. Drain well, and put in blender or food processor, or chop fine. Beat eggs, add cream and seasonings. Sprinkle bottom of pie shell that has been partially baked (10 minutes at 450°) with a little of the cheese. Add egg mixture combined with the broccoli. Cover with remaining cheese. Bake at 400° until custard is set. Make ahead of time and reheat if you wish, or make, refrigerate, and bake when needed.

FETA CHEESE PIE

FOR SIX

1 cup light cream
1 pound feta cheese, crumbled
3 eggs
1 teaspoon cornstarch
Pinch of thyme
1 clove garlic, minced
9-inch pie shell

Mix cream, cheese, and eggs in blender. Add cornstarch, thyme, and garlic, and mix until light and smooth. Bake pie shell 10 minutes at 350°. Cool. Add mixture and continue baking until custard is set. Serve as is or sprinkle with ripe olives sliced thin.

BRIE QUICHE

FOR SIX

4 egg yolks
1½ cups half-and-half
1 pound Brie (mashed)
⅛ teaspoon salt
4 egg whites
8-inch piecrust

Beat the egg yolks with the cream; add the cheese and salt. Mix thoroughly. Beat the egg whites until stiff; stir one-third into the mixture and fold in the rest. Pour into an 8-inch torte pan lined with partially baked piecrust (10 minutes). Bake at 350° for 30 minutes or until custard is set. Cut in eighths or less and serve as is or with caviar. It may also be put into barque or tart shells for a cocktail-party delight. I like to eat it as a dessert with a cold Delicious apple. Try it.

MUSHROOM RAREBIT (OR *RABBIT*)

FOR SIX

I have had this recipe a long time, and just got around to serving it, and what a hit! A luncheon for ladies, a buffet supper for men, both will go overboard.

1 cup medium Cream Sauce
1 can cream of mushroom soup
1 teaspoon Worcestershire sauce
4 drops Tabasco sauce
½ teaspoon salt
½ cup sliced sautéed mushrooms, fresh or canned
1 cup small sautéed mushrooms, fresh or canned

Mix and cook in a double boiler. When hot add:

½ pound grated or chopped sharp Cheddar cheese
2 tablespoons dry sherry

Heat and serve on toasted and buttered English muffins, and garnish with a slice of egg and sliced black olives, or truffles, if you are that extravagant. You know, black olives are called California truffles.

EASY WELSH RAREBIT (OR *RABBIT*)

FOR EIGHT

4 tablespoons butter
1 teaspoon salt
½ teaspoon paprika
¼ teaspoon cayenne pepper
½ teaspoon prepared mustard
1 teaspoon Worcestershire sauce
1 pound sharp Cheddar cheese, grated
About 1 cup beer or ale
2 eggs, slightly beaten

In double boiler, melt butter; add seasonings and cheese. Stir until cheese is soft. Add some beer or ale tablespoon by tablespoon, stirring gently. Mix the slightly beaten eggs with a little of the beer and add last, stirring until the rarebit is smooth. Serve on French bread cut rather thick and oven-toasted, or on slices of broiled tomatoes.

CREAM PUFFS

TWELVE MEDIUM PUFFS

You can make any filling go much further in a small cream puff than in a sandwich — and for some reason guests think fewer calories.

1 cup boiling water
½ cup butter
1 cup flour
½ teaspoon salt
4 eggs

Put water in a saucepan, and as it boils add butter. Continue heating until butter is melted. Add flour and salt all at once. Stir until dough forms a ball. Remove from heat. Add 1 egg, beat, let stand 5 minutes. Add remaining eggs one at a time, beating after each addition. Let stand 10 minutes. Drop on ungreased baking sheet by level teaspoonfuls for small puffs — 2 inches apart. Bake at 375° for 20 to 25 minutes.

The surest way to test is to remove one, and if it collapses, it is not done. When cold, split and fill with salad; or cottage cheese and red caviar is delicious too. Dip stuffed edge into chopped parsley.

CHEESE CUSTARD

FOR FOUR OR SIX

I get carried away with cheese dishes — but who doesn't like them? I have a frequent visitor to my home who says he dislikes cheese — but he eats my soufflés and custards with relish.

1 cup sour cream
½ cup grated Swiss cheese
¼ teaspoon paprika
½ teaspoon salt
3 egg yolks
3 egg whites
½ teaspoon salt
2 tablespoons grated Parmesan cheese

Mix the sour cream, Swiss cheese, paprika, and salt. Add the egg yolks beaten until light. Pour into a buttered casserole and place in a pan of hot water. Bake at 375° for 20 minutes. Beat the egg whites until stiff; fold in salt and cheese. Pile on top of the custard and return to oven for 8 minutes or until meringue is brown.

SOUFFLÉS

Because the soufflé is considered one of the prima donnas of the culinary world, it has intimidated many otherwise intrepid cooks. Perhaps to dispel the traditional fear of failure with the soufflé, Helen Corbitt adopted it as one of the standbys of her professional menus.

She found it one of the most useful and versatile dishes. And she created them using many ingredients not customarily associated with soufflés. At least twenty-five were in fairly regular use on her menus. She preferred a soufflé to "carry" Chicken Oriental, à la king foods, and any creamed dish.

Some of her most spectacular successes were with dessert soufflés, eight of which appear in the Desserts chapter.

ABOUT SOUFFLÉS

There are many things you may do with a soufflé besides baking it in a soufflé dish. I like to pour it into a partially baked pie crust for a cheese soufflé pie and bake at 350° until set, about 30 minutes. Use it as a carrier for any creamed food, or you may serve it simply as a soufflé pie. It is delicious topped with broiled mushrooms or broiled shrimp for a less caloric item. You may bake a soufflé in individual casseroles for a seated luncheon. Use your basic soufflé recipe and put on the bottom a layer of sautéed sliced mushrooms, sautéed thinly sliced onions, shrimp, or spinach or ham soufflé and bake together. Use a glass soufflé dish and watch your soufflé come to life with the added color. Before cooking, ring the dish with buttered bakers' sheet paper for a higher soufflé (do not use foil). Bake in a shallow casserole for a buffet and cut in serving portions. Use a soufflé in place of a vegetable. Serve it with cold boiled salmon, and pass the melted sweet butter, as the Danish do. With cold baked ham it is divine. Use the leftovers in an omelet, in macaroni and cheese, in an oven-toasted cheese sandwich. Just use soufflés, for they are delicious.

CHEESE SOUFFLÉ I

FOR SIX

3 tablespoons butter
¼ cup flour
1⅞ cups milk
1 teaspoon salt
A dash of cayenne pepper
1 teaspoon prepared mustard
2 drops Worcestershire sauce
1 cup grated American cheese, packed
6 eggs, separated

Make a cream sauce by melting the butter and blending in the flour. Cook until bubbly. Add the milk, salt, cayenne, mustard, and Worcestershire sauce, and bring to a boil, stirring constantly. Boil 1 minute. "Time it!" Remove from heat and cool slightly. Add the cheese. Beat the egg yolks until thick, and add the cheese mixture, stirring constantly. Beat the egg whites until stiff. Fold into the cheese mixture carefully; pour into a well-buttered baking dish (three-fourths full). Bake at 300° in a hot-water bath for 2 hours, or until a silver knife inserted into the center comes out clean. This soufflé keeps a day in the icebox after baking, so it can be a leftover successfully. I use this as a base for Chicken or Seafood Oriental, à la king foods, and any creamed dish.

CHEESE SOUFFLÉ II

FOR FOUR

This soufflé is easy, but must be eaten as soon as it is ready. It approaches the French soufflé in texture and appearance.

4 tablespoons butter
4 tablespoons flour
1 teaspoon salt
Cayenne
1½ cups milk
½ pound Cheddar cheese, grated
6 eggs, separated

Melt butter in top of double boiler. Blend in flour, adding salt and a few grains of cayenne. Add milk gradually, blending well. Heat to boiling point; cook, stirring constantly until the sauce is thick and smooth. Boil at least one minute after you think it is enough. Add cheese and continue cooking, stirring frequently, until cheese is melted. Remove from heat and slowly add beaten egg yolks, blending them in well. Let mixture cool. Start oven at slow (300°). Pour cooled cheese mixture into stiffly beaten egg whites, cutting and folding thoroughly together. Pour at once into ungreased casserole. Run tip of a teaspoon around the mixture 1 inch from edge of casserole, making a slight track, or depression. This forms the "top hat" on the soufflé as it bakes and puffs up. Bake in slow oven 1 hour and 15 minutes. Carry soufflé in baking dish to table and serve immediately. The straight-sided French casserole is best for this, but not necessary. Be sure you cook your cream sauce until thick, then start counting.

SWISS CHEESE SOUFFLÉ

FOR SIX TO EIGHT

½ cup butter or margarine
6 tablespoons flour
2 cups milk
2 cups grated Swiss cheese (I find French Emmenthal especially good for a soufflé)
8 egg yolks (use eggs left at room temperature overnight)
1½ teaspoons dry mustard or 1 tablespoon Dijon mustard
⅛ teaspoon cayenne pepper
1 teaspoon salt
8 egg whites (add 4 more for a lighter soufflé)
Parmesan cheese (may be omitted)

Melt the butter; add the flour and cook slowly until mixture foams. Do not brown. Add the milk and bring to a boil; use low heat to ensure the flour and milk being thoroughly cooked. The sauce should be smooth and thick. Remove from heat. Add the cheese and stir until blended.

Cool slightly. Beat the egg yolks and add to the mixture. Add the mustard, cayenne, and salt. Let mixture cool until you can place your hand on the bottom of the container without feeling any heat. Beat the egg whites until stiff but not dry. (Tip the bowl and if the whites do not slide out, they are ready.) Gently stir about one-third of the egg whites into the mixture; then fold in remaining egg whites until well distributed. Pour into a 2½- or 3-quart buttered soufflé dish sprinkled lightly with Parmesan cheese or into two 1½-quart ones. Bake in a 350° oven for 30 minutes if you are going to eat at once, or place in a pan of hot water and bake 1 hour, and it will hold awhile.

CREAM CHEESE SOUFFLÉ

FOR EIGHT

A fine and unusual accompaniment to a main course.

4 eggs, separated
A pinch of salt
1 teaspoon flour
¼ teaspoon dry mustard
A pinch of cayenne pepper
¾ cup cream cheese, softened to room temperature
1 cup sour cream

In a big bowl, beat yolks of eggs until light and creamy. Add salt, flour, mustard, and cayenne. Blend cream cheese and sour cream until smooth. Add to egg yolks and beat with electric beater until smooth. Beat egg whites until stiff but not dry, and fold into yolk mixture. Transfer to ungreased 1½-quart soufflé dish. Place dish in pan of water and bake at 300° for 1 hour.

Variation:

Substitute 1 teaspoon sugar for the mustard and pepper, and serve it hot as a dessert — with puréed fresh strawberries or raspberries (strain to get rid of the raspberry seeds!).

ARTICHOKE SOUFFLÉ

FOR EIGHT

3 tablespoons butter
3 tablespoons flour
¾ cup milk
2 teaspoons grated onion
1 teaspoon salt
6 egg yolks
2½ cups mashed canned or freshly cooked artichoke bottoms
7 egg whites

Melt the butter; add the flour and cook until bubbly. Pour in milk and cook until thick. Remove from heat. Add onion, salt, egg yolks, and mashed artichokes. Let mixture cool (until you can put your hand on bottom of pan). Beat egg whites until stiff. Stir in one-third of them; fold in the rest. Pour into a buttered 2-quart casserole. Bake at 350° for 35 to 40 minutes, or set in a pan of hot water and bake 1 hour, but test with a toothpick or cake tester. Serve as is or with hollandaise.

BROCCOLI SOUFFLÉ

FOR SIX

1 10-ounce package frozen broccoli
3 tablespoons butter
3 tablespoons flour
1 teaspoon salt
1 cup milk
⅛ teaspoon nutmeg
1 teaspoon lemon juice
4 egg yolks
4 egg whites

Cook broccoli; drain and chop fine or put through a food mill. Melt butter; add flour and salt and cook until bubbly, and add the milk. Cook until thick; add nutmeg, lemon juice, and broccoli. Cool slightly and add egg yolks, beaten. Beat egg whites until stiff, and when broccoli mixture is cool, fold egg whites into it. Pour into a buttered 1½-quart casserole; place in a hot-water bath and bake at 325° for 1 hour, or until firm. Serve plain or with a sauce consisting of half sour cream and half mayonnaise with a dash of curry powder.

CHICKEN SOUFFLÉ

FOR SIX

1⅓ cups thick Cream Sauce
½ cup fine white bread crumbs
1½ cups finely chopped cooked chicken or turkey
1 teaspoon lemon juice
⅛ teaspoon pepper
½ teaspoon finely chopped parsley
½ teaspoon salt
2 eggs, separated

Mix the cream sauce, bread crumbs, chicken, and seasonings together. Add well-beaten egg yolks; then fold in stiffly beaten egg whites. Pour into individual buttered custard cups or a shallow 2-quart baking dish. Place in a pan of hot water and bake at 325° until puffed and brown, about 40 minutes. Baked in a ring mold it makes a pretty dish. Serve with any sauce, such as fricassee sauce with slivered almonds, green peas or asparagus in a thin cream sauce, or fresh mushroom sauce. For a luncheon serve the individual soufflés on a slice of broiled pineapple, or on asparagus spears with a thin cream sauce to which slivered toasted pecans have been added. This recipe may be used for any cooked meat or fish.

CRABMEAT SOUFFLÉ

FOR EIGHT

1⅓ cups grated Cheddar cheese
1½ cups thick Cream Sauce
1 pound crabmeat (approximately 3 cups; pick shell pieces out carefully)
4 eggs, whites and yolks beaten separately

Melt cheese in cream sauce. Add crabmeat and egg yolks. Fold in the stiffly beaten egg whites, pour into buttered baking dish or individual casseroles, set in a pan of hot water, and bake at 325° for about 1 hour. This is a light, delectable soufflé. Serve on slices of broiled canned pineapple, or with a thin cream sauce (made with cream) and bits of finely chopped watercress.

SQUASH SOUFFLÉ

FOR EIGHT

Large squash, no longer delicate, can be used successfully

½ cup finely chopped onion
4 tablespoons butter
4 pounds yellow or white squash
1½ cups fine bread crumbs
4 tablespoons chopped pimento
1 tablespoon salt
¼ teaspoon pepper
2 eggs, whites and yolks beaten separately

Sauté onion in the butter until soft and light brown. Wash and slice squash. Cook in boiling salted water until soft. Drain and put through food chopper, electric blender, or food mill. Add sautéed onion, bread crumbs, pimento, and seasonings. Add egg yolks and combine thoroughly. Fold in beaten egg whites. Pour into a well-buttered casserole and bake at 350° for 30 minutes.

VEGETABLE SOUFFLÉ

FOR EIGHT

¼ cup butter
½ cup flour
1 teaspoon salt
1½ tablespoons sugar
1¾ cups milk
3 cups finely chopped cooked vegetables
3 eggs, separated

Melt butter in a saucepan; stir in flour, salt, and sugar. Add milk and cook until thick and smooth. Stir in the 3 cups of cooked vegetables — it's a wonderful way to use up leftover vegetables (except tomatoes and beets) or any one vegetable like squash or corn or broccoli — anyhow, stir in vegetables and well-beaten egg yolks. Beat egg whites until stiff and fold into the vegetable mixture. Pour into a well-buttered pan or casserole and bake in a hot-water bath about 45 minutes at 350°.

SALMON SOUFFLÉ

FOR FOUR OR SIX

3 tablespoons butter
3 tablespoons flour
½ teaspoon curry powder
Pinch of thyme (you may omit)
Salt and pepper
1 cup milk
1½ cups fresh or canned salmon flakes
4 eggs, separated

Melt the butter; add the flour and seasonings and cook until bubbly. Add the milk; bring to a boil and boil for 1 minute, but start counting when it boils, stirring constantly. Remove from stove. Add egg yolks beaten until light and the salmon flaked and free from bones and skin. Cool. Fold in the egg whites stiffly beaten. Pour into a buttered casserole and bake at 375° for 45 minutes in a hot-water bath. (Use the same recipe for leftover chicken or ham or any cooked fish.) Serve with:

BENGAL SAUCE

1 tablespoon butter
1 tablespoon flour
1 cup half-and-half (or whole milk)
Salt
½ teaspoon curry powder
2 teaspoons grated coconut
¼ cup slivered blanched almonds

Melt butter, add flour, and cook a few seconds. Add milk and cream mixture and cook until smooth and thickened. Add seasonings, coconut, and nuts. A good sauce for any soufflé or for croquettes.

FILET OF SOLE SOUFFLÉ

FOR SIX

3 tablespoons butter
3 tablespoons flour
1 cup milk
1 egg yolk
¼ teaspoon dry mustard
1 teaspoon salt
2 teaspoons lemon juice
¼ teaspoon Worcestershire sauce
1 pound cooked, flaked filet of sole
6 egg whites
⅛ teaspoon cream of tartar
2 tablespoons Parmesan cheese

Melt the butter; add the flour and cook 1 minute. Add the milk and cook until thick. Use your French whip to stir in the egg yolk, mustard, salt, lemon juice, and Worcestershire. Remove from stove; add flaked fish. Cool until you can put your hand on the bottom of the pot; then beat the egg whites with the cream of tartar until stiff. Stir one-third of the egg whites into the mixture and fold in the rest. Pour into a 2-quart buttered shallow casserole. Sprinkle with the Parmesan. Bake in a 375° oven for 30 minutes or until puffed and lightly browned. As a variation, put soufflé into individual custard cups or coquilles and use as a first course or luncheon entrée. Serve with:

SHRIMP SAUCE

3 tablespoons butter
1 cup chopped raw shrimp
¼ teaspoon dry mustard
3 tablespoons flour
1½ cups milk
½ cup clam juice
1 teaspoon lemon juice
1 teaspoon chopped chives or dill
Salt and white pepper

Melt the butter; add the shrimp and mustard. Cook 1 minute. Add flour and cook until bubbly. Pour in milk and clam juice; cook until thickened. Mix in lemon juice and seasonings.

I use this sauce on poached salmon or red snapper, filet of sole roulades, or any seafood soufflé; sometimes on an individual cheese or mushroom soufflé; for a luncheon entrée; and on seafood crêpes, too, although I add some whole shrimp to the sauce.

LETTUCE SOUFFLÉ

FOR SIX OR EIGHT

1 large head iceberg lettuce, slivered
1 tablespoon grated onion
½ cup whipped butter or margarine
5 tablespoons flour
1½ cups skim milk
6 egg yolks, beaten
Salt and pepper
6 egg whites

Pour boiling water over lettuce and onion; let drain. Melt butter; add flour and cook until bubbly. Pour in milk; cook until smooth and thick. Add egg yolks slowly, beating all the time. Cool, add lettuce, and, when you can hold your hand comfortably on bottom of pan, season with salt and pepper. Beat the egg whites until stiff. Stir one-third of them into the mixture; fold in the rest. Pour into a buttered 2-quart soufflé dish. Bake at 350° for 35 to 40 minutes.

RICE SOUFFLÉ

FOR SIX

A rice soufflé is an impressive accompaniment to any entrée and a good lower-in-cost carrier for any creamed food. I like it with prime rib of beef.

¼ cup butter
3 tablespoons flour
1 cup milk
1 teaspoon salt
⅛ teaspoon white pepper
1 cup cooked rice
4 eggs, separated
Few drops Worcestershire sauce
1 tablespoon Parmesan cheese (you may omit)

Melt butter; stir in flour and cook until bubbly. Add milk and stir with a French whip until smooth and thick. Remove from heat; add seasonings, rice, and beaten egg yolks. Beat the egg whites until stiff. Stir 2 tablespoons into the rice mixture; fold in the rest. Pour into an ungreased 2-quart casserole and sprinkle Parmesan cheese on top. Bake at 350° about 45 minutes.

MUSTARD CREAM

TWO CUPS

Many Corbitt menus include entrées using soufflés and soufflé pies combined with Mustard Cream, Chicken or Seafood Oriental, and other special sauces and creamed mixtures. The recipe for Mustard Cream is here with the soufflés where it can inspire you to some interesting combinations of your own.

I do not think anyone can really enjoy the flavor of mustard in a sauce if a Dijon mustard is not used. Personally, I think the Maille mustard the best. It is found in good food shops, and if you do not have it in your area, keep asking.

4 tablespoons butter or margarine
2 shallots or green onions, finely minced
3 tablespoons flour
2 cups half-and-half
½ teaspoon salt
2 tablespoons Dijon mustard
2 tablespoons dry white wine

Melt the butter; add the shallots or green onions. Cook until yellow. Add the flour; stir and cook until bubbly. Pour in the half-and-half. Cook and stir with a French whip over low heat until smooth and thickened. Add salt, mustard, and wine. Cook about 5 minutes more. For a thinner sauce, add a little more half-and-half or some chicken broth.

To the sauce I add 1½ cups of slivered ham, chicken, sliced shrimp, or crabmeat. Cut the soufflé pie, then spoon over the sauce.

This method may be used as a basis for making any sauce: i.e., in place of mustard, add capers, parsley, chives, mixed herbs, slivered vegetables, chopped eggs, seafood — you name it.

Rice and Pasta

Rice and pasta played major roles in Helen Corbitt's menu planning through the years. She was devoted to both of them, regarding them as versatile, useful in many ways, and able to "carry" other foods. Both are compatible with many textures, flavors, and temperatures. And both can be served hot, cold, or at room temperature.

Rice she always cooked in a covered casserole in a 350° oven for 45 minutes. She had a superb collection of rice recipes, many of which are included here. Pasta, which Helen called "mama food," was capable, she thought, of "making even the simplest meal a joy to remember."

Helen often said, "People look at you with love in their eyes when you serve a good fettuccine."

RICE RING

FOR EIGHT

2 cups uncooked rice
2 teaspoons salt
4 cups cold water
½ cup grated Cheddar cheese
Butter or margarine

Cook rice, as follows: Put rice, salt, and water into a large saucepan and cover with tight-fitting lid. Set over a hot flame until it boils vigorously. Reduce heat as low as possible and steam for 14 minutes; then remove lid and turn off heat, to permit the rice to steam dry. Stir in grated cheese and pack into buttered 8- or 8½-inch ring mold. Bring rice well up to the brim of the mold, or the ring will break when it is turned out. Put mold into pan of hot water, cover with foil or waxed paper, and allow to stand until serving time. Before unmolding, loosen ring edges with knife. Unmold on hot platter by turning platter over mold and inverting both quickly. Fill center of rice ring with vegetables or chicken or seafood.

RICE AND CHEESE CASSEROLE

FOR EIGHT

3 cups sour cream
1 4-ounce can green chile peppers, sliced and chopped, no seeds
4 cups cooked rice, packed
Salt and pepper
¾ pound Cheddar cheese, grated

Mix sour cream and peppers. Season rice with salt and pepper. Put a layer of rice in bottom of a 1½-quart casserole, then a layer of sour cream and a layer of cheese. Repeat, ending with cheese on top. Bake at 350° about 30 minutes, or until bubbly. Make ahead of time, refrigerate, and bake when ready to serve.

EXOTIC RICE

FOR SIX OR EIGHT

1¼ cups rice
¼ cup butter
2½ cups chicken bouillon
½ cup toasted almonds
¼ cup golden or white raisins
Salt and pepper

Brown rice in butter; add chicken bouillon, cover, and cook in a 350° oven for 40 minutes. Add rest of ingredients and press into a buttered ring mold. Bake at same temperature for 10 minutes. Unmold carefully and fill center with buttered fresh green beans either frenched or cut diagonally. I think this rice is wonderful with everything.

SAFFRON RICE

FOR FOUR

1 cup long-grain rice
1 tablespoon butter
1 tablespoon olive oil
2½ cups chicken bouillon, boiling
¼ teaspoon saffron
¼ cup white wine
Salt and pepper

Brown rice in the butter and olive oil. Add the chicken bouillon, saffron, and wine. Cover and cook over low heat until liquid is absorbed, 20 to 30 minutes. Season with salt and pepper.

ORANGE RICE

FOR SIX

¼ cup butter
1 cup rice
½ teaspoon salt
2 cups chicken broth
½ cup dry white wine
Juice of 1 orange
Grated rind of 1 orange
Salt and pepper
Chopped parsley

Place butter, rice, salt, broth, and wine in casserole. Cover and bake at 350° until light and feathery, about 45 minutes. Add juice and rind; return to oven for 10 minutes. Season to taste with salt and pepper, toss with a fork, and sprinkle with chopped parsley or slivered almonds.

RICE WITH CURRIED FRUIT

FOR TEN TO TWELVE

½ cup chutney, finely chopped
2 cups melon balls (not watermelon)
1 cup diced fresh pineapple
1 banana, sliced
1 cup other fruit such as peaches, pears, or grapes
2 cups chicken broth
2 teaspoons cornstarch
2 tablespoons curry powder or less
¼ cup pistachios
½ cup slivered toasted almonds
¼ cup plumped raisins (cover with warm water and let stand a few hours, then drain)
4 cups cooked rice, hot
Finely chopped parsley

Mix chutney, melon balls, pineapple, banana, and other fruit and chill well. Mix chicken broth with cornstarch and curry powder and simmer until thickened. Add the nuts and raisins to the chicken-broth sauce. Place the hot rice on a heated platter and top with the chilled fruit; then cover the fruit and rice with the curry-flavored sauce. Sprinkle with finely chopped parsley.

This dish is to be a contrast of flavors and textures. The rice and sauce should be at the boiling point, whereas the fruit should be chilled so that you get the contrast in the hot and cold ingredients. Unfortunately, this dish is not designed for buffet or leisurely serving — it should be eaten immediately upon preparation.

MUSHROOM RICE (RISOTTO WITH MUSHROOMS)

FOR EIGHT

¼ cup butter
¼ cup thinly sliced onion
¾ cup thinly sliced mushrooms (about 4)
½ cup dry white wine
1 cup rice
2½ cups beef or chicken broth
½ teaspoon salt
2 tablespoons grated Parmesan cheese

Melt butter; add the onion and sauté until soft, but do not brown. Add mushrooms, pour in wine, and cook until the liquid has evaporated. Add rice; cook 1 minute. Pour in broth, cover, and bake at 350° about 45 minutes or until rice is tender. Remove from oven; add salt and cheese; fork-stir before serving. (I save my mushroom stems for this recipe and chop instead of slice.)

SPANISH RICE

FOR SIX

While I was manager of the Houston Country Club I served many dishes with south-of-the-border flavor, so Mrs. Albert Jones sent me her Spanish Rice recipe. I have never used any other since. You won't either, once you try it.

1 cup chopped onion
½ cup chopped green pepper
1 cup uncooked rice
2 tablespoons olive oil
2 cups canned tomatoes
2 tablespoons vinegar
Salt and pepper

Sauté the onion, green pepper, and rice in the olive oil until the rice is brown. Add tomatoes, vinegar, and seasonings and cook until the rice is done, about 25 or 30 minutes. If I finish it in a casserole after it is cooked, I sprinkle with grated Provolone cheese and bake at 400° until the cheese is brown and bubbly.

EMERALD RICE

FOR EIGHT

4 egg yolks
4 cups cooked rice
1 cup raw spinach, minced
½ cup green pepper, minced
¼ cup onion, minced
1 cup whipped cream
⅓ cup grated Parmesan cheese
½ teaspoon paprika
1 teaspoon salt
4 egg whites
Sour cream
Chives

Beat egg yolks; add rice, spinach, green pepper, onion, whipped cream, grated cheese, paprika, and salt. Mix thoroughly. Fold in stiffly beaten egg whites. Pour into 1½-quart mold. Place in a pan of hot water and bake at 350° for 45 minutes. A variation is to scoop out tomatoes, fill with rice mixture and bake until puffed and lightly browned. Serve either preparation with sour cream and chives on top.

RICE WITH PINE NUTS

FOR SIX

¼ cup butter
2 tablespoons minced onion
1 cup rice
2½ cups beef or chicken consommé
4 ounces pine nuts, toasted
¼ cup chopped parsley
Salt and pepper

Melt butter, add onion, and sauté 1 minute. Add rice and consommé. Cover and bake at 350° for 45 minutes. Stir in pine nuts and parsley. Season to taste.

RICE CAKES

FOR EIGHT

2 cups cooked rice
2 egg yolks
1 teaspoon salt
⅛ teaspoon cayenne pepper
3 tablespoons grated sharp Cheddar cheese
½ cup thick Cream Sauce (2 tablespoons flour, 2 tablespoons butter, ½ cup milk)
1 egg white, slightly beaten
Dry white bread crumbs

Mix rice and egg yolks, seasonings, cheese, and cream sauce. Chill. Shape into flat cakes. Dip in the egg white and dry crumbs. Fry until light brown, or bake on a buttered cookie pan at 375° until light brown. I like to serve them with melted butter and grated orange or lemon peel.

PARMESAN RICE

FOR SIX

1 cup rice, browned in butter with a little chopped onion

Add:

2 cups water
1 teaspoon salt
1 tablespoon lemon juice

Bring to a boil, cover, and turn heat as low as possible. Cook about 20 minutes, then add:

4 eggs, well beaten
¼ cup salad oil
¾ cup grated Parmesan cheese

Pour into a buttered 1-quart casserole and sprinkle with fine buttered bread crumbs and cheese, half and half. Bake at 325° for 40 to 50 minutes.

CURRIED RICE

FOR SIX

2 tablespoons chopped onion
1 clove garlic, crushed
¼ cup salad oil
1 cup rice
1 teaspoon salt
1 tablespoon curry powder
2 cups boiling water

Sauté the onion and garlic in the oil until the onion is soft. Remove the garlic; add the rice, salt, and curry powder, and cook over low heat until the grains are yellow. Add the boiling water, cover, and cook over low heat until dry, about 30 minutes. Nice with seafood.

WILD RICE WITH GRAPES

FOR EIGHT TO TEN

2 cups wild rice, washed thoroughly
4 cups hot chicken broth
1 cup white wine
½ cup butter
2 cups canned seedless grapes, or fresh grapes, peeled and seeded
½ cup dry sherry
4 tablespoons chopped parsley

Put the rice, broth, and wine in a covered casserole and bake at 400° until tender, about 1 hour. Melt the butter, add the grapes, and sauté 1 minute. Add the sherry and bring to a boil. Toss into the rice, add the parsley, fork-stir, and serve. Or make a ring out of the rice, and put the grapes with the wine and butter in the center.

WILD RICE AND APPLES

FOR EIGHT

1½ cups wild rice, washed thoroughly
3 cups hot beef or chicken consommé
1½ cups dry white wine
3 Delicious apples, peeled, cored, and sliced thin
⅓ cup butter
2 tablespoons brandy

Put rice, consommé, and wine in a buttered 1½-quart casserole. Cover and bake at 400° for 1 hour or until rice is tender. Sauté the apples in the butter until soft but not mushy. Fork-stir into the rice; add lighted brandy and serve. You may substitute grapes, toasted almonds, mushrooms, cooked peas — anything your heart and stomach desire — for the apples. The apple version is especially delicious with duck.

WILD RICE CURRY

FOR SIX TO EIGHT

¾ cup wild rice
6 slices bacon, diced
½ cup chopped onion
½ cup grated raw carrots
2 egg yolks
1 cup light cream
1½ teaspoons curry powder
½ teaspoon salt
4 tablespoons butter

Cook the wild rice until done, following the directions on the box. Drain, wash in cold water, and set aside. Fry the bacon, add the onion and carrots, and sauté until soft. Place the rice and onion-and-carrot mixture in a buttered casserole. Beat the egg yolks, add the cream and seasonings, and pour over all. Dot with butter and bake at 300° in a hot-water bath until set, about 30 to 35 minutes. I like this with coq au vin or any other chicken.

RICE SALAD

FOR SIX TO EIGHT

3 cups chilled cooked rice
1 cup chilled cooked peas
½ cup chopped Major Grey's chutney
½ cup finely chopped celery
⅓ cup chopped fresh parsley
1 tablespoon finely chopped onion
1 tablespoon salad oil
1 tablespoon wine vinegar
⅔ cup mayonnaise or half mayonnaise and half sour cream
Salt and white pepper

Combine the first six ingredients by tossing lightly with a fork. Add the oil, vinegar, and mayonnaise. Season to taste. Spoon into a 1½-quart mold lightly rubbed with mayonnaise. Refrigerate for a few hours for a better mingling of flavors. Turn out onto a chilled serving platter or fill thin slices of ham or Swiss cheese with it, and roll up like an enchilada.

RICE SALAD WITH SHELLFISH AND HAM

FOR TEN TO TWELVE

4 cups cooked rice, chilled
1 cup chopped crab, lobster, shrimp, or crayfish
½ cup slivered ham (Virginia, if available)
1 cup *finely* chopped celery
3 hard-cooked eggs, finely chopped
2 tablespoons chopped chives
⅓ cup chopped parsley
2 tablespoons olive oil
2 tablespoons wine vinegar
½ cup mayonnaise
Salt and freshly ground pepper

Combine by tossing lightly the first seven ingredients. Sprinkle with oil and vinegar. Add mayonnaise and season. Let stand in refrigerator a few hours for a more tangy flavor. (Better made the day before; however, salt and pepper just before serving.) Try as an entrée with sliced cantaloupe and honeydew.

WILD RICE SALAD

FOR EIGHT TO TEN

1 clove garlic
3 cups cooked wild rice
2 tablespoons sliced scallions
1 cup cooked peas
8 cherry tomatoes, cut in half
1 8½-ounce can artichoke hearts, cut in half
¼ cup Sherry French Dressing
Chopped parsley
Salt and pepper

Rub your wooden salad bowl with a clove of garlic. Add the rest of the ingredients and toss lightly. Correct seasonings and serve at room temperature.

JAMBALAYA

FOR EIGHT

½ cup salt pork
½ cup diced ham
½ cup chopped onion
1 garlic bud
2 cups canned tomatoes
1 cup raw rice
2 cups water
1 teaspoon salt
1 pint oysters
1 pint raw shrimp, peeled and cleaned

Dice the salt pork, add the ham, and fry slowly until crisp. Add the onion and garlic; cook until soft. Remove garlic; add the tomatoes and simmer slowly until thick. Add the raw rice, water, and salt. Cover and cook for 10 minutes. Add the oysters and shrimp and cook until the rice is done, about 45 or 50 minutes. Don't like seafood? Add 2 cups of slivered lean ham or chicken.

MUSHROOMS AND NOODLES AU GRATIN

FOR SIX

1 cup Mornay Sauce
1 cup medium Cream Sauce
3 cups cooked fine noodles
½ cup sautéed sliced mushrooms
1 tablespoon dry sherry
Butter
6 sautéed whole mushrooms
Parmesan cheese
Paprika

Mix the Mornay Sauce, Cream Sauce, noodles, and sliced mushrooms together. Add the sherry and pour into a buttered shallow casserole. Place the mushrooms on top, sprinkle with Parmesan cheese and a little paprika, and run it under the broiler until brown. Serve with asparagus tips and broiled thick slices of ripe tomato. I sometimes substitute rice or spinach for the noodles.

LASAGNE VERDE AL FORNO

FOR TWELVE OR MORE

The following recipe was brought to me by my favorite wine merchant, Tony LaBarba, from one of his many trips to Europe. An Italian-American, he recognized its worth.

Bolognese Sauce:
½ pound ground salt pork
1½ pounds ground top round of beef
½ pound ground lean veal
2 cups thinly sliced onion
2 carrots, thinly sliced
2 stalks celery, diced
2 cloves
2 cups beef consommé
2 tablespoons tomato paste
1 teaspoon salt
Few twists from pepper grinder
1 cup water
½ pound mushrooms, diced
4 chicken livers, diced
1 cup heavy cream

Put salt pork into a deep skillet and fry until brown. Pour off the melted fat. Put in beef and veal, onions, carrots, celery, and cloves. Brown over low heat. Add the consommé and cook until it evaporates. Add tomato paste, salt, pepper, and water. Cover skillet and cook at low heat for 1 hour. Add mushrooms and chicken livers and cook 15 minutes longer. Just before assembling lasagne add cream and reheat.

Béchamel Sauce:
4 tablespoons butter
3 tablespoons flour
2 tablespoons finely chopped onion
2 cups chicken broth or milk
Salt and pepper
¼ cup heavy cream

Melt the butter. Add flour and cook until bubbly. Stir in onion and cook 1 minute. Pour in broth or milk, stirring constantly with a French whip until thickened. Season to taste. Add cream and simmer until thoroughly heated. Strain.

NEXT:

1 pound spinach lasagne noodles or strips
2 cups grated Parmesan cheese
2 cups grated Gruyère cheese

Cook noodles in boiling salted water until just tender, but not soft. Drain, but do not rinse. Place a layer in a shallow 3-quart oblong casserole. Cover with a layer of the meat sauce (Bolognese), then a layer of the Béchamel, then grated cheeses. Continue layering in the same order, ending with grated cheese on top. Bake in 375° oven until brown and bubbling, about 25 or 30 minutes. Let stand outside of oven 10 minutes before serving.

Prepared and baked ahead of time, it freezes well. If you cannot find spinach lasagne noodles, use plain ones.

FETTUCCINE ALFREDO

FOR EIGHT

1 pound fettuccine
1 cup butter, softened
1 cup cream at room temperature
2 cups grated or shredded Parmesan cheese

Cook pasta in 8 quarts of boiling water to which 2 tablespoons salt have been added, about 8 minutes or until *al dente.* Drain pasta, but do not rinse, and immediately pour it onto a heated platter or into a heated bowl. Toss with butter, cream, and cheese until the cheese and butter are completely melted. Serve at once.

TONNARELLI

FOR FOUR

½ pound package very fine egg noodles
1 4-ounce can mushrooms or 1 pound fresh
3 tablespoons butter
½ cup slivered leftover ham (you may omit)
1 cup cooked peas
½ cup Parmesan cheese

Cook noodles until tender. Drain but do not rinse. Slice the mushrooms; if fresh, sauté in butter. Add to the hot noodles with butter, ham, peas, and the cheese, and toss until everything is well coated with the cheese. I have had guests ask if there were leftovers to take home — so it must be good.

NOODLES À LA CRÈME

FOR EIGHT

1 pound vermicelli noodles, cooked and drained
½ pound bacon, cooked crisp and crumbled
3 cups creamy cottage cheese
3 cups sour cream
2 cloves garlic, crushed
2 cups finely chopped onion
1 tablespoon Worcestershire sauce
2 teaspoons salt
3 tablespoons horseradish
½ cup grated Parmesan cheese

Combine all the ingredients except the Parmesan cheese. Put into a buttered 3-quart casserole. Cover with Parmesan cheese and bake at 350° for 40 minutes or until hot and bubbly.

STUFFED MACARONI WITH SPINACH

FOR TWELVE

This is one of my favorite company pasta dishes that you can do ahead of time. Freeze if you wish, and then bake.

12 No. 20 macaroni shells
3 quarts boiling water
1 teaspoon salt
1 teaspoon salad oil
1 pound spinach (fresh preferred)
2 cups dry cottage cheese or ricotta
½ cup grated Parmesan cheese
2 eggs, lightly beaten
Pinch of nutmeg
Salt and pepper
2 cups thin Cream Sauce (2 tablespoons butter, 2 tablespoons flour, 2 cups milk)
1 cup grated Gruyère cheese

Cook macaroni in the boiling water with salt and oil until *al dente,* 15 minutes. Drain, rinse, and drain again. Wash spinach and put in a covered pot; cook for 1 minute only. Drain and put in blender until chopped but not liquid. Combine with the dry cottage cheese (or ricotta), Parmesan cheese, and the eggs and nutmeg. Mix thoroughly.

Season to your taste. Stuff the mixture into the cooked macaroni and place in a buttered shallow casserole. Pour over the Cream Sauce (seasoned with salt and pepper). Sprinkle with the Gruyère cheese and bake. This is a rich, delicious pasta and one shell per person should be enough as a side dish with a full dinner.

CHITARRA WITH MUSHROOMS AND PEAS

FOR EIGHT

---

1 pound chitarra (guitar-string noodles)
½ pound fresh or canned mushrooms, quartered
¼ cup butter
1 cup fresh or frozen peas, cooked 3 minutes only
⅓ cup grated Romano cheese
Cracked or freshly ground pepper

Cook the noodles in boiling salted water (4 quarts water, 2 tablespoons salt) until *al dente.* Drain, but do not rinse. Sauté mushrooms in butter. Add peas and noodles. Toss lightly with cheese until completely blended. Add a good amount of pepper, and salt if needed. Serve at once.

Or sauté ½ cup thinly sliced onions, add fresh spinach, shredded. Cook 1 minute and add hot noodles and 2 eggs, beaten. Toss with ½ cup freshly grated Parmesan cheese. Serve with crisp bacon.

RICOTTA PASTA

FOR FOUR

A very simple pasta to serve with anything you choose — or eat it alone with a glass of good red wine.

⅔ cup ricotta (or cottage cheese)
½ cup grated Parmesan cheese
Salt and freshly ground black pepper
A pinch of nutmeg
1 8-ounce package macaroni or any pasta
2 tablespoons butter

Mash the cheeses together; add the seasonings. Cook the pasta in boiling salted water, and place in a *hot* buttered serving casserole. Stir the cheese mixture into it. Add the butter, and place in a 350° oven for 5 minutes. Nice with broiled chicken. There is a pasta called wagon wheels — do it this way for a fun dinner.

MACARONI AND CHEESE

FOR EIGHT

Macaroni and Cheese made the old-fashioned way is always an easy dish to prepare; it keeps hot and everyone likes it.

½ pound macaroni
1 tablespoon butter
1 egg, beaten
1 teaspoon salt
1 teaspoon dry mustard
3 cups grated sharp Cheddar cheese
1 cup milk

Boil the macaroni in water until tender; drain thoroughly. Stir in the butter and egg; mix the mustard and salt with 1 tablespoon hot water and add to the macaroni. Add the cheese, leaving enough to sprinkle on the top. Pour into a buttered casserole, add the milk, sprinkle with the cheese, and bake at 350° for about 45 minutes, or until the custard is set and the top crusty.

MY FAVORITE NOODLES

FOR EIGHT

2 cups thinly sliced white or yellow onions
½ cup butter
2 cups sliced fresh or canned mushrooms
1½ cups heavy cream
1 1-pound package noodles, fine or fettuccine
Salt and cracked pepper

Sauté onions in the butter until yellow, not brown. Add mushrooms and, if fresh, cook until translucent. Add cream and bring to a boil. Cook the noodles in salted water (1 tablespoon salt to 1 gallon water) until *al dente*. Combine with the cream mixture. Season with salt and pepper. You may cut down on the cream if you wish a dryer noodle, but I don't.

MIXED NOODLES

FOR FOUR

1 8-ounce package fine noodles
5 tablespoons butter
¼ cup half-and-half
¼ cup grated Swiss cheese
Salt and cracked pepper
1 cup uncooked fine noodles

Cook the 8 ounces of noodles in boiling salted water until tender. Drain, but do not rinse. Add 2 tablespoons butter, half-and-half, and cheese. Season to your taste. Fry the uncooked noodles in 3 tablespoons butter until brown. Toss with the hot cooked noodles.

HOMEMADE PASTA

4 cups sifted all-purpose flour
3 eggs
1 teaspoon salt
1 teaspoon olive oil
Cold water, about ¼ cup

Put flour on a board in a mound or in a large bowl. Make a well in the center and add the eggs, salt, oil, and water. Mix with a fork or your hands until the dough forms a ball. Knead and add more flour if necessary; the dough must be very stiff. Divide the dough into at least four pieces. Roll the first piece with a floured rolling pin on a floured board into a thin smooth sheet. Set aside under a towel for 30 minutes while you roll out the other pieces in the same way. Or you can use a pasta machine. When ready to cut the noodles, roll each sheet as you would a jelly roll and cut into the widths you prefer. Let dry at least 30 minutes hanging over a chair back or a pasta-drying rack.

Cook in a large pot of boiling water (about 8 quarts for 1 pound of noodles) to which 2 tablespoons of salt have been added. Cook until *al dente,* just tender. Drain, do not rinse, and pour onto a heated platter. Toss with 1 cup soft butter, 1 cup cream, 2 cups grated Parmesan cheese until butter is completely melted. Serve at once on warmed plates.

Breads and Muffins

ABOUT YEAST BREADS

Your bread recipe reads: "knead until smooth and satiny." How long is that? You've never made bread before! Most doughs require from 8 to 10 minutes of kneading before you recognize a smooth and satiny surface. After 10 minutes, grasp the dough in one hand, squeezing it slightly with your fingers. If fully developed, the opposite side of the dough ball should feel smoothly taut; you will see bubbly blisters under the surface.

Yeast bread likes a warm, draft-free, and moist place for rising. If you don't have a cozy, private nook for "proofing" (rising) dough, make a "mini-sauna" of your oven. Turn your oven to 400° for one minute only and then turn it off. It should have reached a temperature between 80° and 100° — just what the dough likes. Situate your dough in the warm oven so it has plenty of room to rise. Place a pan of hot water on the oven floor before closing the door. Or place dough in bowl beside your stove, turn one burner on to low. Be sure to cover the bread with a towel or napkin if proofing outside the oven.

Almost any yeast dough or batter may be refrigerated if the amount of yeast in the recipe is doubled. A sweet dough, that is, high in sugar, refrigerates best. You can refrigerate the dough immediately after mixing and kneading or after it has risen once and been punched down. Proofing before refrigeration, however, helps the dough retain its rising power.

If storing the dough in the refrigerator, grease the bowl well. I use butter or margarine and cover with plastic wrap or a tight bowl cover. The best refrigerator temperature is 45° to 50°. Most refrigerator doughs may be kept three or four days with portions removed as desired. Some rising will take place in the refrigerator, but the dough can be punched down if it gets too high.

After refrigeration you can either shape the dough immediately or allow it to come to room temperature — about 1 to 3 hours — before shaping. Then let the shaped dough rise again before baking at the required temperature for the specified time.

BASIC BREAD RECIPE

TWO LOAVES

I think it confusing to have a different bread recipe for each idea you have. A few good basic ones are enough. This recipe can be used for bread, rolls, sweet rolls, or any variation you would care to make. It takes little time; it's worth the little effort. A hamburger or frankfurter eaten on a roll from this dough will make you wonder why you'd ever bought cardboard market buns.

1 package dry yeast
¼ cup lukewarm water
1 cup milk
¼ cup shortening
¼ cup sugar
1 teaspoon salt
4 cups sifted flour (about)
2 eggs

Soften yeast in water. Heat milk and shortening together until melted. (Do not boil.) Measure sugar and salt into large bowl; add hot milk mixture, stir until dissolved, and cool to lukewarm. Add 2 cups flour to milk and mix until well blended, 1 minute on electric mixer. Stir in softened yeast and eggs, beat well, and add more flour to make a thick batter. Beat thoroughly until smooth and elastic, 2 minutes on electric mixer. Cover and let rise in warm place (80° to 85°) until bubbly, about 1 hour. Stir down. Put on a floured board, knead lightly, and shape dough into desired form; let rise in warm place for 30 minutes. Bake in moderate oven (375°) for 20 to 30 minutes or until golden brown.

Variations:

Marmalade Rolls: Follow Basic Recipe through stir-down step. Prepare muffin pans by placing ½ teaspoon melted butter or margarine and 2 teaspoons of any kind of marmalade in each cup. Drop dough into greased muffin tins, one-half full. Let rise and bake as for Basic Recipe. Invert pans and remove rolls immediately after baking. Makes two dozen rolls. Make them in small muffin tins (48 to 60 rolls) for your morning coffee parties

Honey Cinnamon Buns: Mix ½ cup brown sugar, ½ cup honey, 1 teaspoon cinnamon, and ¾ cup pecans thoroughly and divide it among the twelve cups, already well buttered, of a muffin pan. Proceed as in Basic Recipe.

Marble Nut Coffee Cake: Follow the Basic Recipe through stir-down step. Combine ⅓ cup butter or margarine, melted, ⅔ cup brown sugar, and 2 tablespoons water. Spread half of mixture in each of two 9-inch round pans. Divide batter in half. To one-half part add ½ cup brown sugar, ½ cup chopped nuts, and 1 teaspoon cinnamon. Beat until thoroughly blended. Divide both parts of batter in half again, making four equal parts. Combine 1 plain part of batter with 1 brown sugar part by lightly stirring them together for 15 seconds. Spread batter evenly in prepared pan. Repeat. Bake as for Basic Recipe. Invert pan and remove coffee cake immediately after baking. Makes two 9-inch coffee cakes.

Merry Christmas Coffee Cake: Follow Basic Recipe through stir-down step. Combine ½ cup sifted flour, ¼ cup fine bread crumbs or nut meats, ¼ cup butter or margarine until mixture is crumbly. Drop batter by tablespoonfuls into crumbly mixture and gently roll to form coated balls. Shape two coffee cakes by arranging balls a layer deep on greased baking sheet or in a round pan. Let rise and bake as for Basic Recipe. Decorate with Confectioners' Sugar Icing: beat together ½ cup confectioners' sugar and 1 to 2 teaspoons milk until smooth; add candied fruit and halves of pecans. Makes two coffee cakes.

Sausage Bread: Use a mildly smoked sausage (the kind that comes by the foot), beef stick, or salami. Roll out the Basic Recipe dough to desired length. I make it about 12 inches long. Put the meat in the center and form the bread dough around it, about ½ inch thick. Let rise to double in bulk and bake at 375° until golden brown. If I use a beef stick (hickory smoked) or salami, I trim it to about 1 inch to 1½ inches in diameter. The trimmings I use for omelettes or in scrambled eggs or sandwiches. Don't throw them away. Serve the bread warm, sliced about ½ inch thick. 'Tis tasty-nice with cocktails, too.

WHEAT-GERM BREAD

TWO LOAVES

2 packages dry yeast
¼ cup warm water
1½ cups hot tap water
3 teaspoons sugar
2½ teaspoons salt
⅜ cup butter or margarine, room temperature
⅓ cup molasses
1 cup wheat germ
¾ cup milk, heated
4 cups whole-wheat flour
1 to 2 cups all-purpose flour, approximately

In a large bowl dissolve the yeast in the warm water. Stir briefly and let stand for about 3 minutes. In a saucepan mix the hot water, sugar, salt, butter, and molasses. The water should be sufficient to warm the mixture and melt the butter. If not, place it over low heat until the butter is softened. Allow the mixture to cool to lukewarm. Meanwhile, measure wheat germ into a small bowl and pour milk over it. Let it stand until the liquid has been absorbed by the wheat germ, and is only warm to the touch. Stir molasses mixture and wheat-germ mixture together in the large bowl that contains the yeast. Stir mixture well and add 2 cups of whole-wheat flour and 1 cup all-purpose flour; stir together with a wooden spoon for 150 strong strokes. Stir in the remaining whole-wheat flour and sufficient all-purpose flour to form a rough ball of dough. If the ball is sticky, add ½ cup or more all-purpose flour. Turn the dough out on a floured work surface — counter top or bread board — and with a strong push-turn motion knead the dough until it is smooth and elastic. Place dough in a greased bowl, cover tightly with plastic wrap, and move to a warm, draft-free place until the dough has doubled in bulk. Punch down the dough, work it briefly under your hands, and divide it into two equal portions. Shape these into loaves and place in the pans. Cover the pans with wax paper and return to the warm place until the dough has risen to 1 inch above the edge of the pan or doubled in bulk.

Preheat the oven to 400°. Place the loaves in the oven. When tapping the bottom crust yields a hard and hollow sound, they are done. Remove bread from the oven and turn the loaves out on metal racks to cool.

REFRIGERATOR WHEAT BREAD

TWO ONE-POUND LOAVES

3½ to 4 cups white flour
2 packages dry yeast
2 cups milk
¾ cup water
¼ cup salad oil
3 tablespoons sugar
1 tablespoon salt
4 cups whole-wheat flour
Oil or melted butter

Mix 2½ cups white flour with yeast. Heat milk, water, ¼ cup oil, sugar, and salt over low heat until warm (120° to 130°). Add liquid ingredients to flour-yeast mixture and beat 3 minutes on high speed of electric mixer. Add whole-wheat flour; gradually stir in more white flour to make a stiff dough. Turn out onto lightly floured surface and knead 5 to 10 minutes. Cover dough with bowl or pan; let rest 20 minutes. Divide in half. Roll each out to 7-by-14-inch rectangle. Roll from narrow side, pressing dough into roll at each turn. Press ends to seal and fold under loaf. Place in 2 greased 4½-by-8½-inch loaf pans. Brush loaves with oil or melted butter. Or make into rolls, two dozen medium size. Cover with plastic wrap and refrigerate 2 to 24 hours. When ready to use, let stand at room temperature 10 minutes. Puncture any gas bubbles with skewer. Bake in 400° oven 40 minutes. Remove immediately from pans and brush with oil or butter. Cool on wire rack.

OATMEAL BREAD

TWO LOAVES

Oatmeal Bread is good hot out of the oven, and toasted is good enough for the gods.

1 cup quick-cooking oatmeal
2 cups boiling water
½ cup molasses
1 tablespoon salt
2 tablespoons melted shortening
1 package dry yeast
½ cup warm water
6 cups flour

Place the oatmeal and boiling water in a bowl. Stir and let cool. Add the molasses, salt, and shortening. Dissolve the yeast in the warm water. Add to the oatmeal mixture, and then add the flour. Combine thoroughly. Cover with a towel or wax paper and let rise to double in bulk. Punch down, knead slightly, form into two loaves, and put into tins greased with shortening, not butter. Let rise for 2½ hours and bake at 375° for 50 minutes.

FRENCH BREAD

FOUR THIN LOAVES

1 package dry yeast
1 tablespoon sugar
2 teaspoons salt
2 cups warm water, 110° (check on a candy thermometer)
4 or 5 cups all-purpose flour
1 egg white, well beaten with ½ teaspoon salt
Cornmeal

Dissolve yeast, sugar, and salt in warm water. Let stand 10 minutes. Stir in 4 cups flour. Turn out on floured board. Knead for 10 minutes, adding more flour if necessary until dough is smooth and elastic. Put in greased bowl. Cover and let rise in a warm place for 45 minutes, or until double in bulk. Turn out, pat flat, and fold in a quarter circle.

Return to bowl. Cover and let rise 30 minutes. Turn out again on floured board and cut into four equal parts. Let rest for 5 minutes, then flatten and form into loaves. Put on a cookie sheet or flat pan dusted with cornmeal. Let rise 30 minutes. Brush with egg white and water, slash diagonally once or twice, or prick with a fork. Bake at 450° for 20 or 25 minutes. Turn loaves upside-down on oven rack and bake 5 more minutes at 400°.

SOURDOUGH BREAD STARTER

Sourdough Bread is the most sought-after bread in America. This recipe is good.

2 cups flour
1 package dry yeast
2 cups warm water

Combine ingredients in large bowl (not metal); mix together until well blended. Let stand uncovered in warm place (80° to 85°) for 48 hours; stir occasionally. Stir well before use. Pour out required amount and replenish remaining starter by mixing in 1 cup each flour and warm water. Let stand uncovered in a warm place a few hours (until it bubbles again) before covering loosely and refrigerating. Use and replenish every two weeks.

SOURDOUGH BREAD

TWO LARGE LOAVES

3 cups plus 3½ cups flour
1 cup starter
2 cups warm water
2 tablespoons sugar
1 tablespoon salt
1 teaspoon baking soda
Cornmeal
Melted butter

Measure 3 cups flour, starter, water, sugar, salt, and baking soda into large mixing bowl (not metal); beat until smooth. Cover loosely with waxed paper and let stand in warm place (80° to 85°) at least 18 hours. Stir batter down. Mix in more flour (about 3½ cups) to make a moderately stiff dough. Turn onto lightly floured surface and knead until smooth and satiny, about 8 to 10 minutes. Shape dough; place on greased baking sheets that have been sprinkled with cornmeal; brush with butter. Cover and let rise in warm place until doubled, about 1½ hours. Bake in 400° oven 40 to 50 minutes or until done. Brush with butter after baking.

CHRISTMAS FRUIT BREAD

TWO MEDIUM-SIZED LOAVES

½ cup shredded citron
½ cup chopped raisins
½ cup chopped candied cherries
1 tablespoon grated lemon rind
½ cup chopped blanched almonds
1 teaspoon cinnamon
½ teaspoon ground cloves
½ teaspoon nutmeg
¼ cup water or brandy
1 package dry yeast
2 tablespoons lukewarm water
1 cup milk
⅓ cup shortening
¼ cup sugar
1 teaspoon salt
1 egg, well beaten
4 cups enriched all-purpose flour
Melted butter

Soak the fruit, nuts, and spices in the ¼ cup of water or brandy overnight. The next morning soften the yeast in the lukewarm water. Scald the milk; add to it the shortening, sugar, and salt, and cool to lukewarm. Add the yeast, the egg, and 2 cups of the flour. Beat thoroughly, then add the rest of the flour. Allow to rise in a warm place until double in bulk; turn out on a floured board and knead, adding more flour if necessary to make a medium-firm dough. Allow to rise again; knead the fruit into the dough and form into loaves. Place in well-greased loaf pans and allow to rise again until double in size. Brush tops with melted butter. Bake at 400° for 10 minutes; reduce to 350° and bake for 50 minutes. Cool and frost with a thin icing made with confectioners' sugar and water flavored with almond extract.

STOLLEN

You can use the recipe for Christmas Fruit Bread, form it into crescent-shaped loaves, frost while warm, decorate with pieces of candied fruit and nuts, and call it Stollen.

It makes a wonderful sandwich with the turkey leavin's, Christmas night, and though it sounds impossible, thin slices of ham with this bread and prepared horseradish and butter are wonderful. Both the recipe and the ham-and-horseradish idea came from the family of a Viennese girl* with whom I shared an apartment at one time.

SALLY LUNN

ONE CAKE

1 package dry yeast
1 cup milk, lukewarm
3 tablespoons butter
3 tablespoons sugar
2 eggs
3½ cups flour
1¼ teaspoons salt

Soften yeast in lukewarm milk. Set aside. Cream together butter and sugar. Add eggs and mix well. Sift flour, to which the salt has been added. Add to shortening mixture alternately with milk-yeast mixture. Beat well. Let rise in a warm place until double in bulk. Knead lightly. Put into a well-buttered Sally Lunn mold or bundt pan. Cover. Let stand and rise again until doubled. Bake 1 hour at 300°.

PLAIN ROLL DOUGH

TWO TO THREE DOZEN ROLLS

6 tablespoons butter
4 tablespoons sugar
1 teaspoon salt
1 cup scalded milk
1 package dry yeast
¼ cup lukewarm water
4 cups all-purpose sifted flour
1 egg, well beaten

Add the butter, sugar, and salt to the milk. When it has cooled to lukewarm, add the yeast dissolved in the warm water, and 3 cups of flour. Beat thoroughly, cover, and let rise until light.

Cut down and add the well-beaten egg, and 1 cup of flour. Turn onto a floured board and knead until smooth. Put in a greased bowl, cover with a towel, and let rise to double in bulk. If you do not use all the dough at once, spread with melted butter, cover with wax paper, and refrigerate.

Rolls are something like biscuits. You can roll anything you like into

*The girl, Adelaide Brady, who lives in Pittsburgh, remained a close friend of Helen's through the years. She recalls the file box of special recipes Helen prepared for her when she got married.

them, from cheese to candied ginger, spices, herbs, parsley, watercress, jelly, your favorite marmalade. It is only you who stops the ball from rolling.

ORANGE ROLLS

TWO TO THREE DOZEN

Orange Rolls have had the number-two place in the gastronomical affections of my customers.

1 cup confectioners' sugar
⅓ cup butter
1 tablespoon grated orange rind
2 tablespoons orange juice, or enough to moisten

Mix and form into small balls. Form rolls (use Plain Roll Dough) around them and place the rounded side down in a buttered muffin tin. Small rolls are better than large, and should be eaten as they come out of the oven.

ICEBOX ROLLS

TWO TO THREE DOZEN

For those who asked.

1 cup boiling water
1 cup shortening
1 cup sugar
1½ teaspoons salt
2 eggs, beaten
2 packages dry yeast
1 cup cold water
6 cups unsifted flour

Pour boiling water over shortening; add sugar and salt. Blend and cool. Add eggs. Let yeast stand in cold water 5 minutes, then add to mixture. Add sifted flour. Blend well. Set in refrigerator. Make into rolls 1 to 2 hours before baking. Bake at 350° to 370° for 20 minutes.

STICKY ROLLS

TWO TO THREE DOZEN

I know everyone wants the Sticky Roll recipe I have used so many places.

Roll Plain Roll Dough out in a rectangular sheet, spread with softened butter, sprinkle with brown sugar, and roll up like a jelly roll. Cut in ¾-inch pieces. Heavily grease a baking pan with shortening, not butter, and completely cover with a layer of dark Karo syrup. Sprinkle a little brown sugar on top of the syrup. Place the rolls, close together, cut side down. Let rise to double in bulk, and bake at 400° for 20 minutes. You may vary them by adding cinnamon to the brown sugar you roll with, or add pecans or raisins to the pan with the syrup.

BRIOCHE

ABOUT THREE DOZEN SMALL

1 package dry yeast
½ cup warm water
¼ cup sugar
2 teaspoons salt
6 eggs, at room temperature
1 cup butter or whipped margarine, softened
4½ cups sifted flour
1 egg yolk, mixed with 2 teaspoons water

Sprinkle yeast over water in large bowl of electric mixer; stir by hand with a wooden spoon until yeast is dissolved. Add sugar, salt, butter, eggs, and 3 cups flour. Beat at medium speed 4 minutes, occasionally scraping side of bowl and beaters with rubber scraper. Add remaining flour. Beat at low speed until smooth (dough will be soft). Cover bowl with foil. Let rise in warm place free from drafts until double in bulk, about 1½ hours. Using a rubber scraper, beat down dough. Then refrigerate, covered with foil, overnight.

Next day, generously grease small brioche, tart, or muffin tins. With a sharp knife cut off pieces of dough about the size of an egg or 2 ounces in weight. On a slightly floured board shape into a ball. Fit balls into the greased pans. With your fingers make a slight indentation in each center. Insert a small ball of dough for the cap. Cover with a towel; let rise in a warm place until dough reaches top of pan, about 1 hour. Beat egg yolk with water. Brush caps only. Bake at 375° for 10 minutes. Cover loosely with foil and bake about 20 minutes longer, or until cake tester inserted in center under the cap comes out clean. Let stand in pan for 10 to 15 minutes. With a spatula carefully loosen each brioche from side of pans, then remove.

Variation:

To make rum buns with this dough ice while warm with:

2 cups confectioners' sugar
2 tablespoons dark rum
¼ teaspoon vanilla
2 drops lemon extract
Enough hot water to make a soft icing

HOT CROSS BUNS

TWO TO THREE DOZEN

For Good Friday and Ash Wednesday.

1 cup scalded milk
¼ cup butter
¼ cup sugar
1 package dry yeast
3½ cups flour
1 beaten egg
1¾ teaspoons salt
⅛ teaspoon nutmeg
1 teaspoon grated lemon rind
2 tablespoons chopped citron
½ cup seedless raisins

Mix the scalded milk, butter, and sugar together and cool to lukewarm; then add the yeast. Add 1½ cups flour and beat vigorously. Cover and put in a warm place until light and full of bubbles; then add the egg, salt, nutmeg, lemon rind, and 1 more cup of the flour. Beat until smooth; then add remaining flour, citron, and raisins. Knead lightly and place in a buttered bowl and let rise until double in bulk. Punch down in bowl and pinch off pieces the size you want with buttered fingers, and form into biscuits. Place in a buttered pan 1 inch apart, lightly cut a cross on top of each, and brush with a beaten egg. Bake for 20 minutes at 375°.

Make an icing for the cross with:

3 egg whites (or 2 if eggs are large)
1½ cups confectioners' sugar, sifted
1 tablespoon lemon juice

Put egg whites, unbeaten, in a bowl and gradually add most of the sugar. Beat after each addition. Add the lemon juice, then add more sugar, until the icing is stiff enough to hold its shape after being forced through a pastry tube. Decorate each bun by filling the cross with icing.

This icing may be used for all kinds of decorations.

RAISIN BREAD

THREE LOAVES

For sandwiches or for morning toast. Homemade, it's best!

6¼ cups all-purpose flour (measure after sifting)
2½ teaspoons salt
2¼ tablespoons baking powder
2¼ cups sugar
2¼ cups raisins
2 eggs
2¾ cups milk
7 tablespoons butter

Sift dry ingredients and add the raisins. Beat the eggs and add the milk and butter, melted. Combine the flour and milk mixtures lightly. Turn into greased and floured loaf tins and bake at 325° for about 2 hours. Freezes well.

ORANGE NUT BREAD

TWO LOAVES

I have many recipes for orange nut breads, but I find that Derelys Hungarland in Huntsville, Texas, has a better one. It freezes well and can be sliced very thin for sandwiches. Plain sweet butter or cream cheese and preserved ginger makes yummy sandwiches. You can make the sandwiches, wrap in plastic, and either refrigerate or freeze.

Boil until tender 1 cup water, 2 teaspoons soda, and the outer peelings from 4 to 5 oranges. Drain and mash. Add:

¾ cup water
1 cup sugar

Cook until consistency of thick apple sauce — almost crystallized. Set aside. Mix:

1 cup sugar
2 eggs, well beaten
1 cup milk
3¼ cups flour
3 teaspoons baking powder
2 tablespoons melted butter
½ teaspoon salt
1 cup broken nutmeats

When mixed thoroughly, combine with the peel mixture. Mix well but do not beat. Pour into two well-buttered loaf tins and bake at 325° for 35 to 40 minutes or until a cake tester comes out clean.

APRICOT NUT BREAD

ONE LOAF

½ cup diced dried apricots
1 egg
1 cup granulated sugar
2 tablespoons melted butter
2 cups sifted flour
3 teaspoons baking powder
¼ teaspoon soda
¾ teaspoon salt
½ cup strained orange juice
¼ cup water
1 cup sliced Brazil nuts or almonds

Soak apricots in water for half an hour. Drain and grind. Beat egg until light, stir in sugar, and mix well. Stir in butter. Sift flour with baking powder, soda, and salt; add to egg mixture alternately with orange juice and water. Add nuts and apricots. Mix well. Bake in a 9-by-5-by-3-inch loaf pan at 350° for 1½ hours.

This bread put together with a cream-cheese-and-candied-ginger spread makes a delightful tea sandwich.

PRUNE BREAD

ONE LOAF

2 tablespoons shortening
1 cup sugar
1 egg
½ cup prune juice, heated
1 cup sour milk or buttermilk
1 cup graham or whole-wheat flour
1½ cups white flour
1½ teaspoons baking powder
½ teaspoon soda
1 cup cooked prunes, chopped but not too fine
1 cup nuts, chopped

Cream shortening and sugar. Add egg and beat. Add prune juice and sour milk and stir. Combine dry ingredients and add to mixture. Dust nut meats with a little flour and add them with the prunes, last. Turn into a 9-by-5-by-3-inch loaf pan. Bake at 350° for about 1 hour.

Prune Bread may be frozen successfully. It's good to keep for emergency entertaining and for the holidays.

CRANBERRY NUT BREAD

TWO SMALL LOAVES

2 cups flour
½ teaspoon salt
1¼ teaspoon baking powder
½ teaspoon (scant) soda
1 cup sugar
1 orange
2 tablespoons shortening
Boiling water
1 egg, beaten
1 cup chopped nuts (preferably pecans)
1 cup raw cranberries, halved

Sift twice the flour, salt, baking powder, soda, and sugar. Then put juice and finely chopped rind of the orange in a cup; add shortening, and fill remainder of cup with boiling water. Add with 1 beaten egg to the sifted dry ingredients. Add chopped nuts and raw cranberries cut in half. Turn into buttered loaf pans (8½-by-4½-by-2½ inches) and bake at 350° for 1 hour.

Use cream cheese and chopped orange peel for sandwich filling.

BANANA BREAD

ONE LOAF

1¾ cups sifted flour
2¾ teaspoons baking powder
½ teaspoon salt
⅓ cup shortening
⅔ cup sugar
2 eggs
1 pound (3 or 4) ripe bananas

Sift together the flour, baking powder, and salt. Beat shortening in mixer bowl until creamy consistency. Add sugar and eggs. Continue beating at medium speed 1 minute. Peel bananas; add to egg mixture. Mix until blended. Add flour mixture, beating at low speed about 30 seconds, or only until blended. Do not overbeat. Scrape bowl and beater once or twice. Turn into a buttered 9-by-5-by-3-inch loaf pan and bake at 350° about 1 hour and 10 minutes, or until bread is done. This keeps well in the refrigerator.

Variations:

Banana Nut Bread: To egg mixture add 1 cup coarsely chopped nuts.

Banana Raisin Bread: To egg mixture add 1 cup seedless raisins.

Banana Date Bread: To egg mixture add 1 cup finely chopped dates.

Holiday Banana Bread: To egg mixture add ¼ cup seedless raisins and 1 cup mixed candied fruit.

VIENNA COFFEE CAKE

TWO SMALL LOAVES

Vienna Coffee Cake was popular at the Palomino Bar at Joske's of Houston. I make the cake in small loaf pans and slice it thick. It is wonderful toasted.

¼ cup butter
1 cup granulated sugar
2 eggs
1½ cups plus 2 tablespoons cake flour, sifted
¼ teaspoon salt
2¾ teaspoons baking powder
½ cup milk

Cream butter and sugar. Add eggs one at a time, and beat until light. Sift dry ingredients together and add flour and milk to egg mixture alternately, starting with flour. (Will curdle if milk is added first.) Turn into greased loaf tins.

For top:

1 tablespoon butter, melted
3 tablespoons sugar
½ cup walnuts, chopped

Spread melted butter over batter; sprinkle sugar and nuts over top. Bake at 350° for 45 minutes.

QUICK COFFEE CAKE

TWO CAKES

2½ cups sifted flour
1¼ cups brown sugar
½ teaspoon salt
½ cup shortening
2 teaspoons baking powder
½ teaspoon soda
1 egg, well beaten
¾ cup buttermilk
½ teaspoon cinnamon
½ cup chopped pecans

Mix the flour, sugar, and salt. Cut in the shortening with a pastry blender until it looks like cornmeal. Take out ¾ cup. To the remaining mixture add the baking powder and soda, and mix well. Stir in the egg and buttermilk. Pour into 2 greased square cake tins. Mix the ¾ cup of flour mixture with cinnamon and nutmeats. Sprinkle over the top of the batter and bake at 400° for 20 to 25 minutes. Serve hot or reheated, but not cold.

HELEN CORBITT'S COFFEE CAKE

FOR EIGHT TO TEN

Expensive but worth it.

1¾ cups sugar
¾ cup butter
1⅛ cups milk
3 cups flour, sifted
4 teaspoons baking powder
1 teaspoon salt
4 egg whites

Cream the sugar and butter until soft and smooth. Add the milk alternately with the flour, baking powder, and salt sifted together. Fold in the egg whites beaten stiff.

Pour into a buttered baking pan and cover with topping made from:

2 cups chopped pecans
1⅛ cups brown sugar
2 tablespoons cinnamon
¾ cup flour
¾ cup butter

Mix together until it looks like cake crumbs. Spread over the top and bake at 350° for 40 to 50 minutes. Cut in squares. If any topping is left, use it for Crumb Pudding or roll balls of vanilla ice cream in the crumbs and serve with Butterscotch Sauce.

DOUGHNUTS

ABOUT THREE DOZEN

Little doughnuts have always been an early-in-the-morning party item, or for awfully late at night. Use a small round cutter, then find something to cut a hole in the center. Fry the hole, too, regardless of size. Why? — for fun.

4 teaspoons baking powder
½ teaspoon nutmeg
1 teaspoon salt
3½ cups flour
1 egg plug 2 egg yolks
1 cup milk
1 cup sugar
3 tablespoons melted butter
Sugar and cinnamon

Sift dry ingredients. Beat the eggs; add milk, sugar, and cooled melted butter. Add the dry ingredients and form a soft dough. Roll out on a floured board; knead and roll out ¼ inch thick. Cut and fry in deep fat at 370°. Turn only once, very carefully. Piercing them will make them heavy and fat-soaked. Roll in powdered or granulated sugar and cinnamon.

IRISH TEA SCONES

ONE DOZEN LARGE

2 cups all-purpose flour
2½ tablespoons sugar
Salt to taste
2½ tablespoons baking powder
¾ cup butter, softened
2 eggs, beaten
Milk to bind

Sift flour, sugar, salt, and baking powder together. Stir into the butter, along with the eggs. Add just enough milk to bind ingredients together. Turn out on a floured board; roll out to about ½ inch thick. Cut into diamonds, triangles, or rounds and bake at 350° for 25 minutes.

BLUEBERRY COFFEE CAKE

FOR EIGHT TO TEN

⅓ cup butter
⅓ cup sugar
2 eggs
¾ cup milk
1½ cups cake flour, sifted
1 tablespoon baking powder
2 cups blueberries, fresh or frozen
1 3-ounce package cream cheese
2 tablespoons sugar
1 tablespoon lemon juice

Cream butter and sugar; add eggs and beat. Add milk and flour mixed with the baking powder. Add 1 cup of the blueberries and mix well. Pour into buttered 9-inch cake pan and sprinkle remaining berries on top. Mix the cheese with the sugar and lemon juice, and spread over top of berries. Place a crumb mixture on top and bake at 375° for 30 minutes. When done, serve as is, or cover with a thin powdered-sugar-and-water icing. Substitute any fruit for the blueberries.

CRUMB MIXTURE

1 cup cake flour
¼ cup sugar
¼ cup butter
¼ teaspoon cinnamon

Work together to make crumbs.

YORKSHIRE PUDDING

There are still those who like Yorkshire Pudding with their beef.

Pour out 6 tablespoons of beef drippings from the roast into a shallow pan and keep hot. Beat 2 eggs until light, add 1 cup milk, and beat until frothy. Stir in 1 cup of sifted flour and ½ teaspoon salt and beat until smooth. Pour into the hot drippings and bake at 450° for 15 minutes; then reduce the temperature to 350° for 15 minutes more.

CARAWAY TWISTS

ABOUT TWENTY-FOUR

I like to remember my Aunt Laura's Caraway Twists that she served with fricasseed chicken. These are superb with chicken salad, or just "as is."

1 cup grated Swiss cheese
2 tablespoons caraway seeds
Your favorite piecrust recipe, using 2 cups flour
1 egg, beaten
2 tablespoons coarse salt

Add the cheese and caraway seeds to the piecrust before adding the liquid. Roll out on a board as thin as you can to handle it easily. Cut into strips ½ inch wide and 6 inches long or longer. Brush lightly with beaten egg. Sprinkle with the coarse salt and twist each strip into a stick, pressing the two flat ends together. Bake on an ungreased cookie sheet at 375° for 8 to 10 minutes. The same proportions of cheese and caraway seed added to a baking powder biscuit recipe, or biscuit, cut and sprinkled with coarse salt and butter before baking, are delicious split and filled with chicken salad for a morning coffee. Plenty of zest, and serve either version hot.

POPOVERS

TEN OR TWELVE

1 cup sifted all-purpose flour
¼ teaspoon salt
2 eggs
⅞ cup milk
1 tablespoon melted butter

Mix the flour and salt. Beat eggs until light, add milk and butter, and add slowly to the flour. Stir until well blended. Beat 2 minutes with a rotary beater or 1 minute with an electric beater. Heavily butter muffin tins or custard cups and put in the oven to get hot. Fill the cups one-third full. Bake 20 minutes at 450 °; then reduce heat to 350 ° and bake 15 minutes more. Don't peek! Serve hot with marmalade.

HOT BISCUITS

TWO DOZEN SMALL

2 cups flour, sifted
3 teaspoons baking powder
1 teaspoon salt
⅓ cup shortening
¾ cup milk

Sift flour, baking powder, and salt together; cut in shortening until mixture resembles coarse cornmeal. Add milk and mix to smooth dough. Turn out on lightly floured board. Knead lightly. Roll or pat ½ inch thick. Cut with biscuit cutter. Place on ungreased cookie sheet. Bake in very hot oven at 450° for 12 to 15 minutes.

With this as a basic recipe, you may do many variations:

Cheese Biscuits: Add ½ cup grated sharp cheese to dry ingredients.

Pineapple Fingers: Add 1 cup diced candied pineapple. Cut in fingers and brush with melted butter and sprinkle with granulated sugar.

Rich Tea Biscuits: Increase the shortening to ½ cup and add 1 egg, beaten.

Herb Biscuits: Add ½ teaspoon of dried herbs for each cup of flour. I add poultry seasoning or sage for cocktail biscuits.

Cinnamon Pinwheels: These are nice to keep in your icebox and bake as you need them. Roll biscuit into an oblong sheet. Brush with melted shortening and sprinkle heavily with cinnamon mixture made by combining 1 cup sugar with 1½ tablespoons of cinnamon. Roll tight as a jelly roll, wrap in wax paper, and chill. Slice thin and bake at 350° until brown, 12 to 15 minutes.

Onion Biscuits: Add ½ cup French-fried onions, chopped fine, to recipe. Really good with chicken and for brunches or cocktail parties with a slice of ham between.

BUTTERMILK BISCUITS

TWELVE LARGE OR TWENTY-FOUR SMALL

2 cups sifted flour
½ teaspoon baking soda
2 teaspoons baking powder
1 teaspoon salt
¼ cup cold shortening
1 cup cold buttermilk or sour milk

Sift dry ingredients together and cut in shortening until mealy. Add milk and mix quickly. Knead very lightly on a floured board. Pat to ½-inch thickness and cut with floured biscuit cutter. Place in greased pan close together for crust on top and bottom only; put far apart if crust is desired on sides also. Bake at once in 450° oven for 12 minutes or until brown.

BLUEBERRY DROP BISCUITS

TWENTY-FOUR SMALL

This recipe is typically Yankee. Serve these biscuits hot and dripping with butter.

2 cups flour
3 teaspoons baking powder
1 teaspoon salt
4 tablespoons butter
1 cup milk
1 cup blueberries, fresh or drained, if frozen

Sift flour twice; add baking powder and salt. Sift again and work in the butter with a fork or pastry blender. Add the milk and berries and drop by tablespoonfuls onto a greased baking sheet. Bake at 375° for about 12 minutes.

MUFFINS

TWELVE MEDIUM OR TWENTY-FOUR SMALL

A standard muffin recipe serves the same purpose as your roll or biscuit recipes.

2 cups sifted flour
4 teaspoons baking powder
½ teaspoon salt
¼ cup sugar
2 eggs, well beaten
1 cup milk
4 tablespoons melted butter

Combine and sift dry ingredients. Mix the egg and milk and stir into the dry ingredients. Stir in the melted butter. Bake in greased muffin tins, three-fourths full, at 425° for 20 to 25 minutes. Do not overmix. Lumpy batter makes perfect muffins.

Variations:

Blueberry Muffins: Use ½ cup sugar. Fold in carefully 1 cup blueberries, fresh or frozen. If frozen, be sure they are thoroughly defrosted and drained.

Orange Coconut Muffins: Fold in 2 tablespoons grated orange peel plus ½ cup Angel Flake coconut; ½ cup toasted chopped almonds are nice, too, with the orange.

Bacon Muffins: Fold in 6 strips of bacon, fried crisp and chopped and dried.

Cinnamon Muffins: Sprinkle top with cinnamon and sugar, half and half, a goodly amount, too.

Fruit Muffins: Candied pineapple, ginger, in fact, any fruit, ½ cup; if fresh, 1 cup.

Nut Muffins: Add ½ cup chopped toasted nutmeats.

Guava Jelly Muffins: Put ¼ teaspoon of guava jelly on top of each small muffin.

LEMON MUFFINS

TWO DOZEN

1 cup butter or other shortening
1 cup sugar
4 egg yolks, well beaten
½ cup lemon juice
2 cups flour
2 teaspoons baking powder
1 teaspoon salt
4 egg whites, stiffly beaten
2 teaspoons grated lemon peel

Cream butter and sugar until smooth. Add egg yolks and beat until light. Add the lemon juice alternately with the flour (which has been sifted with baking powder and salt), mixing thoroughly after each addition (*do not overmix*). Fold in stiffly beaten egg whites and the grated lemon peel. Fill buttered muffin tins three-quarters full and bake at 375° about 20 minutes. These freeze well, and are nice split and toasted with salads.

ORANGE MUFFINS

THREE DOZEN SMALL

These make a good picnic dessert.

1 cup butter or margarine
1 cup sugar
2 eggs
1 cup buttermilk
1 teaspoon baking soda
2 cups all-purpose flour, sifted
Grated rind of 2 oranges
½ cup golden raisins
Juice of 2 oranges
1 cup brown sugar

Cream butter and sugar; add eggs; beat till well mixed. Dissolve the baking soda in the buttermilk, and add it, alternately with the flour, to the egg mixture. Add orange rind and raisins. Fill well-buttered muffin tins two-thirds full and bake at 400° for 20 to 25 minutes. Mix orange juice with brown sugar. Spoon over muffins and remove them from tins immediately.

Variation:

Use pecans in place of the raisins. I like to make small muffins and freeze them and eat them frozen. They taste like candy.

BANANA BRAN MUFFINS

TWELVE MEDIUM OR TWENTY-FOUR SMALL

1 cup sifted flour
½ tablespoon salt
½ tablespoon soda
¼ cup shortening
½ cup sugar
2 eggs, well beaten
2 cups bran
½ cup buttermilk
6 bananas, diced

Sift the flour, salt, and soda together. Cream the shortening and sugar; add the eggs, bran, and buttermilk. Add the bananas and stir into the flour mixture. Drop into greased muffin tins three-fourths full and bake at 375° for 30 to 35 minutes.

CREOLE CORN MUFFINS

TWO DOZEN

2 eggs, well beaten
1½ cups milk
¾ cup shortening, melted
2 tablespoons chopped green pepper
2 tablespoons chopped onion
2 tablespoons chopped pimento
¾ cup grated American cheese
2½ cups flour
1 teaspoon salt
2 tablespoons baking powder
4 tablespoons plus 1 teaspoon sugar
4 tablespoons plus 1 teaspoon cornmeal

Mix the eggs, milk, and shortening. Add the green pepper, onion, pimento, and cheese to the flour, salt, baking powder, sugar, and cornmeal. Add the milk mixture and stir only enough to mix. Bake at 400° for 25 to 30 minutes.

CORN CRISPS

TWO DOZEN

1 cup boiling water
⅞ cup cornmeal
½ teaspoon salt
2½ tablespoons melted butter
⅛ teaspoon cayenne pepper
Poppy seeds

Pour boiling water over cornmeal and stir. Add salt, 2½ tablespoons melted butter, and cayenne. Drop from teaspoon onto a buttered cookie sheet; then flatten with a spatula dipped in cold water. Brush with more melted butter. Sprinkle with poppy seeds and bake at 350° until brown around the edges.

SPOON BREAD

FOR SIX TO EIGHT

4 cups milk
1 cup cornmeal
2 teaspoons salt
1 teaspoon baking powder
1 teaspoon sugar
4 tablespoons melted butter
6 eggs, separated

Scald milk, add the cornmeal and cook until thick. Add the salt, baking powder, sugar, and butter. Beat the egg yolks and add to the cornmeal mixture. Beat the egg whites until soft peaks form and fold into the batter. Pour into a well-buttered 3-quart casserole and bake uncovered in a 375° oven for 25 to 30 minutes. Grits may be substituted for the cornmeal.

RICE SPOON BREAD

FOR SIX TO EIGHT

1 cup boiling water
1 cup cornmeal
2 cups cooked rice
2 eggs, separated
1 cup milk
3 tablespoons melted butter
½ teaspoon salt
½ teaspoon sugar

Pour boiling water over cornmeal. Mix with the rice and egg yolks beaten with the milk. Add melted butter, salt, and sugar. Cool. Beat egg whites until stiff and fold in. Pour into a buttered 1-quart casserole and bake at 350° for 45 to 50 minutes.

JOHNNYCAKE

ONE DOZEN

¾ cup cornmeal
1¼ cups flour
¼ cup sugar
½ teaspoon salt
4 teaspoons baking powder
1 cup milk
1 egg
1 tablespoon melted butter

Mix all the dry ingredients. Combine all the wet ingredients. Mix together and beat. Pour into a buttered shallow pan or muffin tins. Bake at 375° for about 20 minutes.

Part 4

Fish and Shellfish
Chicken and Turkey
Other Birds, and Game
Dressings for Fowl

Fish and Shellfish

ABOUT BUYING AND COOKING FISH

Delectable fish dishes can be served from the tiniest kitchen — if the desire is great enough. But fish should be treated with respect, never overcooked, and always eaten when ready. It is not a "keep hot in the oven" dish.

And they say it is good food for thinking! Anyhow, catch (or buy) it and *cook* it; don't keep it. Quick-frozen fish has the original flavor, but as soon as it comes into the kitchen, *cook* it.

In buying fish, allow from ½ to ¾ pound per serving with the bone in — or ¼ pound boned. Wash it well inside and out and wipe dry.

TO BROIL FISH

To pep up melted butter for any broiled fish, add to each ½ cup of butter:

1 teaspoon anchovy paste
or
2 tablespoons chopped chives
or
¼ cup any shellfish, cut fine
or
1 tablespoon browned grated onion
or
½ cup browned finely chopped almonds
or

2 teaspoons prepared mustard
or
1 tablespoon lemon juice and 1 teaspoon grated lemon peel
or
2 tablespoons finely chopped parsley or watercress.

TO BAKE FISH

Whether for a whole or fileted fish, I start it in a 350° oven with salt and butter sprinkled over and a little water in the bottom of the pan. If it is a "pale" fish, I sprinkle it lightly with paprika, but no pepper. (New York restaurateur George Rector told me a long time ago not to pepper fish. I was convinced, and have never done so since.) When the fish is tender (it will take from 15 to 20 minutes, depending on its thickness), add more butter and place 2 inches below the broiler heat to crisp on top. Remove and serve at once with more melted butter and lemon or lime.

TO POACH FISH IN COURT BOUILLON

Poaching fish takes a bit of patience. If you have the time, poach it in court bouillon:

3 quarts water (for the sophisticated palate, use half dry white wine and half water)
1 tablespoon butter
1 tablespoon salt
2 tablespoons lemon juice and the sliced rind of the lemon
3 peppercorns
1 bay leaf
¼ cup sliced onion
1 piece celery
1 carrot

Combine ingredients and bring to a boil; then cook over low heat for 20 minutes. Place the fish (such as red snapper, salmon, or trout) in the mixture and simmer until done (the flesh should be opaque and flake easily). Remove fish and place on a serving platter. Strain the liquid, add ¼ cup heavy cream for each cup of stock, thicken, and serve over the fish. Or serve with a variety of sauces; for instance:

Hollandaise, plain or with ¼ cup of lobster or shrimp added to each cup of sauce

or

¼ cup heavy cream beaten into Hollandaise

or

¼ cup Hollandaise, ¾ cup medium Cream Sauce

or

½ cup sautéed oysters, or shrimp, or any other shellfish, or a mixture of them

or

½ cup sour cream, 1 cup grated cucumber, 1 tablespoon minced onion, ¼ teaspoon salt, ⅛ teaspoon paprika.

POACHED RED SNAPPER

FOR EIGHT

For one 6-pound red snapper:

Salt and white pepper
1 bay leaf
½ sliced onion
1 stalk celery
¼ sliced carrot
Few sprigs of parsley
Few slices of lemon

Sprinkle fish cavity with salt and pepper and fill with rest of ingredients. Wrap in foil, shiny side in, with foil overlapping on top. Place in a roasting pan on a rack. Pour boiling water over until top of rack is reached. Cover and steam on top of the stove over medium heat for 30 minutes; water should simmer. Test with a fork for fish to flake. (That is why you have the foil overlapping on top of fish.) Remove fish to serving platter, and slip foil out. Remove vegetables and with a sharp knife strip off the skin from the gills to the base of the tail. When serving, cut in portions to the backbone, then remove bone and cut lower half. Use the same method for poaching whole salmon — that is, if you do not have a fish poacher. I personally like a cold sauce with the hot fish — especially Cucumber Sauce.

CUCUMBER SAUCE

FIVE CUPS

3 cups peeled, seeded, and chopped cucumbers
⅓ cup chopped green onion
1½ teaspoons lemon juice
1½ cups sour cream
2 tablespoons mayonnaise
Few drops Worcestershire sauce
Salt and white pepper

Mix and season to taste.

FILET OF SOLE MOLD

FOR EIGHT

4 filets of sole
Juice of 1 lemon
1 cup finely chopped mushrooms
4 tablespoons whipped butter
1 pound white crabmeat or any white fish, flaked
½ cup soft white bread crumbs
¾ cup skim milk
4 eggs, beaten
3 tablespoons melted butter
2 tablespoons lemon juice
Salt and white pepper

Line a lightly buttered 2-quart Pyrex bowl or soufflé dish with the sole filets sprinkled with the lemon juice. Lightly sauté the mushrooms in the butter. Mix with the crabmeat or white fish. Soak the bread crumbs in the milk and squeeze dry. Add to the crab mixture. Pour in the beaten eggs and melted butter. Blend in the 2 tablespoons lemon juice and season with salt and white pepper. Pour into the fish-lined mold. Cover with foil or wax paper. Place in a pan of hot water and bake at 350° for 1 hour. Unmold on a heated serving tray and serve with Shrimp and Dill Sauce.

SHRIMP AND DILL SAUCE

THREE CUPS

2 tablespoons butter
1 cup uncooked small shrimp
2 tablespoons flour
2 cups skim milk
2 teaspoons lemon juice
1 teaspoon dill weed
Dash of cayenne

Melt butter; add shrimp and sauté until pink (about 1 minute). Add flour; cook 1 minute. Pour in milk and cook until thickened. Add lemon juice, dill, and cayenne.

FILET OF SOLE ROULADE

FOR SIX

3 pounds sole (filets of equal size and thickness)
½ pound fresh salmon, boned and fileted
2 tablespoons whipped butter or margarine, melted
1 teaspoon salt
Water
Dry white wine
1 lemon, sliced

Wash sole and salmon in cold water and pat dry. Lay the filets of sole on a piece of foil, and brush them with the melted butter. Sprinkle with salt. Start at narrow end of fish and roll just enough to hold a slice of salmon securely, then finish rolling loosely and insert a toothpick crosswise to hold the roll together. This may be done early in the day and refrigerated. Place in a shallow pan lined with foil, the shiny side up. Cover with half water, half dry white wine. Add the sliced lemon. Bring to a full boil. Lower the heat to simmer; cover and steam for 8 to 10 minutes. Remove with a slotted spoon to a heated serving tray and serve with Caper Sauce.

CAPER SAUCE

TWO CUPS

1 tablespoon whipped butter
1 tablespoon flour
1½ cups yogurt
½ cup liquid from poaching
¼ cup capers
2 tablespoons chopped parsley
Salt and white pepper to taste

Melt the butter, add the flour, and cook until foamy. Add yogurt and liquid; cook over hot water until thickened. Add capers and parsley. Season with salt and pepper. You may substitute small shrimp or thinly sliced cucumbers for the capers.

GRAPEFRUIT FLOUNDER

FOR FOUR

Mild-flavored fish, like flounder or red snapper, have an affinity for grapefruit, especially when combined with white wine.

4½ pounds flounder
Salt
2 tablespoons butter
2 tablespoons olive oil
1 tablespoon chopped onion
1 tablespoon chopped parsley
1 cup dry white wine
12 grapefruit sections

Sprinkle the flounder with salt. Melt the butter with the olive oil; add the onion, parsley, and wine. Lay the flounder in and simmer for 5 or 10 minutes. Place the grapefruit sections on top; put in a 450° oven and bake until the top is brown — about 15 minutes. Serve at once with a wedge of fresh lime in place of the usual lemon.

STUFFED FISH

FOR EIGHT

Stuffed fish of any kind makes it a company dish! You may use this for trout, snapper, or flounder.

2 cups cooked chopped shrimp or crabmeat
1 3-to 4-pound boned trout or snapper
2 eggs
1 cup cream
2 tablespoons butter
½ cup chopped canned or fresh mushrooms
2 teaspoons chopped chives
1 tablespoon flour
Salt and paprika
4 tablespoons dry sherry
2 limes

Mix the shrimp, egg, and ½ cup of the cream together. Melt butter, add mushrooms and chives, and sauté until soft; add flour and cook until bubbly. Add shrimp mixture and cook until thick. Place fish in a buttered baking dish and spread the mixture between the two sides of the fish. Pour over the remaining cream; sprinkle with salt and paprika. Add sherry and bake at 350° for 45 minutes. Serve with fresh lime quarters. When stuffing small flounder (and the ½- to ¾-pound size are best), slit along the backbone and cut the flesh of the fish away from the bone but leave intact. Spoon as much stuffing into slit as possible.

RED SNAPPER WITH COCONUT

Another easy fish dish. Dip filets of red snapper in pineapple juice. Dot generously with butter; sprinkle with salt and paprika. Bake at 300° until partially done. Cover with freshly grated coconut, or Angel Flake. Return to oven until done. Baste frequently. Serve with fresh lime slices.

QUENELLES OF SOLE

FOR EIGHT

1 pound filet of sole
1 cup cold heavy Cream Sauce (made with 3 tablespoons butter, 3 tablespoons flour, 1 cup milk)
Pinch of nutmeg
½ teaspoon salt
1 egg white, beaten stiff

Put the filet of sole through the finest blade of your food chopper twice. Mix with Cream Sauce, nutmeg, and salt. Put through a sieve. Stir in egg white. The mixture should be light and airy. Using two tablespoons, shape into 16 ovals. Put on a buttered pan and refrigerate several hours. Poach in hot water over low heat, not boiling, for 10 minutes. Remove with a slotted spoon and dry on paper towels. You may serve with any cream sauce, but the one I like I call Grenadine. In the strict sense of the word it isn't, but here is how to make it:

GRENADINE SAUCE

2 tablespoons butter
1 tablespoon paprika
2 tablespoons flour
2 cups whipping cream
Salt and white pepper
2 ounces brandy

Melt butter; add paprika and cook 1 minute. Add flour. Cook until bubbly. Add cream and cook until thickened, stirring with your French whip. Season to your taste. Heat the brandy, ignite, and pour into the sauce. As a rule two quenelles are served with the sauce poured over.

I sometimes add Greenland shrimp or Alaskan king crabmeat to the sauce. You may use fish, especially pike, for the quenelles, or raw chicken or veal, free of fat and skin.

GULF TROUT AMANDINE

FOR FOUR

4 filets of Gulf trout (6 to 8 ounces each)
Flour and salt
½ cup butter
½ teaspoon onion juice
¼ cup blanched, finely slivered almonds
1 tablespoon lemon juice

Wash and dry the fish. Dust lightly with salt and flour. Heat half the butter and all the onion juice in a heavy skillet and cook fish until a light brown. Remove and place on a hot serving dish. Pour off the grease left in pan and add remaining butter to the same pan. Add the almonds and brown slowly. Add lemon juice, and when the mixture foams pour it over the fish. Garnish with something green.

ICELAND TROUT WITH MUSTARD SAUCE

Today in most markets you will find a canned fish that is delicious, Iceland trout. There are five in a can. As a first course serve one very cold with a lemon cup filled with Mustard Sauce: 1 cup yogurt, 1½ tablespoons Dijon mustard. You will find yourself using these fish whether you are counting calories or not.

SALT MACKEREL IN CREAM

FOR FOUR

Great for breakfast entertaining.

1 pound salt mackerel
1 cup light cream

Soak mackerel overnight in water to cover. Drain and wash with cold water. Place in a shallow buttered pan or casserole and pour half the cream over the fish. Bake 15 minutes at 375°; add rest of cream and bake 5 minutes longer. Serve with boiled potatoes in butter and chopped parsley.

SALMON TIMBALES

FOR SIX TO EIGHT

2 pounds skinned and boned salmon, fresh or canned
Approximately 2 cups white wine or half water and half wine
1 teaspoon minced shallots or onion
2 egg yolks
1 teaspoon lemon juice
1 teaspoon salt
Few grains cayenne pepper
2 teaspoons cornstarch
1⅓ cups milk
½ cup heavy cream, whipped

Place salmon in a shallow skillet one inch deep with the white wine (or water and wine). Add shallots. Bring to just below boiling point, reduce heat, and cook gently until fish flakes when tested with a fork. Lift out and drain (or use canned salmon, but be sure to remove skin and bones). Combine with the lemon juice and egg yolks and grind in a meat grinder or electric blender; the mixture should become a paste. Add the seasonings and cornstarch. Mix thoroughly. Pour in the milk. Cool and add whipped cream. Fill a well-buttered ring mold or individual custard cups. Set in a pan of hot water. Bake at 350° until firm, or cook covered on top of stove in the hot water at low heat. Turn out at once on hot serving tray. Serve with the sauce you prefer. I like to use slivered cooked fresh asparagus added to a Basic Cream Sauce.

SALMON MOUSSE

FOR EIGHT

1 tablespoon unflavored gelatin, softened in ¼ cup cold water
1 cup hot sour cream (do not boil)
1 pound canned or 2 cups leftover cooked salmon or other fish
¼ cup mayonnaise
1 tablespoon grated onion
¼ cup finely chopped celery
1 cup whipping cream
Salt and white pepper to taste

Add softened gelatin to hot sour cream. Cool. Add the salmon, mayonnaise, onion, and celery. When mixture begins to congeal, fold in the cream, whipped. Season and pour into a wet mold. Chill. Decorate with slices of pimento and black olives.

FRIED FISH

FOR FOUR

If you are in Texas over a reasonable period of time you will, no doubt, find yourself frying fish. Those fishermen think they know how, too. Some insist the fish must have been swimming on its right side going down the left side of the waterway, but be that as it may, *fry* it!

4 Gulf trout or red snapper filets (or whole if small)
1 egg white, lightly beaten
1 cup cornmeal, salted to suit your taste
1 cup shortening or peanut oil

Wash and dry the fish, dip in egg white, then in salted cornmeal. Heat oil in heavy skillet and fry fish in hot fat until brown. Turn once. Serve with lemon and tartar or cocktail sauce.

FISH FILETS THERMIDOR

FOR FOUR

There comes a time when you cannot find the fresh fish you would like to have. This recipe is especially good for frozen fish of a white variety, but you may use any fish.

1-pound package fish fillets
Dry white wine
4 tablespoons butter
4 tablespoons flour
1 teaspoon salt
1 cup milk
1 cup cream
¼ cup dry sherry
1 can sliced mushrooms
½ cup Parmesan cheese

Poach the fish in half water and half wine. Remove, drain, and place in a buttered casserole. Melt the butter; add the flour and salt. Cook until bubbly. Add the milk, cream, and sherry, and cook until thick. Cover the fish with the mushrooms, then the sauce. Sprinkle with the cheese and bake in a 350° oven until brown and sizzling.

FROGS' LEGS

FOR EIGHT

8 pairs fresh frogs' legs
2 tablespoons lemon juice
Flour
¼ cup butter
2 tablespoons olive oil
1 clove garlic, crushed
2 tablespoons chopped chives
2 tablespoons dry white wine
Salt and white pepper
Chopped parsley (optional)

Cover the frogs' legs in water mixed with the lemon juice; soak for 1½ to 2 hours. Dry and dust lightly with flour. Shake off excess. Melt butter; add oil and garlic. Sauté garlic 1 minute. Add chives and frogs' legs. Shake pan while cooking to prevent sticking. Turn once. When golden brown, add wine, season with salt and pepper, and chopped parsley if you wish. Use the same treatment for shrimp or chicken, especially the wings, which make a good cocktail morsel.

KING CRAB À LA HELEN

FOR EIGHT

2 pounds frozen king crab legs, cut in 1-inch chunks
Sherry
1 teaspoon salt
1 cup whipping cream
1 pound Bel Paese or Muenster cheese

Place crab chunks in a lightly buttered shallow casserole or skillet. Sprinkle with sherry and salt. Pour cream over crab to just cover the bottom of the casserole or skillet. (I use my crêpe suzette pan.) Sprinkle heavily with the shredded cheese. Heat until cream is bubbly; then run under the broiler to melt and brown the cheese. Do shrimp and scallops the same way — all divine.

CRABMEAT LORENZO

FOR EIGHT TO TEN

½ cup finely chopped green onions
1 cup finely chopped mushrooms
½ cup butter
½ tablespoon Dijon mustard
½ cup dry white wine
1 cup Cream Sauce (made with 1 tablespoon flour, 1 tablespoon butter, 1 cup milk)
½ cup half-and-half
½ tablespoon Worcestershire sauce
1 pound lump crabmeat
¼ cup finely chopped parsley
Salt and white pepper

Sauté onions and mushrooms in butter until soft. Add mustard, wine, Cream Sauce, cream, and Worcestershire. Heat, add crabmeat and parsley; season with salt and pepper, and keep warm over hot water until served. King crab, shrimp, or mixed seafood may be substituted.

DEVILED CRAB

FOR EIGHT

1 pound fresh crabmeat (approximately 3 cups; pick over carefully for shell pieces)
4 tablespoons lemon juice
2 teaspoons onion juice

Mix and allow to stand. In the meantime, sauté:

2 tablespoons chopped onion, and
2 tablespoons chopped green pepper
in 2 tablespoons butter

Add:

1 tablespoon chopped parsley
1½ teaspoons dry mustard
½ cup bread crumbs mixed into
½ cup mayonnaise
½ cup thick Cream Sauce
2 teaspoons catsup
1 teaspoon Worcestershire sauce
½ teaspoon curry powder

Mix with the crab. Pack crab shells full; sprinkle with mixture of half bread crumbs and half Parmesan cheese and bake at 350° until brown. Or fry in deep fat. Or use china shells. I keep a loaf of French bread in the refrigerator for crumbs. Grate it on the fine side of a four-sided grater.

CRABMEAT NORFOLK

FOR FOUR

1 pound lump crabmeat
3 teaspoons cider vinegar
⅔ cup butter

Place crabmeat in casserole, pour the vinegar over, add melted butter, and place in oven at 400° until sizzling hot. Serve at once with rice and a creamy cole slaw. Before you cook the rice, sauté a few minutes in butter. For an interesting combination, julienne pieces of Virginia ham can be added to the crab just before baking.

CREOLE CRAB

FOR EIGHT

2 tablespoons chopped onion
½ clove garlic
1 tablespoon butter
2 cups drained canned tomatoes
Salt and pepper
¾ cup cream
1 tablespoon flour
1 cup sliced mushrooms, sautéed in butter
2 tablespoons diced pimento
1 pound lump crabmeat (approximately 3 cups; pick out all shell pieces)

Sauté onions and garlic in butter until soft. Remove garlic; add tomatoes and salt and pepper to season. Stir in cream and flour mixed together and cook until mixture thickens. Add mushrooms, pimento, and crabmeat and heat thoroughly. Serve over rice cooked with a little curry in the water.

CRABMEAT CHANTILLY

FOR FOUR OR SIX

1 pound lump crabmeat
2 tablespoons butter
½ cup sherry
2 tablespoons flour
2 cups light cream
Salt and pepper
2 packages frozen asparagus
1 cup whipped cream
4 tablespoons Parmesan cheese

Sauté the crabmeat lightly in the butter. Add the sherry and simmer until liquid is reduced by half. Add the flour and cream (or you might use canned cream of mushroom or celery soup), season, and cook until thickened. (Fork-stir to keep the crabmeat in lumps.) Cook the asparagus and drain. Place in the bottom of a well-buttered casserole. Pour the crabmeat mixture over, spread the whipped cream over, sprinkle with the cheese, and brown under a low flame.

Substitute any seafood, or even chicken, for the crabmeat; add any vegetable in place of the asparagus. Add slices of avocado before spreading the whipped cream — or mushrooms — or browned almonds. It is a versatile dish, high in calories, but worth it. Nice for a buffet supper.

SEAFOOD PILAF

FOR SIX

¼ cup chopped onion
3 tablespoons chopped celery
2 tablespoons butter
2 cups cooked rice
2 cups canned tomatoes
½ teaspoon salt
¼ teaspoon paprika
½ cup grated American cheese
2 cups lump crabmeat, lobster, or shrimp

Sauté the onion and celery in the butter until onion is yellow. Add the rice, tomatoes, seasonings, and half the cheese. Stir until the cheese is melted. Add the seafood. Pour into a well-buttered casserole and sprinkle with the remaining cheese. Bake at 325° until hot and bubbly.

ABOUT LOBSTERS

There is one thing to remember when you buy a lobster: buy the best. Lobsters, if they are bought alive, should be alive, and you will know by the prancing they do; if they are sleepy, leave them alone. If buying a cooked lobster, test it by straightening out the tail. If the tail springs back into a curled position, the lobster was alive when it was cooked. When buying a frozen lobster, be sure you know the reliability of the concern from which you buy it. Frozen lobsters remain in perfect condition for months, but buy only from a reliable firm.

LOBSTER IN SHERRIED CREAM

FOR FOUR OR SIX

2 cups cooked lobster meat (frozen, canned, or fresh)
¼ cup melted butter
1½ tablespoons flour
½ teaspoon curry powder
½ cup sherry
2 cups light cream
2 egg yolks
¼ cup heavy cream
¼ cup freshly grated Gruyère or Parmesan cheese

Sauté the lobster meat quickly in melted butter. Remove lobster from the skillet. Add the flour and curry and rub with a wooden spoon to make a paste. Stir in sherry and light cream. Simmer 3 minutes over very low heat. Mix together the egg yolks and heavy cream. Pour some of the sherry mixture into this, slowly. Stir the egg-cream mixture back into the sauce, add the lobster, and mix well. Bake in a slow (not over 300°) oven long enough to make it bubbling hot, about 10 minutes. Dust the top lightly with freshly grated Gruyère or Parmesan cheese and place under the broiler long enough to brown.

LOBSTER TAIL AU GRATIN

FOR FOUR

4 8-ounce lobster tails
4 tablespoons butter
½ pound fresh mushrooms or 1 cup sliced canned
3 tablespoons flour
2 cups milk or half-and-half
Salt and pepper
¼ cup grated Parmesan cheese
2½ cups canned artichoke hearts, drained
1 cup grated Swiss cheese
Paprika

Boil lobster tails 12 minutes. Remove, cool, and split. Remove meat by running your thumb under thick end to loosen, then pull and slice in ½- to 1-inch thicknesses. Melt the butter, add the mushrooms, and sauté at medium heat for 5 minutes. Remove mushrooms and add the flour. Cook until bubbly. Add milk and cook until thick, stirring constantly. Season with salt and pepper. Return mushrooms to pan. Spread bottom of a buttered shallow 1½- or 2-quart casserole with half the grated Parmesan. Add lobster, artichokes hearts, and Swiss cheese in layers. Cover with mushroom mixture. Sprinkle with remaining Parmesan mixed with a little paprika. Bake at 350° for 30 minutes or until hot and bubbling. Substitute any vegetable for the artichokes and any seafood, chicken, veal, or ham for the lobster.

LOBSTER AND CHICKEN À LA CRÈME

FOR EIGHT TO TEN

½ cup butter
1 tablespoon minced shallots
2 cups uncooked lobster meat, cut in large dice
¼ cup dry sherry
4 tablespoons flour
3 cups half-and-half
4 cups cooked breast of chicken, cut in large dice
Salt and white pepper
Chopped truffles

Melt the butter; add the shallots and sauté 1 minute. Add lobster and sauté 2 minutes, fork-stirring. Pour in sherry, cover, and cook until liquid is reduced. Add flour and cook until bubbly; add cream and cook until thickened. Mix in chicken and heat thoroughly. Season to taste with salt and white pepper. Sprinkle with chopped truffles.

Any time you add foie gras (goose liver pâté) to a meat preparation you will enrich the dish, so save your pennies and have a tin of pâté hidden away for special occasions. Take the same attitude about truffles. Both give meats and poultry a flavor you will enjoy.

TO COOK SHRIMP

1½ pounds shrimp
3 quarts boiling water containing
3 teaspoons salt (1 teaspoon salt to each quart of water) and
3 slices of onion

Boil shrimp for 5 to 8 minutes (depending upon the size of the shrimp), or until the shells turn pink. Drain, rinse with cold water to chill; remove shells and dark intestinal vein running along the back.

You may also clean the shrimp before cooking. Then drop them into the salted, boiling water and simmer until they curl. Cleaned shrimp takes less time to cook.

You really have to watch them or they will overcook, and what is worse than a tough old shrimp?

Shrimp dishes are popular any way, in Newburg Sauce, in Rarebits, Creole Sauce, Curry, and Gumbo. I do like to toss them in a bit of butter before adding to any sauce.

I like Sautéed Shrimp in Sherry. Peel and clean uncooked shrimp, allowing 8 large ones for each serving. Sauté in:

2 tablespoons sweet butter

until they begin to curl. Add:

2 tablespoons dry sherry and finish cooking.

Eat from the skillet you cook them in, so have a presentable one.

You can sauté scallops in sherry by the same method, or make a stew with milk or cream, as above.

A cup of light cream or milk may be added in place of the sherry. Bring to a boil and season with salt and a whiff of cayenne for a good stew.

PAELLA

FOR EIGHT

When I want my guests to watch me cook, which isn't often (the watching, I mean), I do a paella. This could be a one-dish supper with salad and bread, and can be made as expensively or as cheaply as you wish. I recommend it to young brides who want to make their party food appear ample. I always recommend it be brought to the table in the pan it was prepared in, preferably a paella pan, which can be used for other things. I like to use a patchwork quilt for my table (it looks full already), a whole loaf of bread to slice or hard rolls, and perfect peaches used as a centerpiece. Then I tell my guests peaches are the dessert. I find my guests either eat them or take them home, sometimes both.

3 tablespoons olive oil
1 cup diced onion
1 clove garlic, minced
½ pound fresh lean pork, cut in cubes
1 2-pound broiling chicken uncooked, meat cut from bones, or 1 pound uncooked turkey meat
1 cup white rice, uncooked
1 pound sliced mildly seasoned smoked sausage
1 cup peeled sliced tomato, fresh or canned
3 cups chicken broth
½ cup dry white wine
Pinch of saffron
1 pound uncooked shrimp, peeled
1 uncooked sliced lobster tail
2 dozen mussels in shell or littleneck clams
2 tablespoons pimento, chopped
Salt and pepper
¼ cup finely chopped parsley

Heat the oil in the paella pan. Add the onion and garlic, cooking them until soft and yellow, not brown. Remove. Add pork and chicken and sauté at medium heat until brown. Remove from pan. Add rice and sausage and stir until lightly toasted. Stir in tomatoes, the cooked chicken, pork, broth, wine, and saffron; cook covered about 25 minutes. Add reserved onion and garlic, shrimp, lobster, and mussels or clams; cook 6 minutes, stirring with a fork. Add pimento and stir. Season with salt and pepper. Add parsley and serve at once. Paella is best when eaten immediately. Leftovers freeze well, but the seafood will be soft — sorry! You can use whatever proportions of meat, fish, and rice you like, but this recipe is the one I find everyone likes.

GARLIC BROILED SHRIMP

FOR EIGHT

Peel 2 pounds uncooked medium shrimp (15- to 20-count to the pound). Split, remove intestinal vein. Wash well, put in a pan, and cover with:

4 tablespoons finely minced parsley
4 cloves of garlic, minced
1 cup salad oil (olive oil is better, but it is expensive)
Salt and pepper

Leave in refrigerator all day — and night, too, if you have the time. When ready to serve, place on a shallow pan with the oil that clings to them and broil 3 minutes on each side. Salt lightly. Be sure you do not overcook, or they will be tough and stringy. Sprinkle with freshly ground black pepper. Good, too, to charcoal broil out-of-doors. They are still better if you split, wash, and leave the shells on, but you would need to serve finger bowls.

BUTTERFLY SHRIMP

FOR SIX

24 large shrimp, about 2 pounds, shelled and deveined
2 tablespoons soy sauce
2 teaspoons sherry
1 teaspoon salt
½ teaspoon grated ginger
3 eggs, whites beaten separately
3 tablespoons cornstarch
3 tablespoons flour
3 tablespoons cold water
Bowl of ice
Peanut oil

Cut shrimp halfway through on inside curve; spread out to form a butterfly. Pour over the marinade (soy sauce, sherry, salt, ginger). Marinate for 30 minutes. Remove and dry thoroughly on paper towels. Mix a batter with the egg yolks, cornstarch, flour, and water. Fold in egg whites. Place in a bowl of ice to keep cold. I add a couple of ice cubes to be sure the batter is cold. Heat at least 2 inches of peanut oil to 350°. Dip the shrimp in the batter and coat well. Fry until golden brown. Serve at once with a hot mustard dip. I make mine by stirring dry mustard into the syrup left from pickled peaches or watermelon.

SHRIMP, ALMONDS, AND CHIVES

FOR SIX OR EIGHT

I find this a wonderful buffet idea and usually serve it on a cocktail buffet with small silver-dollar-size patty shells (buy them).

2 pounds shrimp (peeled, deveined, quick-frozen ones)
4 tablespoons butter
¼ cup brandy
1 quart heavy cream
½ teapoon paprika
Salt and pepper to taste
1 cup browned whole almonds
¼ cup chopped chives

Defrost the shrimp — or buy raw shrimp in the market and peel. Sauté in the butter until they begin to turn pink. Add the brandy and ignite. When it burns off, add the cream and cook until thick. Season. Add the almonds and chives. Keep hot over hot water.

A bowl of salad greens with slivers of Swiss cheese and ham and a tart French dressing, herb-buttered bread, and partially frozen peaches with lemon ice would make a good combination of flavors.

VOL-AU-VENT VENETIAN SHRIMP

FOR SIX OR EIGHT

½ cup butter
2 pounds shrimp
2 teaspoons capers
2 tablespoons brandy
1½ cups whipping cream
2 peeled, seeded, and chopped tomatoes
2 teaspoons tomato paste (you may omit)
Salt and pepper
Patty shells

Melt butter; add the shrimp and sauté for 3 minutes at medium heat. Stir in capers. Add brandy and ignite. After flame subsides mix in cream and tomatoes; cook at low heat until cream reduces a little. Add tomato paste and seasonings, and heat.

Vol-au-vent is a patty shell filled with a creamed mixture, seafood or fowl as a rule, and covered with the pastry lid. Literally means "windward flight," so be sure the patty shells are light and be sure to heat them.

FRIED SHRIMP

FOR FOUR

2 eggs
1 cup milk
1 pound large shrimp (uncooked)
1 cup flour
1½ teaspoons garlic salt
36 saltines, smashed with the fingers

Beat the eggs and add the milk. Clean the shrimp and split down the back to butterfly. Dip in the flour seasoned with garlic salt, then into the egg and milk, then in the smashed saltines. Fry in deep fat until golden brown. Serve with a good cocktail sauce or Rémoulade.

CURRIED SEAFOOD STEW

FOR EIGHT

¼ cup butter
2 tablespoons onion, chopped fine
2 teaspoons curry powder
½ pound uncooked shrimp, sliced
¼ pound diced sea scallops
½ pound crabmeat (fresh, frozen, or canned) or filet of sole
3 cups milk
2 cups half-and-half
2 tablespoons sherry
6 or 8 saltines
Salt and pepper

Melt butter; add onion and cook until soft. Add curry and cook 1 minute. Mix in the shrimp and scallops and cook 2 minutes. Pour in other seafood, milk, and half-and-half. Bring to a boil, then remove from heat. Add the sherry and let stand over hot water until ready to serve. Crush the saltines and add just before serving. Season to taste with salt and pepper.

CHEESE AND SHRIMP CASSEROLE

FOR FOUR

¼ pound fresh mushrooms
2 tablespoons butter
1 pound fresh cooked shrimp
1½ cups cooked rice
1½ cups grated aged Cheddar cheese
½ cup cream
3 tablespoons catsup
½ teaspoon Worcestershire sauce
½ teaspoon salt
Dash of pepper

Slice mushrooms; sauté slowly in butter 10 minutes or until tender. Mix lightly with shrimp, rice, and cheese. Combine cream, catsup, Worcestershire sauce, and seasonings; add to shrimp mixture. Pour into casserole; chill overnight, if desired. Bake in moderate oven (350°) 25 minutes. A hearty flavor.

BROILED OYSTERS

FOR SIX

Select 3 dozen large plump oysters (watch your fish man count them out). Chop 1 clove of garlic and 2 tablespoons of parsley and mix with the oysters. Place in a bowl and cover with cooking oil (olive oil is best, but not necessary). Let them stand in the refrigerator for several hours, the longer the better. Place on a flat pan with the oil they have soaked in and broil under direct heat until the edges curl. Don't ever overcook this little bivalve — when his body puffs and his edges curl, he is done; take him out quick. Serve at once on bread sautéed in butter, or on a thin slice of ham or Canadian bacon. They are wonderfully good eating. You can also stick a toothpick in them and serve as an hors d'oeuvre, but have plenty of them — they catch on.

BAKED OYSTERS

FOR FOUR

1 cup small white bread cubes
½ cup butter
1 clove garlic, crushed
2 dozen large oysters
Salt
Nutmeg
Light cream

Sauté the bread cubes in butter with the garlic until golden brown. Remove the garlic. Cover the bottom of 4 individual casseroles with a layer of the sautéed bread; place 6 oysters on top, sprinkle with salt and a few grains of nutmeg, cover with cream, and sprinkle the remaining bread cubes on top. Bake at 375° for 15 minutes. Serve at once.

OYSTERS ROCKEFELLER

FOR SIX

36 large oysters in shells
½ cup finely chopped parsley, or raw fresh spinach, or watercress, or all of them
1 tablespoon finely chopped onion
½ cup butter
1 clove garlic, finely chopped
½ cup white bread crumbs (no crust) ground as fine as you can get them
A few drops Tabasco sauce
½ teaspoon salt
A few drops absinthe (if you have it — or skip it)

Have the fish man open the oysters for you. Pack rock salt in 6 pie or cake pans and arrange 6 oysters in a circle on each pan. Put parsley and onion through the meat grinder, using a fine blade, or else chop it by hand into very fine pieces; mix with the butter, garlic, and bread crumbs, and spread this mixture lightly over the oysters. Add seasonings. Bake at 450° for 10 minutes. Then put the pans on dinner plates and serve. Just garnish with a wedge of lemon.

CELESTIAL OYSTERS

FOR EIGHT

Specially special if the night is cool, the spirits high!

24 large oysters
1 teaspoon salt
¼ teaspoon cayenne pepper
24 thin slices cooked turkey
24 thin slices bacon
Toothpicks
2 tablespoons butter

Drain oysters; season with salt and cayenne. Wrap each in a slice of turkey, then in bacon, and secure with a toothpick. Melt butter and pan-broil rolled oysters until the bacon is cooked, turning frequently. Serve with a dish of sparkling cranberry sauce.

SCOTCHED CRAYFISH

FOR SIX TO EIGHT

4 tablespoons sweet butter
½ pound diced fresh mushrooms (you may omit)
2 pounds frozen crayfish, shelled
2 ounces Scotch whiskey
1½ pints whipping cream
2 tablespoons flour
2 tablespoons butter
½ teaspoon Worcestershire sauce
Dash of Tabasco

Melt the butter, add the mushrooms, and sauté for 1 minute; add crayfish meat and cook until hot. Pour in the whiskey and ignite. Add cream when flame subsides and stir while heating, but do not boil. Make a paste (beurre manié) of flour, butter, and rest of ingredients. Add to the cream mixture. Cook for 5 minutes or until thickened. Serve in pastry cups or on rice as an entrée.

Chicken and Turkey

The only way to get good poultry today is to know your dealer (you do not call the man who cuts up your chicken a butcher; he is a dealer) or else resort to the quick frozen. A good young bird, regardless of whether it is a turkey or a chicken, should be plump and have a creamy appearance (because of a layer of fat under the skin), free from blemishes.

In choosing the size, allow three-quarters of a pound per serving. The larger the bird the larger the proportion of solid meat; for instance:

a 4½-pound roasting chicken will provide 6 servings
a 5-pound fowl will provide about 3 cupfuls of diced meat
a 15-pound turkey will provide 20 servings

When buying poultry, have your dealer cut it the way you wish — split it for broiling, cut for frying or fricasseeing — as he can do it more easily than you.

After you get the bird home, wash it thoroughly inside and out under running water, removing pieces of red spongy lung and liver that may be present.

BOILING A CHICKEN

To boil a chicken (or turkey) to use either for fricasseeing or for salads, creaming, and such, you must remember to cook at low heat.

1 4½- to 5-pound fowl, whole or cut up
1 quart hot water
1 piece celery
1 slice of onion
1 sprig of parsley
1 whole carrot
1 tablespoon salt

Clean the fowl and place in a kettle; add the hot water and other ingredients, bring to boiling point, cover tightly, and let simmer over *low heat* until tender, about 1½ or 2½ hours, depending on the age of the fowl. Anyhow, cook it until it is *tender,* and all the time at *low heat;* turning up the gas won't help. Let the meat of the chicken cool in the liquid. And when you remove the bird, use the stock left (you should have at least 2 cups) for fricassee or for soup.

FRICASSEE SAUCE

FOR FOUR

Fricassee Sauce for chicken is so easy; why do so many people try to make it difficult?

3 tablespoons chicken fat from cooked fowl — or butter
4 tablespoons flour
2 cups chicken stock
½ cup cream (you may omit and use ½ cup more of the chicken stock)
Meat from a 4- to 5-pound fowl (boiled)
Salt and pepper to your taste

Melt the fat; add flour and cook until bubbly. Add chicken stock and cook until smooth, stirring constantly. Add cream and continue cooking until thickened and smooth. Season to your taste, pour over the chicken, either removed from the bone and sliced or diced, or cut up in serving pieces. Serve hot, from a deep platter or casserole, with light dumplings or baking powder biscuits on top. A bit of dried sage added to the biscuit gives it a flavor people talk about. Southerners like rice with a fricassee.

SMOTHERED CHICKEN

FOR FOUR

2 1½-pound broilers, cut in half
or
4 chicken breasts, 6-ounce size
Flour
Salt and pepper
Shortening or butter to make ½ inch in the skillet when melted
2 cups Fricassee Sauce

Wash and dry broilers and dust lightly with flour, salt, and pepper. Fry in hot shortening in a heavy skillet until light brown. Remove and drain. Place in a pan, pour Fricassee Sauce over, cover, and bake at 350° for 1 hour, or until chicken is tender. Halves of browned almonds or fresh sautéed mushrooms added to the sauce dress it up for company. I like to serve a slice of broiled canned pineapple on top of each serving, and a medley of peas with white and wild rice.

You may smother chicken in almost any sauce you like, but always brown it first. The baking time is about the same. These variations I have found popular:

Bake in Creole Sauce and serve with Pink Rice.
Bake in Mushroom Sauce; serve on a thin slice of broiled or baked ham.
Bake in Barbecue Sauce; serve with Au Gratin Potatoes.
Bake in medium Cream Sauce sprinkled with grated Parmesan cheese and paprika.
Bake in leftover turkey or veal gravy.
Bake in canned Clam or Crab Bisque, thinned with cream.

Use aluminum foil to cover your baking pan, if you do not have a tight cover; but be sure to turn the corners and seal tightly.

FRIED CHICKEN

A Yankee, misplaced or not, hesitates to mention fried chicken south of the Mason-Dixon line, but I speak up. Choose fryers of not over 2 pounds, allowing half a fryer for each person. Wash and dry, and cut into the size pieces you like. (Bite-size pieces are good for cocktail parties.) Season with salt and pepper, dip in cold buttermilk, sweet milk, or cream, and dust with flour. I like to add a little curry powder to the flour, about ¼ teaspoon to 1 cup of flour. Fry in hot shortening in a heavy skillet until golden brown, turning frequently. Remove and drain on absorbent paper or a clean towel. Place in a pan with just a few drops of water or stock, cover tightly, and place in oven at 350° for 20 minutes. Serve hot with

CREAM GRAVY

Pour all the fat except 2 tablespoons out of the pan in which the chicken was fried. Add 1 tablespoon of flour and cook until brown and bubbly, stirring the crusty pieces of fat that will cling to the skillet into the flour mixture. Add 1 cup of cold milk, stirring constantly until the gravy is thickened, about 5 minutes. Season with salt and pepper to your taste.

OVEN-FRIED CHICKEN

Select broilers and season with garlic salt and pepper; dust with flour and place in a casserole. For each broiler pour ¼ cup of melted butter over. Cover tightly and bake at 350° for 30 minutes. Remove cover and finish cooking to desired doneness.

CURRY OF CHICKEN BREASTS

FOR FOUR

2 tablespoons chopped onion
2 tablespoons chopped celery (may be omitted)
3 tablespoons butter
¼ teaspoon salt
2 teaspoons curry powder
3 tablespoons flour
1 cup milk (or half milk, half chicken stock)
½ cup cream
1 tablespoon dry sherry (may be omitted)
¼ cup diced pickled peaches
4 6- to 8-ounce chicken breasts
1 cup chicken broth
Croutons (you may buy them prepared if you wish)
Parmesan cheese

Sauté onions and celery in the butter until onions are yellow; add salt and curry powder and mix thoroughly; add flour and cook until bubbly. Add milk and cream, stirring briskly until smooth and thick, and cook until all the starchy flavor has disappeared. Add sherry and fruit.

Poach the chicken breasts in chicken broth or water. Add to the curry sauce and simmer for 10 minutes. Spoon over the croutons, sprinkled with Parmesan cheese.

BREAST OF CHICKEN IN ASPIC

FOR EIGHT

8 6-ounce boned whole chicken breasts or half breasts
4 cups chicken broth, consommé, or water
White wine
2 tablespoons unflavored gelatin
Pâté de foie gras
Truffles or hard-cooked egg

Poach the chicken breasts in the chicken broth until tender, about 20 minutes. Remove the skin and any fat clinging to the chicken. Clarify the broth (or used canned chicken consommé). For 2 cups of consommé, pour in ½ cup white wine, heat, and add softened gelatin. Pour a thin layer of the consommé in a shallow pan; refrigerate to set. Place the breasts on top and pour over them a thin layer of gelatin mixture. Refrigerate. Spread a tablespoon of pâté on top of each breast and again pour on a thin layer of gelatin. Refrigerate until set. Decorate with truffles, sliced hard-cooked egg, or both. Repeat with the gelatin mixture. When remaining gelatin becomes syrupy, pour over and chill thoroughly. Remove chicken to a chilled tray, chop the extra aspic, and surround the chicken.

There is a Swiss granulated unflavored gelatin called Lucul in gourmet shops. You can use it for all aspic preparations, and I wouldn't be without it — but then maybe I am a bit lazy.

CHICKEN KIEV

FOR SIX

Chicken Kiev recipes are many; this one I like best.

6 whole breasts of chicken (from 1½-pound broilers), boned
Butter
Flour seasoned with salt and pepper
Egg batter (1 cup milk, 1 egg, 1 tablespoon flour, ½ teaspoon salt)
½ cup sliced mushrooms
1½ cups sour cream
½ cup chives

Wash chicken breasts and dry thoroughly in a clean towel. Split the long way of the breast and insert a pat of butter in each slit. Roll up tight and fasten with skewer or toothpick. Roll in flour, and dip in batter. Roll lightly in seasoned flour again, and fry in butter until brown and tender; or if you are a deep-fat artist, cook in deep fat. Drain off the fat left in the pan and add the mushrooms. Simmer 1 minute; add the sour cream and chives. Simmer until it starts to boil; place in a chafing dish and place the cooked breasts on top. Serve at once, or spill brandy over the top and ignite, then serve. Heat the brandy first and it will light easier. The breasts may be served without the sauce, and will be equally popular. Or place in a casserole and pour the sour cream, sautéed mushrooms, and chives over and bake at 350°, covered, until thoroughly heated.

SUPREME OF CHICKEN, NANETTE

FOR SIX

6 chicken breasts, boned
Salt and pepper
¼ teaspoon marjoram
¼ cup butter
½ cup dry sherry
2 cups cream
3 egg yolks
½ cup crabmeat
1 tablespoon parsley
6 large mushrooms
½ cup grated Swiss cheese

Remove skin from chicken breast. Sprinkle with salt and pepper and rub with the marjoram. Sauté in the butter over low heat until done. Remove, and add the sherry to the pan. Cook until almost evaporated. Add the cream and egg yolks. Cook over low heat until thickened. Take enough of the sauce and mix with the crabmeat and parsley to stick the flakes together. Sauté the mushrooms and fill with the crab mixture. Place the breast in a buttered shallow casserole, with a stuffed mushroom on top of each. Pour the remaining sauce over, add the cheese, and run under the broiler until brown.

BROILED CHICKEN CHALET

FOR FOUR

2 1½-pound broilers, cut in half
Flour, salt, and pepper
1 cup water or chicken consommé
2 tablespoons melted butter

Wash and dry the broilers; roll in seasoned flour and place breast side down in a shallow pan. Add water and melted butter, cover, and bake at 350° for 1 hour, or until soft. Remove; turn the breast side up, sprinkle with paprika, a little melted butter, and salt if necessary. Run under the broiler at medium heat until crisp on the outside. Serve at once.

One nice thing about this recipe: you may do the baking ahead of time and broil the chickens when you need them; in fact, you can keep them in your refrigerator a couple of days before finishing.

BREAST OF CHICKEN À L'ORANGE

FOR EIGHT

8 chicken breasts
½ cup flour
2 teaspoons salt
1 teaspoon paprika
½ cup butter or margarine
2 cups orange juice (or half orange juice and half dry white wine)
Garnish of toasted nuts, avocado, papaya, mushrooms, orange or grapefruit slices (you may omit)

Remove bones yourself if you wish, but buy boneless chicken breasts if possible. Remove skin, dust lightly with mixture of flour, salt, and paprika. Sauté in the butter at medium heat until a golden brown. Add orange juice, cover, and simmer for 15 minutes. Baste once or twice. Uncover; reduce liquid, if necessary, to a slightly thickened sauce. When serving I like to mound whatever I'm serving it with — rice or noodles or vegetables — in the center of my serving tray, and stand the breasts up around it. Pour the sauce over the chicken. Garnish with slices of avocado or papaya, or both, and nuts or mushrooms. If avocado or papaya are not available, use orange and grapefruit sections.

CHICKEN AND GREEN CHILES CASSEROLE

FOR EIGHT OR TEN

1 4-pound chicken or 2 2½-pound frying chickens, or 2 pounds canned chicken, boned

Cover chicken with water plus 1 tablespoon salt. Cook until tender. Cool, and remove chicken from bones. Cut in large pieces.

4 tablespoons butter or chicken fat
1 cup coarsely chopped onion
3 tablespoons flour
2 cups milk
1 cup chicken broth
1 4-ounce can green chiles, seeded and cut in strips
1½ teaspoons salt
½ 10-ounce can Rotel tomatoes with green chiles (you may omit)
10 or 12 tortillas, torn into small pieces
1 or ¾ pound grated sharp Cheddar cheese (4 cups)

Melt the butter or chicken fat. Add the onion and sauté 1 minute. Add flour; cook until bubbly. Pour in milk and broth and cook until thickened, stirring with a French whip. Mix green chiles and salt with the sauce; add the Rotel tomatoes. Place a layer of chicken in the bottom of a buttered shallow 3-quart casserole, then layers of tortillas, cheese, and sauce. Repeat, with cheese on top. Bake at 375° until bubbling. This may be prepared ahead and frozen. For myself I make individual casseroles and freeze to have when I crave a touch of Mexico.

If you like this recipe hotter, add 2 tablespoons slivered jalapeño peppers.

BREAST OF CHICKEN WITH CHANTERELLES

FOR EIGHT

---

8 4- or 6-ounce whole chicken breasts, boned and skin removed
½ cup flour
1½ teaspoons salt
¼ teaspoon paprika
⅔ cup butter
1½ cups chanterelles or thinly sliced mushrooms
4 tablespoons flour
½ cup dry sherry
3 cups half-and-half
½ cup grated Gruyère cheese

Flatten chicken with heel of your hand and lightly dust the chicken in the combined flour, salt, and paprika. Melt butter and sauté 5 minutes, full side down. Turn and cook 5 minutes more. Remove and keep warm. Add chanterelles and cook 1 minute. Add flour; cook 1 minute. Pour in sherry and cream; cook until thickened. Use your French whip and stir constantly to avoid lumps. Add cheese. Return chicken to skillet and heat thoroughly. Correct seasonings, place chicken in a casserole, and pour sauce over. Heat in a 350° oven. You may omit cheese, but the cheese makes it creamier. Sometimes I add slivered cooked ham, about 1 cup for this amount.

For a brunch or supper I cut the uncooked chicken in thin strips and proceed as above, but sauté the chicken only 5 minutes, stirring constantly. I serve the chicken in crêpes (sprinkled with half Parmesan and half Gruyère cheese and heated) or spooned into pastry shells or over spoon bread or whatever suits my fancy at the moment.

Chanterelles are an edible yellow field mushroom with a very short stem. The canned ones from Europe are not too expensive, so you can be as extravagant as you wish in using them. (Be sure to examine them for sticks and stones.) They have a distinct flavor that is especially good with chicken or veal. I like them tossed in a green salad also.

BREAST OF CHICKEN PIQUANT

FOR EIGHT

8 whole chicken breasts, 6- or 8-ounce
1 cup flour
2 teaspoons salt
¼ teaspoon white pepper
⅔ cup butter or margarine
2 tablespoons salad oil
1 teaspoon minced shallots
2 garlic cloves, minced
Juice of 4 lemons
½ cup finely chopped parsley

Remove bone from chicken or buy boneless. Remove skin and flatten chicken with the heel of your hand. Lightly dust with flour and seasonings. Heat butter and oil with the shallots and garlic and add breasts, full side down. Sauté lightly, about 6 minutes. Turn once. Continue cooking. When done, remove to a platter or casserole and keep warm. Add lemon juice to pan and dissolve any cooked brown particles. Boil 1 minute. Correct seasonings, add parsley, and pour sauce over chicken. Serve at once.

BREAST OF CHICKEN PROSCIUTTO

FOR FOUR

4 boned chicken breasts
2 tablespoons flour
4 tablespoons butter
4 thin slices prosciutto (Italian ham)
1 white truffle sliced (you may omit)
¼ pound Mozzarella cheese
¾ cup chicken bouillon or water
½ cup dry white wine
2 tablespoons brandy

Remove skin and flatten chicken breasts with a cleaver, or use the heel of your hand. Dust with the flour, and sauté slowly in the butter until brown on both sides. Place the ham on top of each piece, followed by the truffle and a slice of cheese. Add the bouillon and cook until reduced by one half. Add wine and reduce again. Add brandy and ignite. Serve with the sauce left in the pan. Use thin slices of any kind of ham if you cannot get prosciutto.

Serve the chicken with saffron rice and undercooked green beans tossed with lemon butter.

CHICKEN BREAST IN CREAM WITH APPLES

FOR FOUR

4 broiling-size chicken breasts, or 2 1½-pound chickens, halved
4 tablespoons butter
2 tablespoons minced onion
4 peeled fresh apple rings, ½ inch thick
¾ cup cider
¼ cup brandy
1 cup heavy cream
Salt and pepper

Sauté the chicken breasts in the butter with the onion over low heat. Poach the apple rings in the cider until soft. Add brandy to the chicken and ignite. Always light brandy and burn off. You destroy the raw taste of the brandy. Add cider left from poaching the apples. Cook at low heat until chicken is tender, about 10 minutes. Add cream and continue cooking until the sauce is thickened. Season to your taste. Place chicken on serving platter, a slice of apple on each piece and pour sauce over all. Run under broiler to brown.

COLD CURRIED CHICKEN MOUSSE

FOR SIX TO EIGHT

1 tablespoon unflavored gelatin
1 cup milk
2 tablespoons butter
½ teaspoon curry powder
1 tablespoon flour
½ teaspoon salt
4 cups finely diced chicken
½ cup mayonnaise
½ cup whipping cream, whipped

Dissolve the gelatin in ¼ cup of the milk. Melt the butter, add the curry powder, cook 1 minute, then add the flour. Cook until bubbly. Add ¾

Sauté the onion in butter until lightly browned. Cut chickens in half and brown lightly. Add paprika and lemon juice. Cover tightly and cook over low heat until tender. Remove chicken and keep hot. Add flour to saucepan; season with salt and pepper. Blend in the sour cream, stirring constantly over low heat until smooth and thick. Pour sauce over the chicken. Serve on a hot platter, with fine noodles cooked in bouillon, and peas, mixed together at the last minute.

NO-NAME GEORGIA CHICKEN

FOR TWO

The following was served to me in Georgia. I do not think I ever ate chicken prepared any better. No name to it — but here it is.

1 broiler, split in half
¼ pound butter, melted
2 tablespoons chopped parsley
2 green onions, chopped fine
½ cup mushrooms, chopped fine
¼ clove of garlic, grated
Salt and pepper
Fresh, soft bread crumbs

Place broiler halves in skillet with the butter. Add parsley, onion, mushrooms, and garlic. Cover and simmer slowly, turning occasionally until done. Remove, season, roll in the bread crumbs, return to the skillet, and broil under low heat until the chicken and crumbs are brown. Pour the seasoned butter remaining in the skillet over the chicken as you serve. It was served to me with rice, and the sauce went over the rice instead of the chicken.

CHICKEN AND ARTICHOKE HEARTS IN NEWBURG SAUCE

FOR EIGHT OR TEN

6 tablespoons butter
6 cups cooked chicken, cut in 2-inch pieces
3 tablespoons dry sherry
1½ cups half-and-half
4 egg yolks, well beaten
1 tablespoon plus 1 teaspoon lemon juice
½ teaspoon salt
⅛ teaspoon white pepper
2½ cups canned artichoke hearts

Melt 3 tablespoons of the butter, add the chicken, and heat. Add sherry and ¾ cup of the cream. Let come to a boil. Add rest of cream mixed with beaten egg yolks, stirring all the time. Add lemon juice, salt and pepper, and rest of the butter. Add the artichoke hearts and heat until thickened at low heat. *Do not boil.* This sauce is not as thick as a cream sauce and will take 10 minutes to cook after eggs are added. If you make this dish ahead of time, reheat over hot water.

CHICKEN CRÈME

FOR FOUR

2 1¾-pound broiling chickens, whole
½ teaspoon salt
1 teaspoon curry powder
¼ cup butter
¼ cup chopped onion
¼ cup water or dry white wine
¼ cup brandy
1 cup heavy cream

Rub chickens with salt and curry powder. Put in a casserole with the butter and onion, breast side down. Roast at 350° for 30 minutes; baste with the wine or water. Turn breast side up and continue roasting about 45 minutes or until chicken is done (the leg bone will wiggle). Pour the brandy on and ignite. Remove chicken. Add the cream to juices and cook on top of the stove until a thickened sauce for the chicken is made. Serve on mixed rices with a dish of chutney on the side. This dish may be prepared ahead and reheated.

CHICKEN ALMOND HASH

FOR FOUR

2 cups medium Cream Sauce
1 cup diced cooked chicken
½ cup sautéed mushrooms
½ cup slivered toasted almonds

Combine all ingredients and heat in a skillet. Serve on rounds of oven-buttered-and-toasted bread spread with a thin layer of deviled or Virginia ham.

CHICKEN HASH

FOR TEN OR TWELVE

Hash is good for informal entertaining, a Sunday brunch, or a late supper after football games and such. Spoon Bread or a Grits Soufflé should be somewhere near, too, especially if Texans are present.

4 cups medium Cream Sauce
3 cups finely diced cooked chicken
½ cup finely diced cooked potatoes
½ cup finely diced cooked carrots
½ cup finely diced cooked celery
Salt and pepper

Mix all ingredients together; place in a buttered casserole or chafing dish and set in the oven at 350° until thoroughly hot. Grated Parmesan cheese sprinkled over the top before baking makes it more delicious.

CHICKEN HAWAIIAN

FOR SIX

3 1½-pound broilers
4 tablespoons butter
Salt and pepper
1 cup water or chicken consommé
1 cup shredded pineapple
3 tablespoons chopped green pepper
1½ cups freshly grated coconut

Wash, split, and dry the broilers. Rub with the butter, salt, and pepper. Place in an uncovered casserole and add water or consommé. Bake at 350° until golden brown and tender. Remove casserole from the oven, cover with the pineapple, green pepper, and shredded coconut; place a tight-fitting lid on the pan and return to the oven for 20 minutes.

CHICKEN JAPANESE

FOR EIGHT

Chicken Japanese has a subtle Oriental flavor that is most pleasing.

¼ cup butter
½ clove garlic, chopped fine
¼ cup flour
2 cups chicken stock
1 tablespoon soy sauce
2 cups diced chicken
Salt and pepper

Melt the butter and add the garlic; sauté for a minute; then add flour and cook until bubbly. Add stock and soy sauce, mix thoroughly, and add chicken and seasonings. Serve, as soon as the chicken is added, over fried Chinese noodles and rice.

CHICKEN TERRAPIN

FOR SIX

Chicken Terrapin has always been a favorite luncheon dish, and I like it even better made with smoked turkey.

4 tablespoons flour
4 tablespoons butter
2 cups milk (or half milk, half chicken stock)
3 hard-cooked egg yolks
1 teaspoon dry mustard

Make a cream sauce of the flour, butter, and milk. Mash the egg yolks with the mustard and add to cream sauce; let stand over hot water for 1 hour. Just before serving, add:

3 hard-cooked egg whites, slivered
2 tablespoons lemon juice
1½ cups diced chicken
2 tablespoons slivered ripe olives
2 tablespoons slivered pimentos

Cook over the hot water until hot. Serve in a buttered rice ring, or over pastry. Garnish with tissue-thin slices of green pepper.

CHICKEN IN PASTRY

FOR TWELVE TO FIFTEEN

Many people have asked for the Chicken in Pastry, which is my answer to the leftover problem. For a hostess interested in serving many people at a time, it has possibilities — for church suppers it would be profitable. You can do your pastry many ways. Make individual turnovers to bake or fry; or a dumpling as you would for an apple; or a long roll to bake and slice. You may freeze it successfully, too.

4 cups finely chopped or ground chicken
¾ cup finely diced celery
¾ cup mayonnaise
1 tablespoon salt
1 tablespoon onion juice
2 tablespoons chopped parsley
1 recipe piecrust (as for a 2-crust pie)

Mix all the ingredients and fill the pastry as you wish. If for individual rolls or turnovers, cut pastry in about 5-inch squares; if for cocktail-party size, 2-inch squares (they are extremely popular). Brush with melted butter and bake at 375°; or fry in deep fat. If you wish a roll for slicing, roll out and spread like a jelly roll and serve with any sauce you like. I like it with an assortment of fresh-cooked vegetables added to a medium Cream Sauce, or Fricassee Sauce. Red Hot Apples are good with this, too (apples cooked with Red Hot candies).

Use the same recipe for leftover meats, ham, or turkey.

CHICKEN CRÊPES

FOR EIGHT

2 tablespoons butter
1 tablespoon minced onion or shallots
2 tablespoons flour
1½ cups half-and-half
1 cup diced cooked chicken
¼ cup dry sherry
16 crêpes
¼ cup grated Parmesan and Gruyère cheeses
¼ cup sliced almonds

Melt butter; add shallots and sauté until yellow. Add flour and cook until bubbly; add half-and-half. Cook until thickened and smooth. Add chicken and sherry to half of the sauce. Place 2 tablespoons of chicken mixture in each crêpe, and roll. Place in a buttered shallow casserole. Cover with remaining sauce. Sprinkle with cheese and sliced almonds. Bake at 450° until brown. Substitute crabmeat or tuna or leftover veal for the chicken.

CHICKEN AND NOODLES CASSEROLE

FOR SIX OR EIGHT

Chicken and noodles is the perfect answer for a low-cost supper dish, and no doubt you will have everything in your pantry.

4 tablespoons butter
4 tablespoons flour
2 cups chicken consommé or milk
½ cup light cream
¼ cup dry sherry
1 8-ounce package fine noodles
2 8-ounce cans of chicken
1 can sliced mushrooms
¼ cup grated Parmesan cheese or Gruyère or half and half
¼ cup blanched almonds
1 teaspoon butter

Make a sauce: Melt the butter, add the flour, and cook 1 minute. Add consommé or milk, and cream. Cook until thick and smooth; add the sherry. Cook noodles according to directions on package. Drain, wash, and pour into a buttered casserole. Add the chicken, mushrooms, and cream sauce. Sprinkle with the almonds, cheese, and butter and bake at 350° until the almonds are brown and the casserole is bubbling.

CHICKEN TETRAZZINI

FOR EIGHT

2 cups Mornay sauce
2 cups medium Cream Sauce
1½ quarts cooked spaghetti, well washed and drained
4 cups chicken meat cut from the bones, in as large pieces as possible — or turkey — or shrimp
½ cup sautéed fresh mushrooms (use up your stems this way)
¼ cup dry sherry

Mix together and pour into a well-buttered shallow casserole. Cover generously with Parmesan cheese, sprinkle lightly with paprika, and bake at 350° until brown and bubbly. Vary it by using toasted almonds in place of mushrooms.

ORIENTAL CHICKEN

FOR EIGHT OR TEN

One of the truly delicious luncheon dishes I have eaten is Oriental Chicken served over Cheese Soufflé. It is adaptable for any kind of entertaining and would be especially suitable for a wedding breakfast or luncheon when you wish something light and delicious.

½ cup butter
½ cup flour
1 tablespoon salt
1 cup cream
3 cups milk
2 cups chicken stock

Melt butter in top of double boiler; add flour and salt and cook until bubbly; add cream, milk, and chicken stock, stirring until smooth. Cook over hot water for 30 minutes. Just before serving add, and heat thoroughly:

2 cups diced chicken, large dice
½ cup sautéed mushrooms
½ cup blanched almonds
1 cup sliced water chestnuts
¼ cup pimento, cut in strips
¼ cup dry sherry

Serve over Cheese Soufflé, or in a pastry shell; over rice — or what have you; but over soufflé is the most delightful thing you will ever taste. You may reserve the mushrooms — sauté whole and top each service with one. Fresh asparagus served across a grilled tomato completes a beautiful plate.

CHICKEN MEXICALI

FOR EIGHT

4 cups cooked chicken or turkey, cut in large cubes
4 cups sliced sweet onions, sautéed until brown
2 cups canned tomatoes
4 cups chicken stock or consommé
½ teaspoon Worcestershire sauce
Salt and pepper to taste
24 tortillas, cut in strips and fried in deep fat until crisp
Provolone cheese

Mix together the chicken, onions, tomatoes, stock, Worcestershire sauce, and salt and pepper. Place in a buttered casserole and cover with the fried tortillas. Press them into the mixture until covered with the juices. If it is not moist enough, add more stock — it should be moist. Cover with grated Provolone cheese and bake uncovered at 350° for about 30 minutes or until brown. This has been a most popular buffet supper entrée.

CHICKEN LIVERS AND MUSHROOMS

FOR FOUR

1 pound of chicken livers
Milk
¼ cup butter
2 tablespoons sherry (optional)
2 tablespoons butter
½ pound fresh mushrooms
1 cup sour cream
2 tablespoons sherry
Very thin toast or sautéed eggplant slices

Cover the livers with milk for an hour. Drain, and sauté in the ¼ cup of butter until brown. Add the sherry (or not) and simmer until completely absorbed. Remove from pan, add 2 tablespoons butter, and sauté the mushrooms lightly. Add the sour cream and sherry and heat only until hot. Place the chicken livers on the toast or thin slices of sautéed eggplant and pour the mushrooms and sauce over.

CHICKEN LIVERS WITH APPLES

FOR FOUR OR SIX

1 pound chicken livers
Seasoned flour
½ cup melted butter
½ cup thinly sliced Spanish onion
8 slices peeled and cored fresh tart apples
2 tablespoons sugar

Dredge the livers in seasoned flour (flour, salt, and paprika) and brown slowly in ¼ cup of melted butter. Sauté in another pan the onions in a little butter and spread over the livers. In the onion-sautéeing pan sauté the apple rings, which have been sprinkled with the sugar, in the remaining butter. Arrange on top of the livers and onions and serve very hot on rice combined with browned almonds.

BROILED TURKEY

The palatability of broiled turkey should be considered as the busy housewife looks around for ways to vary her menu. It will soon be a favorite dish with your family and friends, and for outdoor entertaining it will be a welcome change from expensive cuts of meat.

Choose a young turkey of about 4 pounds. Split in half and snap the hip, wing, and drumstick joints to keep the bird flat while broiling. Season with salt and pepper, brush with melted fat or salad oil, and place in a broiler pan skin side down. Place 7 to 10 inches under heat and broil slowly, turning frequently to brush with melted butter. It will take about 1 hour.

When broiling out-of-doors, hang it on a rack over the direct radiant heat from the hot coals, but do not place on the broiler grate.

TURKEY LOAF

FOR EIGHT TO TEN

One usually thinks of turkey or chicken loaf as a leftover, but this recipe was one of the favorite brunch or luncheon entrées in the Zodiac Room at Neiman-Marcus. It was even a welcomed entrée on our Thursday night buffets. I serve it frequently for a buffet and it is always a request recipe. Bake the Turkey Loaf in a bundt pan or angel food pan. It looks more interesting, as does any loaf.

2 pounds raw turkey (or chicken) meat, ground
4 eggs
1 cup undiluted canned cream of mushroom soup
1½ teaspoons salt
2 tablespoons chopped pimento
2 tablespoons chopped green pepper, blanched
1 cup white bread crumbs
¼ teaspoon white pepper
¼ teaspoon Worcestershire sauce
American cheese, sliced

Markets are beginning to sell ground turkey meat. If yours does not, buy the turkey and ask the dealer to grind it for you — or else do it yourself. No skins. It makes a good burger, too. Mix all the ingredients except the cheese. Put half in the buttered pan, then a layer of American cheese. Fill pan with rest of the mixture. Cover and bake in a 350° oven for about 1 hour. Turn out and serve with any sauce you like, but I like:

MUSHROOM FONDUE

THREE CUPS

½ pound fresh mushrooms
¼ cup butter
¼ cup flour
2 cups half-and-half
1 pound Gruyère cheese, diced
¼ cup dry sherry

Wash and dry the mushrooms and cut in fourths, leaving the stems on. Sauté in the butter for five minutes, stirring constantly. Add the flour; cook until bubbly. Add the half-and-half and cook over low heat, stirring rapidly. No lumps! Add cheese and sherry. Keep warm and serve. Any leftover Turkey Loaf makes a good sandwich the following day, and any sauce reheated and poured over makes it doubly so.

TURKEY AND BROCCOLI MORNAY

FOR FOUR

8 stalks of cooked broccoli
8 thin slices breast of turkey
2 cups Mornay Sauce
4 teaspoons Hollandaise Sauce

Place 2 stalks of hot cooked broccoli on each serving plate, or in 4 portions on a platter. Place 2 slices of hot turkey over the broccoli and pour ½ cup of hot Mornay Sauce over each portion. Place a teaspoon of Hollandaise on top of each and run under the broiler, set at low heat, until bubbly and brown. This is a good party dish, as it stays hot while being eaten, but you must start with everything *hot.*

ROULADE OF TURKEY

FOR EIGHT

A beautiful dinner or luncheon dish; tastes good, too! You can serve it at the table, or in the kitchen. For each serving:

1 thin slice of white meat of turkey, on bottom
1 thin slice of baked or boiled ham, next
3 stalks of cooked asparagus, last

Roll up and place in a buttered baking dish. Cover with Mushroom Sauce and bake at 300° for 30 minutes.

SCALOPPINI OF TURKEY

FOR TWELVE OR MORE

4 pounds thinly sliced raw white meat of turkey
Salt and white pepper
¾ cup flour
¼ cup olive oil
3 tablespoons butter
¾ cup dry Marsala or Madeira
¾ cup chicken or beef broth
¼ cup finely chopped parsley
¼ cup softened butter, not melted

Put the sliced turkey between two sheets of wax paper or foil and pound firmly with a cleaver or rolling pin, but do not pound hard enough to break it up. Lightly sprinkling with salt and white pepper, dip each slice of turkey into the flour, shaking off any excess. There should be only a faint coating of flour. Heat the olive oil and butter in a large skillet. Lay the turkey in one layer deep and not overlapping, and cook at medium heat for 2 minutes on each side. The slices should show streaks of light brown. Remove to serving dish. Pour off excess fat, so that you have about ¼ cup left in pan. Add the Marsala and broth. Cook at high heat until it comes to a boil, scraping all the brown particles in the pan into the liquid. Boil 1 minute, add the cooked turkey and cook about 10 minutes at low heat. Test to see if tender enough. Place in a serving dish and cover with chopped parsley. Put the soft butter in the pan, bring to a foamy state, and pour over the turkey. Add sliced mushrooms if you wish. You may substitute dry sherry for the Marsala or Madeira. It all depends on your taste and budget. I usually serve it with green noodles tossed with cream, butter, Parmesan cheese, and leftover minced ham. Scaloppini freezes well. These are good for buffets because they hold well and leftovers may be frozen and reheated. I freeze them in small packages if left over.

STUFFED TURKEY BREAST

FOR TWELVE OR MORE

Even if you do not have an expert carver around, I think you can use a whole turkey breast to great advantage. It is available frozen the year round in all supermarkets today. There are fewer leftovers, if you are as allergic to them as I am. This preparation is excellent for a buffet.

¼ cup butter
½ cup finely chopped onion
½ cup finely chopped celery
2 tablespoons chopped green pepper, blanched
2 cups cooked rice
1½ teaspoons poultry seasoning
1 egg
¼ cup chopped parsley
½ cup chopped nutmeats or raisins (you may omit)
1 8- to 10-pound turkey breast
Salt and white pepper
Dry white wine or chicken broth

Melt the butter. Add the onion, celery, and green pepper. Cook 1 minute; add rice, poultry seasoning, and egg. Mix thoroughly; add parsley and nuts. Season to taste. Cut the turkey in thick slices from the breast bone to the rib cage, keeping the slices attached to the bone. Stuff the rice mixture into the slits. Sprinkle with salt and pepper and wrap in one layer of cheesecloth to hold the rice stuffing intact. Place in roasting pan and roast at 350°, basting frequently with dry white wine or chicken broth. The roasting should take approximately 25 minutes per pound. If browning too quickly, lay a piece of foil over the top. When finished cooking, remove from the oven, and take off the cheesecloth at once or it will stick to the turkey. Let rest for at least 30 minutes before carving. You may prepare this recipe ahead of time and reheat. It is good cold, too. Serve with the juices left in the pan.

TANDOORI TURKEY

For a cocktail party an 18- to 20-pound turkey should be plenty for 35 to 40 people. After all, it is not a dinner party.

1 quart yogurt
1 cup lime juice
12 cloves garlic, crushed
2 tablespoons grated fresh ginger
2 tablespoons ground coriander
1 tablespoon cumin
1 teaspoon cayenne pepper
1 teaspoon powdered anise (you may omit)
1 18- to 20-pound turkey
1 orange, cut in half, and 2 onions
1 cup melted butter

Mix the yogurt with the lime juice and garlic. Heat all the spices in a skillet and add to the yogurt mixture. Rub turkey inside and out with the marinade, then pour rest of it over the turkey. Put 2 orange halves and 2 onions inside turkey. Cover the bird and marinate 24 to 48 hours, turning the turkey a couple of times. Put in a roasting pan and roast at 375° until the leg is tender (or about 5 hours, figuring 15 minutes per pound). Baste with butter and the marinade. Roast with a piece of foil over top of turkey, but not folded over the pan. Serve cold or warm. Leftovers: dice and put in a curry sauce and serve over rice and fried apple rings.

CURRY OF SMOKED TURKEY

FOR EIGHT TO TWELVE

½ cup butter
½ cup minced onion
1 clove garlic, crushed
3 to 4 tablespoons curry powder, heated in a skillet before using
8 tablespoons flour
4 cups milk, half-and-half, or chicken consommé
3 to 4 pounds smoked turkey, cut in large dice
Salt and cayenne pepper
¼ cup dry sherry

Melt butter; add onion and garlic and cook until yellow but not brown. Add curry powder and cook 2 minutes; add flour and cook until foamy. Remove garlic. Pour in milk; cook and stir with a wire whip until thickened. Add the smoked turkey; heat and then season with salt and cayenne pepper. The turkey is salted, so do not salt the sauce before adding the turkey. Add sherry. Keep hot over hot water or cool and reheat.

Use the same basic sauce for seafood or whatever curry. However, when I curry shrimp, I start with raw shrimp and sauté with the onion and garlic, then remove to add later. They will have much more flavor. Sometimes I heat the milk with 2 cups of coconut, cool and strain, and discard the coconut.

We have a tendency to serve curry on rice because we first heard of it served on rice. I like to use fresh, frozen, or canned cling peach halves, in that order. Dust the peaches lightly with flour and sauté in butter until a lacy brown. Serve curry over them or use cornbread in place of rice.

Other Birds, and Game

Ducks and geese are good variety fowl. Specially raised ducks have a fine flavor and are tender; the Long Island variety are the juicier and meatier (and they haven't flown or waddled down from Long Island, either). The skin is white and the fat, too — and if you can get your dealer to let you feel them, they are tender to touch. They should weigh between 3½ and 4 pounds ready to cook; one duck of this size should serve four people, unless you are duck lovers, and then let your conscience be your guide. The dressing for duck should be tart and on the dry side; a touch of apple, orange, or apricot in it is always a help.

ROAST DUCK

Place duck in roasting pan, sprinkle with salt and pepper, and bake, uncovered, for about 2 hours at 325°. Use no water, and you do not need to baste while roasting. Prick the skin around the tail to let the fat drain out. Pour off the excess fat as it bakes. (When it is done, the leg joint will move loosely and the leg meat will feel soft.)

Thicken 2 tablespoons of the drippings in the pan with 2 tablespoons of flour and add enough water to make a thin gravy. Or serve with:

BIGARADE SAUCE

---

1 orange rind
4 tablespoons duck drippings
2 tablespoons flour
½ teaspoon salt
½ cup orange juice
1 cup water (or half water, half white wine)

Parboil orange rind in a little water for 5 minutes. Drain, remove white portion, and cut into fine strips. Heat duck fat, stir in flour, and cook until bubbly. Add salt, water, and orange juice, stirring constantly until thickened and smooth. Add rind and reheat.

□

Leftover duck is good cold, served with, for instance, Green Bean Salad with Sour Cream Dressing, and a hot spiced apricot or peach. Or my favorite:

SALMI OF DUCKLING

FOR FOUR

---

1 cup leftover duck meat, cut into serving pieces
¼ cup sliced, stuffed olives
A few sliced mushrooms, sautéed (but not necessary)
1½ cups leftover duck gravy (this is the "salmi")

Place in a skillet and bake at 350° until hot. Serve over wild rice.

□

Geese are cooked the same as ducks, but they take longer. Use the same test as for ducks and turkey to determine when tender.

ROAST DUCKLING AU NATUREL

FOR TWELVE OR MORE

Depending on how extravagant you are, there are many ways to estimate how many ducks you will need to prepare. If you serve only half of the breast, you will need 4 ducks; if a quarter, using breast and legs, you will need 2.

2 4- to 5-pound ducks (¼ per serving)
2 teaspoons salt
Juice of 1 lemon or lime
1 teaspoon white pepper
1 orange
1 medium-sized onion
Dry white wine or chicken broth
Garlic, if you like (then you would be cooking the ducks Niçoise style)

There are two schools of thought on roasting duck, depending on whether you like the skin crisp or not. (It doesn't really matter to the duck.) Rub the duck with the salt, lemon or lime juice, and pepper. Place on a rack in a pan. Put one half each of orange and onion in cavity (and 1 clove of garlic, if you wish) and roast uncovered at 450° for 20 minutes. Pour off all melted fat. Return to oven, turn down to 325°, and baste with dry white wine or chicken broth. Roast about 1½ hours or until duck is tender. Wiggle the leg bone! Remove duck. If you wish crisp skin, refrigerate duck until cold or overnight, then return to a 375° oven until thoroughly heated. Baste with juices. Pour off the fat from the juices and add, for a plain sauce, enough chicken broth to make 1 cup and 1½ teaspoons arrowroot or cornstarch and cook until thickened and clear. Strain and serve with the duck, or add ¼ cup brandy or Grand Marnier and ignite. I think the sauce should be passed. Most people like to ladle it for themselves. Throw away orange and onion!

PHEASANTS MADEIRA

FOR SIX

Pheasants receive enthusiastic praise when prepared with Madeira.

6 pheasant breasts
Salt
Paprika
Cream
Flour
½ cup butter
6 thin slices ham
1 cup Madeira
6 slices broiled or fried ham
½ cup heavy cream

Remove skin from breasts, sprinkle with salt and paprika, dip in cream, dust in flour, and sauté lightly in 2 tablespoons of the butter. Add the wine and cover with aluminum foil. Bake about 60 minutes at 350°, or until tender. Place each breast on a slice of ham that has been broiled or fried, add ½ cup heavy cream to the sauce remaining in the baking pan, reheat, and pour over the breasts. Garnish according to your budget. I sometimes add white grapes, split and seeded, to the sauce, and whole canned artichoke hearts.

Serve the legs to the family. Skin the legs and brown in butter. Cover with Creole Sauce and bake at 350° until tender. Serve with rice.

GUINEA HEN MADEIRA

FOR TWO OR FOUR

1 2- to 2½-pound guinea hen
2 tablespoons butter
Salt and pepper
2 tablespoons grated orange peel
1 teaspoon paprika
1 tablespoon currant jelly
1 cup chicken consommé
⅓ cup Madeira
1 cup heavy cream

Rub the hen inside and out with butter, salt, and pepper. Roast uncovered at 350° for 30 minutes, basting with more butter and a little water. Add the orange peel, paprika, jelly, consommé, and Madeira to the roasting pan. Turn the hen. Cover and bake 60 minutes longer, basting frequently. Remove from oven and add the cream. Let simmer for 10 minutes on top of stove, spooning the sauce over the hen frequently.

You never go wrong serving wild rice, and I like to toss a few tiny croutons with it, and grated raw carrots. And sometimes snowpeas and peas — mostly because no one expects it.

ROCK CORNISH HENS

FOR FOUR

4 Rock Cornish hens
Butter and salt
1 carrot
1 teaspoon finely minced onion
1 cup chicken stock — fresh, canned, or made from chicken bouillon cubes
1 jigger dry sherry
1 teaspoon cornstarch

Rub the hens inside and out with butter and salt; place in shallow baking pan small enough so that the hens will touch each other; slice the carrot, add the onion, and place in the pan; roast uncovered at 350°, basting several times during the baking with the chicken stock and drippings. When done (in about 1 hour), remove from pan to a heated serving dish. Reduce remaining stock in the pan to ½ cup, and strain. Add the sherry, mixed with cornstarch, and cook until clear. Pour over the hens.

Dress up for company! Add whole mushrooms, sautéed in butter and a little sherry, and sliced truffles or black olives to the sauce. Serve with wild rice if the budget allows, or converted rice swished around in the drippings. I like to serve them with their openings filled with crisp watercress and spiced kumquats split and placed over their drumsticks.

DEVILED ROCK CORNISH HENS

FOR EIGHT

8 10- to 12-ounce Rock Cornish hens
Salt and white pepper
½ cup Dijon mustard
⅔ cup white bread crumbs
3 tablespoons minced shallots
½ cup butter
White wine

Rub each bird with salt, pepper, and 1 tablespoon of the mustard. Sprinkle with bread crumbs. Place in a square of foil and fold to center. Add 1 teaspoon minced shallots, 1 tablespoon butter, and 3 tablespoons white wine to each package. Fold the foil over tightly and bake at 400° about 50 minutes or until done.

Good for informal eat-on-the-floor to watch a television show. No knives and forks. Good cold too, and for picnics, carried in the foil.

SQUAB IN WHITE WINE

FOR EIGHT

¾ cup butter
8 squab, split down the middle
Salt and white pepper
6 tablespoons chopped shallots
1 clove garlic, chopped fine
1½ cups plus 1 cup Sauterne or Chablis
6 tablespoons chopped parsley

Melt butter in a skillet and lightly brown the squab. Put in a shallow pan or casserole, split side up; sprinkle with salt and white pepper. Add chopped shallots, garlic, and 1½ cups wine. Bake at 425° for 30 minutes, or until tender, basting frequently. (Test for doneness by moving leg.) Remove pan from oven; add chopped parsley and rest of wine. Cook on top of stove until sauce is reduced to desired thickness, but do not thicken.

This is an excellent preparation for Rock Cornish hen and a good picnic item also. Lots of flavor.

LEMON-BROILED SQUAB WITH PAPAYA

The flavor of lemon helps one to enjoy any fowl. Prepare for broiling Rock Cornish hens, squabs, or squab chickens by rubbing inside and out with lemon juice to which a little Tabasco has been added (about

⅛ teaspoon to ½ cup of lemon juice). Place fowl on broiling racks bone side up and sprinkle with finely minced shallots, salt, and white pepper. Broil about 5 inches from heat for 15 minutes. Turn, rub again with the lemon juice and seasonings; broil another 15 minutes. If you like a more definite color, rub with paprika also.

WILD DUCK

Clean and wash the ducks and dry well. Rub inside and out with salt and stuff with raw apple and onion. Cover the breast with strips of bacon; put in oven at 500° and bake 30 minutes; reduce heat to 350° and bake another 30 minutes. Add ¼ cup of red wine for every duck, and bake 15 minutes more. It takes less time for sprigs or teal, but mallards take the full time. Remove the apple and onion; serve the ducks whole or split, with the duck sauce *au naturel* — and with plenty of wild rice.

WILD GEESE

Cook the same as wild duck, adding a clove of garlic with the apple and onion to the inside of the goose. Bake for 30 minutes at 500°; reduce heat to 350° and bake about 1½ hours longer, or until tender.

POT-ROASTED QUAIL

FOR EIGHT

16 or more quail (1 for each guest is not enough)
Salt and paprika
½ cup butter, melted
2 tablespoons salad oil
½ cup dry sherry
Juice of 2 lemons
2 teaspoons Worcestershire sauce
3 tablespoons flour
3 cups half-and-half or whipping cream

Wash quail and remove any shot if possible. Sprinkle the bird with salt and paprika. Tie with string. Sauté in the butter and oil until brown on all sides. Cover and simmer slowly for 1 hour. Add sherry, lemon juice, and Worcestershire sauce. Simmer until liquid is almost evaporated. Remove birds and add flour. Cook until bubbly. Add half-and-half; cook until sauce becomes thick. Add quail and reheat.

QUAIL OR DOVES

Quail and doves are good "potted." Wash and dry; rub with salt and flour and sauté lightly in butter. Remove and place in a casserole or iron frying pan. For 4 or 6 birds, lightly sauté

¼ cup finely chopped onion (or less if you prefer)
½ cup finely chopped mushrooms
1 tablespoon parsley

in the butter left in the pan. Pour over the birds with ½ cup of white wine. Cook for 30 minutes, basting frequently; add ½ cup of heavy cream and, when thoroughly hot, serve with wild rice.

Without the cream, broiled orange slices smothered in currant jelly are a nice accompaniment.

ROAST LOIN OR RACK OF VENISON

FOR EIGHT

2 loins or racks of venison
Red wine or half wine and half water
2 bay leaves
2 onions, sliced
A few juniper berries
8 peppercorns
8 springs of parsley
Salt and pepper
½ cup melted butter
1 cup red wine
1 cup currant jelly
2 tablespoons arrowroot

Cover meat with the red wine; add bay leaves, onions, berries, peppercorns, and parsley. Cover and refrigerate for at least 24 hours. Remove, drain, and dry. Sprinkle with salt and pepper and roast uncovered in a 400° oven for 45 minutes. Baste with the strained marinade and butter. Use a meat thermometer and cook (for about 45 minutes) until medium rare (140°). Remove meat and let rest. Add 1 cup wine and the jelly to juices to make 1 pint or more of sauce. Add the arrowroot mixed with a little cold water to make a paste and heat until thickened. Slice meat in thin slices or into chops and serve with sauce, unstrained.

CHUKARS

FOR EIGHT

8 chukars (Hungarian partridges)
2 cups white bread crumbs
Grated rind and juice of ½ lemon
⅓ cup melted butter
1 egg, slightly beaten
1 clove garlic, minced (if you like)
Salt and white pepper to taste

Wash and dry chukars. Mix rest of ingredients and stuff lightly into the body cavity and between the skin and the breast. Never pack, but always stuff any bird lightly. Tie with string and roast, covered, at 325° about 45 minutes. I use my electric skillet for these. Remove and deglaze pan with dry sherry or brandy. Serve chukars whole with juices.

Dressings for Fowl

An important thing to remember about handling any dressing is to have a light hand. If you are in doubt as to your strength, use a fork to stir and mix.

CHESTNUT DRESSING

TWELVE CUPS

1½ cups seedless raisins (white ones are best)
1 cup melted butter
2 tablespoons salt
2 cups cream
2½ quarts crumbled white bread
1½ cups finely diced celery
4 cups chestnuts, toasted and broken up

Mix together and stuff into the turkey cavity, or bake in buttered casserole at 325° for 1 hour. Very rich — and very good!

OYSTER STUFFING

EIGHT CUPS

---

1 onion
½ cup chopped celery
¼ cup butter, melted
1 clove garlic
1 pint small oysters, drained
2 tablespoons chopped parsley
4 cups soft bread crumbs
1 teaspoon salt
¼ teaspoon white pepper
½ cup light cream

Sauté the onions and celery in the butter with the garlic until soft. Remove the garlic, add the oysters and parsley, and cook until the oysters begin to curl. Add the bread crumbs and seasonings. Stir in the cream; stuff turkey cavity, well rubbed with butter.

SAVORY DRESSING

FIVE CUPS

¼ pound bacon
¾ cup chopped onion
2 tablespoons chopped parsley
1 quart white bread, crumbled in small pieces
¼ cup butter, melted
1 teaspoon salt
½ tablespoon poultry seasoning (use more if you like)
¼ teaspoon pepper
1 egg

Dice the bacon and fry with the onions until crisp. Add parsley, crumbled bread, butter, and seasonings. If you like a moist dressing add enough cold water to moisten. Beat and fold in the egg; stuff the fowl with it, or bake in a buttered casserole until brown. I prefer a dry, crunchy dressing, so I do not add any liquid or egg.

CORNBREAD DRESSING

TWELVE CUPS

Everyone has his idea — so have I.

½ cup onion, chopped fine
½ cup green pepper, chopped fine
½ cup celery, diced fine
⅔ cup butter
6 hard-cooked eggs, chopped
½ cup chopped pimento
2 quarts cornbread crumbs (and be sure the cornbread is well browned)
Salt and pepper
Chicken or turkey stock (or canned consommé)

Sauté the onion, green pepper, and celery in the butter; add cornbread, hard-cooked eggs, and pimento. Season with salt and pepper, and moisten with chicken or turkey stock, or canned consommé. Turn into a shallow well-buttered casserole and bake at 350° until brown on top.

Variation:
Half Cornbread Dressing and half cooked wild rice make a delightful dressing.

RICE DRESSING

EIGHT CUPS

This dressing I use for a vegetable at times. It freezes well. In fact, I think it is better if frozen a few days, then baked. Those Texas politicians I fed for three years always thought it was wild rice, so I didn't correct them.

2 cups Uncle Ben's converted rice
3 large onions, chopped fine
4 large stalks of celery, chopped fine
1 green pepper, chopped fine
Ground heart, gizzard, and liver
½ cup butter
1 tablespoon salt
1 tablespoon poultry seasoning
2 eggs
1 cup chopped nuts (preferably pecans)
½ cup parsley, chopped
Oysters and mushrooms to taste, if desired

Cook rice according to directions on the package. While rice is cooking, sauté onions, celery, pepper, liver, gizzard, and heart together in the butter until thoroughly cooked. Add seasonings and mix. Beat eggs until frothy. Remove sautéed onion mixture from heat, add rice, and fold in beaten eggs, mixing thoroughly. Add chopped nuts and parsley. Add oysters and mushrooms if desired. Loosely fill the turkey cavity and roast the turkey as scheduled, or bake the dressing in a buttered casserole for 25 to 30 minutes at 350°.

TOASTED RICE DRESSING

ABOUT TWO AND ONE-HALF CUPS

½ cup uncooked rice
1 cup water
½ teaspoon salt
3 tablespoons butter
1 tablespoon finely minced onion
1 tablespoon finely minced parsley
1 tablespoon finely minced celery
1 cup bread crumbs, toasted and dried in the oven
½ teaspoon baking powder
1 egg, well beaten
1 teaspoon poultry seasoning

Spread the uncooked rice in a shallow pan and place in 400° oven. Toast until a light brown, stirring frequently to prevent burning. Place rice in a saucepan; add water and salt; cover tightly and cook over low heat until dry. Melt the butter, add the onion, parsley, and celery; sauté until tender. Toss in the toasted crumbs, baking powder, and rice. Add the egg and seasoning; stuff lightly into the bird, or bake for 20 minutes at 350° in a shallow buttered casserole.

WILD RICE STUFFING

ABOUT ELEVEN CUPS

Being a wild-rice fan — and who isn't? — I like to extend it (because it costs so much) as far as I can without losing its identity. This dressing is wonderful with duck or turkey.

1 cup wild rice
Giblets (liver, gizzard, and heart)
2 cups hot broth or water
½ cup finely chopped onion
½ cup butter or margarine
2 quarts oven-toasted dry bread crumbs
1 teaspoon salt
¼ teaspoon ground sage
¼ teaspoon pepper
2 eggs, beaten

Cook the rice according to directions on the package. Chop the giblets fine and cook in water until done. Sauté onion in the butter until yellow in color; add the bread crumbs with the giblets and broth. Add the seasonings and mix lightly. Cover and let stand until the bread is moist. Add the wild rice and eggs, and mix lightly. Pour into a buttered baking dish and bake for 25 minutes at 325°.

FRUIT DRESSING

ABOUT ELEVEN CUPS

2 quarts white bread, cubed
¼ cup diced onion
¾ cup butter
2 cups chicken broth
1 tablespoon salt
¼ teaspoon pepper
1 teaspoon poultry seasoning
2 cups diced apples, or prunes, or stewed apricots
1 cup sliced Brazil nuts

Use stale bread and cut into small cubes. Sauté the onion in the butter, add to the bread, and toast in the oven until dry. Moisten with the broth; add the seasonings, fruit, and nuts; mix and stuff turkey or chicken. Nice with duck or goose, roasted veal, or pork.

Part 5

Beef · Pork · Lamb
Veal · Variety Meats

Beef

PRIME RIBS OF BEEF

Three ribs will feed five or six people, depending on how thin you slice it. Rub the roast with salt, lots of salt, and freshly ground pepper. Peel one clove of garlic, if you are so minded, and push it between two ribs. If not, add to the pan a whole onion, a carrot, a sprig of parsley. Roast uncovered at 350°. I am amazed at the people who still think you burn up the outside to start with. For a rare roast, allow 15 to 18 minutes per pound; for medium, 20 to 25 minutes. If you are a "well done" addict, 30 minutes per pound, and you shouldn't try to roast less than three ribs for good results. Use the same procedure for other cuts for roasting.

TENDERLOIN OF BEEF WITH PÂTÉ DE FOIE GRAS

FOR EIGHT

1 trimmed 4- to 5-pound tenderloin of beef
½ cup dry Burgundy
4 ounces pâté de foie gras
Salt and white pepper to taste
Chopped truffles
1 ounce Cognac

Place the meat in a 450° oven and roast for 25 minutes (internal temperature should be 120°). During roasting, baste with the wine. Remove from oven and save juices; let meat rest about 5 minutes and slice in the size slice you wish. Place on your serving tray. Between each filet slice spread the foie gras, pushing the pieces together again. Run under the broiler; baste with wine if you wish. Cover with chopped truffles. (You can buy truffle peelings, which are good for this recipe and less expensive.) Add 1 ounce warm Cognac; ignite. Serve with Béarnaise Sauce. I usually put the sauce in either fresh or canned artichoke bottoms and surround the meat with them. It then serves as a garnish as well as a sauce for both meat and artichokes.

BÉARNAISE SAUCE

ONE-HALF CUP

1 cup tarragon vinegar
1 tablespoon dried or a few sprigs of fresh tarragon
1 slice of onion
6 egg yolks
1 cup butter
Dash of cayenne

Boil the vinegar, tarragon, and onion until reduced to ⅓ of a cup. Strain into top of a double boiler over hot water. Do not let water boil. Add egg yolks to this mixture, beating with a French whip. Melt the butter and pour slowly into the egg mixture, beating constantly. When thick, remove and place in a pan of cold water to stop the cooking. Add the cayenne and keep at room temperature until ready to serve. Béarnaise Sauce complements any vegetable, poached fish, and beef. I like it on eggs Benedict in place of the traditional Hollandaise.

SAUTÉED SLICED BEEF TENDERLOIN

FOR EIGHT

4 pounds tenderloin or sirloin, sliced ¼ inch thick
1 teaspoon salt
Freshly ground pepper
4 tablespoons flour
1 cup dry red wine
1 cup beef broth
¼ cup butter, melted
¼ cup olive oil

Be sure all fat is removed from meat. Mix the salt, pepper, and flour on a flat pan and dust each slice of meat lightly. Shake off any excess. Pour half the butter and oil into a 10- or 12-inch frying pan and set over high heat. When the pan is hot, add half the meat. Sauté no longer than 2 to 3 minutes. Add a little red wine and let it evaporate. Turn into a warm serving dish and repeat process with remaining steak in the same pan. Remove and keep meat warm. Pour the beef broth into the pan. Bring to a boil; scrape and stir constantly to dissolve all the dark particles. Add rest of wine and boil about 3 minutes. Add the cooked meat only to heat, but do not cook further. If you wish your sauce thicker, add a little arrowroot dissolved in ½ teaspoon lemon juice. You may add thinly sliced onions and mushrooms. I sometimes dip each piece of meat in half soy sauce and half dry sherry or bourbon, sauté quickly, but serve no sauce with it.

I prepare this recipe in my dining room in electric skillets and usually some of my men guests say "Let me" — and I do. I always feel a party is a success if someone else gets into the act.

BEEF TENDERLOIN AND CHICKEN LIVERS

FOR EIGHT

2 cloves garlic
¼ cup olive oil
2 tablespoons Dijon mustard
2 pounds beef tenderloin
1 pound chicken livers
8 bamboo skewers
4 slices bacon, cut in 1-inch pieces
Salt and cracked pepper
Brandy

Mince the garlic; mix with the oil and mustard. Cut the tenderloin into ½-inch slices. Separate chicken livers. Place meat and livers alternately with the bacon on a buttered or oiled bamboo skewer. Rub with the mustard mixture and wrap in foil. When ready to broil, sprinkle with salt and pepper. Broil over charcoal about 5 minutes on each side. Ignite some brandy and pour over. Eat off skewer.

BROILED STEAK

Select your steak cut 1½ to 2 inches thick. Allow ⅓ to ½ pound per person. Remove from refrigerator ½ hour before cooking so that meat will be at room temperature when cooking begins. Trim off any excess fat and wipe with a clean cloth. Put meat on broiler rack greased with some of the fat from the steak. Broil under electric or gas grill 2 or 3 inches below the unit. Sear quickly on one side; turn and broil until at desired stage — 12 minutes if liked rare, 20 minutes if liked medium, and 30 minutes if liked well done. Remove to a *hot platter,* spread with softened butter, and sprinkle with salt and pepper. Serve immediately.

If in doubt as to its tenderness, cover steak with beer and refrigerate for a couple of hours before broiling; wipe dry and proceed.

DOUBLE SIRLOIN STEAK

FOR EIGHT

2 32-ounce sirloin strip steaks (no bone)
Salt and freshly ground pepper
1 clove garlic, chopped fine (you may omit)
¼ cup sweet butter, melted
2 ounces brandy

Rub meat on both sides with the salt, pepper, and garlic. Broil steak 10 minutes on each side. Turn off heat and leave in oven for 15 minutes. Remove to serving platter. Pour sweet butter over and add about 2 ounces of flaming brandy. Slice and serve with juices. One steak will serve 4. Increase broiling time if you like your meat well done. I don't. More vitamins remain if you cook the steak rare.

GINGERED RIB-EYE OF BEEF

FOR TEN TO TWELVE

1 8-pound eye-of-the-rib beef roast
1 tablespoon salt
2 tablespoons grated fresh ginger root
½ cup soy sauce
1 cup sliced onion
1 cup dry sherry or beef consommé

Be sure beef is well trimmed. Rub with salt, ginger, and soy sauce. Place in a roasting pan on top of the sliced onions. Roast at 350°, allowing 10 minutes per pound for rare. Baste with the sherry or consommé. Let rest at least 10 minutes before slicing.

FLANK STEAK

We do not use flank steak enough. The flavor is wonderful. What little fat there is can be trimmed off easily along with the tough membrane. I like to marinate flank steak in half soy sauce and half water or white or red wine for an hour, then broil medium rare, 4 minutes on each side; baste once with some of the marinade. Let rest about 3 minutes, place on a board, then slice across the grain in thin slices; start at the small end of the steak, almost paralleling the board. But be sure the slices are thin or the steak will be tough.

ABOUT BRISKET

I happen to like boiled brisket of beef — my Irish Yankee upbringing perhaps, but it has good flavor and is tender if cooked properly. Make sure you slice it thin. With whipped cream heavily seasoned with horseradish and mustard it makes a cocktail party worth remembering. Or serve with whipped butter mixed with Dijon mustard and green peppercorns:

1 cup whipped butter
1 teaspoon Dijon mustard
2 tablespoons green peppercorns

BOILED BEEF BRISKET

FOR TEN TO TWELVE

1 5- to 6-pound piece of brisket
1 large onion stuck with 2 cloves
1 bay leaf
1 piece celery with leaves
2 carrots
Few sprigs of parsley
6 peppercorns
12 ounces beer (you may omit)
1 tablespoon salt

Place the beef in a kettle and cover with boiling water. Add rest of ingredients. Bring to a boil, reduce the heat to simmer, and cook for 3 to 4 hours or until meat is tender. Add 1 tablespoon salt after 1 hour's cooking. Do not overcook or meat will be stringy and will not slice properly. Remove and keep warm. Cut off any excess fat before serving, but leave on while cooking. If you wish brisket for an entrée, strain the juices left from cooking, skim off the fat, and for each cup of liquid, add:

1 cup whipping cream
¼ cup grated horseradish or Horseradish Sauce
1 teaspoon chopped chives
½ teaspoon dry mustard
¼ cup diced apple

Cook until reduced to a thin sauce. Serve over thinly sliced meat.

SPICY BRISKET OF BEEF

FOR FOUR TO SIX

3 pounds fresh beef brisket
1 teaspoon salt
¼ teaspoon pepper
1 sliced onion
1 stalk celery
½ to 1 cup chili sauce
12 ounces beer
¼ cup chopped parsley

Place brisket in casserole. Season it with salt and pepper. Add sliced onion, celery stalk, chili sauce, and ¼ cup water. Roast uncovered in a 325° oven until brown, about 30 minutes. Pour beer over the meat; cover and bake at the same temperature for about 3 hours, or until tender. Remove meat and strain off all fat. Sprinkle chopped parsley over meat. Cut brisket in thin slices and serve with the juices. This is no dish for a weakling, so serve hashed brown potatoes and sugar-buttered carrots and onions with it.

BEEF CARBONNADE

FOR SIX TO EIGHT

I like this because I can put it in the oven and do other things, like get my hair restyled. It can be prepared the day before or can be frozen for a later meal.

4 pounds lean stewing beef, cut in 2-inch pieces
½ cup flour
½ cup salad oil
2 pounds onions, sliced (about 4 medium size)
6 garlic cloves, crushed
3 tablespoons brown sugar
1 bay leaf
1 teaspoon dried thyme
½ cup chopped parsley
1 tablespoon salt
2 10½-ounce cans beef consommé
3 cups beer
2 tablespoons red wine vinegar

Dredge the meat in the flour and brown in the salad oil on all sides in a skillet. Do only a few pieces at a time. Put in a casserole and add the onions. Brown the garlic in oil left in the skillet. Add to the meat with the brown sugar, bay leaf, thyme, parsley, salt, consommé, and beer. Cover and bake at 325° about 2½ hours or until meat is tender. Pour in vinegar and cook on top of stove until bubbling. If you wish a thicker sauce, add a little arrowroot mixed with cold water. You could use this as a basis for a beef pie or add mushrooms if you wish.

BRAISED BEEF, POIVRE VERT

FOR EIGHT

1 5-pound boneless chuck, top butt, or bottom round of beef
Salt and pepper
3 tablespoons cooking oil
2 cups dry red wine
1 cup beef bouillon
2 teaspoons brown sugar
¼ cup very finely chopped onion
1 clove very finely minced garlic
Dash of nutmeg; pinch of thyme
2 tablespoons green peppercorns
4 tablespoons chopped parsley

Rub meat with salt and pepper, using at least ½ teaspoon salt per pound of meat. Brown meat on all sides in cooking oil. When browned, transfer to a baking dish, adding all other ingredients except the green peppercorns and the chopped parsley. Bake at 350° for approximately 2 hours, basting frequently with the pan liquid. Turn meat twice to ensure even cooking. Remove meat and reduce the pan liquid over high heat until slightly thickened. Add green peppercorns to the sauce. Carve the roast into very thin slices and arrange in serving dish. Pour sauce over all and sprinkle chopped parsley on top, or slice at the buffet table and add sauce as served.

OVEN STEW

FOR FOUR OR SIX

2½ tablespoons butter
¼ cup celery, minced
¼ cup green peppers, thinly sliced
1 clove garlic, minced (you may omit)
½ cup onions, sliced
2 pounds beef stew meat or round steak
2½ tablespoons flour
1½ teaspoons salt
¼ teaspoon pepper
½ teaspoon sugar
1 fresh tomato, peeled and diced
1 4-ounce can mushrooms
2 cups broth or water
½ cup dry red wine
½ cup pimento-stuffed, sliced olives

Melt the butter in a skillet. Add the celery, green peppers, garlic, and onions. Sauté until softened and slightly browned. Cut the meat into 1-inch cubes. Dust with the flour and salt and pepper. Add to the skillet; sauté until browned. Stir in the sugar, tomato, canned mushrooms, broth, and wine. Transfer to a buttered 3-quart casserole; cover. Let stand several hours. Bake 2 hours in a moderate oven, 350°. Stir in the sliced olives 5 minutes before completion.

Serve with Carrots in Cognac and wheat pilaf.

BEEF STEW IN BURGUNDY WITH PARMESAN CRUST

FOR EIGHT TO TEN

¼ cup salad oil
4 pounds beef round or tenderloin, cut in 1-inch pieces
2 tablespoons flour
3 cloves garlic, minced
3 cups dry red Burgundy
2 cups beef broth or water
1 stalk celery
Few sprigs parsley
1 carrot
½ pound diced salt pork, sautéed until crisp
20 small white onions, cooked
20 fresh mushrooms, quartered and sautéed in butter
Salt and white pepper
1 piecrust
¼ cup melted butter
3 tablespoons Parmesan cheese

Heat the oil in the pot you will cook the stew in. Add the beef and brown on all sides. Drain the oil. Add the flour and cook until foamy. Stir in garlic, wine, broth or water, and bring to a boil. Add the celery, parsley, and carrot. Cover and simmer about 2 hours or put in a 350° oven to cook until meat is tender. Remove the celery, parsley, and carrot. Add the salt pork, onions, and mushrooms and simmer until thoroughly hot. Skim off any excess fat from the top. Season with salt and pepper. Transfer to a shallow 2½- or 3-quart casserole. Cover with piecrust, brush with melted butter, and sprinkle with Parmesan cheese, freshly grated if possible. Return to oven to bake at 350° until crust is brown (about 10 or 15 minutes). I like to serve this also as a stew over crisp hashed brown potatoes or thin cornbread — but then I like stew.

BRAISED SHORT RIBS OF BEEF

FOR SIX TO EIGHT

8 pounds well-trimmed short ribs
1 cup flour
1 tablespoon salt
½ teaspoon white pepper
¼ pound diced salt pork
2 cups diced onion
1 cup diced carrots
1 cup diced celery
3 garlic cloves, minced
3 tablespoons brandy (you may omit)
4 cups red wine or beef consommé or half wine (or more)
1 bay leaf
½ cup chopped parsley
⅛ teaspoon thyme

Cut the ribs into serving pieces; dredge in the flour, salt, and pepper.

Place in an oiled roasting pan and roast uncovered at 450° for 25 minutes. Drain off excess fat. Brown the salt pork until crisp; remove pork and sauté the vegetables in the remaining fat until yellow. Add to the short ribs. Ignite the brandy and add with the wine, consommé, bay leaf, parsley, and thyme. Cover and bake at 350° for about 2 hours or until tender. Remove ribs, skim off excess fat, and strain the sauce. Correct seasonings. Return meat to pan, pour the sauce over, and add the crisp salt pork just before serving. You can do ahead of time, as short ribs freeze well. Use the same recipe for brisket of beef. Serve with:

HORSERADISH MOUSSE

---

2 teaspoons unflavored gelatin
¼ cup cold water
1 tablespoon butter
1 tablespoon grated onion
1 tablespoon flour
½ teaspoon dry mustard
1 cup half-and-half
½ cup white horseradish sauce
Few drops Tabasco
Salt and pepper
¾ cup whipping cream

Soften the gelatin in cold water. Melt the butter; add the grated onion and cook 1 minute. Add flour and mustard; cook until bubbly. Pour in half-and-half and cook until thickened. Remove from stove; add gelatin, horseradish sauce, and Tabasco. Season with salt and pepper. Cool. Whip the cream and fold into the sauce. Pour into a wet mold and refrigerate until set.

BEEF HASH AURORA

FOR FOUR OR SIX

---

4 cups ground leftover beef
1 small sweet white onion
1 10-ounce can beef broth, undiluted
¼ cup sour cream (or more, if needed)
¼ cup catsup
½ teaspoon sugar
¼ teaspoon garlic powder
Salt and pepper

In a food grinder, using medium blade, grind together all trimmings you can cut from bones, and all leftover pieces of beef. You should have 4 cups of ground beef for 4 servings. Peel the onion and grind with the beef. Moisten the beef-onion mixture with beef broth, sour cream, and catsup. Add sugar and garlic powder; mix thoroughly. Taste for salt and pepper. Add it, if it needs it, for it depends on how the beef was seasoned in the first place. If the mixture is not quite moist, add more sour cream. The best way of mixing this is with your hands; no spoon will do as well. Pile hash in a skillet or casserole. For topping use:

2 ripe tomatoes
½ teaspoon salt
¼ teaspoon pepper
½ teaspoon sweet dried basil
½ teaspoon sugar
4 tablespoons sour cream

Slice each tomato into 2 thick slices. Arrange these on top of hash. Combine and sprinkle over all the salt, pepper, basil, and sugar. Place a tablespoon of sour cream on top of each tomato. Bake in a hot (425°) oven until heated through and bubbly. The sour cream should be slightly brown; if it isn't, slide the casserole under the broiler for a moment, to finish browning. Serve directly from casserole.

STROGANOFF

FOR SIX

With a leftover roast of beef or veal there is no better dish than this.

4 cups cooked beef or veal
2 tablespoons olive oil
2 tablespoons butter
1 cup thinly sliced and coarsely chopped onion
1½ cups sliced mushrooms
1 cup beef stock or consommé
1½ tablespoons flour
1 teaspoon salt
½ teaspoon whole caraway seeds
A dash of nutmeg
2 cups sour cream

Trim all fat from the meat and cut in strips, about 1 inch long and ¼ inch wide. Heat oil and butter in a skillet; add onions and mushrooms and sauté at low heat until soft. Add meat and continue cooking for 10 minutes; add stock or consommé and cook for 30 minutes. Mix flour and seasonings with the sour cream and add to first mixture. Cook slowly until thick, but do not boil. Remove from direct heat and keep over hot water. I like to serve Stroganoff with fine noodles, well buttered and seasoned with chopped parsley and combined with peas; or add potato balls, cooked in consommé, to the Stroganoff just before serving.

CORNED BEEF
the good old Irish way

To begin with, I say buy good corned beef.

For eight hungry people you use a 4-pound piece of corned beef. I think the brisket is the best; the streak of fat through it helps the texture and flavor. Wash under running water and cover with cold water; bring to a boil slowly and cook 5 minutes, removing the scum that will come to the top of the pot. Then cover and simmer until the meat is tender — about 3 hours, but it could take longer. Cool in the stock until easy to handle. Slice with a sharp knife the long way of the piece of meat and place on a hot platter with just enough of the stock to keep it moist.

Twelve minutes before you are ready to sit down to eat it, cut a medium-sized head of cabbage in eighths, add to the liquid and boil uncovered. Twelve minutes only! Remove and place around the corned beef and eat at once. Just boiled potatoes is the accepted accompaniment; and horseradish or mustard sauce.

Corned beef is one meat I have found that cooking in aluminum foil will do wonders for — just wrap it up and proceed as outlined; just takes twice as long.

MEAT LOAF

FOR EIGHT

Meat loaf can be a sorry concoction or a thing of gastronomical delight. The trouble is that most people overcook it, or rather they use too hot an oven so it is dry and hard on the outside. Good meat loaf is made from fresh-ground beef.

2 pounds chopped beef
¼ pound salt pork, chopped fine
2 eggs, slightly beaten
1 cup milk
3 tablespoons melted butter
1 tablespoon prepared horseradish or 3 tablespoons catsup
2 tablespoons minced onion
¼ teaspoon pepper
1 tablespoon salt
1 cup soft bread crumbs
2 strips bacon

Mix meat and salt pork with the eggs, milk, butter, horseradish or catsup, onion, seasonings, and bread crumbs. Pack in a buttered loaf tin (8 x 4 inches) and cover with the strips of bacon. Bake at 350° for 60 minutes, or until it is well browned and shrinks from sides of tin.

Or dress it up by putting half the meat in the tin and placing three hard-cooked eggs end to end through center of pan, or slices of aged American cheese; pack the rest of the meat in and bake as above. Remove to a hot platter and slice as served, using any sauce you like, or French-fried onion rings and scalloped or au gratin potatoes. Oversized Idaho potatoes baked, split, and topped with thick sour cream, salted and peppered, does it well, too.

Helen's meat loaf baked in an angel food cake pan captured the imagination of cooks and food editors alike. It is handsome and the texture is light.

SWEDISH MEATBALLS

FOR SIX

Swedish Meatballs for a buffet supper are inexpensive and good fare. This recipe was given to me by a good Swedish hostess in Atlanta, Georgia.

2 pounds chopped beef
2 cups soft white bread crumbs
2 tablespoons finely chopped onion
2 teaspoons salt
½ teaspoon nutmeg
4 tablespoons butter

Mix ingredients and roll into walnut-sized balls. Brown in oven at 350°. Cover with beef stock or consommé, seal top of pan tightly with aluminum foil, and continue baking until soft (about 45 minutes). Serve with:

NOODLE CUSTARD

1 package fine noodles
4 eggs
1 teaspoon salt
4 cups milk
A pinch of nutmeg

Cook noodles in boiling salted water until tender. Rinse and drain. Pour into a buttered 2-quart casserole. Mix eggs, beaten until lemon colored, with salt and milk and pour over the noodles; sprinkle with nutmeg and bake at 375° in a pan of hot water until set, about 25 minutes.

Variation:

Combine cooked meatballs with

1 pound sautéed chicken livers
1 pound sautéed whole mushrooms
1 cup Burgundy
2 cups sour cream

Simmer for 10 minutes.

BEEF PATTIES MADEIRA

FOR FOUR

2 pounds ground lean beef
1 teaspoon salt
½ cup Madeira
Cracked pepper
⅛ pound (½ stick) butter
4 slices toast, cut to fit the patties
1 small can liver pâté
4 mushroom caps, browned in butter

Mix beef with 1 tablespoon butter and the salt. Form into 4 patties. Marinate the patties in the Madeira for at least 1 hour. Remove. Sprinkle with cracked pepper and sauté in the remaining butter over high heat for 3 minutes on either side. Remove from pan. Place toast in the butter and sauté. Arranging on an oven-proof dish, place a pattie on each toast slice and cover with a slice of the liver pâté. Top each with a mushroom cap. Pour the remaining Madeira marinade into the pan and simmer for 3 minutes. Pour over patties and place in a 400° oven for 3 minutes. Do tenderloin steaks the same way.

SPICED BEEF

I once suggested that the Neiman-Marcus Epicure Shop list a spiced beef in their Christmas catalog for a gift idea. They had to cut off the orders, as no one fully anticipated its appeal. I received as many, if not more, requests for the recipe. You can wrap and keep it refrigerated for a long time, or freeze. It is worth the effort.

1 pound beef suet
2 ounces ground allspice
2 ounces cayenne pepper
1½ ounces ground pepper
2 ounces ground cloves
2 ounces ground cinnamon
2 ounces ground nutmeg
1 12- to 14-pound top butt of beef or sirloin tip roast
4 to 6 jars saltpeter (buy in a drugstore)
Cracked pepper

Melt suet; add spices and heat 5 minutes. Cool slightly. Punch holes through beef and pour mixture into the holes. I use a wooden-spoon handle to punch the holes. Tie and wrap beef in cheesecloth. Make a brine of saltpeter and water (enough to float an egg). Soak beef for 2 or 3 weeks, refrigerated. Simmer on top of stove in fresh water for approximately 2½ hours. Remove and, while still hot, take off cheesecloth and sprinkle the beef heavily with cracked pepper. Rewrap and refrigerate. Serve cold, thinly sliced, with sliced breads or hot biscuits.

HAMBURGERS

FOR SIX

1½ pounds chopped beef (bottom round, if you can inveigle your butcher to fresh-grind it)
2 teaspoons salt
1 teaspoon Beau Monde seasoning
¼ teaspoon cracked pepper
2 tablespoons cream

Mix meat with seasonings and cream; form into cakes about ½ to 1 inch thick. Preheat the broiling oven for 10 minutes; place hamburgers on buttered broiling rack 3 inches from heat. Broil about 6 minutes on each side, or you may broil in a hot skillet or over charcoal outside. Spread with softened butter and serve with toasted buns or anything your heart desires.

HUNGARIAN GOULASH

FOR FOUR

2½ pounds beef, rump or round, or veal
⅓ cup suet, chopped
½ cup chopped onions
½ clove garlic, crushed
2 cups water
1 cup catsup
½ teaspoon dry mustard
1 tablespoon paprika
2 tablespoons brown sugar
1 tablespoon salt
1 teaspoon Worcestershire sauce
1 teaspoon vinegar
2 tablespoons flour
1 package fine noodles

Cut meat into 1-inch cubes. Brown in suet with onion and garlic. Add water, catsup, and seasonings. Cover and cook at low heat until the meat is tender, about 2 hours. Mix flour with ¼ cup of water and add to the hot mixture, stirring constantly, and cook until thick. In the meantime, cook noodles in boiling salted water. Drain, mix with part of the sauce from the meat, and serve with the meat over them.

Pork

The "little pig who goes to market" saw America first some 400 years ago with the Spanish explorer, De Soto. Since then there has been more controversy over how to cook it, and when, or *if*, you should eat it, than time allows to tell. By all means eat pork — when it is economical to buy it — and cook it well.

STUFFED PORK CHOPS

FOR SIX

The young fry of today are the gourmets of tomorrow, and that goes for some of them right this minute. Every so often I am thrown for a recipe for the under-twelve set, who are bored with the same old thing. Let's face this interest of theirs with foods that are different in both appearance and taste.

3 strips bacon
2 tablespoons chopped onion
1 cup soft bread crumbs
1 cup peeled, chopped raw apple
¾ cup chopped cooked prunes
6 pork chops cut 1-inch thick
Salt, pepper, and flour
½ cup pineapple juice
½ cup Sauterne

Mince bacon and cook until almost crisp. Add onion and cook 3 minutes (medium heat). Add crumbs, apple, and prunes. Cut a slit in each chop and fill with the stuffing and fasten with a toothpick. Sprinkle with salt, pepper, and flour. Brown in a heavy skillet, pour off fat, and add the pineapple juice and wine. Cover and either bake at 325° or cook on top of the stove at low heat until tender, about 1 hour. Add more juice if necessary, or water.

DEVILED PORK CHOPS

FOR SIX

2 tablespoons butter
½ cup chili sauce
½ cup catsup
2 tablespoons Worcestershire sauce
4 tablespoons prepared mustard
1 teaspoon salt
⅛ teaspoon cayenne pepper
6 pork chops, cut 1½ inches thick
½ cup water

Mix butter, chili sauce, catsup, Worcestershire sauce, mustard, salt, and cayenne to make a paste. Spread over chops. Place in skillet and run under broiler and broil at low heat for 5 minutes. Spoon any remaining sauce over chops, add water, and cover. Bake at 350° for 2 hours. Serve from a hot platter. If serving sauce with the chops, be sure to skim all possible fat from top before using.

Do the same as above with Barbecue Sauce.

PORK LOIN

FOR SIX OR EIGHT

Marinate a 5-pound boned pork loin in 2 cups dry white wine overnight with fresh herbs. I like a bit of thyme, rosemary, and tarragon. Remove the herbs; save marinade. Rub pork on either side with 2 tablespoons salt, 2 tablespoons Dijon mustard, and 4 tablespoons brown sugar. Place in roasting pan with clove of garlic, 1 stalk celery, 1 onion, 1 carrot. Bake at 450° covered for 30 minutes. Remove cover, baste with marinade, reduce heat to 350°. Roast uncovered and baste frequently, about 2 hours. Remove meat and pour off excess fat. Add 1 tablespoon flour mixed with 1 tablespoon butter. Cook until brown. Add juices and half water, half beef consommé, to make 1 cup for this amount of flour. Season with more salt and white pepper, if necessary. I like to add a little apple or currant jelly, about 1 tablespoon for each cup of sauce.

The easiest way to remove fat is to pour all the drippings into a glass. The fat comes to the top so you can see it. Spoon off as much as you wish.

PORK TENDERLOIN

FOR FOUR

Pork tenderloins lend themselves to wintry entertaining, and this recipe I particularly like.

2 2-pound pork tenderloins (1½ pounds is average weight)
Salt and pepper; dry mustard
2 tablespoons butter
¼ teaspoon rosemary (optional)
¼ cup butter
½ cup currant jelly
1 cup cream
1 tablespoon flour

Rub the tenderloins with salt, pepper, and dry mustard, and brown in the 2 tablespoons of butter in a skillet. Sprinkle with rosemary (or skip it), the ¼ cup butter, and jelly. Cover and bake for 45 minutes in a 300° oven. Add the cream mixed with the flour and continue baking 15 minutes longer. Serve from the skillet or remove and place on a heated platter with rice and serve with the cream sauce.

FLORIDA PORK LOIN

FOR FOUR OR SIX

Pork has an affinity for fruit, especially citrus.

1 3-pound piece of pork loin, boned or not (there is always more flavor if the bone is left in)
2 teaspoons salt
½ teaspoon Tabasco
¼ cup finely chopped onion
½ cup orange juice
½ cup water
1 lemon, sliced thin
Cornstarch or arrowroot

Rub the pork with the salt and Tabasco. Place in a skillet with the onion and brown on both sides. Remove and pour off the fat, and return to skillet. Baste frequently with the orange juice and water, and bake uncovered for 2 hours at 300° or until done. Add the lemon slices on the top side the last 30 minutes. Drain off the excess fat and thicken the juices with a very little cornstach or arrowroot — about ½ teaspoon to 1 cup of liquid.

HONEY AND MUSTARD SPARERIBS

FOR EIGHT

1 tablespoon dry mustard
1 teaspoon chili powder
1 teaspoon sage
1 tablespoon salt
10 pounds spareribs, cut in 3-inch pieces (the butcher will do it for you)
12 ounces beer
1 cup honey
1 tablespoon lemon juice

Mix the spices and rub on the ribs. Mix the beer, honey, and lemon juice. Pour over the ribs and marinate overnight. Roast uncovered at 350° for 2 hours. Baste with the leftover marinade.

SWEET AND SOUR PORK

FOR EIGHT

2 pounds boneless pork loin
2 tablespoons dry sherry or rice wine
4 tablespoons soy sauce
4 tablespoons flour
2 tablespoons cornstarch
Peanut oil

Cut pork in 1-inch cubes. Flatten with palm of your hand. Mix with sherry and soy sauce. Roll in flour mixed with cornstarch. Fry in peanut oil at 375° until brown and crisp, about 5 minutes.

Bring to a boil:

¾ cup sugar
½ cup soy sauce
2 tablespoons dry sherry or rice wine
4 tablespoons vinegar
4 tablespoons tomato purée (canned)
4 tablespoons catsup

Add:

2 tablespoons cornstarch
1½ cups water

Cook until clear.

Heat in a large skillet or wok:

4 tablespoons oil

Add:

4 slices canned pineapple, quartered
2 green peppers, cut into chunks

Cook at high heat for 2 minutes, stirring constantly. Add the pork and the sauce; cover. Cook at medium heat for 2 or 3 minutes. Serve on hot white rice. Sound complicated? It isn't.

HAM

The language of "ham" has become more and more complicated as the advertising companies have worked overtime to sell ham to the housewife. I have been asked the difference between "tenderized," "ready-to-eat," and "fully cooked" so many times that I am confused myself. Personally, I think all hams need more cooking for a well-done texture and full ham flavor, and I have found these cooking times successful: *Tenderized hams* should bake 4 hours at 300° uncovered. *Ready-to-eat hams* should bake 2 hours at 300° uncovered. *Home-cured hams* need soaking in cold water overnight, and then should be placed in a kettle of simmering water so that ham is just covered. Allow 25 minutes per pound for cooking time. Cool in the water in which it was cooked, remove, peel off outer skin, then bake for 2 hours at 300° with whatever juices you choose. *Fully cooked* and *canned hams,* as well as imported — from Poland, Denmark, Westphalia, or Holland — hams should at least be heated through thoroughly unless they are to be served cold; and both the flavor and texture is improved if baked at least 2 hours at 300°, then allowed to cool before slicing or for sandwiches.

Varying the juices, or the "baste" you use, will keep you "ham-happy." For a 10- to 12-pound ham:

2 cups maple syrup
or
2 cups barbecue sauce
or
1 cup any fruit juice, plus 1 cup light Karo or honey
or
1 cup light Karo, plus 1 cup bourbon or dry sherry
or
2 cups ginger ale
or
Juice of 2 oranges, ½ cup pineapple juice, and ½ cup Karo, plus ½ cup brown sugar
or
2 cups milk

For a quick glaze, melt a cup of currant jelly, add 1 tablespoon cornstarch, and cook until clear. Spread over either hot or cold ham.

For everyday baking of hams, as I have done in the food operations I have managed, I use beer as the "baste" and sprinkle with brown sugar. I use it regardless of the kind of ham — and everyone asks how!

If I ever want to dress it up for a buffet or such, I spread over for the last half hour of cooking 1 cup of preserved fruit such as gooseberry, black cherry, orange marmalade, chutney, jelly, or whatever I happen to light upon.

Sometime boil a cured or fresh ham with enough water to cover and add 2 cups sliced apples to it. Use the apple-ham juice as a sauce to serve with it.

GLAZED HAM BALLS

FOR EIGHT

For a cool evening supper, try glazed ham balls and baked beans.

1½ pounds ground cured ham
1½ pounds ground fresh ham
1¼ cups milk
2½ cups bread crumbs
1½ cups brown sugar
¾ cup vinegar
¾ cup water
1½ teaspoons dry mustard

Mix first four ingredients and let stand for 1 hour. Form into balls. Melt brown sugar in skillet; add vinegar, water, and mustard. Boil 15 minutes and pour over the ham balls. Cover and bake at 350° for 30 minutes. Uncover and bake 30 minutes longer.

BARBECUED FRESH HAM

TWENTY-FIVE SERVINGS

Barbecued fresh ham is a welcome change from the cured ham that finds its way to the buffet supper and cocktail tables too many times. Serve warm with hot biscuits with chopped, sautéed onion added to them. Leftovers, cold, with applesauce and hoecakes.

2 cups brown sugar
2 cups wine vinegar
2 cups water
2 cups chicken consommé
1 teaspoon mustard seed
½ teaspoon celery seed
½ teaspoon cracked pepper
1 12- to 13-pound fresh ham

Bring to a boil the sugar, vinegar, water, consommé, and seasonings. Pour over ham that has been slit about ½ inch deep across the top several times with a sharp knife; let ham stand overnight, or at least 5 hours before you bake it. Bake at 350° 4 or 5 hours, basting frequently with the liquid it has soaked in. When finished, cook remaining liquid down to a thick sauce and pour over the ham.

HAM STEAK À LA BOURGUIGNONNE

I suggest you buy a whole bone-in ham and have the butcher cut two 2-inch steaks through the center. You can use the rest of the ham for baking or broiling. Rub the steaks with Dijon mustard, cover with honey and dry red wine, and marinate for several hours or overnight. Place on your broiling rack and broil for 20 to 30 minutes, 5 inches from heating element, basting frequently with marinade. Slice thinly and serve. You may do ahead of time and reheat. Cover with mushrooms sautéed in butter and red wine. I use the entire mushroom, split in half; allow 3 mushrooms per person. I also like to stuff prunes with sharp Cheddar cheese and marinate with the ham; broil the prunes with the ham the last 5 minutes.

HAM STEAK WITH ONION GRAVY

FOR SIX TO EIGHT

6 tablespoons butter
8 6-ounce ham steaks, horseshoe-cut ½ inch thick
¼ cup hot coffee
2 cups thinly sliced onion
1 tablespoon flour
1 cup sour cream

Melt the butter in a skillet, add ham steaks, and pan fry at medium heat until lightly browned. Baste with the coffee. Remove and keep warm on serving platter. Add the onion to the pan and sauté at low heat until soft and yellow. Add the flour and cook until bubbly. Add the sour cream, and thoroughly heat. Pour over the ham steaks; run under broiler for a few seconds.

ASPARAGUS AND HAM AU GRATIN

FOR FOUR

4 thin slices boiled or baked ham
16 stalks cooked asparagus
4 poached eggs
1½ cups medium Cream Sauce with ½ cup Gruyere cheese blended in
Parmesan cheese

Place the ham in the bottom of an oven-proof casserole; place 4 stalks of asparagus on each slice, and a soft poached egg on top of the asparagus. Cover with Cream Sauce, sprinkle Parmesan cheese on top, and bake at 350° until brown, about 20 or 25 minutes.

HAM CRÊPES

FOR SIXTEEN

16 thin crêpes
16 thin slices baked or canned ham or prosciutto
16 thin slices Gruyère cheese
4 tablespoons butter
4 tablespoons flour
4 cups milk or half-and-half
¼ cup Cognac
Salt and white pepper
Grated Parmesan cheese
Paprika

Place a slice of ham and cheese the same length on each crêpe and roll. Place crêpes in a shallow casserole. Melt butter, add flour, and cook 1 minute. Pour in milk; cook until thickened. Heat Cognac, ignite, add to sauce, and cook 5 minutes. Season with salt and pepper to taste. Pour sauce over crêpes. Sprinkle with Parmesan cheese and paprika. Bake at 350° until brown (20 to 25 minutes). You may prepare the day before and reheat, or freeze for a few days. A thin slice of chicken may also be added to the crêpes. Substitute sour cream for the sauce sometime!

COLD HAM MOUSSE

FOR SIX TO EIGHT

An elegant Ham Mousse artfully served on a handsome tray with parsley sauce can be a masterpiece.

1 tablespoon plus 1 teaspoon unflavored gelatin
¼ cup dry white wine or water
2 tablespoons butter
1 tablespoon flour
1 cup half-and-half or chicken broth
¼ cup mayonnaise
2 teaspoons Dijon mustard
2½ cups finely diced or ground cooked ham, or more if you wish
½ cup whipping cream
Salt and pepper

Soften gelatin in wine. Set aside. Melt the butter, add the flour, and cook until bubbly. Add the half-and-half; mix and stir with a French whip and cook over low heat until thickened. Add the gelatin. Cool. Mix the mayonnaise, mustard, and ham; add to the sauce. Chill. As it becomes thickened and cold, fold in the cream, whipped. Season with salt and pepper to taste. Pour into a 1½-quart mold lightly rubbed with mayonnaise. Chill in refrigerator until firm. Unmold onto a chilled serving tray and serve with:

PARSLEY SAUCE

TWO CUPS

½ cup mayonnaise
1 cup sour cream
¼ cup finely chopped fresh spinach or watercress
¾ cup finely chopped parsley
Few drops onion juice
Salt and white pepper

Mix, season, and serve cold with the mousse.

CARAMEL HAM LOAF

FOR SIX

½ pound ground beef
1 pound ground ham
5 slices bread soaked in 1¼ cups milk
3 beaten eggs
½ teaspoon salt
½ teaspoon dry mustard
⅓ cup brown sugar
Whole cloves

Mix meats, soaked bread, eggs, salt, and mustard. In bottom of a buttered loaf tin sprinkle the brown sugar and a few cloves. Pack meat on top and bake at 350° for 1 hour. Do in individual custard cups for parties.

HAM LOAF

FOR SIX

2 eggs
1 quart ground ham
1 teaspoon baking powder
1 teaspoon Worcestershire sauce
1 cup bread crumbs
1 cup light cream

Beat eggs; add ham and rest of ingredients; mix thoroughly. Butter a

2-quart loaf pan and line with waxed paper. Fill and spread with mixture of:

½ cup brown sugar
1 teaspoon flour
1 teaspoon prepared mustard
Vinegar enough to moisten

Set pan in hot water and bake at 375° for about one hour.

Lamb

Spring lamb is an overworked expression, but if it makes everyone feel better, more power to the lamb. However, facts about lamb are good to know. The meat from lambs three to five months old is known as spring lamb, and is in season from April through June. Because of the preference for the taste of lamb, rather than mutton, most of the sheep are killed before they are a year old, as the younger the animal, the more delicate the flavor. The flesh of both lamb and mutton should be fine-grained and smooth, the color of lamb a deep pink, and of mutton a dark red. The fat of lamb should be white and firm, and of mutton the fat is pink and really hard.

HERBED LEG OF LAMB

FOR EIGHT

1 5- to 6-pound leg of lamb, trimmed for the oven
1 clove garlic
1 teaspoon salt
½ teaspoon dried oregano
¼ teaspoon thyme
¼ teaspoon ginger
½ teaspoon white pepper
8 canned Elberta peach halves
1 cup dry red wine
2 tablespoons currant jelly

Cut a slit at base of roast, near the bone, and place the garlic clove in it. Mix the dry ingredients and rub thoroughly over the meat. Place lamb in a roasting pan on a rack and roast uncovered in a 300° oven about 2 hours (165° on a meat thermometer) for well done, less for medium rare. Surround lamb with peach halves the last 20 minutes. Baste frequently with the cooking juices and the wine. Remove lamb and peaches to a serving platter. Remove garlic bud and let lamb stand a few minutes before carving. Strain the fat from the juices, add the jelly, and heat until melted. Serve jelly with the thinly sliced lamb. The taste of both roast lamb and veal are improved with thin slicing and lamb should always be hot or cold, but never warm. Flame with a jigger of gin, if you like to show off.

LEG OF LAMB, MUSLIM STYLE

FOR EIGHT

---

2 tablespoons grated fresh ginger
3 cloves garlic, crushed
1 cup yogurt
1½ teaspoons salt
¼ teaspoon black pepper
Juice of 2 limes
1 4- to 5-pound leg of lamb
1 tablespoon ground coriander
½ teaspoon cayenne pepper
½ teaspoon ground cinnamon
½ teaspoon ground cloves
½ teaspoon ground cardamom

Mix ginger, garlic, yogurt, salt, pepper, and lime juice. Make several gashes in the lamb and spread mixture over the surface. Marinate overnight. Mix spices and put into a small skillet on medium heat. Cool; sprinkle over lamb. Roast at 450° for 15 minutes. Reduce heat to 350°, and roast for 40 minutes longer, for medium rare (150° on your meat thermometer), longer if you wish it well done (165° on your thermometer). Remove, let rest. Slice thin and serve with strained juices from roasting pan.

LEG OF LAMB IN PASTRY

FOR EIGHT TO TEN

---

1 boned leg of lamb, 5- to 6-pound size or smaller
2 cloves garlic
Salt and pepper
2 teaspoons dried or 2 sprigs fresh rosemary
2 tablespoons melted butter
White wine or consommé
Piecrust
1 egg mixed with 2 tablespoons cold water

Rub leg with garlic, salt, and pepper. Cut a few slivers of the garlic and insert into slits here and there in the flesh. Sprinkle with the rosemary and butter. Roast uncovered in a 450° oven for 15 minutes. Reduce the heat to 375° and roast about 10 minutes for each pound or 140° on your meat thermometer. Baste frequently with the wine or consommé. Remove from oven and cool. Shape the meat as well as you can to look like original leg. Roll out piecrust about ⅛ inch thick, large enough to cover the meat; allow 3 inches in length and 2 inches in width to overlap. Place seam side down on an ungreased cookie sheet. Roll out some of the dough and cut into decorative pieces and fashion over the pastry. Bake at 425° for 10 to 15 minutes. Brush with egg and cold water and return to oven. Continue to bake until pastry is brown, brushing once more during baking with the egg wash.

BROILED LEG OF LAMB

FOR EIGHT TO TEN

1 5- to 6-pound leg of lamb, boned and butterflied
2 cloves garlic or more, minced
1 tablespoon salt
¼ cup dried rosemary, crushed
1 cup gin, bourbon, or beef consommé
2 tablespoons butter

Pull off the thin skin that covers the fat of the lamb leg. Rub lamb with garlic, salt, and rosemary. Let this rest at room temperature for at least 1 hour. Place fat side up in a buttered pan. Broil for 15 minutes. Remove, pour over half the gin, and ignite. (Do not put it back under the broiler before igniting or you'll burn the house down.) Turn the lamb, and broil 15 minutes more. Remove, pour over rest of gin, and ignite. Add the butter. Turn off the broiler and return to stove to keep warm. Slice thin and use juices as a sauce. Well done? Just increase broiling time.

STUFFED LAMB SHOULDER

FOR SIX OR EIGHT

1 3- to 4-pound lamb shoulder, boned
1 cup finely chopped chicken livers, about ½ pound
¼ cup finely chopped mushroom stems
2 tablespoons butter
2 tablespoons chopped parsley
2 tablespoons finely chopped ham
Juice and grated peel of 1 lemon
1 egg yolk
Salt, pepper, and paprika
½ teaspoon rosemary, crushed
½ cup dry white wine or water

Sauté the livers and mushroom stems in the butter until soft. Add parsley, ham, lemon juice and peel, and egg yolk. This will be a coarse paste. Place in center of lamb, and roll, tie, or fasten with skewers. Rub with salt, pepper, paprika, and rosemary. Roast uncovered at 300° for 2 hours (or the doneness you like) and baste with the wine. Add more if you need it. Drain off excess fat and slightly thicken the juices with arrowroot, or serve au naturel. Good cold, too!

CROWN ROAST OF LAMB

FOR EIGHT

The elegant look of a Crown Roast of Lamb can never be lauded enough. Fill the center with a Mushoom Soufflé and your taste buds and your eyes will love this entrée.

1 crown roast of lamb, consisting of 16 well-tied chops
Salt and pepper
1 clove garlic, slivered

Sprinkle lamb inside and out with salt and pepper. Trim all fat. Insert garlic here and there. Place an empty can in center to make a smooth well to hold the mushroom soufflé. Cover the chop ends with foil. Roast at 400° for 20 minutes. Remove from oven. Remove can. Pour off all fat. Cut out a circle of foil to cover bottom of roast and place the roast on it. Fill the center with the following Mushroom Soufflé.

MUSHROOM SOUFFLÉ

1½ pounds fresh mushrooms
¼ cup finely diced onion
1 teaspoon salt
Pinch of thyme
6 tablespoons butter
4 tablespoons flour
1½ cups hot milk
8 egg yolks, beaten
8 egg whites, beaten stiff
2 tablespoons grated Parmesan cheese

Wash, dry, and finely chop the mushrooms. Sauté with the onion, salt, and thyme in the butter until the onions are soft. Add the flour and cook until foamy. Cook 1 minute more. Add hot milk and cook until thickened, stirring constantly for about 5 minutes. Cool slightly and add the beaten egg yolks. Cool and stir in one third of the beaten egg whites. Fold in the rest, and pour into the lamb-roast cavity. Sprinkle with Parmesan cheese. Return lamb to oven and bake at 350° for 40 minutes. Remove to a heated platter; remove foil and strings.

The following sauce may be passed with the lamb and soufflé: Add 1 cup beef consommé to roasting pan, and cook for 5 minutes. Add 1 tablespoon currant jelly, 1 tablespoon red wine vinegar. Cook until jelly is melted. Carve 1 double chop for each guest, including some of the soufflé. Pass sauce. There will be more than enough soufflé to fill the lamb; put the rest in a buttered soufflé dish and bake along with the lamb.

This is a good way to use up mushroom stems also. And use this recipe any time, lamb or no.

LAMB DIJON

FOR EIGHT

---

3 tablespoons Dijon mustard
3 teaspoons salt
2 cloves garlic, minced
⅓ cup olive oil
3 single racks of lamb, trimmed for the oven
1½ cups dry red wine
2 tablespoons honey

Mix mustard, salt, garlic, and oil. Rub over the racks and let stand for several hours. Roast at 375° for 40 minutes, basting with the wine and honey. Serve with juices. Cook longer for well done, but I think you will enjoy lamb pink — at least give it a try.

LAMB CHOPS SUISSE

FOR EIGHT

---

8 double loin lamb chops
2 teaspoons salt
½ teaspoon pepper
2 cups coarsely chopped mushrooms (use stems)
¼ cup butter, melted
½ cup dry sherry
16 very thin slices Swiss cheese

Broil chops 8 minutes; turn and broil 8 minutes or longer if you like well-done lamb. Sprinkle with salt and pepper. Sauté the mushrooms in the melted butter. Add the sherry and cook until sherry is reduced. Pile on chops, cover with the cheese, and bake at 350° for 10 minutes.

STUFFED LAMB CHOPS

Have the butcher cut lamb chops thick — at least 2 inches. Split the lean part of the meat in half, cutting to the bone. Chop 2 fresh mushrooms and 2 chicken livers per chop and sauté in butter until done, but not brown. Season with salt and pepper and stuff in the chop. Sprinkle with garlic salt and rub with olive oil. Repeat for as many chops as desired. Broil under a high heat on both sides until brown. Turn only once. Serve with fresh undercooked spinach that has been finely chopped in an electric blender and dressed with heavy cream and Parmesan cheese. This is my favorite lamb dish.

LAMB CHOP GRILL

A good company dish. For each serving use:

1 lamb chop (1 rib)
1 tablespoon butter
2 links pork sausage
1 chicken liver
1 slice bacon
2 mushroom caps

Brush the chop with butter and place under broiler for 5 minutes on each side. Pan-fry sausage and chicken liver. Roll bacon into a curl and sauté until crisp. Sauté mushroom caps in butter. Arrange on a hot platter and serve with thin blueberry pancakes with whipped lemon butter.

CURRY OF LAMB

FOR EIGHT

¼ cup butter
¾ cup diced onion
1 teaspoon sugar
1 teaspoon salt
3 pounds lean lamb, cut in 1-inch pieces
¼ cup diced preserved ginger
2 tablespoons curry powder
1 teaspoon chopped mint, fresh or flakes
1 tablespoon flour
2 cups chicken broth
1½ cups half-and-half
¼ cup shredded coconut
2 tablespoons lime juice

Melt the butter; add the onion, sugar, and salt. Sauté until yellow. Add the lamb and cook at medium heat until lamb is tender (an hour or more). Add ginger, curry powder, and mint. Cook 1 minute. Add flour and cook 1 minute. Pour in chicken broth and cook until liquid is reduced by half. Stir in 1 cup half-and-half and coconut. Cook until thickened. Add lime juice and rest of half-and-half. Heat thoroughly, but do not boil. You may prepare ahead and freeze.

We are prone to serve curry on rice, but it is more interesting served on cornbread, sautéed peaches, or small crisp croutons.

IRISH LAMB STEW

FOR FOUR

Irish Lamb Stew as my mother made it has always been popular with my men customers on St. Patrick's Day — and other days. I'm sure it isn't because I am Irish, either.

2 pounds lamb breast or shoulder, cut in 1-inch cubes
2 onions, quartered
4 small whole carrots
8 small whole potatoes
½ head cabbage
1 teaspoon salt
⅛ teaspoon pepper
1 cup cooked green peas

Cover lamb with water and simmer, skimming off scum as it appears. Add onions and carrots and continue cooking slowly until meat is tender (an hour or more). Add potatoes and when almost cooked add cabbage, cubed. Cook for 12 minutes longer and thicken slightly with a little flour moistened with cold water. Season and serve on a hot platter with the peas sprinkled over.

Veal

ROAST VEAL WITH MORELS IN CREAM

FOR EIGHT TO TEN

1 6-pound boned and tied loin or leg of veal
½ cup thinly sliced onion
¼ cup diced carrots
¼ cup diced celery
Few sprigs parsley
1 clove garlic (you may omit)
Salt and white pepper
1 cup dry white wine

Place veal in a shallow pan, uncovered. Put in a 450° oven for 15 minutes. Remove from oven and put vegetables and parsley around the veal. Sprinkle with salt and white pepper; return to oven turned to 350°. Pour some of the wine around the veal after 15 minutes. Baste frequently with the rest of wine and drippings. Roast about 1 hour if a loin roast, about 1 hour and 20 minutes if cut from the leg. The temperature on a meat thermometer should be 170°. Do not overcook. Remove strings and transfer to a warm serving platter or tray. Serve with the juices and morels in cream:

½ pound dried morels
3 tablespoons butter
1 tablespoon flour
1 cup whipping or sour cream

Rinse morels thoroughly many times until all sand is removed and let soak for several hours in cold water.

Melt butter; add drained morels and sauté until they are shiny. Add flour and cook 1 minute. Add cream and simmer for 5 minutes. You may use canned morels, chanterelles, or fresh mushrooms in place of dried morels.

Morels are edible wild mushrooms with spongy oval caps. They must be carefully cleaned and cooked for a long time if fresh or dried. Very expensive, but worth it at times, I think.

HUNGARIAN VEAL CHOPS

FOR FOUR

4 veal chops, 1 to 1½ inches thick
Salt and pepper
2 tablespoons olive oil
¼ cup chopped onion
½ cup sliced raw carrots
1 cup fresh tomatoes, peeled and quartered
⅓ cup dry sherry
1 cup sliced mushrooms
2 tablespoons butter
1 tablespoon chopped parsley

Sprinkle chops with salt and pepper and brown in oil with the onion; add carrots, tomatoes, and sherry; cover and simmer slowly for 1 hour. Sauté mushrooms in the butter and add, with the parsley, to the chops. Cook another 5 minutes and serve with a green vegetable dressed with butter and Parmesan cheese.

VEAL À LA CRÈME

FOR EIGHT TO TEN

2 teaspoons sugar
½ cup thinly sliced onion
4 pounds lean veal stew meat
3 cups chicken broth
1 tablespoon butter
1 tablespoon flour
1 cup whipping cream
Salt and white pepper
1 teaspoon grated lemon peel
1 tablespoon slivered lemon peel
Chopped parsley

Put the sugar and onion in a heavy skillet and cook slowly until the onions are glazed and soft. Add the veal and chicken broth. Cover and simmer until the veal is tender (approximately 1 hour). Mix the butter and flour together and blend with some of the liquid — then add to the rest of it. Cook until thickened. Add the cream, seasonings, and grated lemon peel. Turn off the heat and let stand for at least 1 hour. Then reheat and serve with the slivered lemon peel and parsley sprinkled on top if you like. If prepared ahead, this dish has more flavor. It freezes well. I like to serve it with brown rice or mixed noodles.

LOIN OF VEAL WITH SHALLOTS AND MUSHROOMS

FOR TEN TO TWELVE

½ cup butter
1 clove garlic, crushed
2 onions, sliced
2 carrots, sliced
2 3- to 4-pound loins of veal, boned and tied
½ cup beef broth
½ cup dry white wine
6 shallots, finely minced
2 tablespoons butter
8 mushrooms, sliced
½ cup dry sherry or broth
Arrowroot

Melt the butter in roasting pan. Add the garlic, onions, and carrots. Put in 375° oven for 10 minutes. Place meat on top and roast at 375°, basting with the butter, beef broth, and wine, for about 1 hour or until meat thermometer registers 145°. Remove meat to serving tray. In a separate pan sauté the shallots in the butter and cook until soft. Add mushrooms and cook until translucent. Pour sherry into pan drippings and cook, stirring in all the brown bits that cling to the pan. Add a little arrowroot (1 teaspoon for each cup of liquid) and cook until clear. Strain, add mushrooms and shallots, and serve over the meat. For variety, substitute red wine for white or omit wine entirely. Use same recipe for rack or leg of veal.

VEAL AND MUSHROOMS

FOR SIX TO EIGHT

This recipe takes less than thirty minutes and is delicious. Good, too, for buffet suppers.

2 pounds thinly sliced veal cutlets
½ cup butter or margarine
½ cup thinly sliced onion
½ pound fresh mushrooms, sliced, or 1 can sliced mushrooms
1 tablespoon flour
1 cup cream
1 cup dry white wine (chicken consommé for those who do not like wine)
2 tablespoons chopped parsley
Salt and pepper

Cut the veal into 1-inch strips and sauté in the butter with the onion and mushrooms over low heat until brown. Blend the flour into mixture and stir until completely blended. Add the cream and simmer until veal is tender, about 5 minutes. Add wine and parsley and season to taste. Simmer for 5 minutes. Leave out the cream if you like and add consommé. Have a bottle of chilled Chablis with it.

VEAL CHOPS IN SOUR CREAM

FOR FOUR

Veal chops make a dinner fit for a king, especially when done with sour cream.

4 veal chops ½-inch or more thick
Salt and flour
¼ cup butter or margarine
1 cup sour cream
2 tablespoons lemon juice and finely slivered rind of 1 lemon

Sprinkle the chops with salt and dredge them lightly in flour. Shake off all you can. Sauté lightly in butter for 15 minutes. Turn once. Add the sour cream to the skillet and cook over very low heat until the sauce is yellow. Add the lemon juice and rind and simmer a minute. Serve at once.

VEAL CUTLET FONTINA

FOR FOUR

8 thin slices of veal
Flour, salt, and pepper
3 tablespoons butter
1 cup cream
¾ pound Fontina cheese
1 cup julienne of ham (prosciutto if possible)
3 tablespoons Parmesan cheese
3 egg yolks

Dust the veal cutlets with flour seasoned with salt and pepper and sauté in the butter until light brown. Mix rest of ingredients and cook in a double boiler until thick. Spoon over the veal, brown under the broiler, and serve on noodles or rice.

VEAL BIRDS WITH MUSHROOM SAUCE

FOR EIGHT

2 pounds lean veal, cut into 16 thin even-sized slices
1 teaspoon salt
¼ teaspoon sage
16 small pieces Swiss-type cheese
4 tablespoons whipped butter or margarine
2 tablespoons chopped shallots
1½ cups chicken consommé
¼ cup Madeira
2½ cups canned sliced mushrooms
2 tablespoons chopped parsley
Salt and white pepper

Place each veal slice between two pieces of foil and pound with a wooden mallet until very thin. Sprinkle with the salt and sage. Place a small finger of cheese in center of veal; roll up and tie each piece with a string. Melt the butter in a skillet. Add the shallots and cook 1 minute. Add the veal and brown quickly over high heat, turning once. Transfer to a shallow casserole. Add the consommé to the skillet and bring to a boil. Pour over the veal with the wine. Bake at 350° for 30 minutes, basting frequently. Add the mushrooms and heat only. Remove from oven; take off strings and sprinkle veal with the parsley. Season with salt and pepper to taste. Serve from casserole or transfer to a hot platter. Allow two per person.

VEAL PICCATE

FOR SIX TO EIGHT

2 pounds thinly sliced veal cutlets
1 cup flour
1 tablespoon salt
½ cup butter
¼ cup olive oil
1 cup chicken broth
¼ cup lemon juice
2 lemons, sliced very thin
Salt and pepper
½ cup finely chopped parsley

Place cutlets between two pieces of foil and pound until they are thin but not torn. Dredge in the flour and salt; shake off all excess flour. Heat the butter and oil and sauté the veal about 5 minutes over medium heat, turning the meat only once. If skillet is not large enough, as soon as first slices are done, pile on a plate and keep warm. Then return all veal to the skillet and add the chicken broth. Simmer until the liquid is reduced by half. Add the lemon juice and the slices of lemon. Heat only until lemons are hot. Season to taste. Add parsley at the last minute. Serve with the sauce poured over and garnish with the hot lemon slices.

VEAL PAPRIKA

FOR FOUR

¼ cup tissue-thin sliced onions
3 tablespoons butter
1 pound of veal cutlets, sliced ¼ inch thick and cut in ¼-pound portions
¼ cup flour
1 teaspoon salt
⅛ teaspoon pepper
1½ cups chicken stock
¾ cup sour cream
1 teaspoon paprika

Sauté onions in butter; remove and brown cutlets that have been rolled in the seasoned flour. Add stock and onions and simmer, covered, for 1 hour. Add sour cream and paprika and cook slowly until well blended. Serve with buttered fine noodles or rice.

VEAL SCALOPPINI

FOR SIX

Over the years my cooks have greeted me with "What do we scaloppini today?" Since I like the flavor, I really do scaloppini almost every cut of meat and poultry.

¼ cup flour
½ cup grated Parmesan cheese
1 teaspoon salt
⅛ teaspoon pepper
1½ pounds veal cutlets, sliced ¼ inch thick and cut into 2-inch strips
2 tablespoons olive oil
1 clove garlic
½ cup dry white wine
½ cup chicken consommé or stock
1 tablespoon lemon juice
Parsley

Mix flour, cheese, salt, and pepper together. Wipe meat dry, sprinkle with flour mixture, and pound it into meat with a potato masher or edge of a heavy plate. Heat olive oil with garlic and brown meat lightly on both sides. Remove garlic; add wine, stock, and lemon juice. Cover and simmer slowly for about 30 minutes. Sprinkle with chopped parsley and serve from a hot platter.

OSSO BUCO

FOR SIX

10 pounds veal knuckles (each knuckle could weigh ½ pound, so allow 2 per person)
1 cup flour
1 tablespoon salt
½ teaspoon white pepper
½ cup butter
½ cup olive oil
3 cups sliced onion
4 garlic cloves or more
8 ripe tomatoes, peeled and quartered
2 cups dry white wine
Chicken broth to cover
2 bay leaves
1 cup parsley pieces
12 peppercorns
Rind of 3 lemons

Dredge knuckles in the flour, salt, and pepper. Melt the butter in a skillet, add the olive oil, and brown each knuckle. Place in a large roasting pan. Add the onion and garlic to skillet and cook until onion is soft. Add to meat with butter left in skillet. Stir in the remaining ingredients and cover. Use foil if you do not have a cover. Simmer at low heat until meat is tender and bone is soft. Add more liquid if necessary. Remove meat; strain the sauce. Correct seasonings. Pour sauce over the meat and let stand in the liquid until ready to serve. Allow about 3 hours for this preparation. You may simmer (covered) in a 250° oven also. Add thin slices of lemon just before serving — and I add boiled little white onions. Serve a cocktail fork along with so the marrow inside the knuckle can be eaten.

VEAL PATTIES SCALOPPINI

FOR EIGHT

2 pounds ground veal stew meat
½ cup finely minced onion
1 small clove garlic, finely minced
2 teaspoons salt
½ teaspoon white pepper
2 eggs
½ cup flour
½ cup grated Parmesan cheese
½ cup butter
¼ cup olive oil
1 cup Marsala wine
½ cup chicken broth

Mix the first six ingredients and form into patties, 2 inches in diameter (sixteen 2-ounce patties). Flatten with palm of your hand. Dust lightly with mixture of flour and Parmesan. Let stand at least 1 hour. Sauté in butter and olive oil until brown. Remove from pan. Add Marsala and chicken broth to pan. Cook until slightly thickened. Correct seasonings. Pour sauce over patties. Allow at least two patties for each serving.

ROAST ROUND OF VEAL

FOR FOURTEEN TO SIXTEEN

1 10- or 12-pound veal round (rump and shank off, be sure)
2 teaspoons white pepper
2 tablespoons salt
2 teaspoons ground cinnamon
3 medium-sized onions
2 carrots
Few sprigs of parsley
Grated rind and juice of 4 lemons
1 quart dry white wine or water
¼ cup butter
Arrowroot
1 lemon, sliced thin
¼ cup finely chopped parsley

Place meat in a roasting pan. Mix together the pepper, salt, and cinnamon and heat in a skillet. Pat over the veal. Add the onions, carrots, and parsley to the pan. Roast uncovered at 350° for 1 hour. Add lemon rind and juice. Baste frequently with wine or water and juices. Roast about 25 minutes per pound, or until a fork comes out easily when tested (185° on meat thermometer). Strain juices and serve plain or slightly thickened with arrowroot and very thin slices of lemon and the parsley. Let meat rest at least 30 minutes before carving. This is an especially good preparation for a buffet.

FRENCH VEAL STEW

FOR SIX

4 cups water
2 pounds veal stew meat cut in 2-inch pieces
½ cup sliced onion
¼ cup sliced carrots
1 bay leaf
3 peppercorns
2 teaspoons salt
1 cup sliced mushrooms
4 tablespoons butter
¼ cup flour
2 tablespoons lemon juice
1 tablespoon chopped parsley

Simmer first seven ingredients at low heat, skimming off scum that appears. When meat is tender (about 1½ hours), remove bay leaf and peppercorns. Sauté mushrooms in the butter, add flour and lemon juice, and add to meat and cook until sauce is thick. Serve from a hot platter, parsley sprinkled over, with boiled little white onions, new potatoes, and peas. A little white wine added will not hurt it a bit.

I like to cook veal stew as I do fricassee of chicken and serve it over hot biscuit, and with a hot spiced peach or apricot.

Variety Meats

BROILED SWEETBREADS

Parboil and split; brush with butter or salad oil; sprinkle lightly with flour, salt, and paprika. Broil under direct heat until golden brown, about 10 minutes, turning once. Serve with melted butter.

Sprinkle with Parmesan cheese before broiling, for a change.

Crisp bacon is always a good accompaniment to sweetbreads; and I like to add grilled fresh pineapple or apples.

CASSEROLE SWEETBREADS AND DRIED BEEF

FOR FOUR

2 pairs sweetbreads
Juice of ½ lemon
½ cup butter
1 4-ounce jar dried beef
3 tablespoons flour
3 cups half-and-half or milk
Salt and pepper
2½ cups canned artichoke bottoms (usually 8 in a can)
2 tablespoons Parmesan cheese
2 tablespoons grated Swiss cheese

Soak sweetbreads in cold water for 30 minutes. Drain; cover with fresh cold water and lemon juice. Simmer just under boiling for 20 minutes. Remove, cool, discard membranes, and slice as thin as possible without breaking. Melt the butter, add the sweetbreads, and sauté until a light brown. Add dried beef cut into ½-inch strips. Heat only. Remove, add flour to the same pan, cook 1 minute. Add half-and-half and cook until thickened, stirring with a French whip until you have no lumps.

Return sweetbreads and beef to the pan and heat thoroughly. Season to taste. Place the drained artichoke bottoms in a buttered shallow casserole and spoon the mixture into them. Sprinkle with the cheeses mixed together and bake at 350° until bubbly. Run under broiler to brown if necessary. Substitute sliced hard-cooked eggs for the sweetbreads if you are budget-minded, or substitute leftover ham for the beef. I'm extravagant at times — I use prosciutto!

SWEETBREADS WITH MADEIRA AND ALMONDS

FOR FOUR

Since the beginning of time, sweetbreads have been served in cream sauce in a patty shell — but this version is good.

2 pairs sweetbreads, soaked, parboiled, and skinned (see preceding recipe)
2 tablespoons butter
½ cup almonds
⅓ cup Madeira
¼ cup sliced stuffed olives
2 cups medium cream sauce
Patty shells (buy them)
Paprika

Prepare sweetbreads and slice. Sauté in the butter with the almonds. Add the Madeira and continue cooking until reduced by half. Add olives and cream sauce. Dip rims of patty shells in paprika and put in oven to heat. Serve the creamed mixture over them. Fingers of hot pineapple, baked in the oven with rum, brown sugar, and butter sprinkled over, go well with them.

In the Zodiac Room I served this over eggs deviled with minced ham added to the yolks, for a brunch, along with tomato halves baked and piled high with cooked frozen peas put through a Foley mill, seasoned with a pinch of nutmeg.

SAUTÉED SWEETBREADS WITH MARRONS

FOR SIX

3 pairs trimmed calves' sweetbreads
Flour, salt
¼ cup butter
1 tablespoon finely minced shallots or onion
¼ cup Madeira
1 cup chicken stock
12 preserved marrons
12 thin slices Canadian bacon

If possible, obtain the heart sweetbread, which is round in shape. Soak and precook as in recipe for Casserole Sweetbreads. Remove all connective tissue and membranes. Slice thin and sprinkle with flour and salt. Melt the butter; add the shallots and cook until yellow. Add sweetbreads, cook 1 minute, turn, and cook 1 minute more. Pour in wine and stock. Simmer at low heat about 10 minutes. Add marrons and continue cooking until marrons are hot. Correct seasonings. Place sweetbreads on a serving platter or in a chafing dish layered with lightly sautéed Canadian bacon. Pour over the marrons and juices. I sometimes serve them on sautéed pineapple rings. All the ingredients have an affinity for pineapple. I find this a good buffet supper dish.

SWEETBREADS SAUTÉED IN WINE

FOR TWO

1 pair sweetbreads
Salt and paprika
Flour
4 tablespoons butter
4 tablespoons dry sherry

Prepare sweetbreads as in Casserole recipe, discarding membrane. Split sweetbreads. Sprinkle with salt and a pinch of paprika, dust lightly with flour, and sauté slowly in butter until golden brown on all sides. Remove. Add wine to the butter and cook until reduced by half. Spoon over the sweetbreads and serve on slices of broiled Canadian bacon or sautéed ham.

CALF'S LIVER IN WINE

FOR FOUR

8 slices liver, cut ⅛ inch thick (be sure it's skinned)
Flour, salt, and pepper
3 tablespoons butter
1 cup beef consommé
1 cup sherry or Burgundy
1 cup water
2 tablespoons chopped parsley
1 teaspoon salt

Dust liver lightly with seasoned flour and sauté in butter until light brown. Pour over the rest of the ingredients, cover, and bake at 350° for 45 minutes. Serve on a thin slice of broiled ham or Canadian bacon.

TONGUE

FOR SIX TO EIGHT

1 4-pound fresh beef tongue
2 carrots
2 stalks celery
1 onion
1 bay leaf
Few sprigs parsley
3 cloves
1 clove garlic
½ teaspoon sugar

Place the tongue and rest of ingredients in a large kettle. Cover with cold water and bring to a boil. Skim the froth from the surface and simmer covered for 3 to 4 hours or until tongue is tender. Remove tongue, rinse with cold water, and take off the skin. When tongue is cold, slice in ¼-inch slices and re-form as a whole tongue. Garnish with watercress and serve with a sauce or with Mustard Mousse.

MUSTARD MOUSSE

1 tablespoon unflavored gelatin
2 tablespoons cold water
2 tablespoons dry white wine or champagne
2 cups sour cream or whipped cream
¼ cup chopped chives
¼ cup Dijon mustard
½ teaspoon hot dry mustard
1 tablespoon lemon juice
Few drops Tabasco

Dissolve gelatin in cold water. Heat gelatin mixture and pour in wine; add to sour cream mixed with rest of ingredients. Pour into a 1-pint mold and refrigerate until set. Good also with ham. You may omit the gelatin and use this as a sauce.

VEAL KIDNEYS IN COGNAC

FOR TWO TO FOUR

2 small veal kidneys
¼ cup butter
2 tablespoons Cognac
¼ teaspoon dry mustard
1 teaspoon lemon juice
1 tablespoon chopped parsley
Salt and freshly ground pepper

Remove fat and membrane from the kidneys and slice very thin. Sauté quickly in butter. Add the Cognac and ignite. Shake pan while you continue cooking until the brandy is reduced to half the original amount. Remove kidneys to heated platter; add the mustard, lemon juice, and parsley to the remaining liquid. Return kidneys to sauce, season, and serve at once. You have to be brave to serve kidneys, unless you are sure about their acceptance. However, kidneys prepared in this manner will make new friends for yourself and the dish.

ENGLISH STEAK AND KIDNEY PIE

FOR SIX

Every now and then I have a craving for an English steak and kidney pie. I think other people do, too, because so many ask for it — even those who "cannot stand kidneys" eat it and like it.

3 lamb kidneys
1½ pounds top round steak
½ cup sliced onion
1⅓ cups boiling water
1¼ tablespoons Worcestershire sauce
Salt and pepper
2 tablespoons flour
2½ tablespoons butter
Piecrust or baking powder biscuits

Remove skin and fat from kidneys and cut in ½-inch cubes. Cut steak in 1-inch cubes. Brown onion in a little fat from the steak; add kidneys and steak and stir constantly until meat is well browned. Add water, Worchestershire sauce, salt, and pepper; cover tightly and cook over low heat until meat is tender. Make a paste of the flour and butter and add to liquid, stirring rapidly to prevent lumps from forming. Pour into a casserole, cover with piecrust or baking powder biscuits, and bake at 450° until pastry is done. One-fourth cup of red wine added to the gravy helps a lot, but is not necessary.

Part 6

Hundreds of thousands of owners and readers of Helen Corbitt's books associate her name with the color photograph of her on the jacket of Helen Corbitt's Cookbook. *In that photograph, widely circulated since 1957, she is graciously presiding over a candlelit table of desserts: elaborate cakes, tempting tarts and cookies, crystal dishes of berries, and a row of the famous Corbitt Flowerpots.*

Helen's dessert recipes have been celebrated for the past forty years. My task of choosing the desserts for this collection has required time, study, and wise counsel.

The consensus of advice has been to include a very large assortment of Helen's desserts, from simple fruit desserts to her most extravagant creations, and to have a generous sampling of her soufflés, pies, cakes, cookies, puddings, and sauces.

The reasoning is that as closely as many cooks are now monitoring the calories in everyday fare, those same cooks want the Corbitt dessert recipes available for entertaining, for holidays and festive occasions.

Helen made a point of serving at least two desserts at her dinner parties, one a low-calorie fruit dessert or ice, and the other chosen for the way it tasted as well as for how it complemented the menu and for the color and beauty it added to the table.

Cookies

A cookie jar filled to the brim is a symbol of peace and security. The child who does not know the joy and comfort of reaching into a well-filled cookie jar has missed one of youth's greater compensations. And, too, cookie making can be child's play — and what a way to keep their idle hands busy.

There are so many kinds! From honest-to-goodness filler-uppers to the delicate fantasies one likes to serve at parties. And a box of homemade cookies makes your most difficult neighbor a slave forever. One piece of advice: Stir but do not beat cookie mixtures.

ALMOND COOKIES

FOUR DOZEN

1 cup butter
1 cup sugar
1 egg yolk
¾ teaspoon vanilla extract
2 cups sifted cake flour
⅛ teaspoon salt
1 egg white
½ cup finely sliced almonds
3 tablespoons sugar
½ teaspoon cinnamon

Butter a flat 10-by-16-inch pan. Put in refrigerator to chill. Cream butter; add the sugar and beat well. Add egg yolk and vanilla. Add sifted flour and salt. Spread mixture in pan. Beat egg white stiff and spread over cookie mixture. Sprinkle with mixture of almonds, sugar, and cinnamon. Bake in a preheated oven at 400° for 15 to 20 minutes. Cut in strips and remove from pan while warm.

BACHELOR BUTTONS

FIVE TO SIX DOZEN

¾ cup butter
1 cup brown sugar
1 egg, unbeaten
2 cups sifted flour
1 teaspoon soda
¼ teaspoon ginger
¼ teaspoon cinnamon
¼ teaspoon salt
1 teaspoon vanilla extract
1 cup chopped nuts

Cream butter, add sugar gradually, and beat well. Add unbeaten egg. Sift flour with dry ingredients and add to butter mixture. Fold in vanilla and nuts. Chill for several hours. Make into small balls; dip in granulated sugar; place on buttered cookie sheet, and press down with a fork. Bake in preheated oven at 375° until nicely browned, about 15 or 20 minutes.

BOURBON COOKIES

ABOUT SIX DOZEN

2 cups brown sugar
1 cup butter
4 cups flour
4 eggs
1 teaspoon nutmeg
1 teaspoon cloves
1 cup bourbon
3 teaspoons soda dissolved in 2 tablespoons buttermilk
¼ pound citron or candied fruit
2 pounds pecans, chopped
1½ pounds raisins

Mix in order given and drop by half teaspoonfuls on buttered cookie sheet. Bake at 350° for 10 to 15 minutes. Keep this recipe in mind for Christmas.

BRANDY SNAPS

TWO DOZEN

Brandy snaps were a childhood favorite that never had time to get to the cookie jar.

¼ cup butter or margarine
¼ cup sugar
2 tablespoons cane syrup
½ cup flour
¼ teaspoon ground ginger
1 teaspoon brandy
¼ teaspoon grated lemon rind

Cream butter and sugar; add rest of ingredients and mix thoroughly. Drop by half teaspoonfuls on cookie sheet and bake at 350° for 10 to 15 minutes, until golden brown. Bake only a few at a time, as they spread out and must be rolled up while hot. You may fill them with butter cream frosting.

BUTTERSCOTCH BROWNIES

ABOUT THREE DOZEN

One can usually eat a chocolate brownie and rest his conscience, but a butterscotch one — no — you always want one more.

4 tablespoons melted butter
1 cup dark brown sugar
1 egg
½ teaspoon salt
¾ cup flour
1 teaspoon baking powder
½ teaspoon vanilla
¼ cup shredded coconut
½ cup broken nutmeats

Mix and spread in a buttered 8-by-8-inch square pan. Bake at 350° for 25 minutes. Cool and spread with Caramel Icing.

CHINESE ALMOND COOKIES

ABOUT TWO DOZEN

2 cups all-purpose flour
½ teaspoon baking powder
1 cup butter or margarine
1 cup sugar
1 egg, beaten
½ teaspoon almond extract
½ teaspoon vanilla extract
2 dozen whole almonds, blanched

Sift flour and baking powder. Add butter, sugar, and egg. Mix and knead until dough is firm. Roll out to ½-inch thickness. Cut with cookie cutter the desired size. Place an almond in center of each. Place 1½ inches apart on pan. Bake at 450° for 10 minutes, or until cookies begin to brown. Reduce to 250° and bake 20 minutes more.

CHOCOLATE CHIP MERINGUES

TWO DOZEN MEDIUM OR THREE DOZEN SMALL

4 egg whites
¼ teaspoon salt
¼ teaspoon cream of tartar
1½ cups sugar
1 teaspoon vanilla extract
1 cup broken pecans
1 6-ounce package semisweet chocolate chips

Beat egg whites until stiff; add salt and cream of tartar. Continue beating, adding the sugar a little at a time. Continue beating. Add vanilla; fold in pecans and chocolate bits. Drop by tablespoonfuls onto a pan lined with foil, shiny side up. Bake at 300° for 25 to 30 minutes, until dry. Cool slightly and pull off the foil.

Omit the nuts and chocolate for Kiss Meringues.

CHOCOLATE CHIP NUT BARS

ABOUT FORTY BARS

1 cup cake flour, sifted
½ teaspoon baking powder
¼ teaspoon salt
⅛ teaspoon soda
⅓ cup shortening (butter preferred)
1 cup brown sugar, firmly packed
1 egg, slightly beaten
1 teaspoon vanilla
1 6-ounce package semisweet chocolate chips
1 cup finely chopped walnut meats

Sift flour once, measure, add baking powder, salt, and soda; sift again. Cream shortening, add sugar gradually, and cream together until light and fluffy; add egg and vanilla and mix well after each addition. Then add chocolate chips and nuts; blend. Turn mixture into greased 11-by-7-by-1-inch pan. Bake in 350° oven 25 to 30 minutes. Cut into bars. Remove from pan and cool on cake rack. Cut as large or small as you wish. They are wonderful with any fruit or ice cream.

CHOCOLATE FRUIT BARS

ABOUT TWO DOZEN

½ cup brown sugar
¼ cup butter
½ teaspoon salt
2 eggs
¼ cup milk
1 cup flour
½ teaspoon baking powder
½ teaspoon baking soda

1 cup pecan halves
1 cup candied pineapple
1 cup candied cherries
1 6-ounce package semisweet chocolate chips

Cream sugar, butter, and salt until fluffy. Blend in eggs, one at a time; add milk. Stir together flour, baking powder, and soda; combine with butter mixture. Fold in remaining ingredients. Spread in greased 11-by-8-inch pan. Bake in 350° oven for approximately 25 minutes. Serve as is or dribble lemon-juice-and-powdered-sugar icing over the top.

CHOCOLATE COCONUT COOKIES

THREE DOZEN

These were a great favorite with my men customers at Neiman-Marcus.

2 cups flour
2 cups sugar
½ teaspoon salt
1 cup butter or margarine
3 tablespoons powdered cocoa
1 cup water
2 eggs, beaten
½ cup buttermilk
1 teaspoon soda
1 teaspoon vanilla extract

Sift together flour, sugar, and salt. Set aside. Mix butter, cocoa, and water. Bring to a boil; pour over flour mixture. Add well-beaten eggs, buttermilk, soda, and vanilla. Pour into two buttered shallow 9-inch square cake pans. Bake at 375° for 30 minutes.

Topping:
Mix and bring to a boil ½ cup butter, 6 tablespoons half-and-half, and 3 tablespoons cocoa. Add mixture to 2 cups powdered sugar, ½ teaspoon vanilla, 1 cup shredded coconut, 1 cup chopped nuts. Mix and spread over cookies as they come from oven. Cut in squares. This is a good picnic cookie — and a nice change from brownies.

CLARISSA ANN COOKIES

THREE DOZEN

½ cup brown sugar
½ cup white sugar
1 cup Rice Krispies
1 cup chopped pecans
A pinch of salt
1 egg white, stiffly beaten

Mix together all ingredients but egg white. Fold mixture into stiffly beaten egg white and drop from teaspoon onto buttered cookie sheet. Bake at 350° for 10 to 15 minutes, until lightly browned.

DATE SQUARES

TWO DOZEN

Cook in saucepan until thick:

2 cups dates, cut fine (to cut dates, dip scissors in warm water)
½ cup brown sugar
1 cup water
1 tablespoon flour

Combine:

1 teaspoon vanilla
1 cup flour
1 teaspoon soda
2 cups Wheaties
1 cup brown sugar
¾ cup melted butter

Spread half the flour mixture in a buttered 9-inch pan (square if possible) and cover with the date mixture. Spread the other half of the flour mixture on top. Bake at 350° for 20 minutes. Cool and cut in squares.

FILBERT COOKIES

ABOUT SIX DOZEN

Tom Hunt, one of my cooking-school angels, brings me these for Christmas. I do not give a single one away, but keep them all for me.

1 pound shelled filberts, not blanched, but coarsely ground (2 pounds filberts in shell will equal 1 pound shelled filberts)
1 pound light brown sugar
4 egg whites, stiffly beaten
1 teaspoon vanilla
Granulated sugar

Mix ground filberts and brown sugar thoroughly. Add beaten egg whites and vanilla; mix very well. The batter should be stiff enough to leave side of bowl clean; if not, add a small amount of ground pecans or English walnuts. Shape into marble-sized balls, roll in granulated sugar, and bake on greased cookie sheets 15 minutes in 350° oven. These will brown very slightly with the top showing lots of cracking.

FLORENTINES

ABOUT THREE DOZEN

½ cup whipping cream
3 tablespoons sugar
¼ cup flour
⅓ cup slivered almonds, blanched
¼ pound diced preserved orange peel
4 ounces semisweet chocolate, melted

Mix first five ingredients together. Spread a cookie sheet with unsalted shortening and flour lightly. With a teaspoon drop the batter; allow ample space between each cookie. Bake the cookies in a 350° oven until golden brown, from 8 to 10 minutes. Cool. Spread the cookie bottoms with the semisweet chocolate.

FROSTY BUTTER COOKIES

THREE DOZEN

1 cup butter
4 eggs, separated
2 cups sifted all-purpose flour
1 teaspoon baking powder
1 cup sugar
1 cup ground blanched almonds
Grated rind and juice of 1 lemon

Cream butter, add egg yolks, and mix thoroughly. Sift flour and baking powder and stir into the butter-egg mixture. Wrap dough in wax paper and chill in refrigerator for 2 hours or longer. Roll out ⅛ inch thick on lightly floured board, and cut into rounds. Beat the egg whites until stiff and gradually beat in the sugar. Stir in almonds, lemon juice, and rind; cover each round with a layer of this meringue and bake at 350° for 12 minutes.

FUDGE BROWNIE FINGERS

THREE DOZEN

2 eggs
1 cup sugar
½ cup melted butter
2 squares unsweetened chocolate, melted
¾ cup sifted all-purpose flour
½ teaspoon salt
1 cup finely chopped nuts (walnuts or pecans usual; black walnuts divine)
1 teaspoon vanilla extract

Beat eggs slightly; add sugar and stir. Add melted butter and chocolate. Mix flour, salt, and nutmeats and add to egg mixture. Add vanilla and stir until well blended, but do not beat. As I said before, never beat a cookie mix. Pour into a well-buttered 9-inch pan. Bake at 325° for 30 to 35 minutes. Cool and cut in 2-inch fingers. Roll in powdered sugar.

Incidentally, when making your favorite brownie recipe, coconut substituted for the nuts is a nice change, too.

FRUITCAKE COOKIES

TEN DOZEN

These take the place of the traditional fruitcake — and are easier.

¼ cup butter
½ cup brown sugar
¼ cup jelly (any flavor; grape is good)
2 eggs
2 teaspoons soda
1½ tablespoons milk
1½ cups flour
½ teaspoon allspice
½ teaspoon cloves
½ teaspoon cinnamon
½ teaspoon nutmeg
1 pound broken pecans
1 pound seedless raisins
½ pound candied cherries, chopped
½ pound candied pineapple, chopped
½ pound citron, chopped

Cream butter, sugar, jelly, and eggs. Dissolve soda in milk, and add to creamed mixture. Gradually add half the flour, sifted with the spices. Dredge nuts and fruits with remaining flour and stir into batter. Mix well. Drop from spoon onto buttered and floured cookie sheet and decorate tops with sliced candied cherries, if desired. Bake at 300° for about 20 minutes. These cookies ripen just as fruitcake does.

CHARLOTTE'S GINGERSNAPS

FOUR DOZEN

1 cup sugar
1 cup lard
1 cup dark molasses
1 tablespoon allspice
1 tablespoon ground ginger
1 tablespoon soda in 4 tablespoons boiling water
2 cups flour or more

Preheat oven to 350°. Line a cookie sheet with aluminum foil, shiny side up. Mix sugar and lard until light. Add the molasses, allspice, and ginger. Stir in the soda and water and the flour. Roll as thin as possible on a well-floured pastry cloth with a well-floured rolling pin. Cut with a round cookie cutter. With a wide spatula transfer cookies to the lined cookie sheet, placing them close together. Bake 8 minutes or until cookies darken slightly. Remove with spatula to a rack to cool. Store in an airtight container to retain crispness.

LACE COOKIES

FIVE DOZEN

3 eggs, well beaten
¾ teaspoon salt
1½ cups sugar
1½ tablespoons melted butter
1½ teaspoons vanilla extract
¼ teaspoon grated nutmeg
4 teaspoons baking powder
3½ cups uncooked oatmeal

Beat the eggs with the salt; add sugar gradually, then stir in remaining ingredients. Drop by teaspoonfuls onto a well-buttered cookie sheet. Bake at 350° for 10 minutes or until a delicate brown. Remove from pan at once.

LEMON CRUMB SQUARES

TWO DOZEN

My favorite cookie.

1 15-ounce can condensed milk
½ cup lemon juice
1 teaspoon grated lemon rind
1½ cups sifted flour
1 teaspoon baking powder
½ teaspoon salt
⅔ cup butter
1 cup dark brown sugar, firmly packed
1 cup uncooked oatmeal

Blend together milk, lemon juice, and rind. Set aside. Sift together flour, baking powder, and salt. Cream butter; blend in sugar. Add oatmeal and flour mixture and mix until crumbly. Spread half the mixture in an 8-by-12-by-2-inch buttered baking pan and pat down; spread condensed-milk mixture over top and cover with remaining crumb mixture. Bake at 350° until brown around edges (about 25 minutes). Cool in pan at room temperature for 15 minutes; cut into 1¾-inch squares and chill in pan until firm.

MADELEINES

TWO DOZEN

A very popular French sweet. Madeleine shell pans are sold in gourmet shops.

4 eggs
¼ teaspoon salt
⅔ cup sugar
2 teaspoons grated fresh lemon peel
1 cup flour
½ cup melted butter, cooled

Beat the eggs with the salt until frothy. Gradually beat in the sugar until very thick and lemon-colored. (Use your mixer.) Add the lemon peel. Fold the flour into the egg mixture a little at a time. Fold in the melted butter. Fill buttered and floured shell tins three-quarters full. Bake 8 to 10 minutes at 400°. Remove at once and cool. You may add a few drops of food coloring to tint them if you wish.

If you dislike grating lemons and oranges as you need them, do a bunch some day and freeze.

OATMEAL CRISPS

THREE DOZEN

½ cup butter or other shortening
1 tablespoon light Karo
½ cup brown sugar
1 teaspoon vanilla extract
1¾ cups uncooked oatmeal
¼ teaspoon baking powder
¼ teaspoon salt
⅓ cup shredded coconut

Melt butter (or other shortening); add Karo, brown sugar, and vanilla. Mix oatmeal, baking powder, salt, and coconut and add to the butter mixture. Pat thin (about ¼ inch) into a buttered shallow pan. Bake at 325° 15 or 20 minutes. Watch them! Cut into narrow fingers. They are crunchy and wonderful for tea parties.

ORANGE MARMALADE COOKIES

TEN DOZEN MEDIUM-SIZED

½ cup butter
1 cup sugar
2 eggs, well beaten
3 cups sifted flour
½ teaspoon soda
½ teaspoon salt
1 cup thick orange marmalade

Cream butter, add sugar, and cream until light and fluffy. Mix in eggs. Mix flour, soda, and salt and stir into egg mixture. Add marmalade and blend. Drop by teaspoonfuls 1 inch apart on well-buttered cookie sheet. For small cookies, half a teaspoonful. Bake at 350° for 12 to 13 minutes. Remove and cool. If you wish, cover with orange icing.

PECAN BALLS

ABOUT FIVE DOZEN

½ cup shortening
½ cup butter
½ cup sugar
2 egg yolks, beaten
2 tablespoons grated orange peel
2 teaspoons grated lemon peel
2 teaspoons lemon juice
2½ cups cake flour
½ teaspoon salt
2 egg whites, slightly beaten
1½ cups finely chopped pecans
½ pound glazed cherries (you may omit)

You may substitute margarine for the shortening, but the texture and flavor is better if you do not. Cream the shortening, butter, and sugar. Add egg yolks, peels, and juice; stir and add flour and salt. Stir, but do not beat. Chill for 30 minutes. Form into small balls. Roll in the egg whites, then in the nuts. Place on a greased cookie sheet. Make an impression in the center of each ball. Cut the cherries in half and press into the cookies. Bake at 325° for 25 minutes. A favorite party cookie, and nice for Christmas.

PECAN DAINTIES

THREE DOZEN

One of the most popular cookies on the tidbit tray at "Teatime in the Zodiac" at Neiman-Marcus.

1 egg white
1 cup light brown sugar
1½ cups pecan halves

Beat egg white until stiff. Add brown sugar gradually, beating constantly. Work in the nuts and drop from a teaspoon onto a greased cookie sheet. Bake at 250° for 30 minutes. Remove from cookie sheet immediately and cool.

PECAN PUFFS

FOUR OR FIVE DOZEN

½ cup butter
4 tablespoons granulated sugar
1 teaspoon vanilla
1 cup pecans, ground
1 cup sifted cake flour
Confectioners' sugar

Cream butter and granulated sugar; add vanilla. Mix together pecans and flour and add to butter mixture. Roll into small balls and bake on a greased cookie sheet in 350° oven for 12 to 15 minutes. While still hot roll in confectioners' sugar.

PEANUT COOKIES

SIX DOZEN SMALL

1 cup chopped dry-roasted peanuts
1 cup shortening
½ cup brown sugar
1 tablespoon corn syrup
1 tablespoon peanut butter
1 cup flour
¼ teaspoon baking powder

Mix, knead, and roll out dough ¼ inch thick. Cut cookies and bake on a lightly greased cookie sheet at 350° for 20 to 25 minutes.

PRALINE COOKIES

ABOUT TWO DOZEN

1½ cups sifted flour
½ teaspoon salt
¼ teaspoon cinnamon
½ cup butter
¾ cup sugar
2 eggs yolks, beaten
2 tablespoons milk
½ teaspoon lemon extract
½ teaspoon grated lemon peel
¼ cup confectioners' sugar
¼ teaspoon cinnamon
2 egg whites, slightly beaten
⅓ cup chopped blanched almonds

Sift together dry ingredients. Cream butter, add sugar gradually, and continue creaming until light. Combine egg yolks, milk, lemon extract, and peel. Add to butter and sugar mixture. Add liquid to dry ingredients and blend thoroughly. Turn into two greased 8-inch square pans.

Add confectioners' sugar and cinnamon to egg whites and stir until blended. Spread over surface of dough. Sprinkle nuts on top. Bake in moderate oven (350°) 25 to 30 minutes. Cut in squares while warm.

PLAIN SUGAR COOKIES

ABOUT SIX DOZEN

Don't you sometimes want just a plain sugar cookie? A delightful neighbor of mine, Ethylleen Dodson Wright, who believes in grandmothers, gave me her recipe.

Cream together 1 cup sugar and 1 cup butter. Add ½ teaspoon salt, 1½ teaspoons baking powder, and 3 cups sifted flour. Beat one egg with 3 tablespoons cream (I substitute 1 teaspoon vanilla for part of the cream). Mix well and turn onto well-floured board. Roll about ⅛ inch thick, cut, and bake carefully in 350° oven on a buttered cookie sheet until lightly browned (8 to 10 minutes). Sprinkle with granulated sugar before baking if you like.

RUM BALLS

FOUR DOZEN

You may always have Rum Balls on hand, holidays or no. Or use bourbon and call them Whiskey Balls.

3 cups rolled vanilla wafers
1 cup powdered sugar
1½ cups finely chopped nuts
1½ tablespoons cocoa
2 tablespoons light Karo
½ cup rum

Mix thoroughly and form into small balls. Roll in powdered sugar and wrap in wax paper. These freeze well.

SAND TARTS

FOUR DOZEN

Everyone south of New York makes these at Christmastime. They keep forever.

½ pound butter
½ cup sifted confectioners' sugar
2 cups sifted cake flour
1 cup chopped pecans
1 teaspoon vanilla extract

Cream butter; add sugar. Stir well and add flour, nuts, and vanilla. Shape into balls or crescents and bake on ungreased cookie sheet at 325° for 20 minutes or until a light brown. Roll in powdered sugar while warm.

ROLLED NUT COOKIES

ABOUT THREE DOZEN

Any cookie tray looks better with some rolled cookies on it. They are not hard to do, but you have to be quick in their preparation.

⅓ cup shortening
1 cup light brown sugar
2 eggs
½ cup flour
¼ teaspoon salt
½ cup finely chopped pecans
½ teaspoon vanilla extract

Cream shortening, add sugar, and beat until light. Beat eggs well and blend into the sugar mixture. Add flour and salt. Mix thoroughly. Add pecans and vanilla. Drop from tip end of teaspoon on a lightly greased cookie sheet, which is turned flat side up so you can remove cookies easily when they are done. Put only two or three at a time on the sheet, as they spread very thin. Bake at 325° for 5 to 8 minutes. Remove with spatula and roll over the handle of a wooden spoon on a chopping board — be quick! If you do not roll the hot cookie, you will have a crisp lace wafer.

SPICE COOKIES

FOUR DOZEN

No Christmas cookie tray should be without a spice cookie, decorated with silver dragées, colored sugar, and all the things to add sparkle to your table. This is a good one. You can also use them on your Christmas tree.

½ cup butter
½ cup sugar
⅔ cup New Orleans-type molasses
1 egg
2¾ cups flour
3 teaspoons baking powder
½ teaspoon salt
1½ teaspoons allspice

Melt butter slowly in large saucepan; cool. Add sugar, molasses, and egg; beat well. Sift flour, baking powder, salt, and allspice into first mixture. Mix well. Roll in waxed paper; chill. Roll dough out evenly ⅛ inch thick on lightly floured baking sheet. (Cookies hold shape better if you roll dough out on baking sheet and remove the trimmings instead of rolling it on a board and transferring the cookies to the baking sheet.) Cut in shape of Santas, stars, or trees. Lift excess dough from around cookie shapes. Decorate with silver dragées, cinnamon drops, and colored sugar. If cookies are to be used for Christmas-tree decorations, make a hole in each with a skewer; enlarge holes so they won't close in baking. Bake at 375° for 8 to 10 minutes. Remove from baking sheet immediately and cool on cake racks.

SPRITZ COOKIES

FOUR DOZEN

1 cup butter
¾ cup sugar
1 egg
2½ cups sifted flour
½ teaspoon baking powder
⅛ teaspoon salt
1 teaspoon almond extract

Cream butter and sugar until fluffy. Add egg and beat. Mix sifted flour, baking powder, and salt and add to butter mixture. Add flavoring. Stir thoroughly; put into cookie press and shape as you wish on a buttered cookie sheet. Bake at 375° for 12 to 15 minutes. Press bits of candied fruit in center, or brush with unbeaten egg white and sprinkle with slivered blanched almonds before baking. At Christmastime ice with colored icing and decorate with silver dragées.

Cakes and Icings

SHERRY-GLAZED APPLE CAKE

1 cup butter
2 cups sugar
3 eggs
3 cups sifted flour
1½ teaspoons soda
½ teaspoon salt
1 teaspoon cinnamon
⅛ teaspoon nutmeg
3 cups peeled and chopped apples
2 cups chopped nutmeats, walnuts or pecans
2 teaspoons vanilla extract

Cream butter and sugar until well blended. Add the eggs, one at a time, beating after each addition. Mix dry ingredients and add gradually. Add the apples, nuts, and vanilla. Pour into a greased and floured 10-inch tube pan or bundt pan. Bake at 325° about 1½ hours or until a cake tester inserted in center of cake comes out clean. Let stand 15 minutes and turn out.

For the glaze, mix 1½ cups sugar and ½ cup dry sherry and stir over low heat constantly until syrupy. Pour over cake. This would be a great neighborhood gift at Christmastime — or any other time for that matter.

ALMOND CREAM CAKE

1 cup whipping cream
2 eggs
¼ teaspoon almond extract
1½ cups sifted flour
1 cup sugar
2 teaspoons baking powder
⅛ teaspoon salt

Whip cream until soft peaks form. Add eggs, one at a time, beating well after each addition. Stir in the almond extract. Sift together the flour, sugar, baking powder, and salt. Add to the cream mixture and stir only until blended. Pour into a buttered and floured 8-inch springform pan. Bake at 350° for 45 minutes or until lightly browned on top and toothpick inserted in center comes out clean. During the last 10 minutes of baking time prepare the topping:

2 tablespoons butter or margarine
⅓ cup sugar
¼ cup blanched, slivered almonds
1 tablespoon whipping cream
1 tablespoon flour

Mix all ingredients together and stir over low heat until well blended. Pour over cake and bake 10 minutes at 350°. Serve as is or with whipped cream. I sometimes bake this cake in a 9-inch pie tin and serve warm.

BOURBON NUT CAKE

The *Houston Post* started me on the road to writing about food. The food editor, Ann Valentine, sent me this cake recipe. Good for holiday snacking and gifts.

1 cup margarine
2 cups sugar
6 eggs
4 cups sifted flour
2 teaspoons baking powder
2 teaspoons nutmeg
¼ teaspoon almond extract
1 teaspoon vanilla extract
1 cup bourbon
1 pound finely chopped pecans
3 tablespoons coconut
7¼ ounces dates, chopped

Cream margarine and sugar, add eggs one at a time, and stir after each addition. Add flour, baking powder, nutmeg, almond extract, vanilla, and bourbon. Flour nuts; add nuts, coconut, and dates and combine lightly. Pour into buttered and floured angel food tin. Cook in slow (250°) oven for 6 hours. Place a pan of water in the oven to keep the cake from cracking. Also cover cake with aluminum foil for the first few hours of the baking period.

BRANDY ALMOND CAKE

1 cup butter
1½ cups sugar
4 eggs, separated
3 tablespoons light cream
½ cup brandy
2 tablespoons lemon juice
Grated rind of 1 lemon
2 cups flour
2 teaspoons baking powder
1 cup slivered untoasted almonds
Sifted confectioners' sugar

Cream butter and sugar; add egg yolks beaten until light. Add cream, brandy, lemon juice and rind, and flour sifted with the baking powder. Then add the almonds. Fold in egg whites, beaten stiff. Bake in a greased square cake pan at 325° for 1 hour, or 15 minutes longer if using a greased tube pan. Cover with brown paper while baking. If you are unsure of your oven temperatures, put a layer of brown paper in bottom of a pie tin and put tube pan on it. In other words, the cake should be a very light brown when finished. Sprinkle with sifted confectioners' sugar while warm. This is a great, not too sweet, cake for the holidays (especially with eggnog).

CHOCOLATE CAKE

This was my Aunt Laura's chocolate cake, black and moist. I love it with Colonnade Icing and bitter chocolate dribbled over. During the depression, while I was at the Presbyterian Hospital in Newark, New Jersey, I used to get up at three o'clock in the morning every Saturday and make these for anyone who could afford to buy them. And quite a few could.

2 squares unsweetened chocolate
½ cup boiling water

Cook and cool. Then mix:

2 eggs, well beaten
1½ cups sugar
A pinch of salt
½ cup butter

Then add:

Cooled chocolate mixture
1 teaspoon vanilla extract
¾ cup buttermilk
1 teaspoon baking soda

Last, add:

1½ cups sifted flour

Bake in two 9-inch layers at 375° for 35 to 45 minutes.

CARROT CAKE

3 cups sifted flour
1½ teaspoons soda
1 teaspoon cinnamon
½ teaspoon salt
1½ cups liquid corn oil
2 cups sugar
2 cups grated raw carrots
1 8½-ounce can crushed pineapple with juice
1½ cups chopped pecans
2 teaspoons vanilla extract
3 eggs

Sift flour, soda, cinnamon, and salt. Mix oil and sugar. Add half the dry ingredients. Mix well and beat in carrots, pineapple, nuts, and vanilla. Add remaining dry ingredients and beat until well blended. Drop in eggs one at a time, beating after each addition. Pour batter into well buttered and floured 10-inch tube pan. Bake at 350° for 1½ hours. When done leave in pan for 10 minutes, then remove. Cool thoroughly before icing with Cream Cheese Icing.

CHERRY NUT CAKE

2 cups butter or margarine
2 cups sugar
6 egg yolks
3 cups cake flour
¾ pound candied cherries
¼ pound candied pineapple
5 cups broken nutmeats, pecans or walnuts
2 tablespoons lemon extract
6 egg whites

Cream butter; add sugar and mix until smooth and light. Beat egg yolks and blend into butter mixture. Sift the flour over the fruit and nuts, and toss together until well coated. Stir into the butter-and-egg mixture. Add lemon extract. Beat egg whites until stiff but not dry and fold into batter. Pour into a well-buttered 10-inch tube or bundt pan and bake at 300° for 1¾ hours. Let cake cool on a rack for 10 minutes.

Remove from pan and cool completely before slicing. When wrapped, this cake keeps for days and freezes well. No icing is necessary. Sometimes I pour over the top a lemon-juice-and-sugar glaze.

COFFEE ANGEL FOOD

The most talked-about cake at Neiman-Marcus.

1½ cups sifted sugar
1 cup sifted cake flour
½ teaspoon salt
1¼ cups egg whites (10 to 12)
1¼ teaspoons cream of tartar
½ teaspoon vanilla extract
1 tablespoon powdered instant coffee

Add ½ cup of the sugar to flour. Sift together 4 times. Add salt to egg whites and beat with flat wire whisk or rotary egg beater until foamy. Sprinkle cream of tartar over eggs and continue beating to soft-peak stage. Add the remaining cup of sugar by sprinkling ¼ cup at a time over egg whites and blending carefully into, about 20 strokes each time. Fold in flavorings. Sift about a quarter of the flour-sugar mixture over egg whites at a time and fold in lightly, about 10 strokes each time. Pour into ungreased round 10-inch tube pan. Bake at 350° for 35 to 45 minutes. Remove from oven and invert pan on cooling rack.

Ice with Butter Icing, adding 2 tablespoons of powdered coffee to the recipe. Whip until light and fluffy. Spread and sprinkle generously with slivered or chopped toasted almonds.

FRUITCAKE

SIX POUNDS

1 pound dates
½ pound coconut
1 pound glazed cherries
½ pound natural glazed pineapple
½ pound green glazed pineapple
2 pounds large shelled pecans
1 can condensed milk
1 teaspoon vanilla or rum extract

Mix and pack in foil pans. Decorate or not with glazed fruit. Bake at 250° for 2 hours. Fill small foil cups about 2-ounce size for a gift package. Eight of them are equivalent to one pound and they can be made into an attractive package — Thanks! Al Black.

POPPY SEED CAKE

Cakes without icing are becoming the usual, and this was a recipe sent to me many years ago. I have used it for entertaining, as a neighborly gift, and for travelers to munch on. It freezes well and wrapped in clear plastic will keep for days in the refrigerator.

¾ cup poppy seeds
¾ cup milk
¾ cup butter, margarine, or vegetable shortening
1¼ cups sugar
3 eggs
1 teaspoon vanilla extract
2 cups flour
2 teaspoons baking powder
½ teaspoon salt

Soak poppy seeds in milk overnight. Set aside. Cream butter and sugar. Add eggs one at a time, beating well after each addition. Add vanilla, milk and poppy seeds, then flour sifted with the baking powder and salt. Mix well. Pour into a well-buttered 9-inch tube or bundt pan and bake at 375° for 30 to 40 minutes. For a lighter cake, separate the eggs and fold in the stiffly beaten egg whites at the end. This cake may be served plain, with confectioners' sugar sifted over, or with a lemon-juice-and-granulated-sugar glaze.

LEMON ICEBOX CAKE

This recipe came from Margaret Gillam, who was my "boss lady" at the Society of the New York Hospital. I learned many things from Miss Gillam, but best of all that there is no substitute for quality.

1 cup butter
1 cup sugar
3 egg yolks
Juice of 1½ oranges, plus the grated rind
Juice of 1 lemon, plus the grated rind
3 egg whites
Sponge cake or ladyfingers

Cream the butter and sugar together and add the egg yolks and fruit juices. Beat the egg whites until stiff and fold into the butter mixture. Line a mold or cake tin with sponge cake cut in fingers, or ladyfingers, and cover with the mixture. Repeat for as many layers as you wish, ending with the cake on top. Refrigerate overnight or deep freeze. It freezes beautifully. I keep one on hand at all times.

NUT CAKE

You can bring out this nut cake from your deep freeze for dessert, for tea parties, for any special treat. The recipe came from Catherine Cutrer, the wife of a Houston mayor, through Margaret Hull, my favorite recipe gossiper.

1 pound butter
2 cups sugar, sifted
6 eggs, separated
3 cups cake flour
¾ pound candied cherries
¼ pound candied pineapple
5 cups nuts, broken
2 ounces lemon extract

Cream butter and sugar. Add beaten yolks, flour, finely chopped fruit, nuts, and lemon extract. Beat egg whites until stiff but not dry, and fold into batter. Bake 1 hour at 300°. Can be baked in four small loaf pans or one large pan.

ORANGE CHIFFON CAKE

2¼ cups cake flour
3 teaspoons baking powder
1½ cups sugar
1 teaspoon salt
½ cup salad oil (not olive oil)
5 egg yolks
¾ cup water
2 teaspoons grated orange peel
1 cup egg whites (7 or 8 eggs)
½ teaspoon cream of tartar

Sift the dry ingredients together. Pour in the oil, egg yolks, water, and orange peel. Beat until smooth (2 minutes with an electric beater). Set aside. Beat together egg whites and cream of tartar until stiff. Pour mixture over egg whites a little at a time, gently folding in with a rubber scraper. Do not beat. Pour into a 10-inch unbuttered tube pan and bake at 325° for 50 minutes. Increase to 350° and bake an additional 15 minutes, or until the top springs back when you dent it with your finger. Turn pan upside down onto platter. Let stand until cold before removing pan. Cover with the following icing.

COFFEE BUTTER CREAM ICING

½ cup butter
2 cups confectioners' sugar
1½ teaspoons instant coffee
½ teaspoon vanilla extract

Beat the butter until creamy. Add rest of ingredients and beat until light and fluffy.

Cover the iced cake with shaved semisweet chocolate.

PRINCE OF WALES SPICE CAKE

This spice cake has always been popular as a "groom's" cake at weddings, and for tea parties. I always ice with Colonnade Icing flavored with lemon juice and grated lemon peel.

1½ cups sugar
⅓ cup shortening
3 eggs, well beaten
1½ tablespoons molasses
1½ teaspoons baking soda
1½ teaspoons cinnamon
¾ teaspoon cloves
¾ teaspoon nutmeg
3 cups sifted cake flour
1½ teaspoons baking powder
1½ cups sour milk

Cream shortening and sugar; add well-beaten eggs, then molasses. Sift dry ingredients together three times. Add to creamed mixture alternately with sour milk. Pour into well buttered and floured 9-inch cake pans. Bake at 350° for 20 to 25 minutes.

SOUR CREAM POUND CAKE

1 cup butter
1½ cups sugar
4 eggs
2 cups flour
¾ teaspoon soda
½ teaspoon salt
¾ cup currants
½ cup sour cream
1 tablespoon Cointreau

Cream butter; add sugar and mix thoroughly. Add eggs and beat mixture until light. Sift flour, soda, and salt together; add currants. Stir into the egg mixture alternately with the sour cream. Add the Cointreau and pour into a buttered and lightly floured angel food or bundt pan. Bake at 350° for 1 hour or until cake tester comes out clean. Turn out and while cake is warm pour over a lemon-juice-and-sugar glaze.

RUM CAKE

Rum cake is a favorite all-year-round cake. This recipe is the one I use. It freezes well, too.

1 cup butter
2 cups sugar
4 eggs
1 cup milk
3½ cups sifted flour
3 teaspoons baking powder
¼ teaspoon salt
1 teaspoon rum flavoring

Mix butter, sugar, and eggs thoroughly. Add milk and flour mixture (flour, baking powder, and salt sifted together) alternately and mix. Add rum flavoring and pour into well buttered and floured 9-inch square cake pans. Bake 1 hour at 325°. Use the following icing:

1 cup brown sugar
1 cup white sugar
½ cup water
A pinch of salt
1 teaspoon rum flavoring or 2 tablespoons dark rum

Mix all together, except flavoring, and boil well. Add flavoring and pour half the icing over hot cake while still in pan. Let cake cool, then turn upside down on plate and pour remaining icing over the cake.

WHITE CHOCOLATE CAKE

Mrs. John Yeazel from Omaha, Nebraska, sent me this recipe for which I will be eternally grateful.

1 cup butter
2 cups sugar
4 eggs
¼ pound white chocolate melted in ½ cup boiling water
2½ cups cake flour
1 teaspoon soda
1 cup buttermilk
1 teaspoon vanilla extract

Cream butter and sugar. Add eggs one at a time, beating well after each addition. Cool the melted chocolate in the water and add to the egg mixture. Add the flour, soda, and buttermilk alternately to the chocolate mixture. Stir in the vanilla. Pour into well-buttered 9-inch layer cake pans and bake 40 minutes at 350° or until done. You may vary this recipe by the following:

Add only egg yolks to butter and sugar. Use baking powder in place of soda. Then add beaten egg whites to mixture just before vanilla. Fold in 1 cup finely chopped pecans and 1 cup coconut. Bake in two layers. Frost either version with Colonnade Icing or Chocolate Fudge Icing.

CHEESE CAKE

This will not fail; and you may freeze it with great success.

1 pound cream cheese
4 tablespoons flour
1 tablespoon cornstarch
2½ tablespoons sugar
1 whole egg
½ teaspoon salt
½ tablespoon butter
¼ teaspoon vanilla extract
¼ teaspoon almond extract

Mix together and beat for 2 minutes. Add slowly while beating:

6 tablespoons sour cream
1 cup milk

Beat to a peak:

½ cup egg whites

Add, beating thoroughly:

2½ tablespoons sugar

Fold beaten egg whites into the cheese mixture and pour into an angel food tin or springform pan that has been greased with butter and dusted with graham cracker or vanilla wafer crumbs. Bake at 250° until done, about 2 hours. When cool, invert on a serving tray and spread with whipped sour cream. Can be served plain, or as a nice variation with a faint sprinkling of cinnamon or walnut meat dust.

ICEBOX CHEESE CAKE

For the crust, mix:

1½ cups graham cracker crumbs
¼ cup melted butter
1 tablespoon sugar
1 teaspoon cinnamon

Press onto the bottom and sides of a well-buttered 9-inch springform pan. Bake at 400° for 10 minutes. Cool and chill.

3 egg yolks, beaten
½ cup sugar
½ cup hot water
1 tablespoon plus 1 teaspoon unflavored gelatin
¼ cup cold water
2 8-ounce packages cream cheese
½ teaspoon grated lemon peel
1 teaspoon lemon juice
4 egg whites
1 cup whipping cream

Mix egg yolks with sugar; add hot water and cook in a double boiler over boiling water for 3 minutes, stirring constantly. Add the gelatin softened in the cold water. Stir in the cream cheese softened at room temperature. Mix thoroughly and strain. Add lemon peel and juice. Fold in stiffly beaten egg whites and cream, whipped. Pour into cold shell and refrigerate for several hours. A dash of Cointreau won't hurt it either.

SEA FOAM ICING

½ cup brown sugar
1 cup white sugar
4 tablespoons hot water
2 tablespoons strong coffee
¼ teaspoon cream of tartar
2 egg whites, stiffly beaten
¼ teaspoon salt
½ teaspoon almond extract
¼ teaspoon baking powder

Boil sugars, water, coffee, and cream of tartar until the mixture spins a thread, or 248° on your candy thermometer. Remove from heat and pour very slowly into stiffly beaten egg whites, continuing to beat until thick. Add salt, almond extract, and baking powder, and beat until spreading consistency. Pile on the cake thickly, but do not use a heavy hand.

BUTTER ICING

½ cup butter
¼ teaspoon salt
2½ cups sifted confectioners' sugar
3 to 4 tablespoons milk
1 teaspoon vanilla extract

Cream butter; add salt and sugar, a small amount at a time, beating all the while. Add milk as needed, and flavoring. Beat until light and fluffy. Vary your flavors with almond extract, orange juice in place of the milk, and 2 teaspoons of grated orange peel; lemon juice and peel likewise. Add powdered coffee, 2 tablespoons. Add 2 squares of melted unsweetened chocolate. Add whatever you like.

CARAMEL ICING

½ cup butter
½ cup brown sugar
¼ cup milk or half-and-half
1¾ to 2 cups confectioners' sugar
1 teaspoon maple or vanilla extract

Melt butter until brown; add sugar and cook, stirring until sugar is completely melted. Pour in milk and stir. Cool. Add sugar and extract; beat until thick enough to spread.

COLONNADE ICING

4½ cups sugar
1 cup water
6 tablespoons light Karo
6 egg whites, stiffly beaten
⅜ cup confectioners' sugar

Mix sugar, water, and Karo, and cook to soft-ball stage, 238° on your candy thermometer. Add slowly to egg whites, which have been beaten stiff but not dry, beating thoroughly until the icing is like cream. Add confectioners' sugar. This is a soft-on-the-inside, crusty-on-the-outside icing that never fails. Leftovers may be refrigerated, then heated in warm water to lukewarm and used as needed. This icing goes on all the cakes you have liked, with variations:

With fresh coconut or toasted coconut flakes on chocolate or yellow cake.

Unsweetened chocolate melted and dribbled over for a chocolate or angel food cake.

Split layers of yellow caked filled with lemon pie filling, and iced lightly but deep with Colonnade Icing.

Flavored with fresh lime or lemon juice, and the grate rind, for angel food cakes.

Dusted with slivered nuts of all kinds for chiffon, layer, and angel food cakes.

Fresh or frozen strawberries added for angel food and chocolate cakes.

Flavor with anything you like, peppermint, crème de cacao, or powdered coffee (add with the confectioners' sugar).

ORNAMENTAL ICING

2 cups sugar
1 cup water
3 egg whites
¼ teaspoon cream of tartar

Boil sugar and water until it forms a thread, or 240°. Pour the syrup gradually onto beaten egg whites, beating constantly. Add cream of tartar and continue beating until stiff. Use it with a pastry tube when making flowers — it never melts or spreads.

WHIPPED CREAM FROSTING

Being a country girl, I like whipped cream frostings. Be sure to refrigerate cake after icing.

1 cup whipping cream
2 teaspoons sugar
½ teaspoon vanilla extract

Mix and beat until thick. Spread thickly on any kind of cake.

To vary it: Add 1 teaspoon powdered coffee, whip and swirl crème de cacao through, or add any fresh fruit, especially strawberries when icing a chocolate cake.

Pies and Pastry

PLAIN PASTRY

Everyone has her own recipe for plain pastry. This is mine.

2 cups sifted flour
1 teaspoon salt
⅔ cup shortening
6 to 8 tablespoons cold water

Sift the flour and salt together; cut in the shortening quickly and lightly with a pastry blender or your fingers. Stir in the cold water as lightly as possible to form a smooth ball. Roll out on a lightly floured board to as thin a pastry as you like. This will make one 2-crust pie, or 12 individual tart shells, with a few scraps left over. Roll these out for cheese straws, or cut with a small round cutter for bases for cocktail spreads. Keep a container in your refrigerator for such things. Wrap unbaked dough in waxed paper and chill until you need it. Remember to handle as little as possible, so the pastry will be light and flaky.

□

Any cream or chiffon pie may use these two crusts; and they are good for ice-cream pie.

TOASTED ALMOND CRUST

1 cup sifted flour
½ teaspoon salt
¼ cup slivered, lightly toasted almonds
½ cup shortening
2 tablespoons cold water

Mix flour, salt, and nuts. Cut in the shortening and add the water. Mix to form a ball. Roll thin and fit into a 9-inch pie tin. Bake at 400° until light brown.

GRAHAM CRACKER CRUST

1½ cups graham cracker crumbs
½ cup confectioners' sugar
½ cup melted butter

Mix and press firmly into a 9-inch pie tin. Sprinkle lightly with cold water and bake at 300° for 8 minutes.

COCONUT BUTTER CRUST

The quickest pie you can make for company is with a Coconut Butter Crust. Use for a cream or chiffon pie.

2 tablespoons butter
1½ cups shredded packaged coconut

Spread the butter evenly on the bottom and sides of an 8- or 9-inch pie pan, completely coating the pan. Sprinkle with the coconut, and press evenly into the butter. Bake at 300° for 15 to 20 minutes (until brown).

COCONUT CRUMB CRUST

1½ cups tender-thin flaked coconut
2 tablespoons butter, melted
2 tablespoons sugar
¼ cup finely crushed graham crackers, gingersnaps, vanilla wafers, or chocolate wafers
A pinch of cinnamon

Combine coconut and butter and mix well. Add sugar and cookie crumbs, mixing thoroughly. Press firmly on bottom and sides of 9-inch pie pan. Bake in moderate oven (375°) for 10 to 12 minutes or until lightly browned. Cool.

Fill crust with ice cream. Serve immediately, or deep freeze to serve later. An all-time favorite is coffee ice cream in Coconut Crumb Crust with butterscotch sauce and whipped cream. Or fill with chiffon or cream pie filling and chill until firm.

GINGERSNAP CRUST

35 gingersnaps
¼ pound butter, melted
1 tablespoon confectioners' sugar

Roll gingersnaps with rolling pin to make fine crumbs; add melted butter and sugar and mix well. Press firmly into a 9-inch pie tin. Bake at 300° for 5 minutes.

It is good to have crumb crusts stored in your deep freeze. (Put wax paper or foil between them.)

ICE-CREAM PIES

Fill any crust with your favorite ice cream and freeze. When ready to serve, cut and serve with your preference of sauce or fruit poured over, and whipped cream, if you wish.

Strawberry Ice-Cream Pie has always been a favorite.

1 9-inch Graham Cracker Crust
1 quart strawberry ice cream

Press the ice cream into the shell and freeze. Serve with strawberries, fresh or frozen, and unsweetened whipped cream.

Other great combinations:

Lemon ice cream in Gingersnap Crust, served with fresh peaches or blueberries slightly mashed and sugared.

Coffee ice cream and raspberry sherbet in Toasted Almond Crust with Fudge Sauce and whipped cream.

Vanilla, or a combination of flavors, packed in a baked pie shell and piled high with a meringue made with 3 egg whites and 6 tablespoons of sugar. Brown in a 450° oven and place in the freezer. Serve with hot Fudge Sauce or Melba Sauce.

TOASTED ALMOND TARTS

FOR TWELVE

A delectable party dessert.

Pastry dough
⅔ cup sugar
½ teaspoon salt
2½ tablespoons cornstarch
1 tablespoon flour
3 cups milk
3 egg yolks
1 tablespoon butter
½ teaspoon almond extract
1 cup toasted slivered almonds
1 cup cream, whipped and flavored with vanilla extract

Line tart tins with pastry and bake at 400° until done (12 to 15 minutes, watching carefully). Remove from tins and cool. Mix the sugar, salt, cornstarch, flour, and milk and cook over low heat until thick. Boil for 1 minute. Remove; add the egg yolks and butter and cook again until the mixture boils. Remove and add the almond extract and ½ cup of almonds. Cool mixture, fill tart shells, spread lightly with whipped cream flavored with vanilla, and cover with the rest of the almonds. Serve cold.

MY FRENCH APPLE PIE

1 cup butter
2 cups sugar
4 pounds green apples, Winesaps or McIntosh
¼ teaspoon cinnamon
2 teaspoons lemon juice
Pie dough
1 cup sugar

Spread a 10-inch pie tin with ½ cup of the butter, about ¼ inch deep. Pour ½ cup sugar over. Peel and slice thin the apples; mix with the remaining 1½ cups of sugar. Pile into the pie tin; it will be high with apples. Dot with remaining butter and sprinkle with cinnamon and lemon juice. Roll out pie dough and cover the apples, pressing loosely on the sides of the pie tin. Put in a 450° oven and bake 20 minutes. Reduce heat to 350° and bake until apples are soft. Remove, cool slightly. Place a serving plate on top of the pie and invert. Cool. Caramelize 1 cup sugar and pour over apples. Serve with whipped unsweetened cream if you wish. I don't.

This is really my version of Tarte Tatin and I like it better than the original. Funny thing, M. Carrère of the famed Maxim's did too.

fluffy. Melt the gelatin over hot water and add. Pour into baked pie shell sprinkled with the nutmeats. Chill. Cover with whipped cream mixed with instant coffee and confectioners' sugar. Refrigerate.

LEMON PIE

9-inch pie shell, baked

Filling:

4 tablespoons cornstarch
4 tablespoons flour
½ teaspoon salt
1½ cups sugar
1½ cups boiling water
2 tablespoons butter
5 egg yolks
⅓ cup lemon juice
1 tablespoon grated lemon peel

Combine the first five ingredients and cook over hot water for 20 minutes or until thick. Remove from heat and add butter and yolks. Continue to cook over hot water until thick. Cool and add lemon juice and lemon peel. Pour into pie shell.

Topping:

5 egg whites
½ cup sugar
1 teaspoon lemon juice

Beat the egg white to the soft-peak stage, then beat in the sugar gradually. Add the lemon juice. Pile on pie, roughly and high. (For sky-high add 2 more egg whites and 2 tablespoons sugar.) Bake about 5 minutes at 425° — but watch it. Or cover the pie with whipped cream instead of meringue.

LEMON CUSTARD PIE

The very best pie I ever ate.

4 large eggs
1 cup sugar
2 teaspoons flour
1 cup Karo (light)
Grated rind and juice of 1 lemon
4 teaspoons butter, just softened
9-inch unbaked pie shell

Beat the eggs; add sugar mixed with the flour. Add rest of ingredients. Pour into shell and bake at 350° for 60 minutes or until a knife inserted in center comes out clean. Do not refrigerate.

COCONUT CREAM PIE

Coconut Cream or Meringue Pie was the golfers' favorite at the Houston Country Club.

1¾ cups milk
¾ cup sugar
½ teaspoon salt
3½ tablespoons flour
2 tablespoons cornstarch
1 egg plus 2 yolks, beaten
2 tablespoons butter
½ teaspoon vanilla extract
¼ teaspoon almond or lemon extract
2 egg whites
¾ cup grated fresh or flaked coconut
9-inch baked pie shell
1 cup heavy cream

Scald half the milk and add ½ cup of the sugar and the salt. Bring to a boil. Mix flour, cornstarch, and beaten egg and yolks with the remaining milk and beat until smooth. Add a little of the hot milk and blend. Combine both mixtures and cook over hot water until thick, stirring frequently. Remove and add the butter and flavorings. Beat until smooth. Beat the egg whites until frothy, add remaining sugar, and beat until stiff. Fold the custard into the egg whites. Sprinkle ¼ cup coconut through the mixture and pour into the baked shell. Whip cream and spread over the top. Cover with rest of the coconut and chill.

When I use meringue as a top, I whip and fold ½ cup cream into the custard after it has cooled, and beat the egg whites with the sugar and pile on top. Sprinkle with coconut and place in a 450° oven until the coconut begins to brown.

PEACH CRUMB PIE

¾ cup sugar
2 tablespoons butter
¼ cup flour
9-inch unbaked pie shell
14 canned peach halves
¼ cup peach juice
2 tablespoons lemon juice

Mix the sugar, butter, and flour into crumbs that look like coarse cornmeal. Sprinkle half the crumbs in bottom of the pie shell, add the peaches, juice, and lemon juice, and cover with rest of the crumbs. Bake at 375° until crust is done and crumbs are well browned, about 1 hour. Do the same with frozen or canned cherries.

FRESH BLUEBERRY TARTELETTES

2 cups sifted flour
1 teaspoon salt
⅔ cup vegetable shortening
1 egg, slightly beaten
2 tablespoons cold water
2 teaspoons lemon juice

Sift flour with salt into mixing bowl. Cut in shortening with a pastry blender or two knives. Mix egg, water, and lemon juice. Sprinkle over flour mixture; toss and stir until mixture is moist enough to hold together. You may need to add a little more cold water. Sprinkle flour on board to roll pastry on. Rub rolling pin with flour. Do not press down too hard on dough, but roll until dough is smooth and thin. Fit crust tightly into each tart tin, fit a second tin into it to hold it firmly in place. Bake at 350° for 10 to 15 minutes, until golden brown. (You could also buy frozen tart shells or use commercial pastry mix.)

Line the shells with the following cream cheese mixture:

1 8-ounce package cream cheese
3 tablespoons sugar
3 tablespoons lemon juice

Mix until consistency of whipped cream and spread generously inside the tart shells. Fill with fresh blueberries. Cover with blueberry sauce:

1 cup fresh blueberries
2 tablespoons sugar or more
2 tablespoons crème de cassis (you may omit)

Crush berries in blender. Add sugar and cassis. Pour over berries. Serve plain or with sour or whipped cream.

DIXIE PECAN PIE

Selma Streit, who was the beloved director of Scottish Rite Dormitory at the University of Texas, gave me my first southern recipe, for pecan pie. I have used it ever since.

3 eggs
2 tablespoons sugar
2 tablespoons flour
2 cups dark Karo
1 teaspoon vanilla extract
¼ teaspoon salt
1 cup pecan meats
9-inch unbaked pie shell

Beat the eggs until light. Mix the sugar and flour. Add to the eggs and beat well. Add Karo, vanilla, salt, and pecans. Pour into pie shell and bake at 425° for 10 minutes; reduce heat to 325° and finish baking—about 45 minutes.

FRESH STRAWBERRY PIE

1½ quarts fresh strawberries
3 tablespoons cornstarch
1 cup sugar
2 tablespoons lemon juice
9-inch baked pie shell

Wash and hull berries and reserve half (the best ones). Mash the other half, add the cornstarch and sugar, and cook until thick and clear. Remove from heat and stir in the lemon juice. Cool; add the whole berries, or if too large, cut in half, but save a few for garnishing. Pour into the pie shell, cover with whipped cream, and garnish. It has a tartness combined with the strawberry sweetness that is interesting. This is the pie President Eisenhower liked.

RASPBERRY OR STRAWBERRY WHIPPED-CREAM PIE

A pretty pie for a luncheon.

1½ cups milk
½ cup sugar
¼ teaspoon salt
3 tablespoons flour
2 eggs
1 tablespoon butter
½ teaspoon vanilla extract
9-inch baked pie shell
1½ cups cream, whipped
1 cup frozen raspberries or strawberries, crushed to a pulp
Shaved bittersweet chocolate

Scald 1 cup of the milk in the top part of a double boiler. Mix dry ingredients, add remaining ½ cup of milk, and make a smooth paste. Pour into the hot milk and stir until thick. Beat eggs and add to the hot mixture and cook for 5 minutes. Remove from heat; add butter and vanilla. Cool and pour into baked pie shell. Pile whipped cream mixed with the fruit on top and sprinkle with shaved bittersweet chocolate.

Variations:

This cream mixture is the base of all cream pies — banana, coconut, toasted almond. Just before pouring into the pie shell whip ½ cup cream and fold in.

For Caramel Cream Pie, caramelize the sugar.

For Chocolate Pie, add 2 squares of unsweetened chocolate and increase the sugar to ¾ cup. Banana Chocolate Pie is good! So are Chocolate Pecan and Chocolate Toasted Almond.

For Coffee Pie, add instant coffee until it tastes as you like it — I like 2 tablespoons. Add toasted slivered almonds to the coffee-cream mixture, too.

BLACK-BOTTOM PIE

---

1 tablespoon unflavored gelatin
4 tablespoons cold water
2 cups milk
½ cup sugar
1 tablespoon cornstarch
¼ teaspoon salt
4 egg yolks, beaten
2 ounces (2 squares) unsweetened chocolate, melted
1 teaspoon vanilla extract

Soften gelatin in cold water. Scald milk in double boiler. Combine sugar, cornstarch, and salt, stir slowly into milk, and cook until thick. Add gradually to beaten egg yolks. Return to double boiler and cook 3 minutes longer. Stir in gelatin to dissolve. Divide in half; add melted chocolate and vanilla to half the mixture to make chocolate layer. Pour carefully into Gingersnap Crust. Let remaining half of custard cool.

Cream layer:

4 egg whites
⅛ teaspoon cream of tartar
½ cup sugar
1 tablespoon rum
1 teaspoon dry sherry
¾ cup heavy cream
1 tablespoon shaved unsweetened chocolate

Beat egg whites until frothy; add cream of tartar; continue beating to a soft peak, and gradually add sugar. Fold meringue into cooled custard; add flavorings. Pour carefully over chocolate layer. Chill in refrigerator until set. When ready to serve, whip cream, spread on top of pie, and sprinkle with shaved chocolate.

ORANGE CHIFFON PIE WITH PRUNE-WHIP TOP

This was the most popular pie for parties at the Driskill Hotel.

1 tablespoon gelatin
¼ cup cold water
4 egg yolks, beaten
1 cup sugar
½ teaspoon salt
1 tablespoon lemon juice
½ cup orange juice
1 tablespoon grated orange peel
4 egg whites
1 Graham Cracker Crust
1 cup heavy cream, whipped
1 tablespoon sugar
¾ cup chopped cooked prunes
1 teaspoon grated lemon peel

Soak the gelatin in the cold water for 15 minutes. Beat the egg yolks until light. Add ½ cup sugar, salt, lemon juice, and orange juice. Cook in a double boiler until thick. Add the grated orange peel. Remove from heat and add the gelatin. Stir until dissolved. Cool. Beat egg whites medium stiff, add the rest of the sugar gradually, and continue beating until stiff. Fold into the orange mixture and place in the Graham Cracker Crust, piling high in the center. Top with the whipped cream, into which the 1 tablespoon of sugar, prunes, and grated lemon peel have been folded.

At the Houston Country Club I used to swirl crème de cacao in the whipped cream and sliver semisweet chocolate on top.

Use the same recipe for Lemon or Lime Chiffon, substituting for the orange juice lemon or lime juice and grated peel of each. Sour cream is an interesting topping for the lemon pie, sprinkled with a fine dust of walnuts.

SOUR CREAM PUMPKIN PIE

12 ounces (4 3-ounce packages) cream cheese
¾ cup sugar
1½ tablespoons flour
1 teaspoon grated orange peel
½ teaspoon grated lemon peel
2 eggs plus 2 yolks
1 cup cooked or canned pumpkin
⅛ teaspoon cinnamon
9-inch Graham Cracker Crust, unbaked

Blend in your electric mixer the cheese, sugar, flour, and grated peels. Add eggs and egg yolks; beat at medium speed until smooth. Mix in pumpkin and cinnamon; continue beating until light and smooth. Pour into prepared crust. Bake at 350° for 40 minutes or until custard is set. Remove and spread with the following mixture:

2 cups sour cream
3 tablespoons sugar
1 teaspoon vanilla extract

Bake 10 minutes longer. Remove from oven, cool, and spread with a thin layer of cold sour cream.

TOM AND JERRY PIE

---

1 tablespoon gelatin
¼ cup cold water
4 egg yolks
1 cup sugar
½ teaspoon salt
½ cup hot water
2 tablespoons dry sherry
1 tablespoon dark rum
4 egg whites
1 cup heavy cream
1 Graham Cracker Crust

Soak the gelatin in the cold water. Beat egg yolks, ½ cup sugar, salt, and the hot water. Cook and stir in the double boiler until thick. Add the gelatin and stir until it dissolves. Cool; add the sherry and rum. When this mixture begins to set, fold in stiffly beaten egg whites to which remaining ½ cup sugar has been added; then fold in ½ cup heavy cream, whipped. Pour all into Graham Cracker Crust. Chill in the refrigerator. When ready to serve, cover with remaining whipped cream and sprinkle a few grains of nutmeg over the top.

LEMON ANGEL PIE

---

4 egg whites
¼ teaspoon cream of tartar
¾ cup sugar

Beat egg whites until frothy. Add cream of tartar. Continue beating, gradually adding the sugar until the mixture is stiff. Spread in a 9-inch pie tin ungreased and bake at 300° for 1 hour. Cool. Cover with the following lemon filling.

Mix:

6 egg yolks
¾ cup sugar
½ teaspoon salt

Add:

3 tablespoons orange juice
3 tablespoons lemon juice
1 teaspoon grated orange rind
1 teaspoon grated lemon rind

Cook over hot water until thick. Cool and spread over top of the baked meringue. Cover with whipped cream and toasted slivered almonds, or fold into the custard.

I also pour the meringue into a partially baked pie crust and bake. Serve with hot Fudge Sauce, Melba Sauce, or fresh fruit.

BAKED ALASKA PIE

Melt ¼ pound butter and 1 ounce unsweetened chocolate in a saucepan. Add 1 cup sugar and mix. Beat 2 eggs until very light. Add ⅓ cup flour, pour in chocolate mixture, and beat. Add 1 teaspoon vanilla. Butter a 9-inch glass pie pan and add mixture. Bake 35 minutes at 325°. Cool. Prepare a meringue — beat 5 egg whites until frothy, gradually add ½ cup sugar and ⅛ teaspoon salt, and beat until stiff and glossy. Pile peppermint candy ice cream on top of pie. Completely cover with the meringue, sealing the ice cream in. Run under broiler to brown. Do ahead and freeze if you like.

FRENCH CHOCOLATE PIE

2 egg whites
⅛ teaspoon salt
⅛ teaspoon cream of tartar
½ cup sugar
½ cup finely chopped walnuts or pecans
½ teaspoon vanilla extract
1 package (¼ pound) sweet cooking chocolate
3 tablespoons water
1 tablespoon brandy
1 cup heavy cream

Combine egg whites, salt, and cream of tartar in mixing bowl. Beat until foamy throughout. Add sugar, two tablespoons at a time, beating after each addition until sugar is blended. Continue beating until the mixture will stand in very stiff peaks. Fold in nuts and vanilla. Spoon into a lightly greased 8-inch pie pan and make a nestlike shelf, building sides up ½ inch above edge of the pan, but not over the rim. If desired, the meringue can be squeezed through a pastry tube to make a fancy edge. Bake in a slow oven (300°) for 50 to 55 minutes. Cool. Place chocolate and water in a saucepan over low heat. Stir until the chocolate has melted. Cool. Add brandy to chocolate. Whip cream to soft consistency. Fold chocolate mixture into whipped cream. Pile into meringue shell. Chill about 2 hours before serving. (Garnish with shaved chocolate.)

Puddings, Custards, Mousses, and Tortes

CAKE CRUMB PUDDING

FOR EIGHT

¼ cup plus 2 teaspoons butter
½ cup sugar
1 egg
½ cup dark Karo or molasses
½ cup buttermilk or sour milk
½ teaspoon soda
½ cup raisins
½ cup pecans
¼ cup cake flour, sifted with 1 teaspoon cinnamon
½ teaspoon cloves
2 cups bread or cake crumbs

Cream butter and sugar; add beaten egg, Karo, and buttermilk mixed with soda; then add raisins and nuts mixed with flour, cinnamon, and cloves. Finally, add bread or cake crumbs. Cover and bake at 350° for 15 minutes. Uncover and bake 15 minutes longer. Serve hot or cold, as is, or with any sauce. I especially like Foamy Sauce.

FLAN

FOR SIX

3 eggs plus 3 yolks
¾ cup sugar
3 cups milk
1 teaspoon vanilla extract
Caramelized sugar
1 tablespoon grated orange peel

Mix the eggs and yolks with sugar and beat until a light yellow. Warm the milk until hot, but do not boil. Add to the egg mixture and continue beating. Add vanilla. Strain through a sieve into a 1½-quart soufflé dish or mold that has been lined with caramelized sugar and the grated orange peel, or you may strain the mixture into individual custard cups. Bake in a 325° oven in a pan of hot water for about 45 minutes or until firm. Chill. When ready to serve, sprinkle with slivered toasted almonds.

This is a pretty dessert if unmolded and surrounded with the melted caramel and whole strawberries dipped in powdered sugar.

CARAMELIZED SUGAR

ONE-HALF CUP

Place 1 cup sugar in a saucepan and cook over medium heat, stirring frequently until it has a wet look. Then stir constantly until a syrup is formed. Add 2 tablespoons of water and continue cooking until syrup is brown, but do not let it burn. Pour this into your soufflé dish, let it harden, sprinkle with the grated orange peel, and then pour in custard.

CARAMELIZED BREAD PUDDING

FOR EIGHT

Put in top of double boiler:

2 cups brown sugar
8 slices white bread, buttered and cut in cubes

Combine:

6 eggs, lightly beaten
4 cups milk
2 teaspoons vanilla
½ teaspoon salt

Pour liquid mixture over bread and sugar. *Do not stir.* Cook over boiling water 1 hour or until custard is formed. Serve warm. The brown sugar in bottom forms sauce. You may put the ingredients in a see-through soufflé dish and proceed as directed.

I like to serve this when I serve an entrée that has a sharp flavor, like the Chicken Piquant or Oriental Roasted Chicken, or when I do not want to spend too much time and money on a dessert. It can look elegant and expensive, too!

SOFT CUSTARD

FOUR CUPS

A jar of Soft Custard in your refrigerator is your answer to making a quick dessert and strictly your own concoction. If one is ill, it is perfect plain. You may combine it with fruit, pour it over ice cream, puddings, and soufflés, or freeze it for a custard ice cream.

6 eggs
½ cup sugar
¼ teaspoon salt
4 cups scalded milk or half-and-half
1 teaspoon flavoring: vanilla, lemon, almond extracts, dry sherry, or brandy to taste

Beat eggs and add sugar and salt; stir in milk and cook over very low heat, or in a double boiler over hot, not boiling, water, until custard coats a spoon. If you have a candy thermometer, cook to 175°. Cool and add flavoring. If you cook it too long or too quickly and it curdles, beat with an egg beater and strain. You may use skim milk and artificial sweetener if you wish to cut calories.

LEMON FLOATING ISLAND

FOR EIGHT

4 cups milk
4 eggs, separated
4 tablespoons confectioners' sugar
½ teaspoon lemon juice
½ cup granulated sugar
Pinch of salt
½ teaspoon lemon extract
Grated rind of 1 lemon

Bring milk to a fast boil in a shallow saucepan or skillet (the milk should be at least 1 inch deep). Reduce heat to simmer. Beat egg whites stiff, add confectioners' sugar slowly, beating each time to stiff again. Add lemon juice and beat about 1 minute. Drop two or three tablespoonfuls into the simmering milk. Cook 1 minute, turn, cook 1 minute more. Do not crowd in the pan, as the mixture will expand. Drain on a clean cloth. Repeat until all egg whites are used. Mix the yolks with the sugar and salt. Pour hot milk slowly into the egg mixture, then return to pan and cook about 3 or 4 minutes until custard coats the spoon. Watch it or you will have scrambled eggs. Remove, strain, and add lemon extract and rind. Cool. Place fruit — I especially like blueberries or peaches, or both — in a bowl, pour custard over, and float the egg whites on top. Refrigerate. Before serving, thread Caramelized Sugar over the top. Omit the lemon if you wish to substitute any other flavoring. Candied violet dust is pretty sprinkled lightly on top. You may prepare this the day before, except for the Caramelized Sugar. Be sure to cover and refrigerate if you make ahead.

COLD ITALIAN MERINGUE

FOR EIGHT

2 cups sugar
½ teaspoon cream of tartar
½ cup water
⅛ teaspoon salt
6 egg whites
1 teaspoon vanilla extract

Mix the sugar and cream of tartar in a 2-quart saucepan. Add the water. Cook slowly until the sugar is dissolved and water begins to boil. Cover and fast boil 3 minutes. Remove cover and boil without stirring to 242° on a candy thermometer or until syrup spins a thread. Add the salt to the egg whites and beat until stiff. Gradually beat in the hot syrup. Add the vanilla and continue beating until very stiff. Pile into a crystal bowl, refrigerate, and serve on crystal plates with Soft Custard and storebought preserved marrons.

BURNT ALMOND SPONGE

FOR EIGHT

Here is the dessert to end all desserts, expensive but worth it.

2 tablespoons gelatin
¾ cup cold water
1⅛ cups sugar
1¼ cups milk
⅓ cup sugar
½ teaspoon salt
1½ cups whipping cream
¾ cup slivered almonds, browned in the oven
½ teaspoon vanilla extract

Topping:

1 cup whipping cream
⅛ cup powdered sugar
¼ teaspoon vanilla extract

Soak the gelatin in the cold water for 15 minutes. Heat the 1⅛ cups sugar in a heavy skillet until dark brown. Heat the milk and add the syrup gradually, stirring constantly. Remove from the stove and add the rest of the sugar, the gelatin, and the salt. Set in a bowl of ice water and stir occasionally until the mixture begins to thicken and is jellylike in consistency. Beat until spongy. Whip the cream until stiff and fold into the sponge mixture; add the almonds and vanilla. Pile into your prettiest glass dishes or saucer wineglasses; top with the other cream, whipped with powdered sugar and vanilla; garnish with anything you like and serve very cold. A bit of dry sherry added to the whipped cream topping is not amiss.

COEUR À LA CRÈME

FOR EIGHT

8 ounces cream cheese
⅓ cup confectioners' sugar
⅛ teaspoon salt
¼ cup slivered preserved ginger
2 cups whipping cream
1 quart large strawberries

Whip cheese with electric mixer until fluffy. Add sugar, salt, and ginger. Whip the cream and mix with the cheese mixture. Pour into a 1½-quart heart-shaped mold, or two smaller ones, lined with wet cheesecloth. Refrigerate overnight. Unmold on a serving tray, peel off the cheesecloth, and surround with berries. Put a few berries in a blender, slightly sweeten, and pass the sauce with the coeur. For a less caloric coeur, substitute 2 cups of cottage cheese for the whipping cream and beat until the consistency of whipped cream.

POTS DE CRÈME

FOR SIX

6 egg yolks
½ cup sugar
⅛ teaspoon salt
1 teaspoon vanilla extract
2 cups light cream

Beat egg yolks until light and lemon colored. Gradually beat in sugar and salt and vanilla. Stir in ½ cup of the cream. Heat remaining cream and gradually stir into the egg mixture. Strain through a fine sieve into the crème pots or custard cups. Cover with the crème pot covers (or foil if using custard cups). Set pots in a pan three-quarters filled with water. Bake at 325° for 1 hour, or until set. Chill before serving.

Variation:
Add 6 ounces semisweet chocolate to the hot milk for Pots de Crème au Chocolat.

CRÈME BRÛLÉE

FOR SIX

Crème Brûlée is a favorite dessert for holidays, and is here in answer to a request.

2 cups cream
4 egg yolks
2½ tablespoons granulated sugar
1 teaspoon vanilla extract
¼ cup sifted light brown sugar

Heat cream in double boiler. Beat egg yolks, adding granulated sugar gradually. Remove cream from heat and pour over egg mixture very slowly. Add vanilla. Pour into a 1½-quart casserole. Place in pan of hot water and bake uncovered at 325°, about 45 to 50 minutes, or until set. When custard is set, sprinkle with the sifted brown sugar. Place under broiler for a minute or so until sugar melts. Chill. This is a rich smooth custard and should be served very cold.

RUSSIAN CREAM

FOR SIX

1¾ cups light cream
1 cup sugar
2 tablespoons gelatin
½ cup cold water
1½ cups thick sour cream
1 teaspoon vanilla extract

Heat light cream with the sugar. Soak gelatin in the cold water and combine with the hot cream. Fold in whipped sour cream and vanilla as the mixture begins to congeal. Pour into a ring or individual molds, and serve with fresh or frosted raspberries. It is strange, but no other berries will do.

MOUSSE AU CHOCOLAT

FOR EIGHT

¾ cup butter
1½ cups sugar
½ teaspoon almond extract
1 tablespoon brandy
3 eggs, separated
½ pound semisweet chocolate or chocolate chips
¼ cup slivered toasted almonds or marrons
2 cups whipped cream

Stir butter until creamy. Blend in sugar, almond extract, brandy, and egg yolks. Melt the chocolate and add with the almonds to the butter mixture. Fold in egg whites beaten stiff. Fold in whipped cream. Pour into a mold, or one lined with ladyfingers. Refrigerate several hours. Unmold and decorate with whipped cream and layers of shaved semi-sweet chocolate. You do this by leaving the chocolate at room temperature for a few hours, then scraping the surface with a heavy sharp knife (or silver one) toward you. Be not stingy! Or you could use toasted natural almonds, but the chocolate is more spectacular. Add a bit of instant coffee to whipped cream to take away what I call the dead taste. Freeze, too, if you wish, before decorating — a nice do-ahead dessert.

RASPBERRY MOUSSE

FOR EIGHT

1 cup milk
4 egg yolks
3 tablespoons sugar
1½ tablespoons unflavored gelatin, softened in ¼ cup cold milk
½ teaspoon vanilla extract
2 cups frozen raspberries (sugared)
2 cups cream, whipped
4 egg whites, stiffly beaten

Mix milk, egg yolks, and sugar. Cook over hot water until a custard is formed. Remove; add gelatin and vanilla. Chill. Purée berries in blender, then strain. Add to the custard. Taste for sweetness; add more sugar if needed. (Some raspberries are not sweet enough.) Return to refrigerator. When mixture begins to thicken, fold in whipped cream and egg whites. Pour into a 2-quart soufflé dish or ring mold. Refrigerate overnight. Serve with puréed strawberries or raspberries and whipped cream. Decorate with fresh berries if available.

TOASTED ALMOND AND ORANGE MOUSSE

FOR EIGHT

1 cup sugar
3 tablespoons grated orange rind
½ cup boiling water
1 tablespoon gelatin
¼ cup cold water
1 cup orange juice
¼ cup lemon juice
¾ cup cream, whipped
1 cup slivered and toasted almonds

CHOCOLATE TORTE WITH SCHLAG

FOR EIGHT

4 egg whites
¼ teaspoon cream of tartar
1 cup sugar
¼ cup cocoa
½ cup finely chopped pecans or almonds
½ teaspoon vanilla extract
Pinch of salt

Beat egg whites with cream of tartar until stiff. Gradually beat in ½ cup sugar. Mix the remaining sugar with the cocoa and fold into the egg white mixture. Add the nuts, vanilla, and salt. Pour into a lightly buttered 9-by-9-inch glass casserole or cake tin. Bake at 325° for 45 minutes. Cool, remove from pan to a serving tray, and cover with 2 cups whipped cream mixed with ¼ cup sugar, ½ teaspoon cocoa, and ¼ teaspoon powdered instant coffee.

Crêpes and Pancakes

SOUFFLÉED CRÊPES

TWELVE MEDIUM OR SIXTEEN THIN

I find that my crêpes are consistently more tender when I use cake flour, but there is no law that says you must. This recipe will do for entrée or dessert crêpes, but for the former, use less sugar.

Crêpes:

1 cup sifted cake flour (spooned into measuring cup)
1 to 1½ cups milk, whole or skim
2 eggs, separated
1 tablespoon sugar
5 tablespoons butter or margarine, melted and cooled

Put flour in a bowl, add 1 cup milk, and stir with a wire whisk until smooth. Add 2 egg yolks and 1 of the egg whites, unbeaten, and beat until well blended. Add sugar and butter. Let batter stand at least 1 hour. Fold in the remaining egg white beaten to soft-peak stage. Pour about 1 tablespoon butter into a hot crêpe pan. Swish around until pan is completely coated. Pour off excess butter. Add about 1½ tablespoons of batter. Tilt pan until bottom is covered. Cook about half a minute, turn with a spatula, cook another half minute. Remove from pan and repeat process. You do not need to add more butter to pan. Pile crêpes on top of one another; it is not necessary to put paper in between them.

If you prefer a thinner crêpe, add the larger quantity of milk. If you're making them ahead of time, wrap them in clear plastic or foil. Crêpes freeze satisfactorily. To use after freezing, defrost at room temperature — do not put in a hot oven or they will melt into one big glop. Regardless of what you put into a crêpe, the important thing to remember is to roll it loosely — both the crêpe and the filling retain their flavor and texture better this way.

Filling:

2 eggs, separated
½ cup sifted all-purpose flour (spooned into cup)
½ cup sugar
1 tablespoon Grand Marnier
A pinch of salt
A drop of vanilla extract
1 cup milk, scalded
Powdered sugar

Mix egg yolks and flour. Add sugar, Grand Marnier, salt, and vanilla. Mix thoroughly. Gradually add the milk, stirring constantly to avoid lumping. Cook over medium heat until mixture thickens. Cool but don't chill. Fold in stiffly beaten egg whites. Spread a little over each crêpe; fold into a pillow shape. Place in lightly buttered casserole and sprinkle with powdered sugar. Reheat for 5 minutes in a 500° oven. Serve at once — with Apricot Sauce.

PANCAKE STACK

Traditionally speaking, pancakes are served at breakfast, but one may use them just about any time of the day. The young-fry, the debutantes, adore them, and as far as I know everyone else does too.

If you do not have a nonsticking electric griddle, you should invest in one, as you may use it for other things, such as hashed browned potatoes, hamburgers, grilled sandwiches. It is well worth the investment.

During my days at Neiman-Marcus the Thursday night buffets became very popular and the pancake stacks were asked for time after time. We made them with various accompaniments: lingonberries and sour cream with beef, orange butter with chicken, maple syrup and ham juices with chicken and ham, cinnamon butter, whatever came to mind, always cut like a pie. The blueberry pancake was used with everything. I have pancake parties at home and have a variety of stacks and only thin-sliced ham or Canadian bacon and creamy cole slaw, but I need someone to help. You would too, unless your guests want to help.

To make a pancake stack, use your basic griddle or pancake mixture, thin it with milk to a thin consistency, then pour the size you wish. I do a 12- or 14-inch one, and use 10 to 12 cakes for a stack. You can make ahead and pile them on top of each other with wax paper between, and cover with a towel to keep from drying. For a blueberry stack, when ready to assemble spread your tray with lemon cream butter, then top with one pancake. Spread it with lemon cream butter and a little of the hot blueberry sauce. Repeat until you have as high a stack as you wish. Pour more blueberry sauce over all and a goodly dollop of the lemon cream butter. Put in a 350° oven for 3 minutes. Cut in narrow pie-shaped portions and pass.

For 10 or 12 thin pancakes:

2½ cups milk (about)
4 tablespoons melted butter
2 eggs, separated
2 cups flour
4 teaspoons baking powder
4 tablespoons sugar
1 teaspoon salt

Mix milk, melted butter, and egg yolks. Stir in the rest of ingredients and the egg whites, stiffly beaten. Add more milk if necessary to make the pancakes thin. Cook and stack.

LEMON CREAM BUTTER

FOR ONE PANCAKE STACK

½ cup butter
2½ cups confectioners' sugar
3 tablespoons lemon juice
Grated rind of 1 lemon

Cream butter; add sugar and beat. Stir in the lemon juice and grated rind. Beat until the consistency of whipped cream.

BLUEBERRY SAUCE

FOR ONE PANCAKE STACK

4 10-ounce packages quick-frozen blueberries
1 cup cold water
3 tablespoons cornstarch
6 tablespoons sugar
2 tablespoons lemon juice

Defrost berries and strain, reserving juices. Combine water and juices, and add the cornstarch and sugar. Cook over low heat until clear and thickened. Add berries and cook 5 minutes. Remove from heat and add lemon juice.

If using fresh berries, mix 3 cups sugar with 3 tablespoons cornstarch; add 1½ cups boiling water. Bring to a boil and let cook for 5 minutes. Add 3 cups fresh blueberries, 1 tablespoon lemon juice. Add more sugar if necessary.

Soften gelatin in cold water. Set aside. Mix egg yolks, lemon juice, salt, and ½ cup sugar. Cook in double boiler until thickened. Stir in gelatin, lemon peel, and lemon extract. Cool. Beat egg whites until soft peaks form. Gradually beat in rest of sugar, and beat until stiff. Whip the cream. Fold egg whites into custard as it begins to congeal, then the whipped cream. Pour into custard cups and refrigerate. Unmold and serve with sauce of apricots puréed in the blender and sweetened to taste. Or pour into a 1½-quart soufflé dish or mold. I like to put a collar of foil around a 1-quart soufflé dish, tie securely, then remove before bringing to the table. This is a delicious soufflé to serve cold with any fruit and flavored whipped cream, if you wish.

You may use the same base for Cold Orange Soufflé, using ½ cup orange juice and 1 tablespoon grated orange peel and omitting the lemon extract.

HOT LEMON SOUFFLÉ

FOR SIX TO EIGHT

2 tablespoons butter
1½ tablespoons flour
½ cup hot milk
5 egg yolks
4 tablespoons sugar
Grated rind of 1 lemon
1½ tablespoons lemon juice
6 egg whites

Melt the butter; add the flour and cook until foamy. Add milk and cook until thick. Remove from heat; add egg yolks beaten with 3 tablespoons sugar. Let mixture cool; add grated rind and lemon juice. Beat egg whites until stiff but not dry, add the last tablespoon of sugar, and beat again until stiff. Fold into the egg mixture. Pour into a buttered and slightly sugared 1-quart soufflé dish and bake at 400° for about 20 minutes, or until puffed and lightly browned. Serve at once. This dessert could bake while dinner is being served. If you wish to have the soufflé cook slower, put in a hot-water bath, and lower temperature to 350°.

FRUIT SOUFFLÉ GLACÉ

FOR EIGHT

I had this dessert every time I saw it on a menu when I was in Switzerland. Willie Rossel, then chef at the Sheraton Hotel, made it for 1200 guests. If you go to Zurich, you'll discover the Dolder Grand Hotel prepares this dessert very well. So can you.

1 cup water
1 cup sugar
8 egg yolks, beaten
2 cups whipping cream
½ cup candied fruit, finely diced
½ cup Grand Marnier
1 teaspoon grated orange rind
Pinch of salt
Violet Dust

Boil water and sugar together 8 minutes. Pour the hot sugar mixture over the eggs slowly. Stirring with a French whip, cook over hot water until thick. Remove and put saucepan with the egg mixture over a bowl of ice to cool. Stir until cold. Whip the cream until stiff and fold into the cold egg mixture. Stir in the candied fruit, Grand Marnier, orange rind, and salt. Pour into individual soufflé dishes or dessert dishes and freeze. Sprinkle top with Violet Dust.

VIOLET DUST

You may purchase candied violets in candy or gourmet shops. Roll out between two sheets of foil until you obtain a fine dust. Keeps indefinitely in a covered container.

CARAMEL SOUFFLÉ

FOR TEN TO TWELVE

2 pounds granulated sugar
12 egg whites
Butter for coating pan

Place 1½ cups of the sugar in a skillet. Heat over medium heat until a brown syrup forms. Do not let it burn. Pour into a 3-quart casserole or bundt pan, coating the sides and bottom. Cool. Rub the entire pan and coating with butter. Beat egg whites until stiff. Add 1 pound of sugar gradually to the egg whites, beating constantly. Put the remaining sugar in a skillet and brown to a syrup. Add a little water and cook until the syrup forms a thread. Pour into the egg whites and beat at medium speed on your mixer. Increase to high speed and beat for 12 minutes. Pour into the buttered container and bake at 300° in a hot-water bath for 1 hour or until firm but light. Turn out onto a serving tray at once. If you wish to prepare the soufflé early in the day, leave in pan and return to a 350° oven for about 20 minutes. It must be hot or warm to come out of the pan. Some of the caramel syrup will stay in the pan. Serve with English Custard.

GRAND MARNIER SOUFFLÉ

FOR SIX

---

2 tablespoons butter
1½ tablespoons flour
½ cup scalded milk
½ teaspoon vanilla extract
4 tablespoons Grand Marnier
5 egg yolks
4 tablespoons sugar
6 egg whites

Melt butter, add flour, and cook until golden. Add scalded milk and cook until thick. Cook 5 minutes, stirring constantly. Add vanilla and Grand Marnier. Beat egg yolks with 3 tablespoons sugar and combine with the cream sauce. Beat 6 egg whites stiff, adding 1 tablespoon sugar. Fold in half the egg whites, then the other half. Pour into a buttered and slightly sugared 1½-quart soufflé dish or casserole. Bake at 400° for 20 minutes. Serve with 2 tablespoons of Grand Marnier added to 2 tablespoons whipped cream or pour on lighted Grand Marnier, or both.

ANGEL SOUFFLÉ

FOR SIX TO EIGHT

---

6 egg whites
Pinch of salt
Pinch of cream of tartar
1½ cups sugar
1 teaspoon lemon juice
1 teaspoon vanilla extract

Beat egg whites with the salt and cream of tartar until stiff. Add sugar gradually and continue to beat until stiff peaks are formed. Add lemon juice and vanilla. Pour into a buttered square 9-inch cake pan or into a ring mold. Bake at 325° for 45 minutes. Cool, slice, and serve with Soft Custard, flavored as you wish, and/or with any fresh fruit.

ENGLISH CUSTARD

FOR TEN TO TWELVE

¾ cup sugar
3 cups milk
2 tablespoons butter
12 egg yolks, beaten until lemon yellow
1 teaspoon vanilla extract
1 cup heavy cream (you may omit)

Cook sugar and milk together in double boiler. When hot, add butter and egg yolks. Stir vigorously and cook until thickened. Remove from stove to cool. Add vanilla and cream, either whipped or unwhipped.

The first time I served this was at a Confrérie des Chevaliers du Tastevin. After submitting the menu to "the committee" I was notified that all was approved except the dessert, which was too feminine, and what was I going to do about it. I said: "Serve it." Every man present had two helpings. It is a divine dessert and can be used with any kind of entrée. I sometimes serve lightly broiled sugared strawberries with it. You may halve the recipe, but why? Regardless of how few guests you have, it will all be eaten. It is one dessert of which seconds are always accepted with glee.

CHOCOLATE SOUFFLÉ

FOR SIX

4 tablespoons butter
5 tablespoons flour
¼ teaspoon salt
1 cup milk
2 ounces unsweetened chocolate, melted
3 eggs, separated
½ teaspoon vanilla extract
½ cup sugar

Melt the butter; add the flour and cook until bubbly. Add milk, salt, and melted chocolate and stir constantly until thick. Cool. Beat egg yolks; add vanilla and continue to beat until smooth and creamy. Fold into the egg yolks the stiffly beaten egg whites, to which sugar has been added as in a meringue. Fold egg mixture into chocolate sauce, pour into a 1½-quart soufflé dish, set in pan of hot water, and bake 1 hour at 350°. Serve with Foamy Sauce.

Ice Creams and Sherbets

There is no time like summertime to get everyone interested in making homemade ice cream. It was more fun when the youngest member of the family sat on top of the freezer to "steady" it and everyone else cranked until their arms gave out. And what has happened to the ice-cream socials that were so much fun?

Everyone who buys an ice-cream freezer today gets a book of instructions, so follow it. And with the advent of the ice-cream makers that you put in your freezer to do all the work, you can have homemade ice cream frequently. In the following recipes, when the instructions say, "Freeze," follow the instructions that came with your ice-cream freezer, whatever kind you own.

These are my favorite ice-cream recipes.

PLAIN OLD-FASHIONED CUSTARD ICE CREAM

THREE PINTS

¾ cup sugar
3 cups milk
2 tablespoons butter
12 egg yolks, beaten until lemon yellow
1 teaspoon vanilla extract
1 cup heavy cream

Cook sugar and milk together in double boiler. When hot add butter and egg yolks. Stir vigorously and cook until thickened. Remove from stove to cool. Add vanilla. Freeze, adding the cream, whipped stiff, for the last 10 minutes.

FRENCH VANILLA ICE CREAM

THREE PINTS

½ cup sugar
4 egg yolks
2 cups scalded milk
2 cups whipping cream
¼ teaspoon salt
2 teaspoons vanilla extract

Mix the sugar with the egg yolks and beat until thick. Pour in the scalded milk slowly, beating with a wire whisk. Simmer over low heat until slightly thickened. Cool and strain; add cream, salt, and vanilla. Freeze.

GINGER ICE CREAM

To French Vanilla Ice Cream add ½ cup crystalized ginger diced fine.

PEANUT BRITTLE ICE CREAM

Use French Vanilla Ice Cream recipe: Omit the sugar and add ½ pound of peanut brittle rolled out into crumbs.

COFFEE BURNT-ALMOND ICE CREAM

To French Vanilla Ice Cream add 1 cup finely chopped toasted almonds and 2 tablespoons instant coffee.

COFFEE CARAMEL ICE CREAM

THREE PINTS

¾ cup sugar
2 cups scalded milk
4 tablespoons instant coffee
4 egg yolks
2 cups whipping cream
¼ teaspoon salt
2 teaspoons vanilla extract

Caramelize the sugar in a heavy skillet and add slowly to the scalded milk and instant coffee. Bring to a rolling boil; add the beaten egg yolks and cook to a soft custard consistency. Strain and cool. Add the cream, salt, and vanilla. Freeze.

LEMON VELVET ICE CREAM

TWO QUARTS PLUS

1 quart plus 1⅓ cups whipping cream
1 quart plus 1⅓ cups milk
Juice of 8 lemons
4 cups sugar
2 teaspoons lemon extract
1 tablespoon grated lemon rind

Mix thoroughly and freeze. It tastes the way it sounds — like velvet.

PEPPERMINT STICK ICE CREAM

ABOUT ONE GALLON

1 quart milk
1 pound peppermint candy, crushed
2 tablespoons flour
½ cup sugar
½ teaspoon salt
2 egg yolks, beaten
2 quarts heavy cream

Heat the milk and candy to scalding. Mix the flour, sugar, salt, and beaten egg yolks; add to the milk and cook until thick. Cool; add the cream and freeze.

PEACH ICE CREAM

THREE PINTS

1½ quarts sliced, peeled fresh peaches
1 cup sugar
2 cups light cream
2 cups heavy cream
½ teaspoon vanilla extract
½ teaspoon almond extract
⅛ teaspoon salt

Sprinkle the peaches with half the sugar and cover. Mix the cream with the remaining sugar and freeze until partially frozen. Stir in the sugared fruit, flavoring, and salt and continue freezing.

Do the same with strawberries.

MOCHA ORANGE ICE CREAM

THREE PINTS

4 tablespoons instant coffee
¾ cup sugar
2 cups scalded milk
4 egg yolks, beaten
2 cups whipping cream
1 tablespoon grated orange peel
2 tablespoons Grand Marnier

Add coffee and sugar to the milk and bring to a boil. Add a little of the liquid to the egg yolks and stir before adding to the hot liquid. Cook to a soft custard consistency. Strain and cool. Add the cream, orange peel, and Grand Marnier. Freeze. I like to sliver some of the orange peel (peel with a potato peeler) and heat in simple syrup (½ cup water, 1 cup sugar) until it is glazed and sprinkle on top of each serving. Sometimes I pack the ice cream in a mold that has been rinsed in cold water and freeze it. Then unmold and sprinkle the glazed orange peel on top and surround with Ferrara brand rum babas.

Keep 1 cup of the cream aside, whip, and add to frozen mixture about 5 minutes before it is finished. You will have a creamier ice cream. This is a good idea for all ice creams.

FROZEN EGGNOG

THREE PINTS

2 cups milk
1 tablespoon cornstarch
¼ teaspoon salt
¾ cup sugar
2 egg yolks
2 cups heavy cream
1 teaspoon vanilla extract
¼ cup bourbon or rum

Scald 1½ cups of the milk; add the remaining milk to the cornstarch, salt, and sugar to make a smooth paste; add to the scalded milk and cook over hot water until thick. Add beaten egg yolks and boil 1 minute. Cool; add cream, vanilla, and bourbon or rum. Freeze. I like to serve this rather soft in parfait glasses with crushed candied violets on top. This is always popular with teetotalers.

COFFEE MARSHMALLOW ICE CREAM

THREE PINTS

¾ pound marshmallows
¼ cup sugar
3 cups hot black coffee
2 cups whipping cream
1 cup light cream
1 teaspoon vanilla extract
¼ teaspoon salt

Add marshmallows and sugar to the hot coffee and stir to dissolve. Chill thoroughly. Add the cream, vanilla, and salt. Freeze.

ICE CREAM WHIP

FOR SIX OR EIGHT

Ice Cream Whip is good to keep on hand all year long, as everyone will love it.

1 quart strawberries or raspberries
Juice of 1 lemon
3 tablespoons sugar
1 cup chopped pecans
1 cup chopped pistachio nuts
½ cup confectioners' sugar
3 cups whipped cream

Mash the berries with the lemon juice and sugar. Let stand ½ hour. Add nuts and confectioners' sugar and stir. Fold in the whipped cream. Pour into loaf pans or an ice-cream mold and freeze in your freezing compartment. Slice and serve. Or substitute peaches for the berries and almonds for the pecans, but keep the flavor of the pistachio.

AVOCADO AND RASPBERRY MOUSSE

FOR EIGHT

2 large ripe avocados, or 1½ cups mashed avocado
2 tablespoons lemon juice
1 teaspoon grated lemon peel
1 tablespoon orange juice
¼ teaspoon salt
1½ cups cream
¼ teaspoon green food coloring
2 egg whites, stiffly beaten
1 package frozen sweetened raspberries

Combine mashed avocado, lemon juice, lemon peel, orange juice, salt, and cream. Add the coloring. Set in a bowl of ice and salt and whip with an egg beater now and then until partially frozen. Then fold in the egg whites. Pour into your freezing tray with alternate layers of frozen sweetened raspberries. Cover with wax paper and place in your freezing compartment for 24 hours. When ready to serve, slice in the tray with a thin-bladed knife dipped in warm water. Remove and serve on chilled plates. If you have any left, just put it back for another day.

AVOCADO SHERBET

THREE PINTS

1½ cups mashed avocado
¼ teaspoon salt
2 cups sugar
Juice of 12 lemons
1 teaspoon grated lemon peel
1 quart milk

Mix avocado, salt, sugar, lemon juice, and peel; add to the milk and freeze. The curdled look will disappear in freezing.

ORANGE CREAM SHERBET

THREE PINTS

2 cups sugar
1 cup water
2 cups orange juice
1 cup light cream
2 egg yolks, beaten
1 cup heavy cream
¼ cup coconut flakes
¼ cup shredded candied orange peel

Boil sugar and water for 5 minutes. Add orange juice. Scald the light cream; add beaten egg yolks and cook until thickened. Cool and add to the orange juice mixture; add the heavy cream, whipped. Freeze. When partially frozen add the orange peel and coconut.

RASPBERRY CREAM SHERBET

THREE PINTS

1 cup sugar
1 quart frozen raspberries
3 cups half-and-half
4 egg whites, stiffly beaten
¼ teaspoon salt

Add the sugar to the frozen raspberries and mash. Put through a sieve. Freeze cream, salt, and egg whites to a mush; add the berries and finish freezing.

THREE-FRUIT SHERBET

TWO QUARTS

Juice of 6 oranges
Juice of 6 lemons
5 bananas, mashed to a pulp
6 cups water
4 cups sugar
1 quart light cream

Mix and freeze. This was a part of my childhood.

CRANBERRY SHERBET

TWO QUARTS

For the holidays.

2 quarts cranberries
4 cups water
Juice of 4 lemons
4 cups sugar

Boil cranberries with the water for 8 minutes. Put through a sieve; add lemon juice and sugar. Freeze.

FRESH LIME CREAM SHERBET

ONE GALLON

2 fresh limes
⅓ cup fresh lime juice
2 cups sugar
4 cups whipping cream
2 cups milk
Few drops green food coloring

Trim off ends of 2 limes. Slice fruit into paper-thin slices, removing any seeds. Chop fine. Mix with juice and sugar. Cover and refrigerate overnight. Mix 2 cups of the cream and all the milk. Add to the lime mixture. Stir well; mixture will thicken. Add coloring. Freeze until sherbet is partially frozen. Whip the remaining cream and add. Continue freezing until solid. Pack to ripen (8 parts ice to 1 part rock salt).

BUTTER PECAN ICE CREAM

THREE PINTS

1 cup coarsely chopped pecans
6 tablespoons butter
3 tablespoons cornstarch
1 cup sugar
¼ cup dark brown sugar
2 cups milk
2 teaspoons vanilla extract
2 cups whipping cream

Toast the pecans in butter in the oven. Mix cornstarch and sugars in a heavy skillet; add milk and cook until thick, stirring constantly. Remove from heat; add vanilla and chill. Add cream and freeze until partially done. Add pecans and resume freezing. Or whip the cream until stiff, fold in sugar mixture and pecans, pour into freezing trays, and put in your deep freeze.

ICE-CREAM BOMBE

3 quarts vanilla ice cream
2 cups cool Fudge Sauce
1 very cold 3-quart melon mold or 2 1½-quart size

Coat the molds with vanilla ice cream about 1½ inches thick. Pack firmly and quickly. Do not let ice cream melt. Fill center with Fudge Sauce and cover with more ice cream. Cover with wax paper and press on the lid. Place in freezer overnight. When ready to serve, run a wet knife around the edge of the mold. Place a hot towel over for a minute, then turn upside-down on a chilled serving dish. Cut in slices at the table and serve with whipped cream and crème de cacao. Use same method for any flavored bombe.

BAKED ALASKA

FOR EIGHT

Place a layer of any white or yellow cake on an oven-proof china or silver-plated tray — not sterling. (I once had a sterling dish which I placed in the oven come out in four little liquid balls.) If you are fond of the flavor of rum or brandy, sprinkle the cake generously with either or both, and a fine layer of granulated sugar. Cover with a thick layer of vanilla ice cream — or any flavor you wish — leaving a half-inch "frame" around the cake. Then pile high and cover completely with meringue made from beating 4 egg whites until stiff and then adding ¾ cup of powdered sugar. Brown quickly in a 450° oven; remove; pour 1 ounce of brandy on the tray, light, and serve at once. This is for 1 quart of ice cream. Still better is to add to the tray or plate, before adding the brandy, black cherries slightly thickened with cornstarch: a more elaborate version of Cherries Jubilee. Or fresh sugared small strawberries may be used before lighting. They smell heavenly.

FLOWERPOTS

Flowerpots are the answer to a party dessert. Actually, they are miniature Baked Alaskas, but you can do so much with them.

At a recent party I built the decorations for the entire meal around the dessert. The tables had centerpieces of red clay pots filled with every kind of garden flower available, one with blue bachelor buttons, one with red geraniums, one with daisies, another with pink roses. Then I made the dessert's flowers fit in with the decorations of each table — a pot with roses went to the table with a bouquet of roses, daisies to the table with a daisy arrangement, and so on. It was most effective, conversationally and decoratively.

The Flowerpot is made by choosing a small clay flowerpot, which is first sterilized. Place a piece of plain cake in the bottom (to cover the hole). Pile with whatever ice cream you like — or sherbet — to three-quarters full. In the middle of each pot force a large ice-cream-soda straw, and cut off even with the top of the pot. Pile meringue around the inside of the pot, leaving space over the soda straw open. Bake at 400° until the meringue is brown. Insert fresh flowers in the soda straw — it looks just like what it is, a flowerpot with fresh flowers. It is especially nice for wedding parties, birthdays, and such, and not too feminine for men. They are intrigued by them.

At holiday time, use holly and tiny red roses or carnations. Place the pots on a large silver tray and surround with sprigs of holiday greens — effective. You can make them ahead of time and store in the deep freeze — all but the flowers, of course.

Fruit Desserts

Everyone has a crystal vase that is kept far back on the pantry shelf. Why? For a really dramatic dessert, bring it out, polish it till it shines, and fill it with layers of fresh strawberries, then a layer of fresh pineapple cubes, then a layer of melon. Sprinkle each layer lightly with powdered sugar. Repeat the layers of fruit until the vase is full, then decorate with sprigs of fresh mint. Chill thoroughly and serve from the table onto cold glass plates. For those who like the flavor of rum, pour rum over before serving with sweetened whipped cream flavored with almond extract. This is a particularly beautiful and spectacular dessert for buffet entertaining.

Slices of melon, peaches, fresh figs, or any other fresh fruit arranged on a silver tray, a pretty, large plate, or a platter and served with a bowl of Cream Cheese Sauce and a bowl of Melba Sauce are a luscious-to-look-at and -to-eat dessert. The Cream Cheese Sauce is made by adding cream to cream cheese and beating with a fork until it is the consistency of cream and easy to pour. The idea is to pass the fruit, let those who partake select whatever they wish from the tray, dip the Cream Cheese Sauce on top, and pour the Melba Sauce over all. I always get a thrill when I serve this because everyone oohs and aahs both before *and* after eating it. It needs a pretty service though, and chilled plates to eat it from.

STAINED-GLASS-WINDOW DESSERT

FOR TWELVE TO SIXTEEN

Why the name? Because this dessert looks like one. At any rate, it doesn't look like fruit gelatin, which it is. But it is fresh tasting and low in calories. It is your imagination that makes it a beautiful dessert.

Serve this on a flat 12-inch round silver or crystal tray.

1 tablespoon unflavored gelatin, dissolved in ¼ cup cold water
1½ cups fresh orange juice
1 tablespoon lemon juice
1 tablespoon sugar
1 orange, unpeeled
4 fresh peaches
1 small cantaloupe, sliced in bite-sized pieces
2 dozen honeydew melon balls
1 dozen large strawberries
½ cup white grapes
½ cup blue grapes, seeded, cut in half

Melt the dissolved gelatin over hot water and add to the fresh orange juice with the lemon juice and sugar. Cut the orange in half lengthwise and slice in thin slices. Use these to form a scallop around rim of tray. Pour enough of the gelatin mixture to hold the orange slices in place. Refrigerate until set. Place half of a freshly peeled peach or plum in center of tray with enough gelatin to hold it. Let it set also; then make a design of the fruit using slices of peaches and cantaloupe, the melon balls and strawberries cut in half and the grapes in a cartwheel fashion. Pour gelatin mixture over, but do not cover the fruit. In season I sprinkle blueberries or raspberries here and there. Refrigerate for several hours until set. Bring to the table and cut like a pie. Pass whipped cream or sour cream sweetened with brown sugar. It is a delightful dessert.

Lazy? Use any flavored gelatin. I use canned pear juice sometimes in place of the orange juice. You may use any fruits.

APPLE BAKLAVA

FOR TWELVE

2 apples, peeled, cored, and thinly sliced
¼ cup sugar
½ teaspoon cinnamon
About ¼ pound fillo strudel leaves (also called phylo pastry leaves)
½ pound slivered almonds
¼ cup melted butter
½ pound slivered almonds, lightly browned
½ cup water
½ cup sugar
½ teaspoon lemon juice

Mix apples, sugar, and cinnamon. Place a sheet of the pastry leaves in baking pan (13 by 9 inches). Brush with melted butter. Repeat twice. Scatter some of the apples and nuts over. Cover with another sheet of pastry and repeat process until apple and sugar mixture is used. Place 6 sheets of pastry on top, brushing each sheet with butter and sprinkling with nuts. End with pastry. Brush with butter. Cut baklava into size portions you wish to serve. Bake at 350° until apples are tender, about 50 minutes. Bring water and sugar to a boil and cook until a syrup is formed. Add lemon juice. When pastry is done, pour syrup over. When cold, recut. Note: Keep leaves moist while you are working by covering with damp towel.

GLAZED APPLES

FOR SIX

6 Winesap or similar winter apples
3 cups sugar
1½ cups water
⅛ teaspoon cinnamon

Pare and core apples. Cut into quarters. Mix sugar and water and boil 10 minutes. Add cinnamon and drop apple pieces into syrup. Cook slowly until transparent. Place apples in a buttered casserole and keep warm. Keep any syrup left for another time.

BOURBON PEACHES

FOR TEN TO TWELVE

½ cup butter
8 fresh peaches, halved
1½ tablespoons grated orange peel
2 teaspoons lemon juice
4 tablespoons light brown sugar
4 ounces bourbon

Melt butter; add peaches and sauté until lacy brown. Add orange peel, lemon juice, and sugar. Cook until thoroughly melted. Add bourbon and ignite. Serve hot or with ice cream. This is also excellent when served with English Custard.

APPLE AND PRUNE STRUDEL

FOR SIX TO EIGHT

4 strudel leaves (buy a frozen package)
3 large Rome Beauty or Greenings apples, sliced thin
½ cup sugar
¼ cup slivered almonds
½ cup chopped stewed prunes
1 teaspoon lemon juice
Grated rind of 1 lemon
⅛ teaspoon cinnamon
½ cup melted butter
1 tablespoon sugar

Unfold 4 leaves of strudel dough from package. Mix the apples, ½ cup sugar, almonds, prunes, lemon juice, grated rind, and cinnamon. Place 1 leaf of the dough on a piece of foil or damp towel. Brush with melted butter. Sprinkle with sugar. Place second leaf on top, and repeat 2 more times. Place apple mixture on top of the leaves and roll like a jelly roll, lengthwise, with the aid of the foil or towel. Place on a buttered tin and brush again with butter. Mark with a sharp knife 8 portions. Bake at 350° until golden brown (about 50 minutes). Cut while warm. Serve with the following sauce.

LEMON HARD SAUCE

½ cup butter
1 cup granulated or 1½ cups confectioners' sugar
1 teaspoon lemon juice
½ teaspoon grated lemon rind

Cream butter; beat in sugar and flavorings.

GREEN GRAPES WITH COINTREAU

FOR SIX

1 pound seedless green grapes
1 pint (2 cups) sour cream
¼ cup light brown sugar
¼ cup cinnamon
Cointreau

Wash and remove stems from the grapes. Add sour cream; stir thoroughly. Serve in sherbet dishes. Pass a small dish of light brown sugar, another of cinnamon, and a bottle of Cointreau. Each person seasons his own grapes and sour cream to his taste.

MELON GLORY

FOR FOUR TO SIX

1 cup cubed watermelon
1 cup cubed cantaloupe
½ cup sliced strawberries
1 sliced banana
1 cup fresh blueberries or raspberries

Or use any combination of fruit you like. Place in a crystal bowl and cover with

2 tablespoons powdered sugar
½ cup Marsala wine
1 jigger of cherry brandy or your favorite cordial

Refrigerate, and serve when you get around to it — today or tomorrow. If you do not like alcohol, cover with maple syrup and ice water — half and half. A quick and refreshing dessert.

GLORIFIED PEACHES

FOR EIGHT

1½ cups canned peach juice
½ cup water
2 cloves
1 orange, sliced thin with skin on
1 cinnamon stick
3 tablespoons honey
8 canned Elberta peach halves
1 quart vanilla ice cream
Cognac
Macaroons

Boil juice, water, cloves, orange, cinnamon, and honey for 10 minutes. Strain, pour over peaches, and refrigerate overnight. Put peaches in a serving dish, top with ice cream, pour sauce over. Heat 2 jiggers of Cognac, ignite, and pour over. Sprinkle crushed macaroons over all.

RASPBERRY FRANGO

FOR SIX

---

1 cup sugar
4 egg yolks
1 cup hot milk

Beat egg yolks; add sugar and hot milk. Cook until thickened. Cool. Add:

1 cup mashed raspberries, fresh or frozen (put in a blender)
1 tablespoon lemon juice
2 cups cream, whipped

Freeze in freezing compartment or in individual servings in your deep freeze. It is a wonderful ending to any meal. Pretty decorated with whole berries.

ORANGE BOWL

FOR EIGHT

Put in a crystal bowl 6 seedless oranges, peeled and sectioned. Cover with:

1 tablespoon honey
1 tablespoon bitter orange marmalade
1 teaspoon Grand Marnier
1 teaspoon Scotch
1 teaspoon lemon juice
1 tablespoon cold water

Refrigerate overnight. Test for sweetness and add sugar if necessary. Serve very cold with almond dust.

HOT FRUIT CURAÇAO

FOR EIGHT TO TEN

1 29-ounce can freestone peaches, drained (reserve syrup)
1 30-ounce can whole apricots, seeded and drained
2 bananas, freshly sliced
3 oranges, peeled and sectioned
Juice of one lemon
Grated rind of one orange plus 2 tablespoons slivered rind
¼ cup curaçao

Place fruit in shallow baking dish. Mix lemon juice with peach syrup and pour over fruit. Add orange rind. Bake at 350° for 25 minutes. Cool slightly, then pour curaçao over. Serve warm or hot, with or without whipped cream. Do not reheat after adding liqueur.

FRESH FRUIT WITH GINGERED CREAM

Gingered Cream:
2 3-ounce packages cream cheese
1 tablespoon lemon juice
2 cups whipping cream
1 teaspoon sugar
3 tablespoons chopped candied ginger
1 tablespoon grated orange rind

Put all ingredients in a mixing bowl and whip until creamy. Serve on or pass with slices of fresh fruit. Sprinkle with chopped pistachio nuts for added color.

SHERRY PEACHES

FOR SIX

⅓ cup butter
¾ cup brown sugar
⅓ cup water
1 teaspoon lemon juice
6 large ripe peaches, skinned
½ cup dry sherry

Melt butter and sugar in a casserole; add water, lemon juice, and whole peaches. Poach peaches slowly, being sure to baste them frequently with syrup. Depending on size of peaches, it takes from 20 to 30 minutes to cook. Add sherry in last 5 minutes of cooking. Serve hot with meats, or warm with cream for dessert.

STRAWBERRIES EXCELLENT

FOR SIX

2½ quarts strawberries
6 tablespoons brandy
7 tablespoons curaçao
1 cup whipping cream
1 pint pineapple ice or sherbet

Wash and hull 2 quarts of the strawberries. Place them in a serving bowl (crystal is prettiest). Cover with the brandy and 6 tablespoons of the curaçao. Let stand in refrigerator for several hours. Whip the cream. Purée the remaining berries in a blender. Fold the purée into the whipped cream and add the tablespoon of curaçao. Just before serving put six scoops of pineapple ice or sherbet on top of the berries. Cover with the whipped cream mixture.

FAVORITE WAY WITH STRAWBERRIES

FOR FOUR

Fresh strawberries are served more ways than you can keep up with; this way I like them when I have beautiful large berries and want to show off.

1 quart strawberries
½ cup powdered sugar

Wash and hull the berries; place in a china or glass bowl and cover with the powdered sugar. Place in the refrigerator and thoroughly chill. When ready to serve, place the bowl of sugared berries in a larger bowl filled with cracked ice and serve at the table in chilled dessert dishes. Pass a bowl containing 1 cup of heavy cream, whipped, with 1 tablespoon of kirsch added. You will never forget them!

With these strawberries, I like at least to think about serving something with a goodly flavor of chocolate — if only store-bought chocolate cookies.

OLD-FASHIONED STRAWBERRY SHORTCAKE

FOR SIX

There is nothing better than a good shortcake, and strawberry or peach is best. I like to make individual ones and serve on 12-inch crystal plates.

2 cups flour
4 teaspoons baking powder
¾ teaspoon salt
⅓ cup sugar
½ cup shortening
½ cup whipping cream or half-and-half
¼ cup water
Sugared strawberries

Mix the flour, baking powder, salt, and sugar. Cut the shortening in with a pastry blender or two knives. Mix cream and water and stir in quickly. Do not overmix. Dump out on a floured board and pat about 1 inch thick. Cut with a 3- or 3½-inch cutter and put on ungreased cookie sheet about 2 inches apart or drop by heaping tablespoons. Bake at 450° for 15 minutes. Split and butter. Cover first layer with sugared strawberries slightly mashed. Cover with other half and repeat with strawberries. Either be generous with the berries (or peaches) or don't make it. Serve with whipped or pouring cream. I like this dessert with lemon ice cream between the halves with the berries.

Dessert Sauces

Sauces — and they should be good ones, used discriminately and with thought as to how and when — add the dash to desserts that the dexterously turned phrase does to conversation.

Combine a highly flavored sauce such as chocólate or caramel with vanilla ice cream because vanilla has the happy faculty of blending with any other flavor. Use sherry- or rum-flavored sauce with plum pudding to bring out the flavor of its fruits and nuts. Do not put sauce on a cake that is heavily frosted. If serving a sauce from the kitchen, it should be ladled on with discretion. If passed, and I think all sauces should be passed so everyone may have as little or as much as he desires, the sauceboat should be easy to handle and a suitably sized ladle chosen to go with it. (Here's another use for your favorite pipkin.)

These are favorite sauces gathered over years of ladling to a sweet ending.

EASY NO-COOK CHOCOLATE SAUCE

THREE-FOURTHS CUP

2 ounces unsweetened chocolate
½ cup sugar
7 tablespoons cold water
½ teaspoon vanilla extract

Put in an electric blender and beat at high speed for 5 minutes — no cooking.

In fact, I make all kinds of sauces in my blender with whatever candy I happen to have around. I usually put 12 pieces in and 2 tablespoons of water or milk, or rum or brandy or however I feel about things at the time. But I always have a dessert sauce on tap.

CHOCOLATE SAUCE

ONE AND ONE-HALF CUPS

¼ cup butter
¼ cup shaved unsweetened chocolate (about ⅔ of a square)

Stir over low heat until smooth, then add:

¼ cup cocoa
¾ cup sugar
½ cup cream
⅛ teaspoon salt

Bring to the boiling point. Remove from heat and add:

1 teaspoon vanilla extract

This sauce may be stored and reheated over hot water as needed.

APRICOT SAUCE

TWO CUPS

1½ cups apricot jam
½ cup water
2 tablespoons sugar

Combine ingredients, bring to a boil, and cook for 5 to 10 minutes, stirring constantly. Rub the sauce through a sieve. You may add 1 or 2 tablespoons kirsch, brandy, or any liqueur.

CLARET SAUCE

ONE AND ONE-HALF CUPS

Claret Sauce will add color to your desserts — and I particularly like it served over baked apples with the center filled with whipped cream cheese.

1 cup sugar
½ cup water
¼ cup claret
1 teaspoon lemon juice

Boil the sugar and water for 5 minutes; add wine and remove from heat. Add the lemon juice and cool. Keep a jar on hand in your refrigerator.

BUTTERSCOTCH SAUCE

ONE AND ONE-HALF CUPS

---

1 cup light cream
2 tablespoons butter
¾ cup brown sugar
1 tablespoon light Karo syrup

Mix in a heavy pot and cook over low heat until the mixture is smooth and thick. Stir frequently while cooking. Serve warm or cold.

CUSTARD SAUCE

TWO CUPS

Custard Sauce has more friends than any other; and why is the new housewife afraid of it?

3 egg yolks
¼ cup sugar
⅛ teaspoon salt
1½ cups milk
1 teaspoon vanilla or lemon extract

Beat egg yolks slightly and add sugar and salt. Place in top of double boiler and stir in the milk. Cook over hot water, stirring constantly, until mixture coats the spoon. Remove and place in pan of cold water; beat in the flavoring and serve cold over gelatin desserts and fresh or canned fruits.

FOAMY SAUCE

ONE AND ONE-HALF CUPS

---

3 egg yolks
¾ cup sugar
½ teaspoon vanilla extract
¼ teaspoon salt
½ cup whipping cream

Beat first four ingredients until lemon colored and fold in cream, which has been whipped. Serve with fruit pudding or dumplings, and with baked apples.

raisins and rum. Cook for 5 minutes. Add vanilla. Remove from heat and add lemon and orange peel. Add nuts and serve warm, over ice cream.

SAUCE LAWRENCE

adapted from the Pump Room and Veronica Morrisey — ONE AMPLE CUP

1 cup Fudge Sauce
¼ cup orange juice
2 tablespoons grated orange rind
2 teaspoons curaçao
A pinch of salt

Heat Fudge Sauce and add orange juice. Reheat and add grated orange rind and curaçao. Serve hot over vanilla ice cream or flambé with brandy before serving. It is a use-it-all-at-one-time sauce.

SUPREME SAUCE

TWO CUPS

1 egg yolk
3 tablespoons dry sherry or rum
⅛ teaspoon salt
1¼ cups powdered sugar
1 egg white, stiffly beaten
½ cup whipping cream, whipped

Beat egg yolk until light yellow; add sherry and salt with sugar and beat until frothy. Fold in stiffly beaten egg white and whipped cream. Serve over canned or fresh fruit or any mild-flavored pudding.

COLD ZABAGLIONE SAUCE

ONE CUP

4 egg yolks
3 tablespoons sugar
¼ cup dry Marsala or sherry

Put egg yolks in top of double boiler; beat until lemon colored. Beat in the sugar. Heat the wine and add gradually. Place over hot water and cook until thick, beating constantly. Do not overcook. Chill.

Part 7

Parties

This and That

Parties

Helen Corbitt was a famous party giver. In her first book she opened a chapter on parties saying simply: "I like to give a party." In 1974 she devoted an entire book, Helen Corbitt Cooks for Company, *to entertaining.*

Helen didn't need an excuse to give a party. An impromptu gathering could be inspired by a gift of a smoked turkey or a Virginia ham or the unexpected arrival of an out-of-town friend. Her freezer was always full of the right ingredients that could, in short order, be turned into delicious dishes.

Although she had planned and executed receptions, seated formal dinners, and galas for hundreds, and created special menus to be served to presidents, governors, foreign heads of state, and dignitaries, her favorite parties were Sunday brunches, Sunday night suppers, kitchen buffets, and picnics.

Holidays had always been important to her, for she remembered how they were traditionally celebrated in the Corbitt family home in upstate New York. She later followed some of those traditions in her Texas home and added many of her own invention.

In this short section on parties I have selected some of Helen's menus for her favorite informal gatherings and for holiday meals for Thanksgiving, Christmas, New Year's, and St. Patrick's Day. Most of the recipes needed are in this collection. For some of the others consult earlier Corbitt cookbooks; a few will depend on the reader's own ingenuity.

SUNDAY BRUNCHES

Bull Shots and Bloody Marys
French goose basket (used for centerpiece also) filled with fresh strawberries, with bowls of raspberry and strawberry purée to spoon over
King crab in cream over poached eggs on Parmesan cheese toast
Sherried chicken livers, apples, and almonds
Thick slices of cold ripe tomatoes
Slivered fresh asparagus, cooked Chinese style
Hot biscuits, whipped butter, lime marmalade
Various cookies

□

Bloody Marys and milk punch poured from pitchers into stemmed glasses. I'm hooked on stemmed glasses. They look elegant!
Slices of ripe melon with a pipkin of fresh lime and mint syrup to pour over
Thin slices of white meat of turkey in lightly curried cream and covered with slices of crisp bacon
Spoon Bread (made with grits it is Grits Soufflé)
Blueberry drop biscuits
Slices of toasted buttered pound cake

□

To invite out-of-staters for a Texas country brunch gives them memories and a little extra weight for a few days!

Bourbon milk punch, strong coffee, and iced tea
Pink grapefruit
Ham Steak with Onion Gravy
Fried chicken livers and giblets
Grits casserole, black-eyed peas
Texas toast (white bread cut thick, buttered, and oven-toasted)
Pear preserves, red pepper jelly
Vienna Coffee Cake, oatmeal cookies

Weather permitting, serve out-of-doors: fresh air will make everyone hungry.

□

My Sunday-before-Christmas brunch I enjoy. The fireplace is filled with poinsettias, fresh evergreens fill the rooms with their fragrance, and small Christmas bouquets in red ribbons hang from my chandelier in place of a table decoration. I set a polished table and let the reflections of the silver and copper I use give off a warm glow to the heavily laden table. I serve bourbon milk punches and Chablis cassis. I think eggnog is not good with food even at this time of year.

Julienne Breast of Chicken and Chanterelles
Spoon Bread, and lots of it
Piperade
Pear halves baked with lemon marmalade and toasted almonds
Baked whole boneless ham, sliced thin at the table
12-inch round Pancake Stack, with butter, real maple syrup, and the juices from the ham poured over (my mother's trick) — then cut like a pie
A molded cream and ricotta cheese with black cherry preserves spilled over
Hot biscuits and Melba toast
Rum cake, apple cake, and Fruitcake Cookies
Coffee

SUNDAY NIGHT ENTERTAINING

Sunday night entertaining should be early, as one must face the new week bright-eyed and cheerful. Somehow I do not like to spend much time in my kitchen on Sunday unless it is cold and rainy, so I plan simply prepared suppers or ones with advance preparation.

Cold boiled salmon with cucumber sauce
Spoon Bread with melted sweet butter to spoon over, lots of both
Rolled Ham and Chicken Crêpes à la Swiss
Spinach salad with Sherry Dressing
Roquefort mold and red caviar
Crescent rolls
Sherry Peaches and Praline Cookies

□

Lobster and Chicken à la Crème
Pastry barques or patty shells spread with pâté de fois gras
Cold sliced rare Rib-Eye en Gelée
Tomatoes filled with Emerald Rice
Romaine and hearts of palm salad, oil and vinegar dressing

Warm buttered hard rolls
(hard rolls get harder if you get them too hot)
Brazil Nut Torte

□

Braised Beef, Poivre Vert
Chicken Crêpes
Cold lobster and king crab on rings of papaya
with curried mayonnaise
Flageolet Salad
Hot bread sticks
Glazed Strawberries

□

Cassoulet
Wilted Spinach and Mushroom Salad
French bread
Raspberry Mousse
Brandy Almond Cake

□

London broil with red wine butter
(Don't pass this by) Mushrooms au Cresson in Crêpes
Jellied Asparagus Salad
Cheesed Bread
Cold Lemon Soufflé

□

Chicken and Artichoke Hearts in Newburg Sauce
in hot patty shells filled with grated Gruyère cheese
Ham salad in parsley aspic
Avocado with Shrimp Mayonnaise
Oven-toasted buttered rolls
Fresh strawberries with rum-flavored Soft Custard and
Mokka Sticks (you buy, Verkade brand)

I like to serve all sauces separately. Some like a lot; some, not any.

□

Chicken Almond Hash
Tomato Medley Salad filled with Russian Salad
Watercress or soft lettuce sandwiches
Coffee Marshmallow Ice Cream

□

Sweet and Sour Pork
White rice
Oriental Vegetable Salad
Cheese biscuits and plum jam
Pineapple ice and almond cookies

□

Curry of Lamb on crisp cornbread
Three-boy relishes: chutney, riced egg and chives, chopped dry-roasted peanuts
Green beans with sautéed onion rings and coconut
Thin-sliced orange bread
Fresh Fruit with Gingered Cream and unsalted crackers

KITCHEN BUFFETS

One of Helen Corbitt's favorite parties was the kitchen buffet. In her lectures on "Fashions in Food" and at her cooking schools she talked about this informal way to entertain and of how much work it saved the hostess. In Helen Corbitt Cooks for Company *she had this to say:*

Entertain in the kitchen? Why not? Kitchens today often get as much thought and careful decorating as the Victorian parlor used to. And if yours isn't a decorator's dream, so what? It is a delightfully informal place to serve a buffet. Using your range to keep the food hot is a lot easier than getting out chafing dishes or warmers. Pots and pans are attractive enough in color and design to put conventional chafing dishes to shame. You can always hide the lids and extra cooking things. I put mine in one half of my double sink, cover them with an attractive towel, and dare my guests to look underneath. Sometimes I fill the other side of the sink with ice to hold my salad bowl or cold soup.

There is a relaxed atmosphere about a kitchen buffet. Guests enjoy it, feeling, I think, that no one is watching them and that they may take what they wish and go back for seconds without urging. I always add a whimsical touch to the range: a skinny vase with one flower, a decorative pepper grinder or candle. There is lots of color on my dining-room table with gay linen, bright colors in china, and the pitchers of wine to be poured by the guests. Sometimes too I let my guests cook their own entrées — when I know my guests well and know in advance they will relish the chance to cook some. Best of all I ask them to bring their soiled dishes back to the kitchen — not always, but usually when I have no one in to help. Every time I have a kitchen buffet it seems to me that people are enjoying this kind of informality more and more.

These are the dinners I have done — and I always serve the first course in the living room.

Cold Yogurt Soup ladled from a crystal bowl into punch cups (I serve this frequently, as it is refreshing and low in calories.)
Thin homemade whole-wheat Melba toast

FROM THE RANGE

Beef Carbonnade
Kasha
Green Bean Casserole
Wilted Spinach and Mushroom Salad
French bread
Peach Crumb Pie

□

Papaya Oriental

FROM THE RANGE

Herbed Leg of Lamb with Cumberland Sauce and brandy, flamed
Peas in Sour Cream
Artichoke Soufflé
Fennel Salad
Thin whole-wheat sandwiches
Raspberry Frango

The leg of lamb I carve and put back together, then pour over the Cumberland Sauce and flaming brandy. I do this for a seated dinner also. It looks so good. I find that Texans who think they hate lamb gobble it up and ask for more. I also like to broil a leg of lamb for this kind of party.

□

Consommé Bellevue with Avocado

FROM THE RANGE

Ham Steak à la Bourguignonne
Onions and Leeks in Cream
Broiled Potato Slices
Tom Hunt's Spinach Salad with Greek olives
Hot biscuits
Whole strawberries with brown sugar and sour cream
Oatmeal Crisps

□

Pickled eggs and okra

FROM THE RANGE

Chicken Madeira with croutons
Yellow squash with mint dressing
Red cabbage, avocado, and grapefruit salad with Poppy Seed Dressing
Toasted Almond and Orange Mousse

□

Spinach Vichyssoise

FROM THE RANGE

Osso Buco
Mushroom Rice
Layered Vegetables
Hard rolls (to sop up the sauce from Osso Buco)
Watercress Salad
Sour Cream Apple Pie

□

Crudités

FROM THE RANGE

Italian sausages
Fettucine Alfredo
Spinach Ring filled with carrots and grapes
Marinated sliced tomatoes and scallions
Italian bread and sweet butter
Petite babas (buy them), split and filled with coffee ice cream, frozen, then served with hot Caramel Sauce

□

Cream of Corn Soup

FROM THE RANGE

Mixed Seafood in Crêpes
Sliced Brussels sprouts in brown butter
Herb Biscuits
Snow Pea Salad with Sesame Dressing
Hot poached peaches with chilled sour cream to spoon over

□

Demitasse of Clear Tomato Soup

FROM THE RANGE

Braised Shortribs of Beef with Horseradish Mousse

Champ
Green Cabbage in Cream
Potato Bread with Raisins
Apple and Watercress Salad
Stilton cheese, Wheaten biscuits

THANKSGIVING DINNER

Pink grapefruit and shrimp cocktail with Green Herb Dressing
Roast Turkey with Cornbread Dressing
Cranberry sauce
Hot kumquats
Scalloped Onions and Peanuts
Brussels sprouts with brown butter
Knob celery salad
Parker House rolls
Sour Cream Pumpkin Pie
Ambrosia

THANKSGIVING BUFFET

Baked ham with preserved orange sauce
Lobster Tail au Gratin
A super sandwich of cold sliced turkey with molded cranberry sauce, thin bread and butter, homemade mayonnaise, pepper and salt
A variety of cheeses with apples and pears
Caramel Soufflé with English Custard
White Chocolate Pound Cake with pecans and coconut

CHRISTMASES PAST

I remember the Christmas season when it began the day before Christmas Eve. My father with my brother and I rode out into the country in the early evening with a horse and sleigh and cut down our own tree. It was usually heavily covered with snow, so never looked quite as good as we thought it would. We dragged it through the front hallway, now decked with holly, to the fireplace, set it up, and said, "What a beautiful tree." I wonder why our house didn't burn down. We were always cold, wet from snow, tired, but always happy. Then we ate heavenly oyster stew and Johnnycake, 'til we bust'.

Christmas Eve we decorated the tree with strings of popcorn we popped ourselves and ornaments from all over the world, which were carefully packed away each year, and we lived Christmas in other lands listening to the best storyteller I ever listened to — my father.

The night of Christmas Eve my brother and I piled our sleds with Christmas bread my mother baked and took it to our neighbors — wrapped in plain white paper, and tied with red satin (real) ribbon and a sprig of balsam, because it smelled so good. The year we stopped, when we were both college age, I thought the town council would take action.

Everyone who believed in Christmas hung a big wreath of evergreen on their front door, and put lighted holy candles in their window. The candles were blessed by the local priest for everyone who believed, regardless of the church they attended. Everyone in town went to Midnight Mass — drunk or sober. Christian or infidel. It was Christmas.

Christmas night we lighted real candles on the tree, no twinkling lights, no colored bulbs, just pretty twisted red and green candles in a reflector holder. What a thrill! What a fire hazard! But even the bucket of water in my father's hand, and the prayer on my mother's lips, could not dim the lovely light.

CHRISTMAS EVE BUFFET

Mushroom Consommé
Roast Veal with Morels in Cream
Scalloped Oysters
Spinach Crêpes Veronique
Spiced cranberries, sherried prunes, and other preserves
Sally Lunn
Fresh pineapple fingers, dusted with chopped pistachios
Pots de Crème

HOLIDAY BUFFET COCKTAIL SUPPER

Baked Ham on one end of table
Roasted Turkey at the other
Hot Sage Biscuits and thin slices of rye and white bread
Hot Oyster Fritters
Small pastry barques filled with deviled crabmeat
Eggs stuffed with wild rice and smoked turkey
Celery filled with sharp cheese and chipped bacon
Crispy rounds of toast browned in the oven with mayonnaise and Worcestershire sauce, piled high with pâté de foie gras
Red cabbage shells filled with avocado mashed with curry and onion juice
Garlic Potato Chips to dip
A demitasse table with Spiced Pecans and Fruitcake Squares
Preserved Guava Shells and cream cheese and toasted water crackers
Eggnog
Coffee

HOLIDAY DINNERS

Chicken and Corn Soup
Cheese Straws
Hot Spiced Pickled Pears
Roasted Tom Turkey with Giblet Gravy
Rice Dressing
Cranberry Jelly
Green Beans with Minted Butter
Onions and Leeks in Cream
A Crisp Raw Relish Tray
Fresh Coconut Cointreau
Coffee

□

Grapefruit Basket with center of Crabmeat Rémoulade
Buttery Crackers, oven browned with Curry Butter
Roasted Hen Turkey with Turkey Gravy

Cornbread Dressing
Spiced Peaches
Potatoes mashed with Cream and Watercress Butter
Oyster and Eggplant Casserole
Molded Cranberry and Orange Salad
Tom and Jerry Pie
Coffee

NEW YEAR'S EVE DINNER

Beef Carbonnade
Cauliflower and snipped green beans
Hearts of palm and avocado salad, oil-and-lemon-juice dressing
Cheeses and hard rolls
Champagne Mousse with puréed strawberries
Champagne

NEW YEAR'S EVE SUPPER

Split Pea Soup made with smoked turkey
Cornbread
Roast Loin of Pork stuffed with prunes and apples
Escalloped Oysters and Eggplant
Raw relishes in ice
Fresh fruit bowl

NEW YEAR'S AFTERNOON BUFFET

Oyster Stew made with half-and-half
Toasted salty crackers
Spaghetti and meatballs
Pickled Black-eyed Peas
Assorted raw relishes
Milk punch
Coffee

LUCK OF THE IRISH

How can one put into words the wonder of being Irish on St. Patrick's Day? It is a day for listening to all living things. It is a day of music as if all the world were in step with the tune that only an Irishman can really hear. It is living a long history of the extensive wrongs and hurts of one's ancestors. It is also the joy of being alive. It isn't simply a realization that one is descended from kings, for on this day every Irishman is a king — or queen.

On St. Patrick's Day the Irish know more sadness, magic, adventure, and gladness than anyone else can experience on any other day. One walks with complete understanding with God and all mankind for twenty-four wonderful hours.

The Irish may destroy themselves the other 364 days of the year, but on St. Patrick's Day they live it up with friends. On this day all other men look deep into their own history and always find a little bit of Irish there, imaginary or not. I like to celebrate my Saint's Day with a hundred welcomes to my friends. I say to them that hunger is bad, but thirst is worse; I say I wish you a long life, and may God give you sense. This is my usual celebration supper that begins and ends with the supper on the table; my guests eat all evening.

Velvet Corn Soup
Smoked salmon (if I have a few extra dollars around;
if not, a cold salmon mousse)
Hot Corned Beef
Hot horseradish apples
Creamy Cole Slaw
Blarney cheese
Wheat and rye breads
Trifle
Irish Coffee

PICNICS AND OUTDOOR PARTIES

Pique-nique, the French for "pick up a trifle" and which means a picnic for you, can range from the elaborate to a delicatessen sandwich or fried chicken in a bucket. At any rate, it is a pack-up-your-food-and-follow-the-action to roadside parks, a football game, the county fair, the beach, the mountains — just go. It is good for you to relax in fresh air. (You can always find some if you look for it.)

It is easy to have a picnic even though it takes some behind-the-scenes planning. We have picnic hampers today — sophisticated ones — or you can use an egg crate and all kinds of styrofoam containers to carry both hot and cold food. You do need a check list: can opener, eating utensils, a knife for slicing, chopping board, ice container, bottle opener, insect repellent, tablecloth and napkins, salt and pepper and such, pot holder, fuel of some kind, matches, paper towels, trash bag, soap, and a bottle of iodine.

I like picnics near a babbling brook, if only for remembering past fun picnics. One beautiful day in Ireland some friends and I sat on a fallen tree trunk and had that wonderful Irish bread with their equally wonderful ham and Blarney cheese. We made our own sandwiches with sweet butter and champagne mustard and had raisin pound cake, as only the Irish can make, fresh cherries and bananas, a white wine cooled in the brook. Simple, but the birds sang, the sun shone, and the whole world looked bright and uncomplicated.

I like to be extravagant when I give a picnic — and I liked this one — as did my guests.

Fresh Caviar with Hot Flageolets
Leg of Lamb in Pastry
Rice Salad
Romaine with fresh mint in Sherry Dressing
Salt-rising bread and butter sandwiches
A well-packed freezer of homemade strawberry ice cream with cones
Peanut Cookies (take lots)
Chablis in ice
Vacuum jug of coffee

□

Take a portable grill, and this menu you could do easily.

Cold Roquefort Soup
Marinated skewered Beef Tenderloin
and Chicken Livers to grill
Garbanzo Salad
Hard rolls with Port Salut cheese
Raw vegetables in ice
Fresh peaches to toast on the coals
White Chocolate Pound Cake
Sangria (It goes so very well with the peaches, too.)

□

For the Fourth of July, why not have an old-fashioned celebration for neighbors and relatives? Out-of-doors, games and songs — a picnic supper.

Fresh vegetables kept cold in a wheelbarrow
filled with ice
Charcoal broiled flank steaks and hamburgers
Potato salad
French Bread and buns to toast
Old-fashioned Strawberry Shortcake
Fresh Peach Ice-Cream cones

□

For an elegant picnic:

Cold boiled lobster tail with lemon mayonnaise
Cold tarragon chicken
Rice Salad
A round loaf of bread hollowed out and the center filled with
cucumber and egg salad sandwiches
(This keeps them moist.)
Almond Cream Cake
Fresh pineapple wedges in ice with brown sugar
A Sancerre or champagne

And perhaps a candelabra, to give it a flair. It goes without saying: no paper plates. And, oh yes, choose a spot away from the noise of moving objects.

□

A menu with a south-of-the-border flavor:

Guacamole, corn chips, cherry tomatoes, green onions, and jalapeños
Flank steaks, marinated with dry red wine, olive oil, and garlic
(Grill with a few jalapeño peppers here and there.)
Shrimp, marinated in olive oil, garlic,
and lots of chopped parsley to grill
Rolls to toast
Soft cheeses, guava jelly, or guava shells and thin crackers
Good chocolate candy
A chilled sparkling rosé

□

Or try:

Deviled Rock Cornish Hens cooked in foil
(carried to the picnic in the same foil)
Cold Ratatouille
Texas Caviar (pickled black-eyed peas)
Loaves of homemade bread with asparagus spears or salami
cooked inside, butter to spread
Rum Cake

This and That

In Helen Corbitt's first book she introduced a section called "This and That" with these words: "This chapter is just what the name implies — this and that about a lot of things . . . They have proved helpful to me; maybe they will to you."

Actually This and That *was the working title Helen used for the entire manuscript of her first book, which she sent to me in 1956. I have always been glad that when the real title-picking time came her editors at Houghton Mifflin and both of us agreed on* Helen Corbitt's Cookbook *as the best title. Then it was natural to turn to "This and That" as the perfect name for the chapter of bits and pieces — kitchen lore, cooking hints, and some recipes.*

Readers, male and female, novice and professional, fell in love with "This and That." The only complaints through the years have been that "This and That" chapters are never long enough.

Many of the favorites from the other books have been chosen for this collection and there are some new ones, which have been combed from Corbitt lectures and letters and from my notes made during twenty-two years of visits and telephone conversations.

Here, then, is the ultimate "This and That."

□

My mother always dipped her teaspoon in almond extract before measuring vanilla or lemon extract. I still do.

□

I like to serve warm corned beef sandwiches made on thin slices of buttered French bread, and hot applesauce flavored with a goodly amount of horseradish with this. For dessert? Irish coffee.

□

Do not partially cook poultry one day and complete cooking the following day, according to the U.S. Department of Agriculture. This is not considered a good procedure, as it gives bacteria an additional opportunity to grow.

The U.S.D.A. also warns against roasting your turkey in the oven all night long at a low temperature. Don't be tempted. Instead, roast the turkey at a proper, higher temperature for fewer hours in the morning. When done, internally it should be 180° to 185°.

□

In making crêpes, if you find yourself with a hole in the crêpe, simply add more batter while the crêpe cooks. Who will know?

□

Choux designates a cream puff mixture. Why? It looks like a cabbage or chow.

□

A light soup the Zodiac customers enjoyed was of thin slices of avocado, mushrooms, and water chestnuts added to chicken broth. We never found a name for it.

□

Danish Kitchen Finesse: Don't weep, says an old Danish proverb, when peeling or slicing onions. Place a small piece of bread between the teeth and breathe through the mouth.

FRUIT SHRUB

---

6 tablespoons crushed frozen or fresh strawberries
1 cup orange juice
1 cup pineapple juice or 2 cups of any mixed fruit juices you might have on hand, like pear, cherry, peach, or spiced juices you have saved
1 tablespoon lemon juice

For each serving, put 1 tablespoon of the fruit in a juice glass and fill with fruit juices, mixed. Thoroughly chill and serve with a sprig of fresh mint on top. The fruit will sink to the bottom, and the juices will blend so that you have a pretty drink.

□

Cut thin slices of refrigerator rye bread; spread with softened butter and sprinkle with Parmesan cheese and garlic salt. Oven-toast at 350° until crisp, and serve with soup or salads.

□

BLUEBERRY GRUNT

FOR SIX

In the blueberry country a favorite pudding during the season is Blueberry Grunt. I never heard it called anything else.

Cook 2 cups of fresh blueberries in a small amount of water until they are soft. Sweeten to your taste (I use about ½ cup sugar). Add 1 tablespoon butter, 1 teaspoon lemon juice, ¼ teaspoon salt. Pour into a deep casserole dish. Make your own baking powder biscuit recipe and pat it out on top of the blueberries. Place the casserole in a pan of hot water; cover and bake 1 hour at 350°, keeping the water within an inch of the top of the casserole. Serve hot with heavy cream, plain or whipped.

□

Making gravy? The real secret of making smooth gravy is to blend flour thoroughly with fat or with cold liquid before combining it with hot liquid.

□

Grated lemon peel gives a delicate flavor to tea, so try serving a dish of grated lemon peel instead of lemon slices at your next "at home"—but you only need a little.

□

Whipped cream mixed with puréed and strained frozen raspberries is divine for icing an angel food cake.

PULLED BREAD

Take a fork and pull out chunks of unsliced bread about 2 inches long and 1 inch wide. Brush with melted butter and sprinkle with salt and paprika. Bake in a 300° oven until golden brown, 20 to 30 minutes. A sort of crazy Melba toast. Before baking I sometimes sprinkle over Parmesan cheese.

□

Serve a scooped-out pineapple lightly packed with orange and grapefruit sections with slivers of chicken on top, accompanied by a silver bowl of yogurt dressing.

□

Parmesan cheese can be sprinkled oh-so-sparingly on green vegetables instead of butter, or lavishly if you don't watch calories.

□

Garnish a melon wedge filled with fresh fruit with a fresh flower or decorative leaves from the garden.

□

Serve gazpacho in red or green pepper shells or tomato shells. Make a molded salad of the leftovers for lots of flavor and few calories.

□

Serve fresh fruit with a warmed poppy seed dressing mixed equally with grenadine. Hot dressing on cold fruits is a pleasant surprise.

□

Hand a guest a box lunch and he is immediately relaxed and will probably sit on the floor.

□

Serve hot Swedish meatballs over cold potato salad and pass rye bread.

CHEESED BREAD

1 loaf unsliced French or Italian bread
1 cup grated Cheddar or Muenster cheese
¼ cup butter
½ teaspoon Worcestershire sauce

Cut the bread in 1-inch slices to the lower crust. Mix the cheese, butter, and Worcestershire sauce and spread on each slice. Push the bread together and wrap in foil. Heat in a 350° oven until cheese and butter have completely melted, about 20 to 30 minutes.

BREAD AND BUTTER PICKLES

ABOUT FIVE QUARTS

My good friend Margaret Hull makes the best Bread and Butter Pickles I have ever eaten. She brings me some every time she visits, and I do not share them with anyone. Her pickled okra is the best, too. Her secret is using small cucumbers and okra.

1 gallon cucumbers (small in circumference), about 6 pounds
2 green peppers
8 small white onions
½ cup salt (do not use iodized salt)

Slice vegetables thin. Cover with salt and stir. Mix ice cubes through and cover with ice. Let stand 3 hours in a cool place. Take ice out and *drain thoroughly*.

Pickling Syrup:

5 cups sugar
1½ teaspoons turmeric
½ teaspoon ground cloves
1 teaspoon celery seed
2 tablespoons mustard seed
5 cups cider vinegar

Boil syrup. Add vegetables and heat to boiling, but do not boil. Put in hot sterilized jars. Cover with melted paraffin. Let stand at least 3 months before using.

PICKLED OKRA

Choose small okra; wash and leave stem ends on. Fill each hot sterilized jar tightly, but do not bruise okra. For each *pint:*

2 teaspoons dill seed
2 strips jalapeño peppers
½ teaspoon red pepper
2 cloves garlic, cut in half

Cover with the following, which have been boiled together:

1 quart *white* vinegar
1 cup water
½ cup salt (do not use iodized salt)

This syrup is enough for 4 to 6 pints. One pound okra fills 2 pints. Seal jars as soon as filled. Pour paraffin on top to seal properly.

RED RELISH

ABOUT TWELVE PINTS

5 pounds red sweet peppers (weigh after seeds and stems are removed and before washing)
3¾ pounds mild white onions peeled and cut in small sections

Grind peppers and onions together, using coarse cutter. Mix well (juice and all). Cover with boiling water and let stand 5 minutes. Drain off as much water as possible; then squeeze dry. To this add:

1 quart vinegar
2 cups white sugar
3 tablespoons salt

If liked hot, grind in a small hot pepper or red pepper or hot sauce. Bring to a boil and cook 20 minutes. Seal in sterilized jars. (If peppers are not a dark, pretty red, add a little red food coloring. In preparing peppers, be sure to cut out any green spots.)

□

If you have only one cookie sheet, cut pieces of foil to fit, shiny side up. You do not have to wait then for pan to cool. Just shift foil onto cookie sheet. Then throw away the foil — no pan to wash.

□

French bread, cut in inch-size hunks, buttered, and dried out in a 350° oven, is good to serve at any meal where rolls are too much trouble.

□

If you don't have time to make bread, decorate bread sticks by rolling them in melted butter and then in a coating such as sesame seeds, Parmesan cheese, or a cinnamon-and-sugar mixture. Then put in the oven to warm.

□

For Singapore Turkey, rub the bird with curry powder, stuff with oranges, and baste with gin.

□

We need more Indians and fewer chiefs. Let's train more good basic cooks who know how to use the utensils and foods properly.

□

Keep boneless, flattened chicken breasts in the freezer. Thaw, spread with a mixture of sweet butter, cream cheese, and chives. Bake in chicken broth plus cream until the sauce is reduced. Add dry sherry or white wine, if desired.

□

Fine bread crumbs used instead of flour for thickening make a sauce or a creamed mixture more delicate.

□

Cooked shrimp, or lobster, or king crab, with slices of cucumber and avocado, make a perfect salad or cocktail. Use either Rémoulade Sauce or French Dressing.

SPANAKOPITA

FOR SIX TO EIGHT

Spanakopita is a Greek spinach dish that goes well with everything and is delicious.

2 pounds spinach, washed and trimmed of heavy ribs
¼ cup chopped onion
1 package strudel leaves
Gruyère cheese

Drain spinach and chop fine with onion or chop in a blender. Brush a shallow 2-quart casserole with melted butter. Cover with a layer of strudel leaves. Brush with melted butter. Repeat 4 times. Place a layer of the spinach, sprinkle with ¾ cup shredded Gruyère cheese. Repeat until spinach is used. Cover with 4 more strudel leaves, each one lightly buttered. Bake at 350° for 40 minutes or until top is golden brown. Cool and serve either hot or cold. The authentic Greek recipe calls for feta cheese, but I like the Gruyère better.

□

If you are looking for a new way with apple pie, omit the butter with which you usually dot the fruit, and pour in 1 cup of thick sour cream before adjusting the top crust — or use part brown or maple sugar in place of granulated sugar.

□

You'll need the following for an inexpensive spaghetti sauce, good for a late supper: 12 slices of bacon, minced and fried in 2 tablespoons olive oil, 3 eggs, ⅓ cup grated Parmesan, salt, and cracked pepper. Beat eggs, add to hot spaghetti, toss and toss. Add bacon and oil, toss again; stir in cheese and salt and pepper. Enough for 1 pound pasta.

□

Flattened, boneless chicken breasts can cook quickly in a skillet when you are in a hurry — or, more important, to help conserve electricity.

□

More conservation of electricity comes from steaming fresh vegetables just a few minutes in a rack over hot water. This method also preserves their flavor and nutritive qualities.

□

Instead of taking candy to a friend who broke his leg skiing, send him a bowl of gazpacho. It will be much better for him.

□

Serve thick slices of cucumber or medium slices of zucchini instead of crackers with a cocktail dip.

□

I never tell what I am serving because somebody would say, "I don't like tomatoes" or "I don't like yogurt." I just wait and as they have a third cup of soup I say, "I'm so glad you like my yogurt soup."

□

Let dark breads rest 15 minutes before kneading. Less flour will be needed during the kneading process because whole-wheat and rye flours contain a high percentage of bran, which absorbs liquids at a slower rate. This rest period helps prevent the mistake of adding too much flour.

□

Turkey stuffing, cold, sliced thin, and put between thin white bread, is delicious — with thin slices of cranberry jelly between, too, it is something special.

□

SPOOM

This may be used as a dessert or with a fish or fowl course. I always serve it in a stemmed glass.

¼ pound sugar
2 tablespoons water
6 egg whites
Lemon sherbet
Champagne

Boil sugar and water to make a clear syrup. Beat egg whites until stiff. Add hot syrup gradually and beat until cold. Fold together equal parts of meringue and lemon sherbet; lace with champagne.

□

Easy things to remember about rice:

One cup rice makes about 3 cups cooked.

Chopped parsley or a pinch of saffron cooked with rice gives a different flavor and nice color for seafood dishes.

Substitute tomato juice for half the water for pink rice.

Garlic salt never hurts rice when you are using it with chicken.

□

Glassware and silver look cool, and a shelf in your refrigerator given over to serving pieces will pay off in cool delight dividends. For the elbow-raising pause in the day, glasses kept in the deep freeze or in the coldest place in your refrigerator will change your way of thinking during all the hot months.

□

When combining seafood and other foods with a sauce, mix with a fork; also use a fork to stir-fry when you want food to be stirred rapidly.

CRANBERRY SAUCE

FOR TWELVE

The easiest cranberry sauce is what we call the ten-minute variety.

4 cups cranberries
2 cups sugar
2 cups water

Wash cranberries, and be sure to remove the bits of stem and wilted berries. Combine the sugar and water and boil for 5 minutes. Add the cranberries and boil without stirring, until the skins burst; remove from heat and let cool.

CRANBERRY-HORSERADISH MOUSSE

2 cups whole cranberry sauce
1 cup sour cream
3 tablespoons horseradish sauce
1 tablespoon lemon juice
¼ cup grated raw carrot
1 tablespoon gelatin
¼ cup cold water

Combine first five ingredients. Add gelatin to water. Heat over hot water until melted. Add to cranberry mixture. Pour into mold and chill.

UNCOOKED STRAWBERRY JAM

5 cups sugar
3 cups crushed strawberries
1 package powdered pectin
1 cup water

Add sugar to crushed strawberries, mix well, and allow to stand 20 minutes, stirring occasionally. Dissolve the pectin in the water, bring to a boil, and boil 1 minute. Add pectin solution to the fruit-and-sugar mixture and stir 2 minutes. Ladle jam into jelly glasses, filling to about half an inch of the rim. Cover and let stand until jellied (may take 24 to 48 hours). Then seal with hot paraffin and cover with metal lid. Put in freezer or refrigerator promptly.

PEACH CONSERVE

Everyone has a favorite peach preserve recipe, but Peach Conserve is the best thing I ever ate with any kind of hot or cold meats, and combined with cream cheese makes a delicious sandwich spread for tea sandwiches.

2 pounds peaches, peeled
1 cup raisins, cut in half
Juice of 1 lemon
Juice of 1 orange
1 whole orange chopped, skin and all, but no seeds
1 pound sugar
1 quart water
½ pound English walnut meats

Cook peaches, raisins, fruit juices, orange, and sugar in water until thick and clear, stirring occasionally to prevent sticking. Add nutmeats and pour into sterilized jars and seal.

GLAZED PICKLES

Make your own pickles! In a hurry, too.

Buy 6 large dill pickles and slice ½ inch thick. Boil 2 cups of sugar, 1 cup of water, and ½ cup of vinegar to a syrup. Add the pickles and heat. Put in a jar and let stand in a cool place until clear.

□

Fresh fruits may be added to salad greens to make a tossed salad. Or arrange them attractively on the greens, in which case you should pass the dressing of your choice.

BOULA BOULA

FOR SIX

Boula Boula is an exotic soup. The simplest way is to go to the corner grocer's and buy a can of green turtle soup and a can of concentrated green pea soup. Combine the two, beat until smooth, and serve hot with unsweetened whipped cream on top, browned under the broiler. May be served cold, but brown the whipped cream the same as when serving it hot.

□

Almonds and filberts bought already sliced or sliced by you, browned in butter and mixed with butter and orange marmalade, and spread on thin slices of white bread of the Pepperidge Farm variety are an interesting tea sandwich.

□

The best dark breads contain some white flour too. White flour adds gluten to the dough, producing a lighter, more attractive and palatable bread. The bran in whole-wheat and rye flour contains less gluten, giving heavier, more compact loaves.

□

Slice vegetables such as leeks, carrots, and onions across and diagonally in several directions and then place them in cold water to unfold as flower garnishes for skewers of marinated chicken, lamb, or whatever.

□

Instead of cooking frozen vegetables in water (if you cannot find fresh ones on occasion), melt some butter in a skillet and toss the vegetables in, stirring all the while for about 4 minutes.

□

Spread slices of bread with butter. Combine in blender with dry bread crumbs and store the result in plastic sacks in the refrigerator for use as topping. A time-saver, since you don't have to dot the dish with butter when you put it in the oven.

□

Sometimes when serving ice cream with fruit why not put the fruit on the bottom and the ice cream on top? A favorite is fresh strawberries with lemon ice cream topped with an almond-flavored custard sauce.

FRIED PARSLEY

Wash and drain 2 bunches of curly parsley and trim the stems short. Form into small bouquets and put in a frying basket or strainer, a few at a time, and fry in hot deep oil at 380° until crisp, about 2 seconds. Drain on paper towels and lightly salt.

□

Your favorite tomato aspic recipe with freshly peeled and chopped tomatoes added to it, ½ cup for each cup of liquid, is a nice change and fresh tasting. Lightly flavor store-bought mayonnaise with curry powder and add chopped raw celery and carrots, young onions, or whatever you like to serve with it.

CRÈME FRAÎCHE

You cannot buy Crème Fraîche in the supermarket, so make it. This recipe is excellent when you want a special sauce for fresh berries, especially wild ones.

2 cups whipping cream
1 tablespoon buttermilk

Mix the cream and buttermilk together. Heat over low flame until just warm, 85° if you have a thermometer (and you should). Remove mixture and put in warm oven; stir every once in a while for 8 hours. It will be thick. Refrigerate before serving.

□

To "frost" a glass: Dip in unbeaten egg white, then granulated sugar. Do the same with grapes or mint leaves for garnishing.

□

To make Melba toast: Slice bread paper-thin (or buy thin-sliced) and place in a preheated 300° oven and immediately turn off the heat. Leave in oven until crisp. May be made with or without crust.

□

Pickle eggs for Easter: Hard-cook, peel, and cover with beet juice and vinegar, half and half. Add a few cloves and onion gratings. Outside of egg is purple, shading to pink, then yellow.

SALAD WITH MINT

Lamb needs a touch of mint, most folks say, so why not in the salad? Mint, by the way, is good with any green salad.

½ cup olive oil
Juice of 1 lemon
1 teaspoon ground fresh pepper
1 teaspoon chopped fresh mint
¼ teaspoon oregano
1 coddled egg

Combine in a bowl olive oil, lemon juice, and seasonings. Add egg and whip. Pour over salad greens.

ROLLED WATERCRESS SANDWICHES

Take 24 thin slices of very fresh bread. Remove crusts and spread each slice with watercress mayonnaise or watercress butter. Roll up the slice and fasten with a toothpick. Place snugly in a pan lined with a damp cloth and cover with damp cloth. Chill well. Remove toothpicks; insert a small spray of watercress in each end of the rolled sandwiches. Makes 24. Do the same thing with asparagus.

□

Try Chocolate Cinnamon Toast. Mix together ½ cup of cocoa, 5 tablespoons of melted butter, 1 teaspoon of cinnamon, and 6 tablespoons of sugar. Spread on hot crisp toast or English muffins.

□

Lump sugar with lemon juice added (just enough to keep it from melting) is nice to serve on your tea tray. Do the same with orange juice or lime juice, or brandy.

TUNNEL-OF-FUDGE CAKE

Beat 1½ cups soft butter at high speed until fluffy. Beat in 6 eggs, one at a time. Gradually whip in 1½ cups sugar: beat until fluffy. By hand, stir in 2 cups flour, 1 package dry frosting mix (Double Dutch), and 2 cups chopped walnuts until blended. Bake in greased bundt or 10-inch tube pan at 350° for 55 to 60 minutes, until top is dry and shiny. Cool in pan for 2 hours.

The frosting mix and nuts are essential for success. Cake has a soft fudgy interior.

□

I've said it before, but I repeat that a freshly cooked chicken (roasted or boiled) makes the best sandwiches or chicken salad if the meat is used without refrigeration. That means planning your cooking to be over about thirty minutes before making the sandwiches or salad.

□

Fresh celery cut slantwise and thin, boiled 1 minute only in salted water, then combined with salted peanuts or pecans and whipping cream or a thin cream sauce, or combined with sliced sautéd mushrooms and browned almonds, or dressed with sweet butter and lots of chopped parsley makes a nice change in the vegetable department.

□

I always say mashed potatoes taste even better if put into a casserole, spread with whipped cream and shredded cheese — then baked until brown on top. And they go especially well with hamburgers or meat loaves. Relishes, hearty ones such as carrot sticks, celery hearts, cherry tomatoes, olives, help you forget a salad. For dessert? Why, anything at all — but à la mode it.

□

Apricot whole fruit nectar, sweet wine, rum, gin, brandy, or fruit juice is often used for liquid in fruitcakes. These liquids are used, too, to dampen cloths that cakes are wrapped in while they ripen.

□

Any fresh fruit piled high in a baked tart shell and covered with a fruit glacé gives a fresh, sweet ending to a meal. The glacé is made by combining any fruit juice you like with sugar and cornstarch: 1½ cups of juice, 1 cup of sugar, and 3 tablespoons cornstarch. Cook until thick; add vegetable coloring if desired; cool and pour over the fruit. If you are really ambitious for a party, make an assortment of tarts for each guest to choose from.

□

A good way to use leftover beef is with mustard. Spread both sides of the thinly sliced leftover meat with prepared mustard and coat with fresh bread crumbs. Sprinkle the slices with melted butter and sauté in more butter until golden brown. Garnish with chopped egg and chopped parsley or not.

□

Lemon Butter balls are nice to serve with fish. These are made by adding a tablespoon of lemon juice and a tablespoon of chopped parsley to 2 tablespoons of butter. Blend well and roll into balls. They are pretty, and the flavor is much more effective than melting the butter and adding the lemon juice.

□

I am becoming fond of pastas made from artichoke flour. Fewer calories! Cook in boiling salted water until tender, drain, do not wash — and toss with dry cottage cheese and cracked pepper until well blended. Low-calorie and tasty. Toss in a few poppy seeds for added flavor.

MY SPECIAL COCKTAIL

FOR SIX

2 tablespoons rum
2 cups cranberry juice
Pineapple sherbet

Mix the rum and cranberry juice and chill thoroughly. Pour into juice or cocktail glasses and float a ball of pineapple sherbet in each glass. Find some kind of green leaf and place under each glass on a serving plate.

□

During the fresh fruit season, slices of chilled melon of any kind go particularly well with chicken dishes or turkey, and the combination of the cold, cold melon and hot fowl is delightful.

□

Then, of course, one should mention canned peaches or pears, filled with tart jelly or a strong cheese — baked or broiled and served hot with any meat — hot or cold. My favorite roast beef or steak garnish is stuffed prunes — stuffed with sharp cheese and then soaked in sherry or any other dry white wine, or stuffed with cream cheese and chutney; I have a hard time deciding.

□

Broiled orange slices and grapefruit sections are good with any of the lighter-flavored fish. It does a certain something to the fish, besides making a pretty dish of it.

□

Salads are a garnish in themselves — pretty, eatable, subtle. If they aren't, make them over.

□

Apple pie with cheese — a great American institution, but sometimes take the time to make Cheese Apples to put on top or at the side. Either cut them with a melon-ball cutter, or better still, mash the cheese and work into balls, apple shaped. Dust one side with paprika, or a little red coloring and granulated sugar, and make a stem of watercress or parsley, or, if you can find it, angelica. Good, too, on hors d'oeuvre trays.

□

Apple pie with Roquefort cheese sprinkled over the crust and returned to the oven to heat will make the lovers of American cheese think twice.

APRICOT DRESSING

Try this on fruit salads when you want to be different.

½ cup apricots (canned or frozen) put through a sieve
Juice of a fresh lime
2 tablespoons mayonnaise
1 cup heavy cream, whipped

Mix the apricots and lime juice and add to the mayonnaise. Fold into the whipped cream. Pile on fresh fruit salad and dust with pistachio nuts chopped fine.

MASHED TURNIPS

FOR EIGHT

You can always fall back on turnips.

Mix 4 pounds white or yellow turnips, cooked and mashed, with 1 tablespoon sugar, ¼ teaspoon mace, ¾ stick butter, ½ cup sour cream, salt, and pepper. Put in buttered casserole and bake at 350° until hot.

□

Don't forget, the secret of barbecuing is a solid bed of glowing coals. Whether charcoal, wood, or other fuel is used, light the fire at least 30 minutes ahead of time so that it will burn down to ash-gray coals before cooking starts.

Rub the outsides of pots and pans with soap before using over an open fire. They will be much easier to clean afterward.

□

Beef patties for outdoor cooking are better, I think, if you add ¼ cup of cracked ice to each pound of meat when you mix.

□

Large dill pickles with the center removed with an apple corer and stuffed with cream cheese mixed with chopped capers and parsley, with flecks of pimento, is good, too, for a cocktail snack.

□

For a sandwich filling, about 2 dozen dried figs, chopped and steamed, 1 pound of cream cheese, and ¼ cup of walnut meats, mixed and seasoned with salt, and made up with whole-wheat bread, will make you both healthy and wise.

□

For dessert, something easy and good is to fill a large tray with whole strawberries, toasted crackers, and a brick of cream cheese that has been rolled in granulated sugar, and let everyone help themselves. They can combine it any way they wish — cheese on strawberries, strawberries on cheese, cheese with crackers, or whatever you serve. I like matzo crackers with it.

□

A favorite dessert among those who like to use their taste buds to full advantage is Broiled Peaches with Rum Sauce. Peel and halve the peach, place flat side up in a pan covered with melted butter. Sprinkle generously with sugar and run under the broiler at low temperature until sugar is melted. Place in a glass serving dish and cover with Rum Sauce.

□

I don't mind cooking for 100, but I hate to wash one dish for myself.

□

Cover corned beef with chutney and bake. Then slice it for a buffet and serve it with a whipped cream–horseradish spread.

□

How do you skin green peppers? Roast the peppers in an oven until the skins are well blistered (no harm will be done if they blacken a little). Then remove them from the oven, put them at once in a pot, and cover. Let the peppers stand (off the heat) for about five minutes. The steam will have loosened the skins and they can be easily removed.

□

Potato salad will have more flavor if you add your dressing and seasoning while the potatoes are hot. The French do.

□

When you want to serve pancakes family-style and prepare them all at once, keep them warm until serving time by placing between cloth towels in a 200° oven.

□

A simple pretty glaze for fruitcake is made by bringing corn syrup to a full boil and then spreading or brushing over the surface of the cake. Then decorate with blanched toasted almonds, candied fruits and peels, and dried fruits.

□

If you store fruits in a plastic bag, wash the fruit first, and make a few small holes in the bag to provide ventilation and let out some of the moisture which accumulates.

□

Shredding cheese? A good rule of thumb: ½ pound of cheese yields about two cups of shredded cheese. If you want to keep a large piece of cheese for an extended time, dip the cut surface in melted paraffin.

□

Hot broiled fruit of any kind is good with ham. And as a cold garnish, canned or fresh apricots stuffed with cream cheese with a touch of horseradish added, and grapes (the long white kind; or black Ribier ones) split, deseeded, and stuffed with Roquefort or Camembert cheese make a very fine decoration with ham, hot or cold. They are especially nice added here and there to an hors d'oeuvre tray too!

□

The most inexperienced bride can do this, so there is no excuse to skip the dessert when she is called upon to entertain her husband's boss.

SABAYON

FOR EIGHT

1 cup powdered sugar
6 egg yolks
1 cup milk
1 cup dry sherry

Beat the sugar and egg yolks until smooth. Place over hot water; add milk and sherry and beat until 4 times its former size. Serve hot in tall glasses, and hot!

□

Light destroys riboflavin. It may also cause an off-flavor in milk products. So don't let milk and cream stand in the light. Put these products in the refrigerator as soon as possible.

STRAWBERRIES ROMANOFF

Whip 1 pint vanilla ice cream until creamy and fold in 1 cup cream, whipped, and 6 tablespoons of Cointreau. Fold in 1 quart of cleaned and slightly mashed fresh strawberries, sweetened with ½ cup confectioners' sugar and 3 tablespoons of Cointreau. Blend quickly and lightly and serve in chilled, stemmed glasses. The hostess should do this at the table. A guest always feels better when he sees his hostess do something special herself. I show off with this dessert frequently, as my friends will testify.

□

For a delightful luncheon, cream mushrooms in just enough sauce to hold them together, in a chafing dish. Sprinkle with Parmesan cheese, brown under the broiler (just take the saucepan — you don't have to take the whole works to the range), then spoon it over asparagus tips. Serve with crisp bacon curls and grilled tomatoes. You make bacon curls by rolling them up, fastening with a toothpick, and either drying them out in an oven or frying them in deep fat. Take the toothpick out before you serve them. Add a molded fruit salad and coffee. You need no dessert.

BANANA CHUNKS WRAPPED IN BACON

Bananas are passed by too frequently. Cut them into 2-inch chunks and wrap in bacon that has been blanched in boiling water for 10 minutes and thoroughly dried. Sprinkle with brown sugar and bake on a rack at 350° until bacon is crisp and sugar slightly carmelized. Good with beef entrées, too!

□

Lemon Jell-O dissolved in 2 cups hot apricot nectar with 1 teaspoon grated lemon rind added for zip makes a perfect base for jelled fruit salads.

□

Canned applesauce, thinned down with maraschino cherry juice and spooned over lemon or orange sherbet, is a pretty and delicious dessert, and lower in calories than many others!

□

Consommé Madrilène à la Russe gives a different twist to the same old thing. Buy the consommé, then three-quarters fill your soup cup, and top with whipped cream or cottage cheese and a dash of caviar.

□

Diced pears, walnuts, and celery tossed with mayonnaise are a nice change from the traditional Waldorf salad. Decorate with slices of avocado for a holiday salad.

□

The term "fry poaching" is rather new. Try it. Melt a little fat in a frying pan over low heat, just enough to grease the bottom of the pan. Add eggs one at a time, pour in two or three tablespoons of water, cover pan tightly, and steam until eggs are done.

□

HOMINY HASHED IN CREAM

FOR SIX

4 cups canned whole hominy
3 tablespoons butter
1 teaspoon salt
1 cup half-and-half

Sauté hominy in butter until brown. Add salt and cream; simmer until thickened.

□

Did you ever melt one square of chocolate and think you would never get it out of the pot so you could use it? Butter the pot a little first and it will pour out quickly. Do the same to the cup when measuring molasses or Karo syrup.

□

Thread on a skewer chunks of pineapple, zucchini, tomatoes, canned mushrooms, green pepper, and onions. Brush with butter, salt, and pepper and sprinkle with brown sugar and broil or bake. A way to tempt children and men who are in a rut as to their vegetable consumption.

□

Have you thought to check the temperature in your freezer lately? The temperature should be 0°.

□

Freezing does not kill the bacteria in food; it simply stops their multiplication. Bacteria continue to multiply after the food is thawed.

□

Cured meats should not be frozen, because seasonings added during curing accelerate the development of rancidity.

□

What is freezer burn? It is the drying out of the surface tissues of food, resulting in a white appearance. Freezer burn is not harmful, but does make the dehydrated area tough and tasteless when cooked.

□

If you're planning to make homemade ice cream, you can substitute chilled evaporated milk (not diluted) in place of light cream. You might call it a weight watcher's ice cream because it is only about 140 calories per serving.

□

Section grapefruit, cover with puréed and strained fresh raspberries, and refrigerate overnight. Both the color and flavor will make them the center of attraction.

□

Try drained canned pears, mixed with marrons and marron syrup and served icy cold. For 1 can of each, heat ¼ cup of brandy, light, and pour over the fruit. While it is still burning serve over coffee ice cream.

HOT CHEESE BALLS

TWENTY-FOUR SMALL BALLS

½ pound grated sharp cheese
4 teaspoons flour
⅛ teaspoon cayenne pepper
1 teaspoon salt
2 egg whites, stiffly beaten

Mix cheese, flour, cayenne, salt, and the stiffly beaten egg whites. Roll in:

1 cup fine dry white bread crumbs

Fry in deep fat at 375° until golden brown. Serve hot on toothpicks.

ORANGE PECANS

1¼ cups sugar
Grated rind and juice of 1 orange
⅛ teaspoon cream of tartar
Pecans

Cook sugar, orange juice and rind, and cream of tartar to soft-ball stage; remove from heat and beat until creamy. Dip pecans into the mixture, forming into small clusters, or coating singly if they are large. Keep mixture in pan of warm water while dipping.

CAKE OF MANY FLAVORS

Use your favorite white cake recipe or mix and prepare six or seven thin layers. Make a Butter Cream Icing and flavor lightly with Jamaica rum. On the first layer sprinkle crème de cacao, then ice with the Butter Cream. Repeat layers with a different liqueur sprinkled on each. Cover the entire cake with the Butter Cream Icing. It depends on how many liqueurs you have and how heavy your hand is for the flavors of the cake, but it is one you will enjoy — but not for children. A nice cake for celebrations.

□

Fresh peaches served with Soft Custard Sauce flavored with lemon extract are a delectable dessert.

□

If you find yourself without time or inclination to make a dessert, compromise with "Grasshopper." My way? One jigger crème de menthe, 1 jigger brandy, 1 scoop vanilla ice cream. Put in an electric blender.

LEMON MARMALADE

---

4 lemons, sliced very thin
5 cups water
4 cups sugar

Cover lemon slices with water. Bring to a boil. Simmer, covered, for 2 hours. Measure, add enough water to make 4 cups of the fruit mixture. Add the sugar. Cook at high heat until the syrup sheets from a testing spoon. Pour into hot clean glasses. Seal.

SHERRY FRAPPÉ

FOR SIX

---

1 bottle dry sherry
2 tablespoons lemon juice
2 cups apple juice

Mix and put in your freezer compartment. When ready to serve, put in blender and beat to frappé consistency. Pour into stemmed glasses. Decorate with a sprig of mint and serve with a short soda straw.

□

Whether you buy or bake cookies, store them properly by keeping them at room temperature: crisp ones in a container with a loose cover, soft ones with a tight-fitting cover. A wedge of fresh apple will keep them moist. If crisp ones become limp, place on an ungreased baking sheet and put in a 300° oven for 5 minutes.

Cookies are a sign of hospitality and are as old as 1563. The American "cookie" comes to us from the Dutch who settled New Amsterdam (New York). The Dutch called a cookie a "koekje," a diminutive of "koek," meaning cake. As in many cases when adopting new food, the English took the sound and gave it their own spelling. The British today call our cookie and/or cracker a "biscuit" and sometimes a "tea cake."

When cutting cookies dip the cutters in flour before pressing into the dough. When rerolling the trimmings, lay them together. Wadding them together before rolling out toughens them.

If you wish to mail homemade cookies to your children, pack them in popcorn to prevent breakage. They can eat the popcorn too.

□

Use cocoa in place of flour to dust pans for chocolate cake.

□

Fresh coconut sometimes stumps the amateur. It is easy. With a sharp-pointed instrument tap the three soft spots at the top of the coconut. Pierce one soft spot and pour off the milk. Save it too — make a curry sauce with it, you'll love it! Move the nut in one hand, tapping the entire surface gently with a hammer. Keep on tapping until the shell cracks and falls off. Don't be too ambitious in tapping; if you hit too hard, the nut meat will stick to the shell when it breaks. Then slice the skin off and there you are! This is what the coconut growers say; and it really works.

FRESH COCONUT COINTREAU

I serve this in a brandy snifter. For each serving use:

1 tablespoon Nesselrode sauce
1 ball vanilla ice cream
2 tablespoons freshly grated coconut
1½ tablespoons Cointreau

Put Nesselrode in bottom of glass, ice cream ball next, grated coconut over all, then the Cointreau. It is a pretty holiday dessert. Put a sprig of holly or green on the plate with it.

□

For a quick and lazy dessert, try lemon ice or sherbet with puréed canned apricots spilled over (put apricots in electric blender), and sugar and lemon juice added to your liking.

□

There is a more subtle flavor in fresh pineapple if covered with a mixture of ice and brown sugar.

□

Would you like to decorate with chocolate leaves? Melt semisweet chocolate, pour over leaves from your garden. Mark veins with a knife. Let chocolate harden, then peel away the leaves.

CHUTNEY SAUCE

TWELVE PINTS

A really good chutney made with green pears comes from Meg Healy of radio fame via Cris Millard of General Foods. I like it as well as the famous Major Grey's — and it's less expensive.

¼ tablespoon Worcestershire sauce
1½ ground green peppers
1 tablespoon cloves
1½ tablespoons ground cinnamon
Dash of red pepper
4½ pounds sliced green pears
4 lemons, peeled and sliced (cut peels in strips)
¾ pound dark raisins
3 pounds dark brown sugar
8 buds garlic
3 large onions, sliced
⅔ cup crystalized ginger, cut fine
7 cups canned pineapple chunks, drained
1 quart plus 1 cup vinegar
3 tablespoons mustard seed
½ cup soy sauce
Tamarind root: boil and use 3 tablespoons of juice (you may omit entirely)

Mix all ingredients and cook slowly until fruit is done, 45 minutes to 1 hour after boiling. This does not spoil and does not need to be sealed. Good with lamb, chicken, roast beef, etc.

EAST INDIAN CHUTNEY

FIVE AND A HALF PINTS

There are as many recipes for chutney as time and people who make it. This one from Mae Walker of Warner Springs, California, has a different taste I like.

3 pounds peeled and cored apples (weigh after peeling)
3 pounds sugar
4 ounces green ginger root, scraped and sliced in long thin slivers
½ ounce red chili, pounded or almost pulverized
4 ounces garlic, peeled and sliced the short way of the small clove
1 tablespoon salt
1 pound apricots, dried and cut in strips, large enough to both see and really taste in the chutney
½ pound raisins, seeded and cut, not put through blender
1 pint apple cider vinegar

Cook apples into an applesauce. Add sugar, ginger, chili, garlic, and salt. Cook down to a jam. Stir from bottom of pot, as this mixture will burn easily. Add apricots and raisins; continue cooking about 20 minutes. Add the vinegar, bring to a rolling boil, and continue cooking until chutney is again jamlike. Pour into jars and seal.

□

When scrambling eggs let your sophisticated imagination run riot. Toss in things like diced avocado, orange sections, and grated orange peel. Toss in lobster, shrimp, or crabmeat with a whiff of garlic. Toss in matzo crackers. Toss in anything.

□

A different twist! Fold horseradish sauce and cranberry sauce into whipped cream to serve with cold turkey.

HOT SLAW WITH APPLE

I like this recipe of Margaret Hull's.

3 cups shredded cabbage
3 tablespoons vinegar
2 tablespoons water
1 tablespoon sugar
2 tablespoons butter
1 teaspoon caraway seeds
1 teaspoon salt

Mix over quick heat until it reaches a boil; reduce heat to low, add 1 large peeled and grated apple, heat 1 minute longer, and serve hot.

□

A famous chef revealed that the secret of his delicious chicken was the soaking of the chicken in buttermilk for several hours before cooking.

□

Season sour cream with a bit of curry powder, or salt and ginger, before adding as a garnish to cream soups.

□

To keep noodles and macaroni from boiling over, put a tablespoon of butter or cooking oil in the water and the pasta will stay in the pot.

□

To me, half an avocado filled with a tart French Dressing and a few anchovy filets is a glamorous dish at any time.

□

On the hottest day you ever felt, a cool and easier-than-ever first course: fill halves of avocado with canned jellied consommé; sprinkle with fresh lime juice and cracked pepper. Garnish with fresh lime.

□

Queen olives in chipped ice with a sprinkling of fresh lime juice are well worth trying for your next cocktail party.

□

Run a hot knife over domestic Camembert cheese or place in oven for a minute until it runs. Guests will think it imported — soft inside and crust on outside. (If you like it, eat all; if not, eat inside only.) Must be kept in good refrigeration.

□

When making rolled sandwiches, it is a good idea to steam the slices of bread in a colander over boiling water for a minute or two. The slightly damp bread will roll easily without cracking.

□

Do you know how to test a pineapple for ripeness? The best way is the "thump" test; the fruit should sound solid when snapped with the forefinger and the thumb. Thump the inner side of your wrist, then the pineapple — if the sounds are similar, then the fruit should be a good one. If your greengrocer says you are crazy, tell him this information comes straight from the pineapple's mouth — in other words, Hawaii.

To prepare a fresh pineapple, cut a thick slice from the top and bottom, and stand the pineapple on a cutting board. Cut the peel off from the top downward, using a strong sharp knife. Cut a thin layer first, and then a deeper one, until you have determined the thickness of the peel, which differs with the variety of the pineapple. Next cut the eyes out around the pineapple. Slice in rounds or wedges, and remove the core.

AMBROSIA

While I am on the subject of pineapple, Ambrosia is always a popular dessert. This is my favorite recipe.

1 ripe pineapple
6 oranges
2 cups freshly grated coconut

Peel and prepare the pineapple, and slice in thin slices. Peel the oranges and cut into sections. Place in layers in a bowl, with ½ cup of powdered sugar; cover with the fresh coconut and chill. You may or may not pour over ⅓ cup of dry sherry or ¼ cup of apricot brandy — or mix the two. Any way it is a wonderful sweet ending to any kind of meal.

□

For highest quality, keep frozen foods frozen until they are defrosted for use. The process of thawing and refreezing does not in itself make fruits and vegetables unsafe, but thawed foods spoil more rapidly than fresh foods and may quickly become unsafe to eat if not refrigerated.

Refrozen vegetables may toughen and refrozen fruits become soft and mushy. It is never a good idea to refreeze meats, fish, or fowl.

□

Ice water or a little milk will keep peaches from turning dark.

FRESH CORN FRITTERS

FOR SIX

1 pint grated fresh corn
½ cup milk from the corn (add milk if necessary to make the ½ cup)
2 eggs, separated
½ cup flour
1 teaspoon salt
1 teaspoon baking powder
1 tablespoon melted butter

The corn is grated off the uncooked cob and mixed with the milk and egg yolks. The flour, salt, and baking powder are mixed together and added, and then the melted butter. The egg whites are beaten stiff and folded in last. Drop them on a greased hot griddle or frying pan and cook like pancakes. Serve with melted butter, syrup, and scads and scads of crisp bacon.

□

Pineapple sherbet served with a tablespoon of good brandy over is an excellent dessert after a flavorful meal. The taste of everything disappears like magic and you feel satisfied but refreshed.

□

To test bread dough to see if it has doubled in bulk, press the tips of two fingers lightly and quickly about ½ inch into the top of the dough. If the dent stays, the dough is light enough to have doubled in bulk.

□

Be sure you do not use cake flour for bread making. Use all-purpose flour because it has the protein to form an elastic framework strong enough for bread making. How is cake flour different from all-purpose flour? Cake flour, milled from soft wheat, is lower in protein than all-purpose flour and usually is not enriched. Cake flour is very fine, uniform, and makes tender, delicate cakes.

□

If you like a brown pie crust, sprinkle a little granulated sugar on the top or brush lightly with an egg beaten with a little water.

□

Eggs are considered a liquid ingredient in recipes, so their size will affect the "wetness" of a mixture. Extra large eggs may necessitate adding a little more flour; very small eggs make it necessary to add less flour than the recipe calls for. A large egg is a safer size.

□

If the meringue topping on your pie shrinks from the crust, it is because you did not seal it properly before putting the pie in the oven. Be sure the meringue touches the edge of the crust.

□

Place baking pans in the center of the oven to permit free circulation of air and heat on all sides. When putting two or more pans in the oven at the same time, stagger them on different shelves, so that one is not directly above the other. There should be at least one inch between two pans on the same shelf; otherwise the trapped heat will cause a "hot spot."

□

Do you bake with your oven light on? If so, the light throws extra heat into that corner of the oven, possibly causing uneven baking.

□

Biscuits will take on a light brown finish if the tops are brushed with milk or butter before baking. If you want biscuits to be crusty, place cut dough one inch apart on baking sheet; if soft, place next to each other.

□

If you cut off the crust before freezing bread, you will find the loaf will not crumble when you slice.

□

Lumpy — that's the batter for perfect muffins. Overbeaten batter will cause peaks, tunnels, and toughness in the muffins because the gluten in the flour is overdeveloped.

PEAR CONSERVE

Pear Conserve is another different sweet that is excellent with roasts of all kinds, and good mixed with cream cheese for a party sandwich.

8 pounds medium-ripe pears, peeled, cored, and sliced
8 pounds sugar
½ pound preserved ginger
4 whole lemons, put through the food chopper or cut fine

Place all ingredients in a kettle and let stand overnight. In the morning bring to a boil; then set in 350° oven and cook for 10 minutes. Reduce heat to 300° and cook until thick and amber colored. Pour into hot sterile jars. Cool and seal. This will make 10 pints or as many small jars as you wish to divide it into. A jar of the conserve, tied up in cellophane with a Christmas green, would be an acceptable Christmas gift for anyone.

□

To convert between self-rising and all-purpose flour or cornmeal, remember that every cup of the self-rising product contains exactly 1½ teaspoons baking powder and ½ teaspoon salt, which must be added or deleted from the recipe, depending on which way you are converting.

□

Here's a biscuit recipe that calls for only two ingredients: 2 cups enriched self-rising flour and 1 cup dairy sour cream! Blend the two together, knead slightly, roll, cut, and bake at 450° for 15 minutes. It's a light, tasty biscuit.

□

Dark or dull pans absorb heat, with the result that foods actually bake faster and crusts are browner than in shiny pans that reflect the heat.

□

Leftover yeast rolls? They will obtain a fresh-baked taste by being sprinkled lightly with water, covered, and rewarmed in a 400° oven. Store-bought rolls likewise.

STRAWBERRY AND PINEAPPLE CONSERVE

A conserve that is also special.

2 cups fresh pineapple, cut in small pieces
6 cups sugar
2 quarts strawberries

Combine pineapple and sugar and simmer at low heat for 10 minutes. Add strawberries, washed and hulled, and cook slowly until thick and clear. Pour into glasses or jars and cover when cool with melted paraffin. It will keep on your pantry shelf.

CRANBERRY ORANGE RELISH

This is a must sometime during the holiday season.

1 quart cranberries
2 large seedless oranges
1½ cups sugar

Wash fruit, peel oranges, and chop rind in very small pieces. Chop orange pulp and cranberries very fine, or put all through the meat grinder, using the medium knife. Mix fruits with the sugar. This will keep in the refrigerator for more than a week without sealing, or pour into hot sterilized jars and seal to keep longer.

□

Individual cheese breads are good with a salad meal. Diagonally slash hard rolls at one-inch intervals. Do not cut all the way through. Place small squares or strips of mozzarella or Swiss cheese in each gash. Warm rolls in preheated 375° oven, 3 to 5 minutes or until cheese melts. Serve hot.

□

Words to the wise cook! Unless it is specifically called for, don't use whipped butter in a recipe, since the shortening power is not the same as for unwhipped butter.

□

What are "pine nuts"? There are many varieties of pine seeds under the name of "pignolas." The most common are "piñon" (Spanish for pine). Add them to rice, noodles, green salads, for a change of flavor.

RHUBARB AND ORANGE MARMALADE

Rhubarb isn't used enough for anything, but definitely not enough for preserves. This Rhubarb and Orange Marmalade will turn you into a fan.

6 oranges, quartered, seeded, and sliced paper-thin

To every cup you obtain add:

2 cups water

and let stand 48 hours; then bring to a boil and add:

4 pounds fresh or frozen rhubarb, cut in ½-inch pieces

Boil 30 minutes; add:

2½ pounds sugar

and simmer slowly until the mixture jells. Pour into hot sterilized jars. Cool and seal with paraffin wax. This will make 12 6-ounce jars.

To test for jelly, dip out a large spoonful and pour slowly back into the kettle. When the last of the mixture separates into two lines of drops which "sheet" together off the edge of the spoon, the jelly has cooked enough.

A WORD ABOUT HERBS

Much has been written about herbs for centuries. Women in Biblical times took them for granted. Through history men have fought wars over them. The modern cook, with an imaginative use of herbs, transforms an ordinary dish into an inspired creation. It has been said herbs are the wit of cooking, but even wit should be tempered. So herbs and spices should be used not with a heavy hand, but with a light and disciplined one, thus producing a subtle delight for the taste buds. Buy as small a package as possible. Keep tightly covered; store away from heat.

Rub a leg of lamb with garlic, then sprinkle with chopped rosemary before roasting.

Try a bit of thyme in making oyster stew.

Add a pinch of dried or fresh rosemary to fish when boiling or broiling.

Stir a little thyme into hamburgers before cooking.

Rub a roast of pork with fresh sage leaves or sprinkle with commercial poultry seasoning.

Add a sprig of fresh mint to water when cooking green peas.

Sauté fresh-chopped basil in butter and add to any green vegetable, especially green beans or peas, and the lowly carrot!

Add chopped basil or chives to stewed or stuffed tomatoes.

Add finely chopped chives to eggs, scrambled, fried, or shirred. A chive omelet is a joy forever.

Chopped parsley added to any fowl, veal, or egg dish gives it both added flavor and color, and who ever heard of a boiled potato without chopped parsley? Only the unimaginative — and chopped watercress is even better.

Chopped chives give the same effect to the center of a baked potato as they do to vichyssoise, only more so.

Rose geraniums make your garden smell heavenly; and a couple in the bottom of your cake pan makes a sponge cake — well, you try it. If you are new-fashioned enough to make jelly, one in the bottom of each jelly glass will make your grandmother feel young again, because her mother used to do it.

Horseradish grated and added to sour cream and poured over hot spinach is wonderful.

I like sage added to hot biscuits to eat with roast pork or fricasseed chicken. About ¼ teaspoon to 2 cups of flour; and likewise, rosemary, and chives — or anything else that grows and is edible.

Certain touches to food give a light, illusive coolness we strive for at times. Touches of parsley, even if not eaten, put you in a better frame of mind. Parsley's history may have something to do with it. During the Reformation in England, parsley was used extensively as an edible herb. Legend spells out that the parsley seed was supposed to go to the Devil seven times before the seed would sprout. The Irish, God bless them, did not believe in its fiendish character and renamed it Our Lady's Little Vine. In ancient times it was woven into the crown of a hero returning from war.

Parsley may be kept fresh a long time if washed and stored in the refrigerator in a tightly covered jar.

Chicory, or curly endive, has a piquant flavor. Pagan custom required every bride to plant chicory in her garden as a symbol of her life-long faithfulness.

A sprig of mint has a pleasant lemony scent, and when added to a drink, salad, or fruit, peps it up as if by magic.

CRISP POTATO RINGS

Slice unpeeled thoroughly scrubbed Idaho potatoes in thin slices. Place in one layer on cookie sheet and sprinkle with salt, pepper, and butter. Bake at 375° until crisp.

□

Peel and section large California seedless oranges. Place in shallow serving dish and sprinkle with brown sugar. Cover with sour cream and shake cinnamon and grated orange peel on top. Garnish with fresh mint if you have it growing in your yard.

GRAPEFRUIT IN HOT CLARET

---

4 seedless Texas grapefruit
1 cup sugar
¼ cup water
1 cup claret
½ teaspoon lemon juice

Peel and section grapefruit. Place in a china or ceramic bowl. Chill. Boil sugar and water. Cool. Add claret and lemon juice. Pour over grapefruit.

□

You can serve any vegetable with salmon, but because my mother served peas with salmon I usually do, combined with cooked fresh white onions or scallions, or canned Belgian carrots, heavily parslied. A cabbage and celery coleslaw lightly dressed is a crunchy salad.

□

Slice Brussels sprouts — they cook better and are pretty to look at, as you have three colors in place of one — then toss with halves of white grapes and sweet butter.

PRALINES

THREE DOZEN SMALL

I am amazed at the requests I receive for praline recipes. I like this one.

2 cups sugar
1 teaspoon soda
1 cup buttermilk
¾ cup butter or margarine
2 cups pecan halves
1 teaspoon vanilla extract

Cook sugar, soda, buttermilk, and butter to soft-ball stage, 240° on candy thermometer. Stir from bottom frequently. Remove from stove; beat for 5 minutes. Add pecans and vanilla. Beat until the mixture drops easily onto wax paper. When cool, wrap individually in clear plastic. These keep indefinitely.

□

The southern hospitality gesture at eating time: "Take two and butter them while they're hot!"

□

To roast almonds, place them in a single layer on a flat pan and roast at 300° about 20 to 25 minutes. Stir occasionally so they brown evenly.

□

I like crème de menthe in the summertime. Dress up your desserts with it, especially fruit or ice cream. For company, pile ice cream on top of any fresh fruit, and pour lighted crème de menthe over.

□

Sour cream combined with mayonnaise, half and half, with a dash of lemon juice and cayenne pepper and salt, makes a delightful sauce for asparagus or broccoli, and for mild-flavored fish.

□

Candied bacon is a wonderful breakfast treat. Blanch bacon in hot water for five minutes, dry, place on broiler pan, sprinkle with brown sugar, and broil.

□

An American Brie cheese that is mighty good is produced in Lena, Illinois — Kalb brand. It is worth your investigation. It would make a nice ending for a meal, with toasted unsalted crackers.

□

When using noodles or any pasta as part of a casserole, reduce the cooking time by one-third. The noodles finish cooking in the oven. Casseroles containing cheese should be baked at low to moderate temperatures.

□

Roquefort Hamburger Buns are sure to make a hit. Make, or buy, regular hamburger buns; split, toast, and butter. Place on each bun a large thin slice of onion; spread with butter and a thin slice of Roquefort cheese; run under the broiler until the cheese is brown and then place the cooked hamburger patty on one of the cheese-toasted halves. Cover with other half and serve while hot. Smaller versions of these are wonderful for outdoor cocktail parties, but you will need tons!

□

Glazed corned beef is good. Cover cooked corned beef with ⅓ cup of brown sugar and stick with whole cloves. Bake at 350° until glazed. Remove the cloves and serve. Really good for a snack with dark rye bread and dill pickles.

□

If you are using canned vegetables such as green beans or peas, drain them and reduce by one-half the liquid they are canned in by cooking it on top of the stove. Then put the vegetables back in pot and heat. Add your seasonings and butter. They will taste better.

□

The magic of vegetables lies in their dressing. Read with your taste buds for a change.

□

Cooked new potatoes can be tossed in a skillet with butter, lemon juice, and grated lemon peel. Add to this chopped olives or parsley or onion flakes, or a little sour cream.

□

Add chopped leftover bits of ham and Roquefort cheese to mashed potatoes and casserole them. Bake at 350° until hot. Add to stuffed potato mixture too!

□

Croutons you make yourself, browned in butter with a pinch of curry powder or oregano, tossed into just undercooked green beans, or over asparagus or broccoli.

□

Top a casserole of mashed potatoes with thick sour cream, and brown in the oven.

□

I find marinated vegetables can fill a need for salad or vegetable without much preparation. Refrigerate overnight cans of whatever vegetables you wish to use. The day you use them, open, drain, and marinate with a good basic French dressing an hour or more. Then drain and arrange on a bed of salad greens in a bouquet fashion. Sprinkle with chopped hard-cooked egg and parsley.

□

I like to use out-of-the-ordinary canned vegetables at times; one that you find in gourmet shops today is cardoons. They look like celery, taste a bit like asparagus, but will keep guests guessing. This recipe is so easy. You merely drain the cardoons, place flat in a buttered shallow casserole or crêpe pan, sprinkle with cream, melted butter, salt, pepper, and freshly grated Parmesan cheese. Run under the broiler until they are sizzling.

□

Prunes, pitted and stuffed with sharp cheese, wrapped in a small piece of bacon, and broiled until the bacon is crisp, are a good snack for morning coffee parties.

□

Stuff cooked large prunes with cashew nuts, American cheese squares, or pineapple cubes. Cover with sweet Madeira, chill overnight; serve with creamy cream cheese (cream cheese whipped with cream to a whipped cream consistency).

□

Prunes in wine — magnificent! Cover a pound of prunes with cold water, and soak them overnight. Sprinkle ½ cup brown sugar into the mixture and stew until soft. Remove from heat, add 1 cup of red wine, and simmer again for 10 minutes. Cool, add ¼ teaspoon vanilla.

□

Plump cooked prunes served ice cold with a tablespoon of crème de menthe over each serving taste amazingly good.

□

Use the refrigerator method of preparing prunes during hot weather. Pour enough boiling water or fruit juice over prunes to cover them. Then cover the container and place it in the refrigerator for 24 hours.

□

Lemon juice added to the water when cooking rice makes it white, and added to the butter in which you sauté mushrooms gives them the high gloss you find in really good restaurants.

□

Fresh tomatoes peeled and chopped fine, seasoned with salt and pepper and frozen to a mush in your ice tray, served in ice-cold cups or glasses with a spoonful of curried mayonnaise, are a delectable summer first course. Festive, too, if served with crisp cheese straws and ice-cold black olives.

□

Surprises with prunes:

When making muffins, fill pans about one-third with batter, drop in a pitted, uncooked prune for each muffin, and add batter to the usual two-thirds level. Sprinkle tops with cinnamon sugar before baking. Fragrant and delicious.

Thread skewers with plump prunes and your choice of the following: cherry tomatoes or tomato wedges, pieces of green pepper, mushrooms, canned whole onions, cooked Brussels sprouts, or marinated artichoke hearts. Brush with melted butter or margarine, broil gently, and serve with any main dish.

□

Vichyssoise combined with minced clams and heavy cream makes a delicious cold soup that needs only a salad and fruit dessert for an exciting lunch.

□

Cream mixed with warm honey is good on waffles and griddle cakes. The honey is warmed by placing the container in hot water.

□

Young whole chickens can be roasted at 400° instead of 325°, the latter being the temperature generally recommended for whole poultry.

□

You can pile poultry dressing between two sections of spareribs, skewer them together, and bake for a company dish.

□

If you wish to keep brownies and similar cookies a long time, cut and wrap individually in foil or clear plastic before storing.

□

Add ⅓ cup of toasted sesame seeds to ingredients for a single piecrust when making a quiche or a meat pie.

□

Celery cabbage is becoming one of my favorite vegetables. Cut in large dices, put in a skillet with very little salad oil or butter, and stir-fry one minute. Cover and cook one minute more. Sprinkle with salt and pepper (or a few drops of soy sauce), and you have a low-calorie, bright green, divine-tasting vegetable.

SALSIFY PERSILLADE AND SNIPPED GREEN BEANS

It is difficult to find fresh salsify in most markets, so use the canned. I drain and wash the salsify and sauté quickly in very little butter. Add enough heavy cream to "stick them." Season with salt and pepper and sprinkle with parsley. I like to make a ring of salsify on my serving tray and fill the center with very finely snipped cut-on-the-bias green beans, cooked about five minutes, and dressed with sweet butter, salt, and pepper. These two vegetables complement each other.

□

To avoid "pulling" an angel food cake down when you cut it, slice with a pronged divider or two forks back to back.

□

Start with a chilled bowl and beaters if you're planning on whipping cream. Cream is easiest to whip when its temperature is 35° to 40°.

□

When heating sour cream, remember that it reacts as milk does to high temperature, and it may curdle. So use medium heat.

□

Add a little warm liquid to slightly beaten egg before combining the egg with a hot liquid or mixture.

□

One of the quick luncheons I like to prepare is to split, butter, and toast either English muffins or hamburger buns. Make a seafood or chicken salad and pile on top. Cover with grated Muenster or Gruyère cheese and run under the broiler to brown.

□

New potatoes cooked in their jackets, sprinkled with Parmesan cheese, and served with any green vegetable go well with short ribs, and boiled fresh white onions simmered in butter with a few raisins give an interesting flavor to the meal — also conversation.

□

Baking custard? Try substituting two leftover egg yolks for one whole egg. It works.

□

To bake a frozen unbaked pie, bake in a 425° oven, adding 15 minutes to regular baking time. If the pie is already baked, thaw at room temperature for ½ hour. Then bake at 375° for 30 minutes.

□

A quick raclette: Place Monterey Jack cheese on an oven-proof plate, bake in a 450° oven until it begins to melt. Serve as a cocktail tidbit with small (hot) boiled potatoes and green onions.

□

If you like the flavor of almonds, grind them in your blender, season with salt, and roll boned and skinned chicken breasts in them. Sauté in butter and serve with the nut-flavored butter they have cooked in.

□

A bit of horseradish sauce added to any salad dressing will give it the push it sometimes needs.

□

In Italy basil is called "Kiss-me-Nicholas" and any girl approaching a favorite young man with her basil sprig is hoping to be kissed.

Ripe olives lend extra-special appeal to any relish or canapé tray. To provide a rich gloss, drain olives well and pat dry with paper towels, then roll in a bowl with a few drops of salad oil. Serve some of the olives with coatings of parsley, toasted sesame seeds, or instant minced onion.

□

The Arabs knew about the lemon a long time before the medical researchers discovered vitamin C. Its culture was preserved in the twelfth and thirteenth centuries in Spain. The Spanish in turn brought lemons to America. In these days of salt-free diets, a squeeze of lemon juice gives the magic that salt normally provides. At any rate, use lemons, vitamin C and all. Flavor water for ice cubes with lemon juice. Combine with a little olive oil for vegetables and fish. Let celery stand in cold water and lemon juice for an hour. The celery will be more crisp, white, and tender. Add lemon juice to water for piecrust. Use it in place of vinegar for dressings.

□

Add a can of beer to meats you boil or braise or roast. It will act both as a tenderizer and a flavor bud.

CHEESE MIX

½ pound aged Cheddar cheese
½ cup finely diced celery
¼ cup chili sauce
¼ cup finely diced onion
½ cup dried beef, chopped fine
Cream

Mix first five ingredients thoroughly and add enough cream to make it spread easily. Good for storing for future use. Really good spread on hamburger buns and grilled for a "quickie" lunch.

CHEESE PASTRIES

1 cup shredded sharp cheese, packed
1 cup shortening
2 cups sifted flour
⅛ teaspoon cayenne pepper
1 teaspoon salt

Work the cheese and shortening into the flour and seasonings until a soft ball is formed. Chill several hours, then roll out and cut in the shape you like, or form in a log and slice. Bake on a lightly floured cookie sheet at 400° for 8 to 10 minutes. The seasoning may be up to you — the cheese is, too. I use cream cheese to serve with fruit salads, Roquefort for cocktails. Sometimes I mix all the cheese I have in the refrigerator together. Garlic salt is good. I use these pastries as a base for Creamed Chicken, Lobster Newburg, and such, or serve them on cocktail trays.

FROZEN LOG

½ pound sharp Cheddar cheese
8 slices uncooked bacon
2 small onions
½ teaspoon Worcestershire sauce
1 teaspoon dry mustard
2 teaspoons mayonnaise

Put first three ingredients through a food chopper. Combine with last three ingredients, mix, and roll into a log the diameter of a 50-cent piece. Freeze. When you get ready to serve, slice, put on top of bread rounds, crackers, or split English muffins, and put under the broiler until brown. Serve with a salad for lunch on a busy day.

PÂTÉ BEAU MONDE

2 3-ounce packages cream cheese
4 tablespoons cream
2½ teaspoons Beau Monde seasoning
¼ teaspoon dried thyme
¼ teaspoon dried marjoram
¼ teaspoon dried summer savory
2 tablespoons parsley, finely chopped

Mix several hours before using, and serve with crackers or thin toast squares.

□

When buying a whole fish in the market, be sure the fish looks you in the eye with a healthy stare. You cannot tell about one that has been skinned or boned, so smell it and cook as soon as possible after you buy or catch, or freeze it. Don't overcook. For once in your life follow the rules.

□

To keep egg yolks in the refrigerator from forming a hard crust, slide them into a bowl and cover with cold water.

Cocktail wafers on tap: 1 cup flour, 2 cups grated Cheddar cheese, ¾ cup chopped pecans, ¼ teaspoon minced garlic, ½ cup margarine. Mix, form into a log, chill. Slice when ready to serve and bake at 350°, 10 to 12 minutes.

□

Chopped thin mints on peppermint ice cream, cinnamon candy stick crumbs on coffee ice cream with crème de cacao, apricot purée mixed with Cointreau on orange ice or vanilla ice cream or both, crushed Almond Roca candy on strawberry ice cream, fresh or frozen blueberries mixed with crème de cassis on lemon ice — all good.

□

Deviled eggs à la king have always been a favorite Friday lunch. Serve the eggs, deviled your own way, chilled, and then placed on hot asparagus tips or chopped spinach, and the hot à la king sauce poured over.

□

An apple tart I like: Line a tart pan with removable bottom with pie crust. Slice apples (Greenings are best) and overlap in circles to fill bottom. Bake at 400° for 10 minutes. Mix ½ cup flour, ½ cup sugar, ½ cup cream, pour over, and bake at 350° until apples are tender.

□

If you cannot find a convenient spot on your buffet table for your forks, stand them up in a vase or goblet. I use an old spoon holder.

□

A celebration dessert to use for birthdays, anniversaries, holidays: Any cake, any pie, strawberry shortcake, anything that will hold extra-long skinny tapers. You merely push them into the dessert and light. It is a blaze of glory, and that is what a celebration should be.

MADEIRA JELLY

FOR SIX

Put 2¼ cups of cold water in saucepan with peel of ½ lemon, 3 whole cloves, peel of ½ tangerine, small stick of cinnamon, and ½ cup sugar. Let simmer over low heat for 8 minutes. Soak 1 tablespoon gelatin in 2 tablespoons cold water and juice of 1 small lemon for 5 minutes. Pour on hot mixture and stir until gelatin is dissolved. Add 1 cup of full-bodied sweet Madeira and let stand until cool. Strain into a covered jar and let stand in refrigerator overnight. Serve with sweetened whipped cream.

□

Making tea correctly is the secret to its popularity, so give it a try. Use a good grade of tea; there is no economy in using poor tea, because the best you can buy costs only a fraction of a cent more per cup. Use an earthenware or china pot that has been rinsed out with boiling water. Use a teaspoon of tea or one tea bag for each cup to be brewed. Always use furiously and freshly boiled water and allow the tea to remain in the pot five minutes before pouring. If you like it weaker in strength, add hot water after the tea is brewed. Serve with lemon or milk. (Cream is considered poor taste, but I like it.)

In serving iced tea, prepare in the same way and pour the hot and freshly made tea into glasses filled with cracked ice.

COLD BANANA BISQUE

The Mauna Kea Hotel in Hawaii has a favorite soup, most often requested. It is good!

1 quart half-and-half
4 large peeled ripe bananas

Put in the blender until thoroughly mixed and creamy. Chill. Serve with cinnamon croutons made as follows:

3 slices thin-sliced crustless white bread, diced
⅓ cup melted butter
3 tablespoons sugar, mixed with ½ teaspoon cinnamon

Place the diced bread in a buttered shallow pan. Mix with the butter and sugar mix. Put in a 300° oven until lightly caramelized, stirring frequently. These are good with cold avocado soup, too.

□

Asparagus or broccoli lightly buttered and sprinkled with toasted sesame seeds, and served with green or egg noodles, are good. Toast sesame seeds in a 300° oven.

□

You do not have to go into a whirl over finding Fontina cheese. Use Bel Paese or Gruyère as a substitute.

□

A Chinese-inspired dinner goes a long way on a small food budget.

□

Grated orange or lemon peel added when using lemon extract, and served over chilled, peeled fresh fruit or berries, is delicious.

□

Suggestion from club fare — a Shrimp Peel. Hot and cold shrimp with sauce, shrimp gumbo, shrimp salad, shrimp Newburg, rice and salad — some or all, if you catch the shrimp; otherwise you need a pot of gold to buy them.

I find that small decorated birthday cakes appeal to children more than a large one. I usually put the candle in a little wooden or ceramic holder for each guest to take home. Children like to carry away something from a party — either decorations or small gifts make them happier than leaving empty-handed.

□

Sauce for steak: 6 ounces Roquefort cheese, 2 tablespoons cream cheese, 1 teaspoon Worcestershire sauce, 1 teaspoon mushroom catsup, 1 garlic clove (minced), few drops Tabasco. Mix.

□

Chocolate, vanilla, and coffee ice cream over fresh fruit marinated in Galliano's liqueur — a nice ending.

□

If you insist on boiling your vegetables, use less water! One-half to one cup water usually is enough water to boil for six servings of fresh, young, and tender vegetables. You must cook over low heat in a pan with a tight-fitting lid. Watch them — they boil fast.

□

How many beans? One cup of uncooked dried beans yields about 2½ cups cooked beans.

□

A bushel of peaches can give you a very fine time, especially during the peach season. It brings a color and flavor to your table that everyone enjoys, and who knows, it may even inspire your mate to pass you the most superb compliment I know: "You look just like peaches and cream."

□

Cantaloupe Cocktail with Orange Sauce for breakfast. Cut the cantaloupe with a ball cutter or dice to make 3 cupfuls. Blend 1 cup orange juice with 2 tablespoons lemon juice and pour over the cantaloupe. Pile in cold glasses and sprinkle with springs of mint dipped in powdered sugar.

□

My favorite dessert for entertaining at home, and for those who love me, is:

A large bowl of vanilla and coffee ice cream
An array of sauces
A bowl of slivered nuts
A bowl of whipped cream
A pipkin of crème de cacao or Benedictine
Fresh or frozen strawberries
Melon balls in Sauterne

Let everyone make his own sundae. Most fun. I call it The Seven Deadly Sins.

□

CARAMEL CUP CUSTARD

FOR FOUR TO SIX

The most popular potluck dessert at Neiman-Marcus is Caramel Cup Custard. Old as the hills — but everyone loves it — young and old.

Mix well: ⅓ cup sugar, a pinch of salt, 3 whole eggs, and ½ cup light cream. Scald 2 cups milk. Add to egg mixture, whipping while you pour. Add ½ teaspoon vanilla. In the meantime, put ½ cup of sugar in a heavy skillet and cook over medium heat, stirring constantly, until it is the color you desire. Add 1 tablespoon of water, and stir until completely blended. Put 1 tablespoon of the caramelized sugar into the bottom of the custard cups and pour the custard on top. Bake in a water bath at 350° until done (about 25 to 30 minutes).

CASSATA CAKE

FOR EIGHT

A choice dessert.

Buy or make a fresh pound loaf cake, about 9 inches long and 3 inches wide
1 pound ricotta cheese (soft)
2 tablespoons whipping cream
¼ cup sugar
3 tablespoons Grand Marnier or Strega or other orange-flavored liqueur
3 tablespoons mixed candied fruit, coarsely chopped
2 ounces semisweet chocolate, coarsely chopped

With a sharp, serrated knife, slice the ends and crusts off the pound cake and level the top if it is rounded. Cut the cake horizontally into ½-inch slices. Beat the ricotta with the sugar, cream, and liqueur, until smooth. Fold in the chopped candied fruit and chocolate. Center the bottom slice of cake on a flat plate and spread it with the ricotta mixture. Keeping sides and ends even, place another slice on top and spread with more filling. Repeat until all cake slices are reassembled and the filling has been used up, ending with a plain slice of cake on top. Gently press the loaf together to make it as compact as possible. Do not worry if it feels wobbly; chilling firms the loaf. Refrigerate for about 2 hours, or until the ricotta is firm.

For chocolate frosting: Melt 12 squares of semisweet chocolate with ¾ cup coffee; remove and beat in ½ pound sweet butter. Beat until smooth. Swirl over the cake, top and sides. Decorate with candied fruit. Cover loosely with plastic wrap, wax paper, or aluminum foil and refrigerate at least 24 hours before serving it — or freeze.

TEXAS TREATS

Historically speaking, Texas is beef-and-hospitality country. Big steaks, big men, big cars, and big the welcome hand to strangers. I should know, it extended a big welcome to me. The hospitality of Texans has not changed and they use any excuse for entertaining — to welcome, to say Godspeed, or just for fun.

TEXAS BARBECUE SAUCE

THREE CUPS

This hot, smoky sauce used by Texans for outdoor picnics may be used as a steak sauce or for oven barbecuing.

1 tablespoon salt
½ teaspoon pepper
3 tablespoons brown sugar
¼ cup catsup
3 tablespoons prepared mustard (brown mustard)
2 tablespoons Worcestershire sauce
1 teaspoon Liquid Smoke sauce
1 cup water
2 tablespoons chili sauce
½ cup vinegar
1 cup melted butter or cooking oil

Mix in order given, using rotary egg beater as oil is added. Simmer slowly until slightly thickened. This makes enough sauce for 6 pounds of meat. Keep hot.

Brown meat over coals of charcoal broiler, add sauce, and bake at 350° until tender. This is for such cuts of meat as shoulder, clods, short ribs, lamb shoulder, and breast, the cheaper cuts of meat. If barbecuing a steak of the cheaper variety, soaking it in beer for a few hours will help tenderize; then swish it around in the barbecue sauce before broiling over the grill. Brush frequently with the sauce while broiling.

CORN STICKS

FOR TEN TO TWELVE

Every other country I know of grows corn for cattle and corn for humans. In Texas, the humans eat the corn for cattle: fried corn, the best you ever ate — and you never find it except in Texas.

2 cups water
1¼ teaspoons salt
1½ cups cornmeal
1 cup grated sharp cheese

Bring the water and salt to boiling. Add cornmeal and mix thoroughly. Cook until the mixture separates from the sides and bottom of pan. Remove from fire, add cheese, and mix. Take mixture out by teaspoonfuls and shape into balls. In the palms of the hands, roll balls to ½ inch thickness, in the shape of small cigars. Fry in hot deep fat (375°) for 2 or 3 minutes. Drain before serving.

TAMALE PIE

FOR SIX TO EIGHT

In Texas one hardly thinks of a potluck supper without a Tamale Pie tucked away somewhere in the recipe file.

12 tamales, cut in 2-inch pieces (canned)
1 quart diced chicken
2 cups chopped corn
2 cups canned tomatoes
½ cup raisins
½ cup sliced stuffed olives
3 slices bacon, fried crisp and crumbled
1 tablespoon chili powder
½ teaspoon salt
1 teaspoon Worcestershire sauce
1 cup chicken consommé
¼ cup butter
1 cup grated sharp Cheddar cheese

Mix the tamales and chicken with the corn, tomatoes, raisins, olives, and bacon. Add the chili powder, salt, and Worcestershire sauce to the consommé. Place the tamale mixture in a buttered 4-quart casserole. Dot with butter. Pour the consommé mixture over. Bake at 300° for 1 hour. Remove. Cover with the cheese and return to oven to brown.

If you are taking the south of the border seriously, you might serve a guacamole salad with this and some canned or frozen pineapple spears, some toasted pecans, and a bit of candy as the ending.

HUSH PUPPIES

2 cups cornmeal
¼ cup flour
1 teaspoon soda
1 tablespoon baking powder
1 tablespoon salt
1 egg, beaten
6 tablespoons finely chopped onion
2 cups buttermilk

Place all ingredients in a bowl and mix. Dip from a teaspoon into hot fat and fry until brown on both sides. These are really the popular hot breads of the Southwest. Good for every occasion from a cocktail item to a formal dinner (in the South).

CORNMEAL BISCUITS WITH GREEN CHILES

FOUR DOZEN SMALL BISCUITS

1 cup flour
1 cup yellow cornmeal
1 teaspoon salt
⅓ cup shortening (half may be butter)
½ cup milk
¼ cup chopped green chiles (Ortega brand is the most common — buy whole and chop)

Mix flour, cornmeal, and salt together; cut in shortening. Add milk and chiles; stir and turn out on floured board. Pat to ½ inch thick. Cut into biscuits. Place on an ungreased cookie sheet. Bake at 450° for 12 to 15 minutes.

TEXAS CORNBREAD

A better-than-best cornbread comes from a Texas ranch, straight from the pretty wife of a west Texas lawyer who ranches on the side. She makes it for the ranch hands. I have adapted it for my own use, and yellow cornmeal sales have increased.

1 cup yellow cornmeal
½ cup flour
1 teaspoon salt

Mix thoroughly; then add without mixing:

1 cup buttermilk (sour milk or half sour cream and milk)
½ cup sweet milk
1 egg
1 tablespoon baking powder
½ teaspoon soda
¼ cup melted shortening

Grease the muffin pans or corn-stick pans well and heat. Stir up the mixtures thoroughly and pour into the hot pans. Bake at 450° until done. The bread will be moist and brown on the bottom.

GRITS SOUFFLÉ

2 cups milk
½ cup grits
1 teaspoon salt
½ teaspoon baking powder
½ teaspoon sugar
2 tablespoons melted butter
3 eggs, separated

Scald milk, add the grits, and cook until thick. Add the salt, baking powder, sugar, and butter. Beat the egg yolks and add to the grits mixture. Beat the egg whites to a soft peak and fold in the batter. Pour into a well-buttered 1½-quart casserole and bake uncovered in a 375° oven for 25 to 30 minutes. Cornmeal may be substituted for the grits.

GARLIC GRITS

Cook together until done:

2 cups grits
1½ quarts water

Add and mix:

½ cup milk
2 rolls garlic cheese
4 eggs, beaten
¼ pound (1 stick) butter
Salt and pepper to taste

Pour into a buttered casserole. Sprinkle with Parmesan cheese and paprika. Bake at 300° for 30 minutes.

LIMPING SUSAN

FOR EIGHT

¼ cup finely diced salt pork
1 cup rice
1 onion, chopped fine
3 cups chicken broth or consommé
2 cups mashed canned tomatoes
2 tablespoons chopped parsley
Salt and pepper
Cooked okra
Slivers of cooked chicken

Fry pork until crisp. Add rice and stir until rice is golden. Add onion and cook until soft. Add broth or consommé (or water). Cover and cook until rice is done, about 1 hour. Add tomatoes and parsley and seasonings — fork-stir and bake uncovered for 30 minutes. Just before serving add cooked okra and slivers of leftover chicken, or not.

HOPPING JOHN

FOR SIX TO EIGHT

4 strips bacon
¼ cup chopped onion
2 cups black-eyed peas, fresh or frozen
½ cup raw rice
2 cups water, boiling
Salt and pepper

Dice the bacon and fry with the chopped onion. Add to the peas, rice, and water. Cover and cook at low heat until the rice and peas are done. Add seasoning.

This is served on New Year's Day in many homes — for good luck, you know!

TURKEY ENCHILADAS

FOR FIFTEEN

Ann Criswell of Houston has a good recipe for Turkey Enchiladas using cooked turkey, developed by the Texas Department of Agriculture.

Oil
2 4-ounce cans green chiles
1 large clove garlic, minced
1 28-ounce can tomatoes, drained and liquid reserved
2 cups chopped onion
2 teaspoons salt
½ teaspoon oregano
½ cup tomato liquid or water
3 cups shredded cooked turkey
2 cups sour cream
2 cups grated Cheddar cheese
1 package (15) corn tortillas

Preheat 2 tablespoons oil in electric skillet at 300°. Rinse seeds from chiles and chop (use rubber gloves and don't touch your eyes). Sauté with minced garlic in oil. Drain and break up tomatoes. Reserve ½ cup liquid. Add tomatoes, onion, 1 teaspoon salt, oregano, and reserved liquid. Simmer at 200° uncovered until thick, about 30 minutes. Remove from fry pan and set aside. Combine turkey with sour cream, grated cheese, and remaining salt. Heat ⅓ cup oil and dip tortillas until they become limp. Drain well on paper towels. Fill tortillas with turkey mixture; roll up and arrange side by side, seam side down in electric skillet. Pour chili sauce over top and cook at 250° until heated through, about 20 minutes. Can be prepared as a casserole in a 13-by-9-by-2-inch baking dish in a 350° oven.

GREEN ENCHILADAS

FOR EIGHT

This delicious recipe is from Lola Hunt of Mexico and Dallas. The day before serving, prepare the following:

Sauce:

1 large white onion
2 4-ounce cans green chiles
½ cup parsley sprigs or raw spinach
2 chicken bouillon cubes
1 can mushroom soup
1 green tomato, if available (otherwise omit)
2 cups whipping cream
Salt and pepper

Put onion, chiles, parsley, bouillon cubes, soup, and tomato in blender. When blended, add the cream. Season with salt and pepper.

½ cup salad oil (not olive oil)
16 soft tortillas or crêpes
1 pound Swiss cheese, grated
Meat from a 3-pound roasted chicken, shredded

Have two small skillets ready. In one heat the oil, in the other ¾ cup of the sauce. Dip each tortilla into the hot oil quickly and drain. Dip into the sauce and stack. When all are ready, put 1 tablespoon of the cheese and some of the chicken on each tortilla and roll. Place in an 8-by-12-inch casserole. Mix rest of sauce with rest of cheese and any of the sauce left from dipping. Pour over the enchiladas. Bake at 350° until hot. When serving, top with sour cream. For a luncheon entrée you could use individual casseroles, serving two enchiladas per person.

JESSIE'S CHILI

FOUR QUARTS

Jessie was one of my cooks at the Driskill Hotel in Austin, and he made the chili. I still use his method and keep the chili frozen. Using this recipe, I have substituted lower-in-calorie chicken and turkey for the beef.

¼ pound chile pods (1 package)
1 quart water
1 pound coarsely ground beef suet
5 pounds coarsely ground beef
3 to 4 cloves garlic, finely chopped, or 1 tablespoon garlic powder
2 teaspoons ground comino (cumin)
¾ cup chili powder
2 cups chopped onion
2 cups canned tomatoes
4 tablespoons cornmeal
2 tablespoons flour
Water
Salt

Boil the chile pods covered in a pot with 1 quart of water for 15 minutes. Remove the pods, and save the water they have boiled in. Remove pods' stems and seeds and slip off the skins. Chop the pods. Sauté the suet, beef, and garlic until meat is thoroughly cooked, about 40 minutes, with the comino and chili powder. Add the onions and cook 10 minutes; add tomatoes mixed with the cornmeal, flour, and chopped pods. Cook another 5 minutes. Add the chile water and enough water to make 2 quarts. Simmer for about 45 minutes or until all the flavors are well blended. Add salt to taste.

When I substitute coarsely ground turkey or chicken for the beef I add ½ cup of butter or salad oil in place of the suet.

□

When I make enchiladas I dip each tortilla in the fat from making the chili, or in broth or salad oil, fill with chili, grated Cheddar cheese (or half Cheddar, half Provolone), and grated onion. Roll up and arrange side by side, seam side down, in a shallow casserole. Pour chili over and sprinkle with grated cheese. Bake at 350° for 15 minutes. Run under broiler until piping hot. Serve right away, but you may assemble them ahead of time and freeze before baking.

GREEN PEPPER JELLY

A nice change and especially good with lamb. This recipe came from Dallas's Suzy Nash, who says it originates from the Higgenbotham family cookbook called *This Little Higgy Went to Market.* It really does not matter where it comes from. It is divine.

¾ cup green bell peppers (about 4 small), seeded and cut up
¼ cup fresh jalapeño peppers
1½ cups cider vinegar
6 cups sugar
6 ounces Certo

Put peppers in the blender with ½ cup of vinegar. Blend well at high speed. Pour into a saucepan, rinse blender with remaining vinegar, and add to peppers. Add sugar and bring to a rolling boil that you cannot stir down. Remove from heat. Let stand 5 minutes. Skim if necessary. Pour in Certo. You may add a little green coloring. Pour into 5 sterilized ½-pint containers and seal.

THE CUP THAT CHEERS

Be it made with spirits or not, the loving cup has its place in every home. For graduation parties, large get-togethers, lounging on the back porch or terrace, after football games, any time more than two people get together.

MINT PUNCH

FOR TWELVE

---

1 cup sugar
½ cup water
Juice of 6 oranges
½ cup of grapefruit juice
Juice of 6 lemons
½ cup crème de menthe
Rind of ½ cucumber
Rind of ½ orange
1 quart ginger ale
¼ cup grated fresh or frozen pineapple

Boil the sugar and water, cool, and add the juice of oranges, grapefruit, and lemons, the crème de menthe, the cucumber rind, and the orange rind. Chill several hours, remove cucumber and orange rind, add the ginger ale and fresh pineapple, and pour over ice cubes.

WHISKEY SOUR PUNCH

FOR FIFTY

---

1 quart lemon juice
1 quart orange juice
1 quart whiskey
3 quarts sparkling water
Sugar to suit your taste

Pour over ice, and sprinkle with slivers of fresh pineapple. Serve in cold glasses.

GINGER ALE FRUIT PUNCH

FOR FIFTY

1½ quarts lemon juice
1½ quarts orange juice
6 quarts water
4 pounds sugar
1 quart pineapple juice
2 quarts ginger ale

Mix first five ingredients and let stand several hours in ice. Add 2 quarts of ginger ale and pour over lime or lemon sherbet. Serve in punch cups.

CHAMPAGNE PUNCH

FOR THIRTY

1 quart Sauterne
2 cups brandy
2 quarts champagne
1 quart sparkling water

Mix Sauterne and brandy. Pour over ice; then add the champagne and sparkling water. Serve right away.

DAIQUIRI PUNCH

FOR SEVENTY-FIVE

2 quarts lemon juice
4 quarts lime juice
4 quarts orange juice
1 pound confectioners' sugar
4 quarts club soda
2½ fifths light rum

Mix fruit juices and sugar and refrigerate several hours. Add soda and rum and serve with cracked ice and fresh mint in cold glasses.

FRUIT PUNCH I

FOR THIRTY

4 cups pineapple juice
4 cups fresh lime juice
1 quart orange juice
2 cups sugar
1 quart orange sherbet
2 quarts ginger ale

Mix fruit juices and sugar and refrigerate. Pour over the orange sherbet and add ginger ale. Garnish with fresh mint and thin slices of orange.

FRUIT PUNCH II

FOR FIFTY

3½ cups sugar
1 pint hot tea
2 cups lemon juice
3 quarts orange juice (frozen)
1 quart pineapple juice
3 quarts ice water
1 quart ginger ale
1 cup sliced strawberries
1 cup shredded fresh pineapple
1 cup sliced white grapes

Dissolve sugar in the hot tea. Cool. Add lemon, orange, and pineapple juice, and ice water. Refrigerate. When ready to serve, pour over ice in a cold punch bowl and add the ginger ale and fruit, and mint leaves if available. This is a pretty and refreshing punch and you may vary the fruit with the season.

WEDDING PUNCH

FOR THIRTY

---

4 cups sugar
Juice of 12 lemons
1 pineapple, chopped fine
3 quarts ice water
1 quart fresh strawberries, sliced
1 quart champagne
1 quart sweet Sauterne

Dissolve the sugar in the lemon juice and add the pineapple and water. Pour over a block of ice in a punch bowl; add the fruit, champagne, and Sauterne.

MAY BOWL

FOR TWENTY

¼ cup powdered sugar
1 jigger Triple Sec
1 quart sliced fresh strawberries
2 quarts May wine

Add the sugar and Triple Sec to the berries. Refrigerate 1 hour. Pour over a block of ice, add the May wine, and serve in cold cups.

CHRISTMAS WASSAIL

FOR TWENTY

1 teaspoon ground ginger
½ teaspoon ground nutmeg
1 teaspoon allspice
2 teaspoons cinnamon
¼ teaspoon ground cloves
¼ cup hot water
4 quarts claret
4 cups sugar
14 eggs, separated

Stir spices in the hot water and boil ½ minute. Add to the wine and heat, but do not boil. Add sugar and stir until dissolved. Beat egg yolks and whites separately, and fold yolks into the whites. Pour in a punch bowl and add the heated wine. Whip with a French whip until frothy. It is very good; and pretty if the bowl is in a bed of holly leaves.

MILK PUNCH

FOR FOUR

3 cups milk
1 cup cream
3 tablespoons sugar
8 jiggers bourbon

Pour into a cocktail shaker or electric blender with a little ice and frappé. Serve in chilled glasses or punch cups and dust with nutmeg. Or pour into a really cold punch bowl with ice cubes and whip with a French whip. This is a wonderful morning drink, especially after a rather large evening.

SPICED TEA

FOR FIFTY

6 quarts boiling water
1½ pounds sugar
2 lemons, juice and rind
4 oranges, juice and rind
4 teaspoons whole cloves
8 sticks cinnamon
12 tablespoons tea

Let first 6 ingredients stand 20 minutes, keeping hot but not boiling. Add tea. Let stand 5 minutes. Strain. Serve from a tea urn in punch or demitasse cups.

HOT CHOCOLATE

FOR TWENTY

⅔ cup cocoa
¾ cup sugar
½ teaspoon salt
1 cup water
3 quarts scalded milk
1 teaspoon vanilla extract
1 cup cream, whipped

Mix cocoa, sugar, salt, and water. Add to the scalded milk and beat with a rotary beater or wire whip. Return to heat and bring to a boil. Remove; add vanilla and pour into warm cups. Put a teaspoon of whipped cream on top. Add a touch of cinnamon to the cream for grownups who indulge.

IRISH COFFEE

FOR ONE

1 sugar cube
4 ounces hot coffee
1 jigger Irish whiskey
Dab of whipped cream

Put sugar in bottom of cup, add the hot coffee, then the whiskey. Stir to dissolve sugar. Add the whipped cream. Do not stir again.

EGGNOG

FOR THIRTY

Eggnog is as personal as you make it. This one is mine. I remember the first time I made it, for the Houston Country Club Woman's Golf Association Christmas party. They were sure a Yankee couldn't, but afterwards this recipe was always used.

24 eggs, separated
2 cups sugar
1 quart bourbon
1 pint brandy
1 quart heavy cream
2 quarts milk
1 quart vanilla ice cream

Beat the egg yolks and sugar until thick. Add the bourbon and brandy and stir thoroughly. The liquor "cooks" the eggs. Add the cream and milk and continue whipping. Break up the ice cream and add, combining thoroughly. Beat the egg whites until stiff and fold in. Refrigerate if possible for 30 minutes before serving. Sprinkle lightly with nutmeg. This is a drinkable eggnog, not too thick, but speaks with authority.

TEA PUNCH

FOR SEVENTY-FIVE TO EIGHTY

Make a syrup of:

8 quarts water
8 pounds sugar

When cool, add:

2 quarts lemon juice (3 dozen lemons)
1 pint orange juice (½ dozen oranges)
¼ pound black tea steeped in 1 pint water (strained)
Rind of 1 cucumber, chopped
¼ teaspoon cayenne pepper, scant (may be omitted)
1 bunch mint, cut fine
2 quarts strawberries
½ pint grape juice
1 can chunk pineapple, sour cherries, or raspberries

Serve over ice and ladle into punch cups.

SUMMER FIZZ

FOR TEN

12 sprigs fresh mint
1 cup boiling water
1 cup currant jelly
3 cups orange juice
½ cup lemon juice
1 cup cold water
1 quart ginger ale

Crush the mint in a bowl with the back of a spoon. Add the boiling water and the cup of currant jelly. When the jelly is melted, cool, and strain out the mint. Add the fruit juice and cold water; just before serving, add the ginger ale. Serve over ice with halves of fresh strawberries and sprigs of fresh mint.

PINEAPPLE LEMONADE

FOR EIGHT

Pineapple Lemonade is refreshing to serve in tall frosted glasses.

2 cups sugar
2 cups water
Juice of 4 lemons
2 cups fresh pineapple, grated

Boil the sugar and water until it spins a thread. Cool; add the lemon juice and grated pineapple. When ready to serve add water to please you, and pour over ice cubes and fresh mint.

SOUTH AMERICAN COFFEE PUNCH

FOR THIRTY

I used to serve this punch for summer afternoon parties around the swimming pool at the Houston Country Club. Really refreshing in hot, humid weather.

8 cinnamon sticks
1 gallon hot strong coffee
1 quart whipping cream
4 teaspoons vanilla extract
2 quarts coffee ice cream
¼ cup sugar

Add cinnamon sticks to coffee. When cold, remove cinnamon and add whipped cream, vanilla, ice cream, and sugar. Float more whipped cream on top. Serve from a punch bowl into tall iced glasses partially filled with finely chipped ice.

CRANBERRY ORANGE PUNCH

FOR TWELVE

6 cups cranberry juice cocktail
1 cup frozen orange juice
3 tablespoons lemon juice
1¼ cups pineapple juice
3 cups ice water

Mix together in order given and pour over an ice block in a punch bowl. Serve plain or with fruit sherbet floating on top. Place your punch bowl in the center of a polished table and surround with greens from your yard or sprigs of holly at holiday time. Or serve as a first-course cocktail.

BORDER BUTTERMILK

FOR FOUR

1 6-ounce can frozen lemonade concentrate
1 lemonade can of tequila

Put above ingredients in blender. Fill with crushed ice. Blend at high speed until smooth and frothy and milky looking.

KIR

FOR ONE

1/5 ounce crème de cassis
3 or 4 ounces Chablis or a dry white wine

Mix and serve very cold in a stemmed glass.

This drink, invented by Père Kir of Dijon in the late 1920s or early 1930s, has become a most popular aperitif.

SANGRIA BASE

There are several ways to make Sangria and only a few ways are good. The classic recipe is the best.

2 large oranges, sliced
3 lemons, sliced
3 limes, sliced
3 quarts water
2 pounds sugar

Slowly boil mixture for 3½ hours or more until it is reduced by half. Cook until syrupy and a bitter taste begins to appear. Cool at room temperature.

To make Sangria for eight: Spoon ⅓ cup of the base into a pitcher; add 1 bottle of an inexpensive red wine. Add 1 dozen ice cubes and about half of a 10-ounce bottle of soda water. Stir well and add diced peaches, strawberries, cherries, or whatever fresh fruit you wish, and thin slices of lemons, oranges, and limes. There is a great difference between the taste of this Sangria and the simple kind. For a white Sangria use a dry white Burgundy wine in place of the red. You may also add brandy or vodka, 1 cup for each bottle of wine.

The simple Sangria, either red or white:

2 oranges, thinly sliced
2 lemons, thinly sliced
1 lime, thinly sliced
½ cup sugar
1 bottle wine
5 ounces soda water
12 ice cubes
Fresh fruit, if you wish

Crush the oranges, lemons, and lime with the sugar and refrigerate for a couple of hours. Remove, add wine, soda water, and ice cubes. Stir well and pour. Of course, add brandy or vodka, 1 cup for each bottle of wine. I sometimes serve this drink in tall glasses over ice with fresh fruit added and a sprig of mint — a type of Planter's Punch!

This keeps indefinitely in a jar refrigerated.

CHAMPAGNE PEACH

ONE FOR EACH GUEST

1 ripe Freestone peach, peeled
Crushed ice
Champagne, chilled

I like to use a whole peach, but you could slice and use less. Place peach in a saucer wine glass. Cover with crushed ice and pour the champagne over. Or half-fill a punch bowl with sliced peaches and proceed. The peaches must be sweet and the champagne not too dry.

COFFEE PUNCH

FOR FIFTY

I recommend this coffee punch for all occasions: cocktail parties, weddings, teas, receptions. High calorie, but some will like it better than whiskey.

2 gallons strong coffee (I add 2 tablespoons instant espresso to the coffee), cooled
2 gallons vanilla ice cream
1 pint half-and-half
Sugar to taste
2 bottles Cognac or brandy (4/5 quarts)

Freeze 1 quart of the coffee in a ring mold. Pour the rest into a punch bowl. Add ice cream, cream, sugar, and frozen coffee. Stir well and add Cognac.

MIMOSA

FOR TEN TO TWELVE

I use this drink frequently for all-women gatherings, especially in the early part of the day. It doesn't tickle your nose as much as plain champagne, but it is better for you to start the day with a little vitamin C.

1 quart cold, freshly squeezed orange juice
1 bottle chilled Brut Champagne

Mix and pour into stemmed glasses; and please, no maraschino cherry. If you have any mixture left, add softened unflavored gelatin (1 tablespoon for each pint liquid) to it and pour over a bowl of fresh fruit for a good dessert.

BRAVE BULL

Mix equal parts of tequila and Kahlua and pour over ice. Add a few twists of lemon peel and stir well. Pour into old-fashioned glasses with an ice cube.

□

The Mexicans have a *dicho* all Americans should adopt: *Salud, amor, pesetas, y tiempo para gozarlos;* which means, "Health, love, wealth, and time to enjoy them." I would add another: Eat with pleasure and moderation in all things.

□

Yesterday has gone by; we can do nothing about it. Tomorrow is not yet here, and we can do something to make it more pleasant, especially gastronomically. Give freely of your own time and prepare delightful meals for your family. It is a loving way to spread health and happiness.

□

The priceless ingredient of any recipe
is a good cook!

Metric Conversion Table

U.S. Standard Measures	Metric Measures
1 ounce	28 grams
3½ ounces	100 grams
8 ounces	227 grams
1 pound	454 grams
1 gallon	3.79 liters
1 quart	.95 liters or 950 milliliters
1 pint	.48 liters or 480 milliliters
1 cup (8 oz.)	.24 liters or 240 milliliters
1 tablespoon	15 milliliters
1 teaspoon	5 milliliters

Index